Culture and Horticulture

A Philosophy of Gardening

by

Wolf D. Storl

BIO-DYNAMIC Farming and Gardening Association
San Francisco, CA

Illustrations by Midge Kennedy
Printed by Thomson-Shore, Inc.

ISBN 0-938250-01-9

Dedicated to the Memory of Robert Elbers
of Warmonderhof, Holland

Acknowledgements.... For many hours spent at the typewriter, I want to thank John Kehoe. I am grateful to Christine Storl, without whose help the book would not have been possible. Special thanks to Lutz Kramer of Rogue Community College for reading the manuscript, and to the students who prompted the writing.

The rushes daily grow taller;
Apricot blossoms daily more lush.
As an old farmer, I enjoy the view;
Everything I do according to the seasons.
I rise early to feed the cows;
Then yoke a pair to farm in eastern acres.
Earthworms crawl in and out of the ground;
Field crows follow me around,
In flocks they peck and cry,
As if to tell me of their hunger.
My heart is full of compassion
Looking at this, I pity both them and myself.
I give my food to the crows;
At dusk I return with an empty basket.
My family greets me with mocking smiles;
But never would I have changed my mind.

Ch'u Kuang-hsi
6th century

TABLE OF CONTENTS

Part II

Culture and Horticulture

A Philosophy of Gardening

PART I

INTRODUCTION

This book is written as an introduction to gardening in its wider aspects, linking it to historical, philosophical and cosmological contexts, taking horticulture from the microscope to the wider cosmos. Surely such vistas are involved when one takes a shovel to hand to turn the soil: eons have formed it; life permeates it in manifold forms; cosmic cycles of sun and moon warm it, circulate water through it, lure out of it the season's vegetation; and man shapes it according to his thinking and willing, plants and husbands it according to his cultural traditions, and finds mental and physical sustenance through it. All that is gardening!

This book is not just a collection of garden facts and practices, for there are enough good books of this kind on the market. It is not written primarily for the seasoned biodynamic agriculturist versed in anthroposophical lore, or for the academic biologist and college-trained horticulturist, who, while dealing with his relevant and irrelevant variables, test tubes, and statistics, loses the total picture. This book does not intend to amass detail after detail, hoping to eventually emerge with the larger concept. Unlike the archeologist who matches potsherds hoping to find and finally reconstruct the complete pattern of the vessel, we hope to approach the subject as one who has glimpsed into the potter's workshop having caught sight of the overall shape of the vessel while lacking knowledge of most of the details. Thus we start with the holistic concept of the archetypal image of the garden, trying to outline, sketch, and accentuate this image by the use of various observed facts, details, and useful analogies. For this reason, if it becomes evident that some of the minor details are mistaken or obscure, as some surely are, it should not detract from the overall concept, the archetypal garden, which is central to our concern. This methodology is a surer way of avoiding the truncations and frankensteinian distortions that have come about by a blind amassing of facts and details without regard to the holistic aspects, and which have eventually been translated into our social and environmental crisis.

The first part of the book is concerned with a philosophical, historical and epistemological setting, and the second part deals with the more practical, down-to-earth aspects of gardening.

Now that a critical "sociology-of-knowledge" is in vogue, an author feels obliged to add a personal note of intent, background and credentials to his writing. This is the intention of the rest of the introduction.

* * * * *

I first came into contact with organic gardening and the *bio-dynamic* method in particular, while I was studying ethnology in Switzerland doing "participant-observation research" in a community where bio-dynamic agriculture provided the subsistence basis. I had gardened before, helping a proverbial "old neighbor" for years to earn pocket-money as a boy and learning many tricks of the trade, including the use of pesticides and ammonia sulfate. Eventually, I enrolled at Ohio State University School of Agriculture to learn forestry. In the first year of general introduction into agriculture, I learned that the old family subsistence farm must come to an end, that the farm should be a production unit like a factory, the work processes must be specialized and technologized so that the farmer can go into his barn wearing a business suit and just push buttons ... otherwise, humanity's exploding population would starve. More or less, that is what one was told.

While strolling through the experimental fields of the college and mentally comparing them to the other soils I had seen in the small Ohio farming community where I had grown up, I noticed their lack of a certain living quality. When I saw more of the research equipment and procedure, when a professor received an award for a starling-killing machine, when I heard of placing windows in the stomachs of experimental animals in order to watch the digestion, I became upset. I could not think of trees as renewable capital or mere, albeit complicated, chemical processes. Though I had been part of a group of honor students, candidates for a technocratic elite that was meant to implement these concepts later, I gave up forestry and studied anthropology instead. I, for the most part, forgot about my early contact with agriculture until the research in the rural community in Switzerland where I found a better way of doing farming and gardening.

The community, Aigues Vertes, near Geneva, is interesting anthropologically because it is not a traditional Swiss village, but a newly founded community that dedicates itself to providing good homes and a sheltered environment for handicapped people, of which there were about fifty at the time I was there. The community's social structure consisted at the time of study of ten households, averaging about eight persons each, workshops (pottery, enameling, weaving, doll making, carpentry, repair shop, etc.), and a basis of bio-dynamic farming and gardening. The village was organized by committees, such as the housewives committee, produce committee, machine and equipment committee, and so forth. A weekly general village meeting was held where the committees reported problems and where projects were discussed and decided upon by unanimous agreement. Except for personal items, major means of production and resources were held in common. The village was one of several *Camphill Villages,* founded in the 1940's by the Viennese child pedagogue and pioneer in curative education, Dr. Karl König. König conceptualized the villages as alternatives to the social arrangements that brought about the excesses of mass society, whether of capitalism, fascism or communism. He utilized the philosophies of the *Bruderhof,* of the Bohemian philosopher Comenius, of Robert Owen, and of the *Threefold Social Order* of Rudolf Steiner. The handicapped villagers were happy and secure and I experienced this as one of the few communal efforts that seemed to be working successfully.

Agriculturally, the community had access to about 80 acres, of which only 32 acres (13 hectares) were in direct production, the rest being occupied by woodland and structures. The garden at the time of the study was a little more than two acres. From this amount of land all the food needed by the villagers was produced, along with some surplus to sell to city people who literally begged for fresh organic produce. The garden yielded a most varied assortment of vegetables the year round. In the winter, the selection narrowed to carrots, leeks, witlof, endives, oysterplants, parsnips, turnips, beets and onions. If there was a good harvest, the cabbage, celeriac, squash and fennel could last well into spring. Five gardeners, three of them mentally handicapped, and occasional student helpers worked in the garden the year round. In the summer, the work was intense from dawn to dusk; in the winter, the work was easier, consisting of cleaning vegetables, fixing tools, working on manure composts, picking up wheelbarrow loads of stones that kept growing like spuds in the moraine soil, planting witlof roots in warmer indoor boxes for sprouting, watering the lamb's lettuce, endives and sugarloaf under the plastic foliage tunnels, and so on. In February, the hot beds were prepared from horse manure and liquid manure, the first sowings were put in, and the constant watering, airing and watching for frosts kept the gardeners on their toes.

The farm was operated by two farmers and four or five handicapped who were skilled milkers and accustomed to a variety of work courses. Eight milk cows, a bull, some heifers, calves, a work horse sometimes with a foal, pigs, chickens, ducks, sheep and rabbits made up the animal helpers. The number of animals was carefully suited to the land and available pasture, so that the whole worked like a self-contained organism. The farm produced all the milk that was needed and all the grain that was baked into bread at the village bakery. Excess milk was turned into cheese, cottage cheese, etc. Eggs, butter, and cheese were sometimes in short supply. Red and black currants, gooseberries, strawberries, elderberries, rowan berries and raspberries were produced in their season, requiring the workers from the workshops to help with the plentiful harvests. From the berries, plums, cherries, apricots, pears and apples, juices and preserves were made in the village, along with pickling and sauerkraut-making. Similarly, during the haying season, potato harvesting or the beet-seedling-thinning, a large reserve labor force could be called upon to do the necessary tasks.

The farm and garden worked closely together. The farmers would supply the cow, horse, pig and chicken manure which the chief gardener and expert compost maker, "Kompostmeister Manfred Stauffer" would bio-dynamically prepare with herbal essences and render into the finest humus substance possible. This composted manure provided the basis for a steadily increasing fertility of the land under cultivation. Originally, the land had not been so productive; the soil is composed of the gravelly moraine of an old Rhone glacier, and the area enjoys the least amount of annual rainfall in Switzerland. One family, prior to the establishment of the village, had failed to make a living on this land trying to raise pigs. The canton of Geneva acquired the land with tentative plans to make it part of an agricultural experiment station or school, but soil tests showed it to be unsuitable. Consequently, it was leased for a nominal sum to the Camphill people. Over the next 15 years, the population of the new community rose from 12 to nearly 100 people, all of whom were fed by the amount of land where before one family had not been able to survive.[1] Of this population, only about 10% were actively and directly involved in agriculture, the rest were able to perform other tasks.

The households ordered their daily vegetables and fruit needs each morning and the freshly harvested produce was delivered by handicapped villagers. The records kept of this and sales outside the village show that production nearly doubled each year for a period of five years, before leveling

---

[1] It must be mentioned that a high investment of starting capital was necessary to get this efficient system going, some of which was derived from donations by parents of the handicapped, or by insurance payments.

off to a steady peak. During that time, the expert handling of bio-dynamic practices had increased the humus content in the soil to a noticeable extent. Before, the soil had been compacted with few earthworms evident; now, the soil became darker, fluffier and more alive with a small fauna. Much of this was due to bringing in outside organic material, a practice that is generally avoided in bio-dynamics, but was initially necessary to raise the humus level on this gravelly soil to keep water from leaching out. For a few francs, city workers, driving truckloads of algae dredged from Lake Geneva, leaves from the parks and dirt from roadside ditches, were persuaded to dump their loads at Aigues Vertes instead of at the city landfill. Nonetheless, the greatest aids in soil-building were cover crops and manure of the livestock. Everything organic was composted, including garbage, old cloth, chicken feathers and leather scraps. Once a visitor accidentally left his coat on a rag pile only to return and find that it had been composted. Another time, a bookstore gave the village a truckload of books, mostly cheap French novels which could have been sold in town at a franc apiece. It was decided to compost these, too. After soaking them to loosen the bindings, it took two years to get a compost that was so full of earthworms (bookworms) that it looked like raw hamburger when disturbed, a fact that made it the favorite exhibit for the many international visitors to the garden. We did not use this compost on the vegetables after second thoughts about the lead contained in the printer's ink.

Experiments were made in the garden house to ascertain the quality of the various composts by seeing how well cress seeds *(Lepidium sativum)* sprouted, how quickly they developed mass, measuring the distance between internodes, etc. Controls were run under identical conditions on various soils and composts. Other tests were done to check quality indications by placing plant saps into test-culture dishes to see when and which kind of bacteria or fungus developed. The composts were applied in a directed way, depending on the preceding crops, the needs of the new crops and the condition of the soil.

Eventually, outside sales brought enough money in to afford the building of a greenhouse and a pond to collect rainwater from the roofs of the village buildings. Rainwater was considered to be better water than well water.

Despite ethnoscientific training, I had, at first, an excruciatingly hard time understanding the motives, postulates and world-view of the community. The results these people were getting in their "treatment" of the mentally handicapped, in their lifestyle were impressive. But, they did not proceed from the scientific methodology that I considered the only basis of reality. Since I was there as an anthropologist doing research, I listened, observed and made notes of ideas about invisible "etheric" forces at work, planetary and lunar influences, "beings" at work in the garden and village, etc. My notebook was filled with observations of the following sort: Mountain crystals were pulverized and buried in a cow's horn in the ground for a year; of this, a pinch the size of a pea was taken and stirred rhythmically clockwise alternating counterclockwise for one hour in a bucket of lukewarm water and then this was sprayed over the fields and gardens. One time, noticing a leaking gutter on the roof, I fixed it. The next rain, it was leaking again and I fixed it again. A third time, the master gardener mumbled disconcertedly something about someone always fixing the gutter. I found out that it was intended to drip on a certain spot where a sheep's skull was buried with oak bark in it. It was supposed to rot there in a certain way for a reason that I did not comprehend at the time. Another time, aphids appeared on the beans and I was ready to counter-attack with tobacco juice (figuring that was the organic way of destroying pests); but the gardener just sat there looking and thinking. "What is there to think about?" I demanded. "There is the problem and here is the solution." The gardener replied that it would be better instead to find out *why* the aphids were there in the first place. "Well, that is simple," I replied, drawing on my natural science studies, "They are most likely windborne or carried by another organism and we had better destroy them before they spread!" He then explained, "No, the reason they are here is more subtle than that; it has to do with how we fertilized the soil, what crop preceded it and what weather patterns exist which weakened the plants that they became susceptible."

Moles and gophers were, at times, a problem in the garden. Once in a while, the gardener's cat would catch one of these rodents. The gardener would then take them, skin them and hang the hides to dry while his wife fried the carcasses for the cats to eat. At a certain time, when Venus was in a particular zodiac sign, he would burn the pelts and sprinkle the ashes over the fields, causing, he claimed, the other gophers to reconsider where they had settled.

I kept notes on all of this and had my own anthropological explanations. By placing the phenomena into categories of "survivals of a primitive early European world-view" or into Sir James Frazer's "homeopathic and contagious magic" I was doing less for anthropology than for my own cognitive dissonance.

Other bio-dynamic gardeners and farmers that I met at this time engaged in strange practices, such as gathering water at the full moon or collecting and using herbs in unusual ways. One farmer boiled the shoots of the "red pine" (Norway spruce – *Picea abies)* for several hours, and, diluting the juice with rainwater, he poured it around his land to keep slugs out. He reasoned that the red pine belongs to Saturn and the slugs belong to the Moon. The characteristics of Saturn are, among others, warmth and dryness, while those of the Moon are wet and cold. The slugs will feel that they are leaving Moon territory and entering Saturn and recoil at the prospect. This explanation, and others like it, seemed like the product of unbridled fantasy and it was hard for me to consider them to be real in the "real" world.[2]

Despite this, Aigues Vertes and other bio-dynamic places were shining examples of good husbandry, of healthy stock and plentiful produce. I stayed nearly three years instead of the one I had originally intended, and found the individuals working in bio-dynamics to be much more sophisticated than I had at first suspected. Rather than working with outmoded, hand-me-down superstitions, they were utilizing a

---

[2] Somewhat later, an agronomist from Oberlin College, who had just spent nine months on a research tour of all the countries engaged in the "Green Revolution" came to visit an old friend at the village. I introduced myself as a fellow academician, eager to tell him about bio-dynamic agriculture and the promise it holds. He was just as incredulous as I had been at first, and after hearing about companion planting, lunar cycles, and medicine for the soil, he refused to even look at the garden. "I don't want to see it!" he exclaimed. "Organic gardening – I know all about it. It does not work! But I do hope you will publish your findings and expose this sort of quackery."

metalanguage, a complicated system of symbols to express and communicate fine and detailed observations about the workings of nature. I found out that many of the practitioners of this method were far from being uneducated; many had impressive academic and scientific credentials. In the meantime, my professor at the University of Bern with whom I was finishing my Ph.D. dissertation and exam, became worried that I had lost my scientific objectivity. He suspected me of the greatest heresy of anthropology: identification with the subjects under study. Besides, I had made none of my research public. I began to feel, however, that I had found a level of cognition superior to the one on which I was operating, and which I attempt to formulate in this book.

Following the apprenticeship years at Aigues Vertes, I tried my own hand at organizing a garden. A small home for the mentally handicapped in Schwarzenegg (Switzerland), trying to achieve self-sufficiency, asked me to set up an organic vegetable garden. I set out to apply all of what I had learned and had good results. Old peasants would come by on their Sunday walks and look at the way things grew, nodding their approval. The weeds left in the garden deliberately for their companion plant effects, however, did not receive the appreciation of the immaculate Swiss peasant who braids his manure piles and stacks firewood in mosaic patterns.

Subsequently, I attended conferences for alternative agriculture. One conference was in Saas, where young people were using the bio-dynamic method to reclaim the abandoned mountain terraces of the Wallis (Valais) Valley. The peasants of this area had undergone modernization within the last fifty years, and the men were catering to the more profitable tourist business or working in a chemical plant in the valley after a highway had been built, while the women tried to carry on a rudimentary agriculture at home. Before returning to the United States, I attended a month-long seminar on bio-dynamics at the Goetheanum in Dornach, Switzerland, and was duly impressed by the thoroughness of the research and the depth of understanding regarding nature. It is out of these experiences that the course at Rogue Community College and this book came about.

CHAPTER I
HISTORICAL SKETCH

Agriculture started about 9000 years ago as archaeological evidence from Asia Minor suggests. Nine thousand years is a long time for observations to accumulate and techniques to develop. Indeed, *agriculture* and *culture* are intimately linked, as anthropologists have shown many times in relating the connection of quality and form of lifestyle with various subsistence patterns. It might be claimed that a healthy agriculture is the basis of a healthy culture and healthy culture implies a healthy agriculture.

Early forms of agriculture include the *irrigation* practices of Mesopotamia, Egypt, the American Southwest and other parts of the world; and *swidden* (or slash-and-burn) systems developed in the forested areas of the world.[1]

Swidden is the cutting or girdling of trees, the burning of the brush, releasing nutrients in the ashes, and the sowing or planting of food plants in the spaces. The soil is usually exhausted after a few years, forcing the primitive agriculturist to move to another location, perhaps after a number of decades, to return to the same plot for a new cycle of clearing, burning and planting. Some of the early American pioneers practiced swidden, as did the Indians, such as the Iroquois, who subsisted on the "Three Sisters," maize, beans and squashes.

---

[1] cf. Carl O. Sauer, *Agricultural Origins and Dispersals* (New York, American Geographical Society, 1957).

Our early European ancestors practiced swidden agriculture until the time that the population increased and a more stable way of life developed, when more permanent forms of agriculture were devised. The fusion of Barbarian and Roman lifestyles brought about the feudalistic, medieval way of life. Most of the population were peasants engaged in agriculture, while a small percentage of the population, the nobility, provided protection, ensuring the peaceful, agricultural cycle would not be unduly interrupted. The clergy provided guidance in the moral and ideological sphere. Generally, land was held in common, with each family tilling what it needed to survive and to pay as tax to the nobility and church. If the family grew larger or became smaller, the amount of tillage in tenure would vary correspondingly. The crops were grown in a *three-field system* of rotation. One field was planted with summer crops, one with winter crops and one lay *fallow.*[2] The fallow field was permitted to be overgrown with weeds which helped restore the fertility to a large extent. The fields were also manured at times. On the average, the yields were low, but the fertility of the soil remained pretty constant. The animals were grazed on the *common lands* beyond the confines of the village and the common woodland served as a source of firewood, herbs, acorns for swine in the fall, etc.

Linked with early agricultural systems was a whole way of life and a cosmology supported by centuries of observations and lifetimes of experience. There was nothing resembling modern scientific research at the time. The closest to such

[2] For a good description of the development of agriculture in the Western World, see: Sir Albert Howard, *The Soil and Health* (New York, Schocken Books, 1972), Chap. 3.

research was the activity in cloister farms and cloister gardens. Here, medicinal herbs were grown, also vegetables such as carrots, leeks, onions, cucumbers, cabbages, lettuce, peas, parsnips and chard as well as some that are nowadays considered weeds, such as mustard, purslane and lambsquarters. Plants for dyeing cloth such as the teasel, mallow and yarrow and flowers, those rich in symbolic meaning, such as the rose, the lily and the violet were tenderly cared for. New insights were gained through meditation, rather than by a method of controlled experiment. Old knowledge, the horticultural and agricultural writings of the old Greeks and Romans (Plinius, Cato, Theophrast, Virgil) were kept by the monks and eventually filtered down to the illiterate peasants in the form of an oral folklore.[3]

The cosmology of the Middle Ages was suffused with the belief in numerous "supernatural" beings. Various elemental spirits were at work in nature: gnomes in rocks, nymphs in water, sylphs in the air and fire spirits in fire and warmth. Each had certain jobs to do; the gnomes helped form the roots, the nymphs the leaves, the sylphs wove the flowers and the fire spirits helped the fruits to ripen. There were other nature spirits, house spirits, seasonal spirits that were taken account of by prayer, propitiation, or magic. Many of these, of pagan origin, had acquired a Christian veneer,

[3] Quite a lot is known of the cloister gardens through the writings of such renowned individuals as Abbot Walafried *Strabo,* whose poem *"de cultura hortorum,"* 842 A.D., describes many of the gardening procedures. *Abbess Hildegard of Bingen* writes extensively of plant cultivation and medical uses. *Albertus Magnus,* in the middle of the 13th century writes of composts and of peasants' sayings. In the 12th and 13th centuries, many Greek and Roman astrological, meteorological and agricultural writings become available via the Arabs and were translated into Latin. Much of this treasure has not yet been translated into modern languages and made available to us.

reappearing as saints or as angels. Each day of the year had a saint's name, rather than merely a number, and the nature of the day was associated with the nature of the saint. Thus, for example, it was noted that the 12th, 13th and 14th of May, bearing the names of Pancratius, Servatius and Bonifacius, usually bring frost. They were known as the "Ice Saints." Some saints had prophetic characteristics, such as St. Urbain (May 29th): Whatever the weather on St. Urbain, it would be the same later during the haying season.[4]

Certain saints' days were good for sowing this or planting that, harvesting this or reaping that. The saint himself was thought to be active in helping the plants sprout, grow, ripen, etc., just as a person born on a certain day would have a special relation to the saint of that day and often would be named after the saint, as is still the custom in rural Latin America. The craft of gardening, especially vegetable gardening, was watched over by St. Fiacre (August 30th), after whom, incidentally, Paris taxi cabs are also named. He is pictured with an open book and a spade. With the saints, one is reminded of the function of the revered powerful ancestors among the agricultural people of Africa and China.[5]

The old gods of the Romans and of the northern peoples did not disappear with the coming of Christianity— how could they, since they symbolized the forces that constitute

---

[4] St. Swithin (July 15th) in England:

St. Swithin's Day, if thou dost rain
For 40 days it will remain.
St. Swithin's Day, if thou be fair
For 40 days 'twill rain na mair.

[5] *Baer's Agricultural Almanac* (Grosset & Dunlap Publishers, N.Y.), is one of the few farmers' almanacs that still provides the name of the saint for the day.

the world! — they continued to exist, metamorphosed into beings acceptable to Christian ideology (e.g. Archangel Michael becomes identifiable as Thor; Gabriel, the messenger, as Mercury, etc.) or, in the later Middle Ages, the gods were associated with the spheres of the seven planets (Saturn, Mars, Jupiter, Sun, Venus, Mercury and Moon) as expressions of the various heavenly spheres. These spheres didn't just exist "out there," but were active on earth as well, through mysterious "influences" (in-flowing) and correspondences. For example, Jupiter's *signature* is found on earth as the color yellow, the organ of the liver, the metal tin, the plants such as the dandelion, maple, liverwort and others, and the psychic characteristic of wisdom. The signature of Mars, to give another example, is found in the color red, the gall bladder, iron, courage, fierceness and plants such as the oak, the nettle, hops, plantain, etc.[6]

[6] Nicholas Culpeper (1616-1654), a British physician, in his *Culpeper's Complete Herbal,* has recorded what planets the various plants are governed by for posterity. His book is and remains a classic on medicinal herbs. cf. *Culpeper's Complete Herbal,* Foulsham & Co. Ltd., new ed. If one were to attempt to apply these principles to the situation in southern Oregon, one could come up with the following analysis: The predominant vegetation in the Grants Pass area is oak, coniferous trees, manzanita, madrone, poison oak, and Saint John's Wort. Oak is ruled by Mars; coniferous trees are ruled by Saturn; poison oak, a *rhus,* is ruled by Jupiter, a lunar one at that; manzanita and madrone, as *ericaceae,* belong to the Sun, as does St.-John's-wort. Decomposed granite, high in silicon content, belongs to the supra-solar planets. Thus, given the vegetation and the soil, one can say that the upper planets, the forces of Mars, Sun, Jupiter and Saturn are predominant, as opposed to the subsolar forces. For the gardener this would mean that what he grows will be highly nutritious, his seeds will be of good quality and he will have to aid the subsolar and lunar forces with the application of some lime and liquid manure. As far as the elemental spirits are concerned, the medieval observer would note that during the dry, hot summer months, the fire spirits and sylphs predominate; while in the rainy season, the nymphs, who are not even there to make dew in the hot season, make a strong comeback and the mosses and lichens are very much Moon. The gnomes, who are associated with the crystal formations of the winter are not very strong. The archangel Michael does not manifest his being with lightning storms, but shows his presence by an occasional falling star that is a spark from his sword as he fights the great dragon. Such a way of looking at nature, quite foreign to us, nevertheless has an attractive imaginative quality.

The planets, operating against the background of the fixed stars, were considered to belong to a higher realm, a more majestic sphere. This region, divided into twelve zones, constitutes the *zodiac,* twelve archetypal forces that influence the events here on earth, modifying and influencing the planetary forces. Thus, a sun shining from Leo (in July) is a different sun than that shining from another background, such as from Pisces (in February). A full moon in Taurus, the Bull, is different from a moon in, let us say, Scorpio. The sphere of the fixed stars, the zodiac, was experienced anthropomorphically as a giant man (Meganthropus). Aries was considered to constitute the head of this macrocosmic man, Taurus, the neck, and so on down to the feet which were in Pisces. Each of these zodiacal signs was assigned to one of the four elements (earth, air, fire, water) and had great relevance as to when anything should or should not be done, when to plant, sow, till, cut nails, cut hair, cut timber, etc.[7]

Predictions and prescriptions based on saints' days, planetary and atmospheric conditions, and also on observations of animal behavior were stated as rules, often fitted into rhymes and couplets and passed on through the centuries, from father to son, by word of mouth. The rules are countless, but we can give a few examples, such as these weather oracles:

St. Vincent's sunshine
brings corn and wine.

(This refers to the prediction that if the weather is clear on

[7] Albert Hauser, *Bauernregeln* (Artemis Verl., Zürich, 1973), also, Jerry Mack Johnson, *Country Wisdom,* (Anchor Press, Doubleday; Garden City, N.Y., 1974).

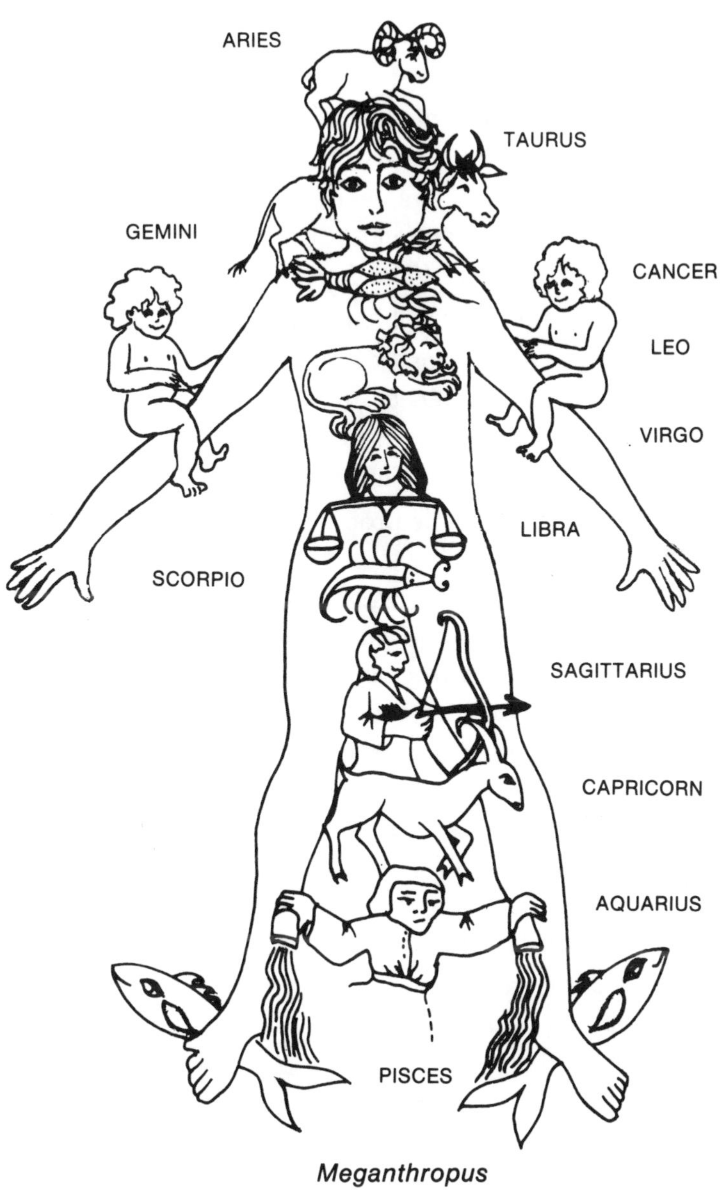

Meganthropus

the 22nd of January, St. Vincent's day, the harvest will be bountiful.)

When April blows his horn (thunders)
it is good for hay and corn.

All the months of the year
curse a mildish Februeer.

Green Christmas, White Easter.

(If Christmas is mild, it will surely snow around Easter.)

When clouds appear like rocks and towers,
the earth's refreshed by frequent showers.

In the waning of the moon
a cloudy morn, a fair afternoon.

Other sayings concern the proper times to engage in this or that activity:

Cut herbs just as the dew does dry
Tie them loosely and hang them high
If you plan to store away
Stir the leaves a bit each day.

Sow peas and beans in wane of the moon
Who soweth sooner, he sows too soon,
That they with the planet may rest and rise
And flourish with bearing most plentiful and wise.

The moon in September shortens the night
The moon in October is hunter's delight.

Fruit gathered too timely will taste of wood
will shrink and be bitter and seldom be good.

At hallow tide (All Saint's Day, November 1st)
slaughter time entereth in
and then doeth the husbandman's feast begin.

As January doeth lengthen

Winter cold doeth strengthen.
The provident farmer on Candlemas Day
(February 2nd)
has half of his fires (wood) *and half of his hay.*
When the likker's low
or ceases to stew,
The farmer doeth know
the winter is through.
Onion skin very thin
mild winter coming.
Onion skin thick and rough
coming winter's cold and tough.

There are numerous sayings that regulate the right time to sow, plant and reap and in which astrological sign to do so; and finally, there are some of definite humor, lest anyone become too serious, for example:[8]

A husbandman can surely know
On the 30th of February there's never snow.
If a rain falls on the rye,
the wheat and clover won't stay dry.
On Sylvester (December 31st) *snow, then clear,*
No more snow the rest of the year.

This, then, is what constituted the "science" of the old agriculturist. It was a science that was not yet divorced from religion, psychology or everyday life; rather, it was part of a holistic way of being. Their agriculture was a sacred way of life, as Jacob Burkhardt once remarked, not just a business to be carried on.

As the peasantry became more literate, these rules found

[8] Schweizer Dorfkalander (Appenzell, 1882).

their way into the *Farmer's Almanacs,* or into almanac-like publications such as Thomas Tusser's *Five Hundred Points of Good Husbandry* (1683) which was a standby for the New England pioneers.[9] It is surprising that, despite education and scientific progress, the almanacs are still being used by a number of farmers and gardeners today, but generally, the users are considered to be backward, quaint and superstitious. These almanacs contain a calendar for the year with the daily corresponding astronomical data, a weather forecast, list of the holidays, tips on gardening, farming, fishing, horoscopes, recipes, weights and measures and other items. Popular almanacs currently printed in the United States include *Old Moore's Almanac,* first published in 1697, *Baer's Agricultural Almanac,* of Lancaster, Pa.; also *Grier's Almanac,* first published in 1807, and *The Old Farmer's Almanac,* in 1792.

The medieval way of life and cosmology did slowly come to an end due to a variety of demographic, socioeconomic and political factors, all of which are common history. Wealthier landowners saw to it that the common land disappeared from the manor by a series of enclosures. Peasants were forced off the land and absorbed as laborers in an industrial revolution that has not come to a halt since. Many peasants emigrated to the newly discovered continents and found themselves in new and unusual ecological and socioeconomic situations. Other factors also helped destroy the old way, such as the calendrical reforms of Pope Gregory XIII in the 16th century, whose replacement of the old Julian Calendar brought about a shift of 11 days and fixed

[9] Eric Sloane, *The Seasons of America Past* (Funk & Wagnalls, New York, 1958).

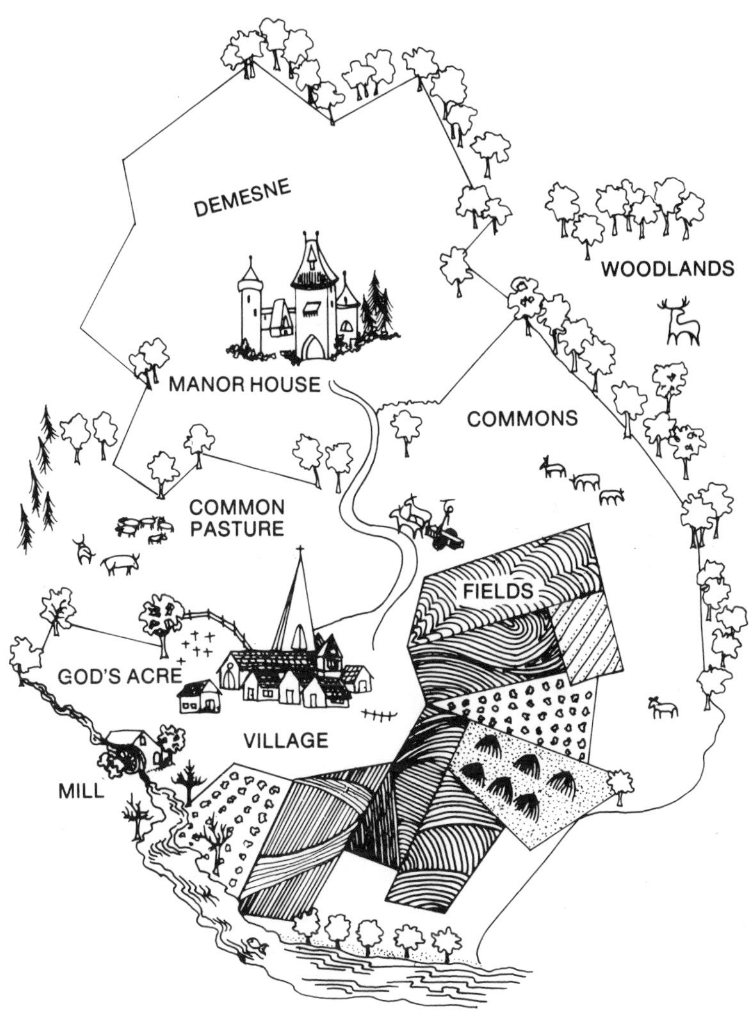

General Outlay of Medieval System of Land Usage

the beginning of the year in January – instead of on March 25.[10] This very much confused such issues as the saints' days. Also, by this time, the gradual shifting of the relative positions of the planetary cycles to the zodiac (e.g. the spring equinox) had caused a discrepancy between the dates of the conventionally fixed signs and what could actually be observed in the night-time sky. Finally, the new skepticism concerning the old traditions, and the empirical-logical scientism of the Enlightenment detracted greatly from the credibility of such peasant rules. Many of the peasant rules were applicable only in certain restricted ecological and geographical regions, and did not lend themselves to the formulation of general rules, as scientific standards demand.

Early settlers brought their rules and almanacs with them to America, but found them difficult to apply under such novel circumstances. Here and there they have managed to hold on to them, and even to found new local adaptations, as with the Amish of Pennsylvania and the mountaineers of Appalachia.

The *Foxfire Book*[11] lists a number of such beliefs among the Appalachians of Rabun-Gap Nacoochee in Georgia. Rules about Ground Hog day, on February 2 (if the ground hog sees his shadow, there will be six more weeks of winter); and about poison ivy (Leaves three, let them be) in the Mid-West are of this nature. In the Williams region, in southern Oregon, there is a rule about Grayback Mountain:

Seven on Grayback, heavy with snow

---

[10] Ibid., p. 32.

[11] Eliot Wigginton, *The Foxfire Book* (Anchor Books, Garden City, NY, 1972). See chapters on Weather Signs, Planting by the Signs, etc.

All summer long, water will flow.[12]

This permits the farmer to plan management of his water resources for the coming summer since it refers to whether the springs will dry up or not. Though here and there these rules live on, a newer philosophy and commercial orientation have little use for such passed-on traditions and home-grown observations that do not lend themselves readily to controlled experiment. And it is not to be denied that many such rules seem trite, redundant or even nonsensical.

The Newer Agriculture

With the rise of the new experimental, scientific spirit, steady improvements in agriculture and horticulture can be registered.[13] Jethro Tull invented the *drilling* of grain instead of broadcasting it, which permitted "interdrilling" or cultivating. At the same time, in the 1730's, Lord Townshend of Norfolk developed a modern system of crop rotation: a four-year rotation of wheat, turnips, barley and clover or beans with manure plowed in to boost production. New varieties of livestock and plants were bred. The yield per acre was significantly increased. In the 1810's, Von Thaer discovered the significance of humus, and legumes were introduced as green manure.

The impetus for chemical agriculture, which became the backbone of 20th century agribusiness, was inadvertently provided by the chemist *Justus von Liebig.* Von Liebig carried on convincing experiments in which he burned plants and analyzed the ashes for their content of elements and

---

[12] Recorded by W. Shampine of Williams, Oregon.

[13] cf. Gordon J. Cook *Our Living Soil* (The Dial Press, New York, 1960), Chap. 1.

minerals. He reasoned that when a crop is harvested a small percentage of nitrogen, phosphorus and potassium (NPK), as well as calcium, magnesium and others is removed from the soil. In due time, the soil will deplete unless these elements are replaced. It would not matter whether these elements are replaced in a chemical form or in an organic form (manures or compost) because nitrogen is nitrogen, phosphorus is phosphorus, and potash is potash, no matter what form they are found in. In 1842, a disciple of Liebig, J. B. Lawes, began to experiment with fertilizers on his estate of Rothamstead in Berkshire. He succeeded in producing and marketing superphosphates extracted from mineral calcium phosphate. In 1843, J. H. Gilbert, a chemist, joined him and helped wed chemistry to agriculture. Continuous experiments have been run in Rothamstead with basically three fields. One field has no fertilization, one is dressed with manure and the other is given pure chemical fertilizer. The chemical fertilizer is holding its own against the manure, while, of course, being a lot cheaper and easier to manufacture and handle. The experiments of Rothamstead seemed to show the way for a future of prosperity; the old peasant dream of the "land of cockaigne," of "Schlaraffenland," or the paradise on earth seemed to come true. The flaws in the theory did not become evident until this century. For the time being, a completely materialistic world-view had it that the plant was considered a chemical factory needing a certain input of NPK, water, CO_2 and energy which provided an output of sugars, starches, O_2, etc.

Phosphorus could be derived as a side-product of the ever-expanding steel production — from the slag. Potassium was found in underground deposits, like those of Strassfurt, Germany. Nitrogen was derived from the sodium nitrate deposits of Chili, the famous Chile saltpeter, and from side-products of the coal-gas production. Farmers were, however, on the whole, slow to take the bait and before the 1890's, few actually used chemical fertilizers.

A big boost to chemical fertilizer usage was given by the First World War. The Allied blockade had successfully cut off the Central Powers from imported food and from the Chili saltpeter. Nitrogen is, of course, the basic ingredient of the ammunition that keeps the armies in the field. German scientists developed a method of fixing nitrogen from the air, which is composed of 79% N as an inert gas. Thus, solving problems in the arms industry and the fertilizer industry was a result of the war, with nitrogen salts becoming readily available and food production being subsumed under the war effort. It is a similar story from the Second World War. Much research had been done in between the wars in chemical warfare materials, and poisons were stockpiled. When the second war broke out, both sides were afraid to use these stockpiles, so they became diverted toward the war against insects. DDT, used for the first time successfully by the Allies to save the liberated city of Naples from a lice and flea epidemic, was the first of a number of chlorinated hydrocarbons that would wage war against a healthy environment. It is only now being realized what the unfortunate and unforeseen effects would be. The Vietnam war was not without its "spinoffs" for agriculture: complicated defoliants and herbicides were developed further and productive capacities expanded. Though that war is over, the stockpiled chemicals are marketed and passed off to the farmer and to county agencies who spray roadsides and irrigation canals, irrespective of the ecological damage incurred. It is not surprising; what other fruits can be borne out of war research which is motivated by fear and hostility?

CHAPTER II
VOICES OF CONCERN AND REFORM

Concern about the quality of the food and health of the people brought a number of reformers at the turn of the century, each with some recommendation of special diets, baths, herbs and nature cures (e.g. Are Waerland, Rev. Kneipp, Graham, etc.).[1] Others were concerned with man's increasing alienation from nature and the countryside, such as Dr. Schreber of Leipzig, who instituted the practice of *allotment gardens* for city-dwellers so common now in Europe. The allotment guarantees every urbanite the right to a small piece of land on the edge of the city, which can be gardened on weekends or in the evenings, for a minimal amount of rent.

There were other voices of concern from those who wanted to go back altogether to a rustic life and turn their backs on the science and technology that seems to have gotten mankind into such straits in the first place. While others, representing the established interests, either held the opinion, "We never had it so good," or, "Sure, there are problems, but more science and more technology will eventually solve these problems." These issues remain pretty much the same today though in an amplified form.

The organic gardening and farming movement, as it was pioneered independently by Dr. Rudolf Steiner and Sir

[1] Paavo O. Airola, *Health Secrets from Europe* (ARC, N.Y., 1970).

Albert Howard, took a more moderate stand. Howard felt it was the misuse of science and a one-sided application of technology, in the interests of the profit-motive, which were at fault. Science should help man to live in a more harmonious way with nature, not alienate him from nature. For example, what could be more scientific than the construction of compost piles, knowing what goes on in each of the stages of decomposition and humus formation, and understanding the action of the humus upon the soil? By contrast, application of chemical fertilizers is not really scientific, because it is harmful, in the long run, to soil fertility and detrimental to the health of mankind; it serves only the interests of a few to whom monetary profits are the major reality.

Rudolf Steiner, also, did not turn his back on science. He warns that an emotional, mystical reaction is as detrimental as a one-sided, coldly "objective" scientific approach. The scientific, rational, objective consciousness is a recent human achievement, whose development has entailed increasing materialism and a dimming of the spiritual vision and soulful experience of the world that once was a part of man's heritage. In the times before the Enlightenment, people had visions, saw angels and elemental spirits, lived by a traditional wisdom rather than by the findings of empirical research, and peasants relied on their folk sayings rather than on the opinions of the remote agricultural experts. These times have slowly faded, in the cities faster than in the country, in America faster than in the old world. Steiner sees this development as a positive necessity; only now, in the twentieth century, has the time come to pick up the older faculties, the soulful, intuitive, and imaginative, and to recombine them with the currently one-sided rational, intellectualistic, scientific faculty to form a whole once again. It is not a matter of going backward and becoming serfs or savages again, but of picking up the baby that has been thrown out with the bath water during the Enlightenment and the scientific development of the last two hundred years. Man is more than just an intellect, wisdom is more than what is garnered by reason; a feeling sensitivity, creative imagination and a good will must be reintegrated into our way of dealing with our world, and with our farms and gardens.

Thus, going back to a neolithic, medieval, and Indian, or an early American pioneer type of existence is not the point of the organic agriculture movement. Given the socioeconomic and demographic situation of today, the attempt to do so would create unimaginable hardships; but even more so will the present course of big business, corporate and chemical agriculture, or the dehumanized, specialized collective farms of the Soviet bloc. Both are blind to the essence of nature and are just about to destroy the ecosphere itself. There is plenty of established scientific evidence and there are countless practical demonstrations in farms and gardens which show that organic gardening does work. The most striking example of this is, of course, China, where as F. H. King reports, farming and horticulture of the most intense sort has been carried on for over four thousand years without depletion of soil fertility.[2] As Rodale and others have reported from modern China, organic agriculture is able to feed a population of nine hundred million people, nearly as many livestock, and three

---

[2] F. H. King, *Farmers of Forty Centuries* (London, 1933, Jonathan Cape Pub).

times the number of hogs, on about the same amount of arable land as is available in the United States. Travelers to China report no starvation, poverty or the like, and all of this without huge doses of chemicals, insecticides and heavy, petroleum-gobbling machines; but by careful composting of all organic stuff and a labor-intensive method.[3] Despite the claims of the U.S. Department of Agriculture that humanity would starve if we "went back" to organics, these facts do not indicate that organic agriculture is primitive. From the author's own experience, as explained in the introduction, the view cannot be shared that organic agriculture would lead to starvation; on the contrary, the more one works in harmony with nature, the better results one can expect. Organic agriculture is not a more primitive, but rather a more advanced form of agriculture based on a deeper and more thorough understanding of the ecological totality. The problems seem to be more those of social, political and world-market economy factors. Organic agriculture is intensive and needs people to share the work; it lends itself better to the type of society that Thomas Jefferson envisioned, i.e. one of local independence, decentralization and self-sufficiency; and this is, of course, at variance with international corporate efforts, world markets and centralized planning. Organic agriculture implies the shared work of several people, similar to the large family, the joint family of bygone days, or perhaps, some newer social form such as the small community, or commune. Here the tasks can be meaningfully divided without the risk of alienating, one-sided specialization. Some people can take care of the livestock, some can gar-

[3] cf. Sterline Wortman, Agriculture in China (*Scientific American*, June, 1975).

den, some can bake bread or make cheese, etc. This kind of work-sharing can lead to the satisfaction of social, psychological and cultural needs much more effectively than the current truncated, isolated family. It is basically this social-political nature of organic agriculture which is threatening to the established interests, and not really the issue of whether it is scientifically sound or not.

History of the Modern Organic Movement

It was Rudolf Steiner who first formulated an organic approach to agriculture in the western world. As stated before, there had been a series of health and nature movements in the latter half of the 19th century, but it was Steiner who saw the problems as related to each other: what one does to nature — to soil — one does essentially to other people and to oneself. An unhealthy agriculture and an unhealthy social and spiritual life have common roots, and his *anthroposophy,* intended to be a superlative of anthropology, tried to deal with all these problems simultaneously. In 1924, the *bio-dynamic* movement of organic agriculture got under way, and despite tension with Hitler's regime, suppression by the Communists and the silent treatment by chemical agriculture, it has developed, over the years, into a strong movement. Its basic philosophy, as we shall see, is somewhat difficult, and an exclusive "in-group" attitude by some of the practitioners has made it, unfortunately, somewhat inaccessible to a lot of people.

Popular awareness about the deterioration of the environment and the possible link to mental and physical health did not reach a wider public until after the Depression and the Dust Bowl in North America. The concept of *conservation* and a number of important publications during this time indicate the concern.[4]

It was during this time that the work of Sir Albert Howard began to be known and in 1940 his *Agricultural Testament* was published, followed by the important *Soil and Health,* in 1947. It was at that time that the organic movement, as we know it today, was born. In America, J. I. Rodale picked up on Howard's work, entertaining contact with the biodynamic movement at the same time, and launched the movement in America with the *Organic Gardening and Farming Magazine* and the book, *Pay Dirt* (1945). Rodale created an experimental farm at Emmaus, Pennsylvania, and was active in organizing *garden clubs* throughout the United States. Similar activity occurred in Britain and Continental Europe, albeit on a lesser scale.[5]

After the activity in the 40's and early 50's, the movement toward organics slowed down, its proponents were classed with the food faddists, the sunshine-and-health types, and all those other quacks and neurotics not to be taken seriously. Bumper crops and a booming unfolding of agribusiness had quieted the concern; it was hardly being noticed that despite ever heavier doses of insecticides, pests

---

[4] All one need do is read the papers about the mismanagement of collective farms, centrally planned by bureaucrats, who know only abstract economic priorities and nothing about local ecological conditions; or read about the grain trade with Russia; the selling of steer manure, by the tons, to Kuwait; the plantation system and the accompanying dehumanization of the workers in the tropical countries, who deliver the raw materials to industrialized society.

[5] In Britain, Lady Balfour wrote *The Living Soil* (1943) and launched the famous Haughly Experiment. Friend Sykes, using his 750-acre organic farm as a basis, wrote *Food and Farming of the Future* (1950). Together, they formed the Soil Association. In Switzerland, the work of Dr. Mueller and Dr. R. Bircher (incidentally, the creator of the Bircher-Muessli); in Germany, the writings of Konemann, Seifert, N. Remer et al, deserve mention. In the U.S.A., the research of Albrecht, Waksman, Pfeiffer and books by E. H. Faulkner, L. Bromfield and others still make important reading.

and diseases were on the increase while major portions of friendly fauna, butterflies, birds and wildlife were being depleted, some to the point of extinction.[6] In 1963, it was Rachel Carson's book, *Silent Spring*, that broke the spell and awakened people to the tragic and alarming state of affairs in agriculture.[7]

This was the start of the *ecology* movement, the beginning of the popular recognition of the interrelatedness of all life on this planet. It became increasingly difficult to scoff at the organic gardeners and farmers.

Concern with organics includes a wide spectrum of people at this point: from patriots, who stress independence, self-reliance and survival, to leftist communards who include organic agriculture as a way of liberation from the "system"; from practical, hardheaded realists, to practical idealists such as those of the New Alchemy Institute, or Alan Chadwick's gardeners at Santa Cruz State University, to those who would incorporate it in a new metaphysics, such as in Findhorn.

---

[6] The American Bald Eagle is one of the number of top carnivorous birds that was brought to the verge of extinction by chlorinated hydrocarbons which interfere with the calcium processes of eggshell formation. In 1973, a delegate from American Indian Tribes was sent to Europe to procure eagle feathers, necessary in the sacred ceremonies, because there were no more eagles to be found in the U.S.

[7] At the time, in 1964, I was enrolled in a course of entomology at Ohio State University. The professor doubled as a pesticide researcher for a major chemical corporation and as a university teacher. When confronted with Rachel Carson's book, he scoffed at the ideas expressed as those of a hysterical woman. For him, it was a matter of total warfare: insects compete with homo sapiens for scarce resources (carbohydrates, proteins, etc.) and one or the other would have to be decimated.

CHAPTER III
THE PIONEERS OF ORGANIC AGRICULTURE

Sir Albert Howard (1873-1948)

Sir Albert Howard, a British mycologist and agricultural lecturer, spent most of his life in tropical countries, mainly India. His astute empirical observations in agriculture led him ever further from the specialist, the "laboratory hermit," and into contact with the practicing peasant. He realized that an isolated laboratory divorced from the multiple functional factors that make up the farm, would lead to erroneous conclusions. He formulated a holistic-ecological approach to farming and gardening, developed the successful *Indore Compost-Making Process,* stressed the need for taking account of and adapting to local situations rather than proceeding from laboratory generalizations.

As Imperial Botanist of the Government of India (1905-1924), he proved in large scale practical farming that composting leads to soil health, and that a healthy soil provides for healthy plants that are wholesome and fit for human and animal consumption, and at the same time disease resistant. He drew attention to the importance of *mycorrhizae,* fungi found in good humus soil that enter into symbiosis with the rootlets of plants. These fungi coat the roots and grow into the roots themselves, supplying growth hormones and organically bound nutrients to the host plants while being provided carbohydrates in return. When the mycorrhizae die, their protein bodies are absorbed by the plant for further nutrition. These fungi, plentiful in humus soil, largely absent in chemically fertilized soil, are, according to Howard, essential to disease resistance and quality in crops. He further proved that livestock fed on organically grown fodder were disease resistant, as were his oxen during an epidemic of hoof-and-mouth disease, In all cases, he kept stressing the importance of healthy soil and the need to cycle organic products back into the soil in the "great wheel of nature." This, and not the constant breeding of new strains or the spraying of poisons, made for healthy plants, and, by extension, for healthy animals and human beings. He drew attention to Darwin's last great contribution to knowledge, the work on the earthworm, that wonderful being that puts tremendous amounts of nutrients into the soil while working and aerating it at the same time.[1] He noted that the application of chemical fertilizer kills the earthworm: the U.S. Department of Agriculture even recommends the use of ammonia sulphate for destroying earthworms on golf putting greens.[2]

Sir Albert Howard exposed the hundred year old experiments at Rothamstead, comparing strips of land chemically fertilized with manured and unfertilized fields. As noted before, carefully kept statistics indicated that chemical fertilizer held its own against manure, while at the same time being cheaper, easier to handle and apply. Howard gave four reasons why these experiments were unsound:[3]

---

[1] Charles Darwin, *The Formation of Vegetable Moulds Through the Action of Worms*, (1882). Darwin estimated that 10 tons per acre passed through the earthworms annually, the resultant castings being much richer in P, K and Ca than the surrounding soil.

[2] Sir Albert Howard, *The Soil and Health*, p. 74.

[3] *Ibid*, pp. 72-75.

1. The experimental plots were too small and the conditions, that is, one hundred years of wheat, were too unnatural to be representative of anything that went on in any farm or garden anywhere.

2. Nature was reacting to the continuous crop of wheat by plaguing the experiments with weeds. The weeds got worse and worse.

3. Since plots were so narrow and no steps were taken to isolate the plot from the surrounding land, that a lot of earthworms would migrate into the plot; though they were periodically destroyed by the application of chemical fertilizer, they themselves were a fertilizing agent.

4. The fourth point is perhaps the most important. New seeds, secured from outside sources, were used each time. Had the seeds from each preceding crop been used, the results would have been different. It would have shown, as other studies indicate, that the vigor, the germination ability and the quality of the resultant plants would have decreased over a period of a few generations. The degeneration of seed stock is, after all, one of the major problems in agriculture today.

Sir Albert Howard was fought by the specialists of the research station and by the fertilizer and chemical companies whos profits were at stake. Fortunately, his influence spread. In Britain, Lady Eve Balfour, sickly since childhood, found that her health improved and so did the health of her piglets after she had turned to the Indore Method. Friend Sykes, a breeder of thoroughbred horses, found that organic fodder insured easier foaling and sure winners. Together, they formed the influential Soil Association in Britain. In the United States, it was *J.I. Rodale* who understood what Sir Albert Howard was saying:[4]

> In the reading of *An Agricultural Testament* (Howard, 1940) I was affected so profoundly that I could not rest until I had purchased a farm in order to assure for ourselves a supply of food raised by the new method. The reading of this great book showed me how simple the practice of the organic method could be.

The result was the *"Organic Farming and Gardening Magazine"* (1942) which by now has a circulation of nearly a million copies per month; the creation of organic gardening clubs; the circulation and publishing of information and new research.

Rudolf Steiner (1860-1925)

Rudolf Steiner was an Austrian philosopher who is known for his contributions to pedagogy (Waldorf Schools), curative education for the mentally handicapped, contributions to medicine, and social science (the Three-fold Social Order). In 1924, he was asked by farmers in Silesia to help provide insights into the problems that had begun to perplex their trade. The Silesian sugar beet growers were confronted with increasing crop disease and pests such as nematodes that were ruining their business. Other farmers had noticed a steady decline in the seed quality. For example, at one time, lucerne (alfalfa) could be grown up to thirty years on the same field while periodically cut for fodder, but then it was only 9 years, then only 7 years, and, at the time Dr. Steiner was confronted, it was only 4 to 5 years. In former times, also, a farmer could use his rye, oats, wheat,

[4] J. I. Rodale, *Encyclopedia of Organic Gardening* (Rodale Books, Inc., Emmaus, Pa. 1973), p. 802.

and barley year after year for seed, but recently, it has been only a few years before he is forced to buy a new variety. The seed quality just "degenerated." At the same time, animal health was getting problematical, with increased barrenness, difficult births, hoof-and-mouth disease, etc.[5] In June, 1924, Dr. Steiner gave a course of eight lectures at Koberwitz, the country estate of Count von Keyserlingk. These lectures provided the basis for the *bio-dynamic movement* in agriculture.[6] Since the lectures a half a century ago, bio-dynamics has grown to a respectable form of organiculture. Many of the indications that Steiner gave have been tested empirically by a number of scientists and have been found sound, as have those of the people who are directly engaged in agriculture, the farmers and gardeners.

Steiner was trained in the natural science tradition, but in order to understand the thought that lies in bio-dynamics, one must realize that he connects also with the insights and terminology of the pre-Enlightenment scientific tradition, in such a way that the modern mind can deal with them, permeating them with intellectual clarity. In this work we feel that we suddenly have access again to ancient traditions, such as the Greek natural philosophers with their teaching of the four basic elements, with Aristotle's *entelechy* and *scala naturae,* with the medieval cloister gardens and the alchemists with their concepts of transmutation of matter, correspondences of the microcosm and macrocosm, the planetary influences; with the Christian

[5] Koepf, Petterson, Schaumann: *Bio-Dynamic Agriculture* (Anthroposophic Press, Spring Valley, N.Y. 1976), p. 14.

[6] Rudolf Steiner, *Agriculture,* transl. by George Adams, 3rd ed. (Bio-Dynamic Agriculture Association, Rudolf Steiner House, 35 Park Road, London N.W. 1, 1974).

mystics such as Jacob Boehme, whose world of nature was the cloak of Divinity filled with spiritual forces; with the natural science writings of the poet Goethe, who refused to lose himself to abstract speculations and complicated instruments; and finally with the tradition of peasant wisdom and the obscure secretive lineage of European herbalists, such as the one in the Vienna Forest with whom Steiner had been in contact as a student.[7]

Steiner felt it was his mission to help recombine these ancient wisdoms and poetic insights with the findings of modern science, testing each for their soundness. Only such a holistic background can give the modern agriculturist the understanding he needs to deal with the complexity and depth of Nature. This should be by no means a purely intellectual exercise; rather, practical work is of major importance. We learn by doing and thinking; hands and heart are as important as the head. At agricultural conferences, at his headquarters in the Goetheanum in Dornach, Switzerland, Steiner insisted that there should be as many peasant farmers as scientists present.

Though one can practice bio-dynamics without specifically going into Steiner's philosophy, it will aid our purposes to list some of the concepts that make up the background of his agricultural lectures.

Bio-Dynamic vs. Organic

Is there a difference between the bio-dynamic method

---

[7] A book that gives some indications of this tradition of Old World folk healers and herbalists is the popular *Of Men and Plants* by Maurice Messegué, published by Macmillan Co., N.Y. 1973.

and the organic method, or are they pretty much different names for the same thing? Although we have mentioned both concepts in the same breath so far, there are a number of differences.

The organic method is ecologically oriented. It tries to replace an overly complex, laboratory-oriented approach with a *common sense* approach which the ordinary gardener and farmer can relate to. In many cases, the organic approach tries to understand how Nature does things, for "Nature knows best," and then tries to do gardening and farming in the most natural manner possible. Insects and diseases are combated by the use of nature's own remedies (ladybugs, trichogramma, preying mantises, garlic and pepper sprays, etc.). The aim is healthy soil for healthy plants for healthy men and animals.

Bio-dynamics is also ecologically oriented, but takes a much wider scope into account, including the sun, the moon, planets and subterranean features, in its effort to understand the totality of all factors. The mental factor is also considered. Bio-dynamics, though not disparaging of common sense, is concerned essentially with consciousness-expansion in regard to plants, animals and soil. The attempt is made to look into the deeper spirit of nature. Out of this deeper awareness, based on exquisite observation of nature, the approach calls for *not* letting things run their natural course, but for intensifying certain natural processes (creating optimal animal populations, making special compost preparations, planting selected companion plants at certain cosmic constellations), aiding nature where she is weak after so many centuries of abuse, short-cutting destructive processes, and using human intelligence, kindness and good will to foster positive developments (planting hedges for birds, planting bee pastures, etc.). Bio-dynamics is a human service to the earth and its creatures, not just a method for increasing production or for providing healthy food. The healthful and bountiful abundance is, so to speak, a natural result of the right view of and treatment of nature. Healthful food is not enough to save humanity; the question is, what are the energies provided by the good food going to be used for? Fighting bugs and disease-prevention are not major concerns for bio-dynamics as they are for the chemical farming method where tons of poisons are used to "solve" the problem, or for the organic method, where natural organic techniques are used for the war on bugs. Bio-dynamics can be summed up as: Putting one's energies into supporting the good, rather than into fighting the bad. Low productivity, insects and disease are not the problem, they are the symptoms. Spraying bugs ground up in a blender, using trichogramma wasps, etc. is treating the symptom, whereas building the soil and one's relationship to the land is treating the problem.

CHAPTER IV
BASIC CONCEPTS

The Four Elements

The concept that everything in Creation is composed of the elements, FIRE, AIR, WATER and EARTH, is ancient indeed, forming a great part of pre-Socratic speculation about the nature of the universe, and continuing through our history until replacement by Mendeleev's Periodic Table of nearly one hundred elements. We feel that we have advanced a long way, and the idea of four elements is rather simplistic. Yet, we ought to be cautious, for what the sages of old meant by an "element" is different from what we mean by an element of the periodic chart.

Aristotle, for example, sees primary matter as a CHAOS, that has only potential existence until it is impressed by the ordering formative forces derived from the COSMOS. These forces have four manifestations in the four elements. Matter is made manifest to us in the continual interplay of fire, air, water and earth.[1] In brief, Cornelius Agrippa of Nettesheim writes:

> There are four elements and primordial basis of all formed things: they are Fire, Earth, Water and Air. All natural things of our world are formed of them not by mere aggregation, but by transformations and intimate

[1] E.J. Holmyard, *Alchemy* (Penguin Books, Middlesex, England, 1968), p. 21.

combinations, which, when destroyed revert back to the original elements. None of the empirically sensible elements are in pure form, all are more or less mixed together ... Plato is of the opinion that ... the elements transmute into earth or into each other. Each element has two specific characteristics, one principle one and the other that serves as a connecting medium to the other elements. Whereas Fire is warm and dry, Earth is dry and cold, Water is cold and wet (moist) and Air is moist and warm. According to these characteristics, the elements form pairs of opposites, such as Fire and Water, Earth and Air. Other ways in which they form opposites are that Earth and Water are heavy while Air and Fire are light, for which reason the Stoics called the former passive and the latter active elements. Plato notes further distinctions, pointing out that Fire is sharp, rare and mobile, whereas Earth is dark, dense and at rest. In that Fire and Earth are opposites . . . etc.[2]

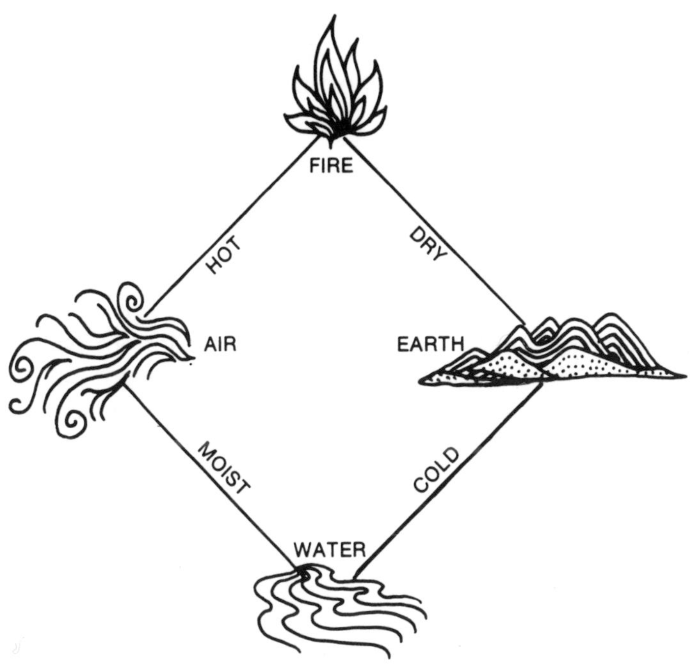

Let us examine this a little more closely: Fire is the least dense element and, hence, the most spiritual. It has a purifying, transmuting character; it is anything hot, colorful, quick, from a burning faggot to a choleric temper. Earth is most dense, and is manifested in anything in a solid, cold and dark state, from a piece of lead to a solid thought.

[2] Agrippa of Nettesheim; *De Occulta Philosophia Magische Werke* (Druck: A. Hain, Meisenheim Glan, 1530), pp. 49-51.

Water, flowing and sensitive, willing to assume all forms, is cold and dark, yet lets light travel through it.[3] Air is found in anything that is light, warm and moving, be it the wind, or in the soul.

The elements are always mixed as, for example, in a wood fire: Fire in the heat and darting flame; Air in the light, smoke and fragrance of the burning logs; Water in the melting pitch; Earth in the ashes.

Water, that is our H_2O, can similarly be found in its earthy elemental state as solidly frozen ice, in its watery state as a liquid, in its airy state as a vapor, and in its fiery state as a boiling substance.

The four elements are not just confined to the inorganic and mineral world, but bring into manifestation the other kingdoms of nature as well. In the plant kingdom, the earth element predominates in the roots, the water element in the leaves and fluid system of the plant, the air in the lightness and fragrance of the flowers, and the fire in the ripening of fruit and seed. We can characterize some plants as having a special affinity to the heavy earth and water element, such as cabbages, potatoes or beets, and others, such as grain and herbs, as having affinity to the light and warmth element.

In the human and animal organisms, we can assign the earth element to bones and nerves, the water element to the lymph and fluid system, the air element to the respiratory system and the fire element to the pulsating of the warm blood. Overall, one can imagine how the earth element predominates in the mineral kingdom, the water

---

[3] Water, as the sense-organ of the earth, in its sensitive, all-pervading form, is discussed in the excellent work, *Sensitive Chaos*, by Theodore Schwenk.

element in the plant kingdom, the mobile air element in the animal kingdom and the fire element in the human kingdom.

Of what use is the concept of the four elements to us as farmers and gardeners? For one thing, *the manifestations of the four elements are directly available to our senses,* while the 100 and some elements that the chemist talks about are not there for us to experience directly. Mendeleev's elements are available primarily to our intellect, but not to our senses. This is not to discount the careful work of diligent scientific specialists, rather it is to point out a way that the ordinary farmer and gardener can sharpen his own observation and trust his own judgment once again. In the four elements, we have a conceptual system that can be applied to everyday work with nature; it worked well in a time of direct unmediated experience and observation, not so much as a theory, as an ideational description of what is already there. As we shall see later, it is a valuable way of describing and experiencing the seasons, the growing habits of plants, the quality of manures, the processes of composts, etc. In farming, one can speak of cold, wet soil such as clay which is too much Earth, or of sandy soil which is too light and heats up too quickly, as too much Air and Fire. A compost can be diagnosed as too watery, too earthy, too airy and too hot; and how such a compost will affect the vegetables can be studied, also, in these terms.

It is a good exercise to practice detecting the four elements and to try to describe all observable phenomena in these terms. Many secrets of nature reveal themselves to the observer, and that without the aid of complicated instruments (microscopes, spectroscopes, soil-test kits) or technical literature that abounds with abstract jargon. If practiced correctly, one has at one's disposal a means of finding the keys to successful gardening without the aid of a distant specialist. This is one way of overcoming the alienation from immediate experience that ails so many modern people. The author has seen traditional farmers look at the sky and know what the weather would be like in the next 48 to 72 hours on the basis of just such repeated observations, while neighbors who had lost self-confidence in their own judgment and observation abilities, would listen to the radio bulletin to find out whether it would rain, to know whether they should hay or not. Since the weather patterns are much influenced by local idiosyncrasies, especially in the mountains, it is little wonder that the traditionalist's judgments were often more to the point than those who relied on experts that were miles from the scene, in some city office where such predictions are made.[4]

The four elements are not obvious and easy to discern at first, but a meditation on water will help, watching it change from ice to water, boil, evaporate, condense and freeze. Then compare dry ice to this. Where is the difference? Cooking, especially on a wood fire, if done correctly, is one of the finest contemplations of the transformations and interplay of the four elements (T.V. dinners do more than give

[4] The kind of alienation from the immediate phenomenological perception and from a confident judgment is instilled at the earliest age into the school child in our modern society: Children are taught that their perception is wrong when they think the sun rises and sets and that, except for hills, the earth is essentially flat. Instead, the child is told that the earth is a ball that orbits around the sun. The latter is intellectually and scientifically sound and is the basic factor that made the rockets and moon-landings possible, but phenomenologically and on the level of down-to-earth decisions, it is *not* true. For the plants in the garden, the sun does actually rise in the morning in the east and set in the evening in the west. R. Steiner would say that both perspectives are necessary and one is not more "right" than the other.

an upset stomach, they also impoverish inner life by depriving one of the chance to experience these elemental transformations). It is in meditations like these that the alchemists experienced their work not only as one of externally changing, transmuting one substance into another (lead into gold, "muck" into humus), but of changing a base mentality into a heart of gold and a mind of crystal.

Barthelemy de Glanville: "Le Proprietaire des Choses" 1487

In the days of yore, the four elements found imaginative personifications as the workings of the gnomes and dwarves (Earth) who worked crystal mines and on plant roots, nixies and undines (Water) found in all water interfaces, sylphs and fairies (Air) and fire spirits and salamanders (Fire).

Nature can correctly and effectively be described in terms of the interaction of such elemental spirits.

When dealing with the four elements, bio-dynamic researchers tend to talk of formative forces, or *etheric formative forces:* the life or earth ether; the chemical, sound or water ether; the light ether; the warmth ether. The ethers are the formative forces whose effects can be read in the forms and appearances in the physical world. In themselves, they are supersensible, or discernible to inner perception if this is trained. By looking carefully at the gesture the plant makes during its growth, one can read what forces were working on the plant to give it the shape and characteristics it has.

Etheric formative forces sculpt our visible world. As a cursory example, let us look at the physiognomy of leaves: for instance, the hemp leaves are worked on by the forces of light and warmth, melting away the substance and leaving only lacy, pointed lances that are filled with resin and aroma. In contrast, one can take the fleshy, succulent leaves of cabbage in which the earth and water forces predominate and swell it with substance. Both are, by the way, good companion plants, complementing each other to

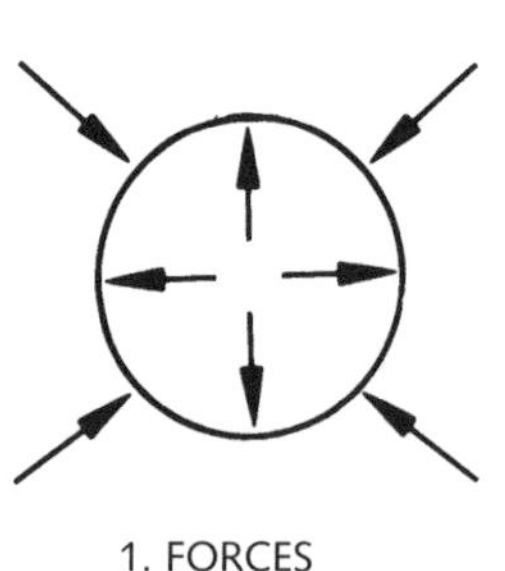

1. FORCES BALANCED

i.e. OAK CABBAGE

2. INNER FORCES STRONGER (EARTH–WATER LIFE–CHEMICAL)

i.e. HEMP MAPLE

3. OUTER FORCES STRONGER (AIR–LIGHT)

keep hungry insects at bay. In the stomach, too, heavy foods such as cabbage and potatoes are best complemented when seasoned with caraway seed, a plant that is formed by light and air ether.

The gardener can see to it that plants with an affinity for the earth and water ether (cool weather lovers) get the moister, cooler spots in the garden, for if the air and light ether become too strong, they will bolt. Those plants that have affinity to the light and air ether should be aided to keep them from getting "stuck." In the *Agricultural Course,* Rudolf Steiner gave hints on how to aid the flow of these etheric forces, by the use of *silica* preparations which aid the light absorption capacity of plants, and the use of calcium and cow manure preparations which strengthen the life and chemical (earth and water) etheric formative forces. These preparations will be discussed in the second part of the book.

A number of researchers have developed methods for making these etheric formative forces visible. The formation of floral and foliar ice crystal patterns on window panes in the winter, and the vibrations from musical instruments that can arrange fine dust on paper into various organic-looking figures (Chladni's figures) are examples of visible indications of these formative forces. The method of *capillary dynamolysis* developed by L. Kolisko, using plant saps to be tested in a solution of silver nitrate, and then studying the characteristic patterns that are created by the capillary movement of this solution up a roll of filter paper, provide pictures of the effect of these etheric forces that are working in substances.[5] Characteristic differences between bio-

[5] L. Kolisko, *Agriculture of Tomorrow* (Kolisko Archives, London, 1939).

dynamically grown food and chemically grown food, between plants germinated during different lunar phases can be shown by this capillary method.

Another method is the *sensitive crystallization* procedure developed by E. Pfeiffer. Here, substances drawn from plant, animal or human tissue are tested by crystallizing them in a solution of copper chloride. The patterns of crystal formation are characteristic. For example, roots will yield more compact crystals than flower extracts. The method is being used in medicine to diagnose for various disorders, by crystallizing blood.[6]

Photographing the characteristic movements of water streams and drops through a viscous fluid, such as glycerine, is a method developed by T. Schwenk to make visible the formative forces of the water element.[7]

Formative forces of sound, such as the spoken word and the sound of musical instruments can be made visible by a sound-sensitive flame.[8]

In a discussion of the basic four elements, the fifth element, or *quinta essentia,* must be included. This fifth element can be interpreted to refer to the human element, human consciousness, as vital an essence as the others, but of a different nature. Thus for a compost, one must have enough solid matter; there must be enough moisture for the metabolism of the small organisms; there must be air spaces for gas exchange; and a heated metabolism must come

---

[6] Ehrenfried Pfeiffer, *Sensitive Crystallization Processes: A Demonstration of Formative Forces in the Blood* (Spring Valley, N.Y.: Anthroposophic Press, 1936).

[7] T. Schwenk, *Sensitive Chaos* (Schocken Books, N.Y., 1976).

[8] Schiller, P.E.; "Untersuchungen an der freien schallempfindlichen Flamme" (Akustische Zeitschrift, 1938).

about. But for all this to be happening properly, it takes the quintessence, the gardener, who arranges the compost heap. All four elements are present on any spot of ground, but by themselves they form no garden: it takes the ordering principle, the quintessence, to arrange the four so that the garden can flourish in harmony. What the gardener is in a microcosmic sense, Christ as the Master of the Elements is in the larger sense, as shown in the illustration above.[9] Considerations like these might provide a key to man's place in nature.

PROCESSES: Sal, Mercurius, Sulphur

Besides the Four Elements and their mutual interactions, the alchemists also talked about basic *processes* which tie in with them. What goes on in the universe as movements, functions, states of being can be understood as essentially three processes: that of the *sal* (salt) process referring to precipitation, crystallization; that of the sulphur process, referring to dissipation, dissolution, going into sublimation; the mercury (quicksilver) process, which mediates the exchanges between the opposite poles, the contracting, centripetal salt process, and the centrifugal sulphur process.

As an example, in the plant, the hard, condensed nature of the gnarled root shows that the salt process is stronger here than in other parts of the plant. The *mercury* process is evident in the leaves and stems with their respiration, assimilation and transport functions; and the *sulphur* process is evident in the delicate flowers and fruit which dissipate themselves in fragrance, pollen and seed. This can be illustrated by an annual weed, noting the difference between

[9] Barthelemy de Glanville, "*Le Proprietaire des Choses,*" (1487).

the lower leaves and the leaves as they move upwards towards the flower; one will observe the leaves becoming lacy, pointed, less substantial, as though the plant is dissipating itself.

In the seasons, we see these processes at work also: winter with its freezing, crystallizing character, drawing all things tightly together, is a salt process; rainy spring and early summer with winds and rapid growth of vegetation indicate a mercury process; while late summer and fall with the heat and the dissolving of the lush vegetation into myriad color and fragrance show a sulphur process. This in turn gives way to a salt process in late fall when the birds gather into tight flocks to fly south and plants retreat into seed, into the roots and bark, or into the ground, hugging it tightly as a rosette formation.

In plants, animals, composts and soils one can detect imbalances in the processes, or abnormal and one-sided expressions of the processes, as for example fruits and vegetables that are too hard and woody, stems that have hard knots on them indicating an excessive sal process. On the other hand, the plant might rot, develop odors and mucus in the stem, leaf or even root area: here we can say that the sulphur process is taking place too early, or is in the plant in the wrong place at the wrong time.

According to Paracelsus of Hohenheim, Sal, Mercur and Sulphur are kept in balance by the *Archeus* (ether body). If this Archeus does not function, the processes will split up, one will burn, another will rot, another dry up; the organism will fall apart.

All this can be carefully observed in Nature. The observations can be diligently practiced at any time without the need for special equipment or instruments. One can see sulphur, mercury and salt in the burning of a log, in the darting flame, the smell and odors of the smoke and the remnant of the ashes. Just as with the four elements, we can meditate on this trinity in cooking, baking, pottery making and, of course, gardening. We can see plants such as the carrot which bring sulphuric color and fragrance all the way down into the tap root. Pines bring the salt process all the way to their flowers (cones) which are dense and woody, while at the same time, the sulphur penetrates leaf, stem and root in the fragrant pitch. Composts in which the sulphur process is too strong smell badly and dissipate their nutrients as methane and ammonia. Earthworms, by carrying decaying organic substance into the ground and mineral substance upwards, carry on a mercurial function in the soil; initiating a sal process by applying ammonium sulphate will drive them off. The examples are endless.

The alchemists found these processes not just on the physical, material plane, but as processes of the mind and spirit, as well. Here, sal is the crystallizing *thought;* mercur, the ever-moving *feeling* and *sensing;* and the sulphur process, the *will.* A good gardener has to know these inner aspects of the processes also, for they are to be found in him who is the quintessence of the garden. These, too, are ingredients in a proper garden as much as water, fertilizer and seeds. There is an *inner gardening* that accompanies the outer gardening; it is perhaps the key to the often talked about "green thumb," the "good vibes" that turn wastelands into gardens of Eden. They might account for the recently discovered phenomenon of the "Backster effect." (Fluctuating electric potential in plants in response to human presence, measurable by a galvonometer.)

Microcosm – Macrocosm

Elements and processes work within the world of Nature and the world of Man. This takes us to another important universal concept found in ancient and primitive man alike, but difficult for the 20th century thinker: that of the *macrocosm* and the *microcosm.* Man is a "little world" that contains all of the elements of the "greater world."[10] Both worlds contain an inner and an outer aspect. Man lives within the outer world of Nature that reaches from the stars

[10] This anthropological insight is expressed in the Hebraic-Babylonian account in Genesis of the creation of Adam from the mud (substance) and the breath (spirit) to form the *imago dei,* in contrast to the other creatures that came into existence by the fiat: "Let there be . . ."

of the heavens to the sand grains of the seashore, and includes minerals, plants and animals; through thoughts, feelings, instincts, through dreams, memories, imaginations and intuitions he perceives the inner side of the macrocosm. Because the microcosm is of the same nature as the macrocosm, man can understand and has affinity with all that exists macrocosmically. As Goethe expresses it: "Thou art like the spirit thou doest comprehend" (Faust I).[11]

Certain Renaissance scholars, such as Giordano Bruno, Agrippa of Nettesheim, Ficino, et al, drawing upon the hermetic-cabbalistic and neo-platonist traditions, postulated a spiritual origin of the Universe, both macrocosm and microcosm, in which the Creator, through His Word, created the universe in a series of pulsations.[12] From the pure Spirit emanated the world of the Soul (World Soul), out of which the ocean of life forces (World

---

[11] 19th century philosophy and, for that matter, western philosophy in general after Descartes, believed the two regions to be entirely separated and "never the twain shall meet." The outer world of nature takes its separate, mindless course, unaffected by the inner world of human thinking, feeling and willing, so the university professors thought. For Kant, thought and even perception were subjective, the "Ding-an-sich," the objective world could not be known in its essence. Of course, shamans, Hopi medicine men, African witch doctors, as well as Shakespeare's witches, and traditionalists would not agree. They always acted as though there were sympathies between people's state of soul and Nature, such as between the inner climate and the weather in nature, and they held that one could affect the other and vice-versa. Sir James Frazer, in his *Golden Bough,* cites numerous examples of primitive "sympathetic" and "contagious" magic. But the enlightened world has split the subjects of study at the universities into sciences and humanities, and the two have ever since had a difficult time communicating. Modern anthropology, as originally conceived by Tylor and Boas, attempted to heal the breach, but it, too, soon fell apart into the specialties of cultural and physical anthropology. Rudolf Steiner's anthroposophy has tried to do the same with more success, showing that the inside and outside are metamorphoses of the same forces and beings.

[12] Frances Yates, *Giordano Bruno and the Hermetic Tradition,* (Vintage Books, New York, 1964).

Ether) emanated, which then crystallized into the physical world. Other thinkers have the microcosm evolve out of the macrocosm, symbolized by an animal recreating itself by laying eggs (the Easter Bunny with his eggs is a remnant of this lofty concept). The same forces that created the universe at large with its kingdoms of nature, created the human being with all of his faculties. Thus, there are *correspondences* and *sympathies* between the world of nature and the world of man all along the line. The one is the mirror-image of the other: "As above, so below," proclaims the meditation formula of Hermes Trismegistus.

What is concentrated in man, the salt (sal) of the earth, is spread out in nature as millions of separate entities. What is laid out before him as the animal kingdom in the macrocosm is found in man's soul as the many passions, desires and feelings seated deep in his blood, respiration and muscle tissues. What is called the plant kingdom in the macrocosm is the endlessly sprouting, growing, wilting, and decaying life of the imagination that is based on the lymph and vegetative system in man. What is the solid mineral kingdom of the macrocosm, obeying rigid physical and chemical laws involving causality and exclusiveness, is in man the faculty for clear, logical thinking that has its physical locus in the bone and nerve tissue which is most mineralized and least alive of the body tissues. This is one of the reasons why the logical, abstracting mind can deal so effectively with the physical, material world; that world can be treated as a mechanism and its laws can be abstractly formulated. However, this faculty is not enough to understand the world of plants and animals which engages the gardener, because these are more than mechanisms, they are living, etheric organisms which can

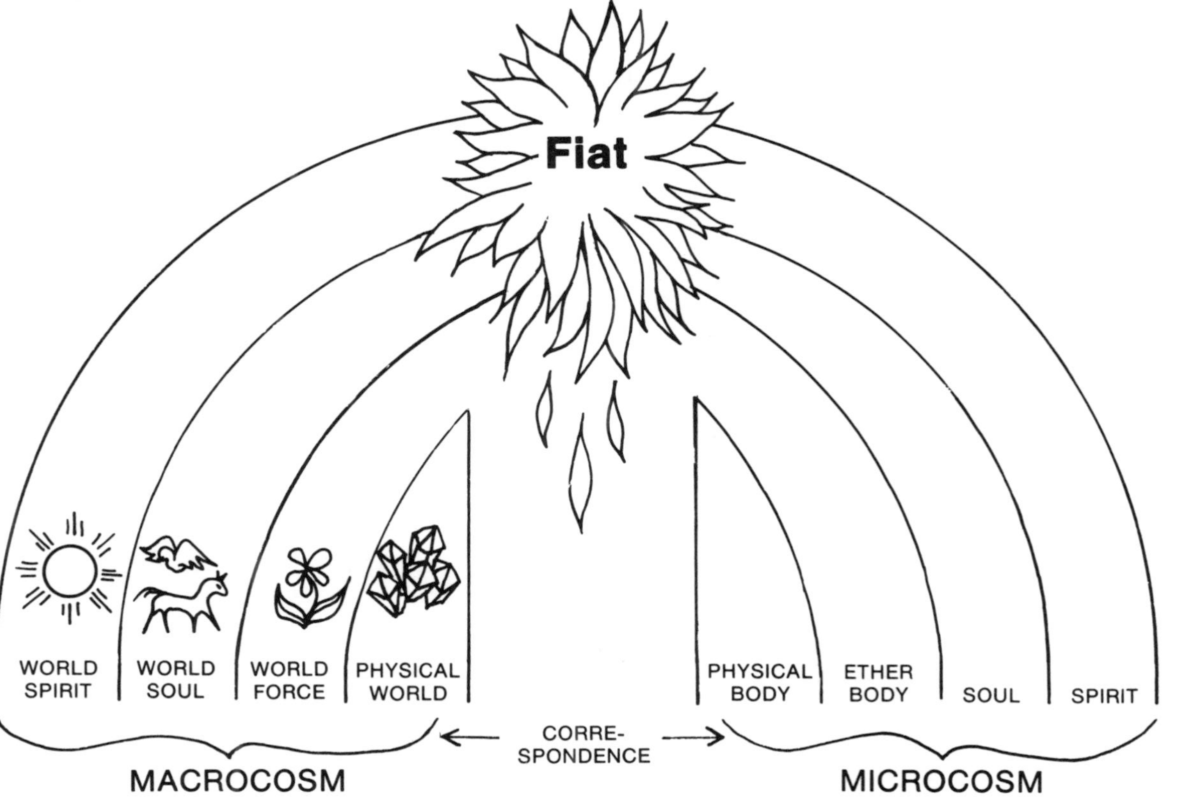
Fiat
WORLD SPIRIT
WORLD SOUL
WORLD FORCE
PHYSICAL WORLD
PHYSICAL BODY
ETHER BODY
SOUL
SPIRIT
MACROCOSM
CORRE-SPONDENCE
MICROCOSM

only be understood when the proper imaginations (image= picture) come to life in the mind.

Nature can be seen as man exteriorized, and man is nature internalized. Because everything found in external nature is found somewhere in man and everything found in man is found in some transformation in the realm of nature, the Renaissance neo-platonists postulated that in order to study the human being one must study nature, and in order to study nature one must study the human being.

The correspondences are found on all levels (physical, etheric, astral, spiritual). We can only indicate here. Again, it takes a lot of practice and imagination to get the feel of what is meant by them. Where, for instance, are the eagles and sparrows found in the microcosm: are they not like high, soaring, lofty ideas or daily little fluttering thoughts? Where are snails or slugs to be found in man: is it not in the tongue? Do snails not go tasting their way through the world and in a deeper sense are they not found in the character trait of slushy indulgence? And thunder and lightning . . . are these not flashes of anger or flashes of insight whose manifestation both externally and internally was personified by the ancients as Thor, Jupiter, Indra, Thunderbird or Michael?

Very archetypal imaginations of correspondences are those of the seven visible planets. Each planet has a *signature,* working through the formative forces into manifestations in nature and in man. Thus, Venus is not just a tiny speck of dead light in the starry sky, but has a macrocosmic signature in the color green, in the metal copper, in sexual attraction and reproduction, in plants such as birches etc., and it is present in the microcosm as love, sensual or aesthetic, negatively in the green of jealousy, in the physical body as kidneys and their function. Jupiter's signature is in the color yellow, the metal tin, in stately creatures such as maples and eagles, in wisdom and justice, in the body in the liver, etc. Mars is found in red, iron, nettles and oaks, in the gall formation on oaks and in animals, in warlike fierceness and courage, etc. The sun's signature is found in gold, uprightness and has the heart as its organ. The moon has silver, growing and decaying, snails, worms, dogs, etc. Mercury has quicksilver, any movement, message bearing, commerce, healing, snakes, etc. among its signatures. Lead, dark colors, pines and beeches, time, old age, etc. are among the signatures of Saturn. The list is endless because the world of phenomena is endless. Neither is it as simple as some astrologers have us believe, because the spheres of the planets interpenetrate each other and the influences are mixed so that seldom does the signature come out clear and unequivocal. Alchemists have always indicated that it is a difficult task to perceive these signatures and correspondences that exist in nature correctly; it takes keen external observation and perception of the senses as well as the inner perception of the proper imagination.

Alchemists agreed that just as it takes clear senses to perceive the external world, so it takes a clear mind, not clouded by wishful thinking, lusts, and bad will to perceive the supersensible qualities of the object under study. For, to the alchemists, the mind does not primarily think, but is a mirror that reflects what exists in the universe into the conscious part of the soul (that is why, for example, the brain was assigned to the lunar sphere which reflects the light of the sun). If the mirror is distorted by virtueless living, the images perceived will also be distorted.

The discussion of *imaginative perception* and of *goetheanistic science* will aid the methodology of our endeavor to understand these images.

Imaginative Perception

Just as there can be logical, clear thoughts that correctly apprehend the phenomena of the physical world, as opposed to illogical, obscure or erroneous thoughts, so there can be living imaginations that apprehend something of the life, soul and spirit of the world. These imaginations must be distinguished from wild and idle fantasies that only confuse and do not explain or point out anything. Logical, discursive thought and imagination are not mutually exclusive; both account for different aspects of the same phenomena.

As an example: walk through the orchard in late fall or early spring, just before sunrise. Delicate frost crystals growing on the bare, black branches sparkle in the light of predawn. Quickly, the first beams ray over the hill and strike the branches. The crystals disappear at the touch of the sunrays, filling the still grove with rustling, sounding like footsteps or squirrels scurrying about, as they fall onto the dry leaf mulch. This lasts for a moment until the sun is up higher and then it is still again. The hoar-frost is gone.

This is a phenomenological vignette of what one might experience. Given the same phenomenon, one can explain it in the fashion of logical, discursive thought that remains on a materialistic level, or one can explain it imaginatively. Both approaches are correct and one is not exclusive of the other.

A materialistic, mechanistic explanation would have the hoar-frost grow due to the special bonding nature of H_2O

when the relative humidity has reached 100% (dewpoint) while the temperature is on or below 0° Celsius. As the position of the earth planet shifts relative to the sun, the solar radiations warm, first of all, the black twigs (black absorbs the entire spectrum, converting the light into thermal units). As the branches heat above 4°C, the portion of the crystals attached to them liquifies, subjecting the remaining crystal structures to gravitational pull. The impact of the crystals on the mulch causes acoustically audible waves. In a matter of a few minutes, the air temperature, generally, has been warmed to such a degree that the fallen crystals liquify, drip off the mulch and, thus, seem to disappear.

An imaginative explanation draws not so much from the abstractly formulated laws of physics and chemistry, but uses the metalanguage of age-old cultural tradition based on visions and images that have been passed through the generations; the explanation of the phenomenon might go like this: Helios, the sun king, is approaching; heralds in pink and tender blue vestments announce his approach. Gnomes and dwarves, who work with the crystallizing forces of nature with ores and precious stones in the dark recesses of the universe, do not like to see the sun directly (they prefer to hear about the sun through what the growing plant roots tell them during the summer). And they certainly are not on speaking terms with the dumb sylphs who dance on the sunbeams. So they scramble back into the earth, causing rustling sounds as they snatch up their precious crystals, losing most of them to the undines, the water spirits, who turn the crystals into liquid.

Sometimes imaginative explanations serve the purpose of obtaining a holistic concept, a gestalt, of what is going on, better than a materialistic abstraction.[13]

In gardening, we are dealing with such innumerable factors, the minerals, insects, birds, plants, weather and cosmic influences, that often imaginative pictures comprehend totality better than a materialistic, discursive form of thinking. Imaginations comprehend gestalts, that is, they grasp totalities. They can deal with aspects that necessarily lie outside the parameters of our limited thinking. The gardener who thinks only materialistically is tempted to treat the soil, the plant, the animal like machines or mechanisms, which they are not; he is tempted to use abstract concepts of chemistry (NPK), fuel-energy, input-output ratio models for the organisms, formulas, etc. in his analysis of his garden or farm organism. This is inevitably harmful, for it does not show understanding of their true nature; living processes must be understood by living thoughts. For bio-dynamic gardening, living picture imaginations are necessary, but they must be correct and fit the phenomena. They must give a clearer concept of reality.

Unfortunately, there is currently much occultist, one-sided, spiritualistic nonsense written about gardening; fantastic accounts of talking with plants, drug-induced dreams of beings and forces that do not connect with the

---

[13] For example, small children have a better idea about where the baby brother comes from when they are told of the stork that flies to the swamp and picks up the baby from among the waterlilies and drops it through the chimney of the house. Included in this true imagination are numerous symbolic elements that satisfy the curiosity of the child without violating its sense of truth, and that avoid the abstract notions of microscopic sperm, ova, zygotes, DNA-RNA, etc. which the child is incapable of comprehending at his age. The stork, a white bird, symbolizes the transcendent origin of the human being; the long, red beak, the depositing of the infant in the family hearth include beautiful imaginations of human sexuality; the primal swamp indicates the frog-like nature of the embryo in the watery environment of the womb, etc.

phenomena, but are idle, fluttering fantasies and illusions that will not help in a realistic way to create beautiful, productive gardens.

The Spheres, or Planes

To aid us in an understanding of what plants, animals, man and minerals are in relation to each other and to the universe, there lingers in the background of bio-dynamic epistemology the concept that the universe is arranged in a series of interacting, interpenetrating planes that are presided over or occupied by a hierarchy of beings, souls, essences and spirits. Earliest cosmologies, similar to those still maintained by shamanistic tribes of Siberia, illustrate it as a Cosmic Tree, at whose roots the primordial dragon dwells, whereas all beings live on some level along the branches, while eagles live at the top.[14] Such cosmologies are again imaginative expressions of contents of inner and outer experience.

Starting with the empirical world, one can experience solid rock formations always on the bottom, followed by a layer of water (lakes, seas), then a level of air (atmosphere) above which light and warmth (sun, moon) originate. This is how one experiences the physical world, not the other way around, though there are many intermediate realms and mixed states. This can be referred to as the *hierarchy of the elements*.

Some creatures are more at home in one element than in

---

[14] A microcosmic version of the tree is seen in the backbone along which the vital organs, with their different faculties, are arranged, starting with the unconscious, wormlike intestinal apparatus and ending on top with the head from which thoughts arise and arrive like flocks of birds. In the Nordic *Voluspa*, the tree, which spans nine universes, is called the Yggdrasil, roughly translated as the "I-carrier."

	SPHERES	MINERALS	PLANTS	ANIMALS	MAN	MODE OF PERCEPTION	HIERARCHIES
SUPER-SENSIBLE WORLD or SUPER-NATURAL WORLD	Higher Spirit Plane	Ego or Spirit of the Mineral				Intuition	Higher Hierarchies Crystal Heaven Logos
	Harmony of the Spheres	Soul of the Mineral	Ego or Spirit of Plants			Inspiration	12 Regions of the Zodiac Cherubim Seraphim
	Astral or Elemental Plane	Ether Body of Mineral	Soul of Plant	Ego or Group Souls of Animals		Imagination	Thrones ♄ Kyriotetes ♃ Dynamis ♂ Exusai ☉ Archai ♀ Arch-Angels ☿ Angels ☽
		Gnomes	Undines	Sylphs	Fire Spirits		
Sensible World (Incarnate)	Earth Plane (Midgard)	Physical Mineral (Inorganic Nature)	Physical and Etheric Body of Plants	Physical and Etheric Body and Souls of Animals	Physical and Etheric Body and Soul and Ego or Spirit of Man MICROCOSM	Physical Senses Reason	Earth
Sub-sensible or Sub-natural World	Sub-terrestrial	Gravity	Electricity	Magnetism	Nuclear Energy	Special Instruments Mathematics	Lower Hierarchies

the other: worms and moles in the ground, fish in the water, fowl and butterfly in the air and light. Though these creatures live in the elements, they are different from them. As living creatures, they express the working of a life force which can get a hold of and utilize the elements in its own construction. This life, or etheric, force creates a level of organization beyond the elements, a level that can be called that of the *formative*, or *etheric forces*. It is characterized by vitality, endless repetition of itself (i.e. plant growing from node to node, mitosis), symmetry and levity (as opposed to gravity). Phenomenologically the living organisms referred to collectively as the vegetable kingdom can be explained in terms of elements (physical body) and life forces (ether body).

Other organisms have something in their makeup that goes beyond the purely etheric forces, something that turns ever-growing life forces into another direction, that stops the endless replication of the formative forces and changes them into sensitivity, feeling, drives and consciousness. These organisms are the animals, where the purely vegetative, unconscious growth has been turned into organs of sensing, nerves and inner organs, which do not have the regenerative powers of purely vegetative cells. In that animals are sensing, feeling and increasingly conscious, they represent a higher state of being, that of the incarnate *soul* (L. anima=Soul). Whereas plants incarnate physically and etherically, animals develop thinking which is used to aid the instincts in meeting the exigencies of life.

In the human being, however, a new level is reached, characterized by symbolic and abstract thinking, impulses of a moral nature and self-consciousness which go beyond the sympathies and antipathies of the soul life. We are here at the state of egohood or self-conscious *spirit*, where the question posed, "Who is it that is thinking, feeling and willing?" is answered by "I am!" Thus, man has a physical body, an ether body, a soul and a spirit.[15]

This, which has just been discussed, makes up the *natural world*, the place that in Germanic mythology was called *Midgard* (the garden in the middle), which was regarded as the proper dwelling place of mankind.

Below the natural world are levels, or spheres, which were in former times imaginatively called the abodes of the demons and devils. These are the realms of sub-material forces that are no longer concrete matter, which the modern scientist perceives using powerful laboratory instruments and advanced mathematics. These forces, gravity, electricity, magnetism and nuclear energy might themselves be reflections of the etheric formative forces, for they are known to have effects on vegetation (i.e. electroculture).[16] These lower levels might be called the *sub-natural world*.

There is also a *supernatural world*. The wisest of humanity have never doubted the possibility that beings can exist in nonphysical manifestation. The possibility opens that elemental spirits, angels and other nonincarnate beings who might have etheric bodies, astral bodies or spirit bodies but not physical bodies, exist, in back of phenomena, and that it is just with our materialistic thinking and physical perception that we do not perceive them. (If we do perceive

---

[15] Max Scheler, *Man's Place In Nature* (Noonday Press, NY, 1962): Scheler sees in the ability of homo sapiens to say "NO" to his drives and passions indications of the spirit.

[16] The many experiments of subjecting soils or plants to electric currents in order to induce more rapid growth are recorded in Tompkins, P. and Bird C.: *The Secret Life of Plants,* chaps. 10 & 11; "Plants and Electromagnetism" and "Force Fields, Humans and Plants."

them with our physical eyes, then we are probably hallucinating.) Already through imaginative thinking one has images of beings that have their effects in the physical world, but are themselves not present in it as incarnate entities. How else does one explain the universality in human culture, attested to in ethnographic literature, of dragons, witches, garden dwarfs, nature spirits, unicorns etc.? Cultural traditions of myth, art and poetry are clothing these nonmaterial beings (essences, forces) in forms that make sense to us. With a developed inner vision, true imagination, one can perceive pictures on the *astral* or *elemental plane.* A higher faculty than the imaginative one is the *inspirational faculty* that perceives what lies beyond the picture images. Real inspiration is said to come from "heaven," a plane beyond the elemental and astral world, which is referred to as the plane of the *Harmony of the Spheres,* or *Lower Spiritual Plane.* Real inspiration is the rare experience of a few gifted people like Shakespeare, Dante, Beethoven. An even higher level of perception than Inspiration is that of *true intuition* which perceives into a world of archetypal images, into the *Higher Spiritual Plane.* Such intuitions, when available to an age through a great human being, are characterized as a great religious-sacred insight, as a major advance of mankind, such as the intuition of Zarathustra, who, according to legends, taught humanity first how to do agriculture.[17]

---

[17] C.F. Rudolf Steiner, *Macrocosm and Microcosm* (Rudolf Steiner Press, London, 1968), p. 206 n. Varying terminology employed for the supersensible worlds:

Oriental: Physical Plane; Astral Plane; Rupa-Devachan or Lower Mental Plane, Arupa Devachan or Higher Mental Plane.

Medieval and Rosicrucian Theosophy: Physical World, Imaginative World, World of Inspiration or Harmony of the Spheres, World of True Intuition.

Others: Little World, World of the Elements, World of Spirit or Heavenly World, World of Reason, World of Archetypal Images.

The various planes can be located in spatial, as well as in inner configuration. Imagination, which perceives the astral plane (Gr. aster=star), is related macrocosmically to the planetary spheres of Saturn, Jupiter, Mars, Sun, Venus, Mercury and Moon. The world of inspiration has its locus in the fixed stars, the zodiac. The world of intuition is born in the realms beyond the fixed stars, the so-called Crystal Heaven. In Christian mythology, as formulated by Dionysius the Areopagite, all these regions are populated by the angelic host, the three major choirs of angels (see chart, p. 68).

It is on the lower level of the supersensible world, the astral plane, that the animals' guiding spirits or their group-egos originate. From the realms stretching from Saturn to the Moon, the forces that so wisely guide the animals are to be found. The migration of flocks, the building of nests, the running of salmon upstream, rutting seasons, the spinning of pupae, paper-making by the paper wasps, etc., are usually referred to as "instinct" or "innate behavior mechanisms" for lack of better understanding. When one looks only at the animal's nervous system and cerebral development, one really cannot explain these complex behaviors. To do so is like looking at the hands of a clock, postulating an intrinsic reason for their movement without taking the background mechanism into account. In earlier times one tried to come to a closer understanding of the guiding forces of the animals by seeing their behavior in light of the rhythms of the sun, moon and the other planets as they move against the background of the zodiacal constellations (Gr. zodiac=animal circle). Thus, it was said that the spirits, or egos, of the animals are not incarnated on the physical plane as are the egos of individual human beings with their self-consciousness. For animals only the physical bodies, etheric bodies, and souls (anima) are incarnated. One can say that there is an ego, or group-spirit, for each group or species of animal. This explains why in primitive tribes, almost without exception, the medicine men and witch doctors claimed in all seriousness to be conversing with animals that appeared to them in (culturally modified) humanoid form. American Indians, for example, would put themselves onto the imaginative plane of consciousness by ritually regulated fasting, isolation, dance or the use of psychotropic herbs, and then would talk to the "grandfather" or "boss" of the animals asking special favors or protection, requesting the grandfathers to release some of their children to be hunted and promising in return to respect certain taboos. Young Indians seeking guidance and a life's mission tried to contact the animal spirits on the supersensible plane. The mind that is incapable of imaginative consciousness considers this to be "superstition" and locates the causes of such behaviors in some intrinsic "socio-psychological behavior mechanism."

Whereas we have our ego consciousness on the physical plane and animals have it on the astral plane, the plants have their egos or group spirits on the plane of the Harmony of the Spheres. This plane is accessible to the form of consciousness referred to by early Rosicrucians as "inspiration" and is located in the realm of the fixed stars which includes the twelve regions of the zodiac. It is from here that the archetypal plants (sometimes called devas) direct their children, who are their physical and etheric bodies on earth. This is expressed poetically in the case of little violets:

When God cuts holes in Heaven
The holes the stars look through,
He lets the little scraps fall down to earth—
The little scraps are you.[18]

This is the "music of the spheres" of Pythagoras that gives the world its geometry; orders and arranges with its musical, rythmical influences everything from the atoms to the harmonious symmetries of the plants, as shown by the correlation of the numerical ratios between the movement of the heavenly bodies, music and plant forms. Here music originates; perhaps this gives a reason why, as a number of studies have shown, plants are influenced by the vibrations of music.[19] It is interesting to note, too, that this region is often seen as the "heaven" where the dead dwell, who then work on the plant growth, on vegetation on the earth below.[20]

---

[18] Alfred C. Hottes, *Garden Facts and Fancies* (Dodd, Mead, & Co., N.Y., 1949), p. 63.

[19] P. Thompkins and C. Bird, *The Secret Life of Plants;* a comprehensive overview is given in chapter 9, "The Harmonic Life of Plants."

[20] Ethnologically it is of interest to note that in most horticultural societies, especially in Africa and E. Asia, the dead, the ancestors, are thought of as working in the ripening of fruits and flowers, grain and seed. One feeds the dead food, shows deference with flowers and sacrifices and they, in turn, working from the macrocosm into the earth, assure the crop. American Indian horticulturists, such as the Iroquois, believed the dead traveled the long road along the Milky Way and lived in villages located somewhere in the fixed stars. According to Mircea Eliade, *Patterns of Comparative Religion,* (Meridian Books, N.Y., 1963), p. 351: "Hippocrates tells us that the spirits of the dead make seeds grow and germinate and the author of the *Geoponica* says that the winds (souls of the dead) give life to plants and everything else." Ancient Germans offered sacrifices to the dead in the spring as sowing began and also at harvest time. The ceremonies surrounding "old corn man" or "old corn mother" among European peasantry have the nature and appearance of ancestor reverence. That we decorate our graves with flowers and that, in popular vulgarized conception, the dead are seen on clouds, playing harps or singing with choirs of angels, is a crude picture image of what used to be perceived as the plane of the Harmony of the Spheres.

The plant spirit-ego, working from the fixed stars, is modified by the effects of the seven movable planets, especially the sun and the moon. The daily and seasonal rhythms of the plant world could not be thought of without regard to the latter.[21] Thus it is in the spheres of the seven planets that the soul of the plant resides. As Paracelsus states in his "De Caducis":[22]

> Where is the workman that cuts out the forms of the lilies and roses that grow in the fields? and where are his workshop and tools? The characters of lilies and roses exist in the astral (star) light, and in the workshop of Nature they are made into forms. A blooming flower cannot be made out of mud, nor a man out of material clay; and he who denies the formative power of the astral light, and believes that forms grow out of the earth, believes that something can be taken out of a body in which it does not exist.

The minerals have their physical bodies on earth, while their life force is found on the higher plane where the animals have their egos and plants have their souls. The soul of the mineral is found in the fixed stars, while their spirits or egos are found in the higher heaven beyond the fixed stars. We can easily follow this in our thoughts, but to "realize" this we must have intuition, the so-called "stone of the wise." This is the sphere that the ancients referred to as the Crystal Heaven, and Australian aborigines express this

[21] This will be expounded upon in a later chapter on the cosmic influences in plant growth.

[22] Franz Hartmann, *Paracelsus: Life and Prophecies* (Rudolf Steiner Publications, Blauvelt, N.Y., 1973), p. 156.

when they claim that crystals found on earth must have broken off the seat of the highest god and fallen to earth.[23]

Although this discussion of levels and spheres might seem complicated, it is nonetheless greatly simplified, for it involves complex cosmologies. We permitted ourselves to peek at these immense worlds because, as holistic gardeners, we do not want to limit our view of plants, bugs, and birds in a narrow and isolating fashion, but we want to explore their proper place in the universe in relation to each other and to man. The chart provided is a crudely simplified approximation to help interpret the interrelationships. The study of the works by Rudolf Steiner and careful investigation of alchemy, ethnographic records, and folklore can help to clear up our fogged vision. Steiner's works contain unusual and interesting philosophical perceptions which he does not ask us to believe as pontifical pronouncements, but as working hypotheses to be tested against our practical work and logical thinking.[24]

If there is truth hidden in these cosmologies, could it be possible to have contact with and "talk" with one's plants and animals? Could one tell the deer's "grandfather" to leave the garden alone, or tell the caterpillar's spirit to go easy on the cabbage; invite the song birds to live in the garden? There are gardeners who claim something to that ef-

---

[23] This again offers interesting insights into the customs of primitive societies regarding sacred stones. The theophany of stones is shown in Bethel, the Rock of Ages, St. Peter, the Muslim's Ka-aba, etc., cf. Mircea Eliade, *Patterns of Comparative Religion.*

[24] Books by Rudolf Steiner that are an aid in this endeavor include: *Knowledge of the Higher Worlds and its Attainment, An Outline of Occult Science, Theosophy, Macrocosm and Microcosm, Nine Lectures on Bees, Agriculture, Man as a Symphony of the Creative Word, Spiritual Science and Medicine,* and others which are available from the Anthroposophic Press, Spring Valley, N.Y., 10977; or from the Rudolf Steiner Press, London.

fect. There seems to be an explanation in this for the unusual garden of Findhorn, where gardeners claim to have contacted friendly nature spirits and are "seeing" them and "talking" with them with the result of growing large, healthy vegetables in cold, inhospitable northern Scotland.[25] And perhaps the Amish are not just stubborn traditionalists when they link the powers of tractors and electricity with a demonic world; certainly the Amish have been able to maintain excellent farms without excessive destruction of the ecology.

In its more esoteric aspects, bio-dynamics works with considerations like these, though a careful attempt is made not to take over unclear, outmoded systems from the Middle Ages, Renaissance, or the Indians; but to bring such ideas into accord with what is acceptable to modern rationality.

[25] Paul Hawken, *The Magic of Findhorn* (Harper & Row, N.Y., 1975).

CHAPTER V

TRANSMUTATION, DESTRUCTION AND CREATION OF MATTER

Alchemy, that ancient science clothed in obscure symbols and surrounded by strange allegories, was practiced in China, India, the Mid-East, and medieval Europe. It concerned itself with the changing of substance (in its visible, as well as its etheric and spiritual, form) into other substances, transmuting it into higher forms, composing and decomposing *(solve et coagula)* it. The aim was to permeate matter with the form-giving spirit, and to provide the spirit with substance. The alchemists studied such natural processes as the metamorphosis of vegetation, the rotting of composts, burning candles and other instances where change of substance could be observed. Chains of transformation were carefully studied, such as when a candle is lit: the ponderable wax, cold, solid, becomes soft and malleable, then it becomes liquid, mobile, creates a reflecting surface, then it vaporizes, becomes bright flame and, finally, dissipates itself into warmth. In steeple bells, the heavier bells give off the lowest tones, the lightest bells the highest tones. Countless observations like these led to concepts concerning matter; rules such that there is a continuity in matter ranging from ponderable, heavy, solid, earthy, crystallized substances to the light, warm imponderables that link into the supersensible, that dissipate themselves into cosmic regions. Candle wax and boiling water are examples of such disappearing matter, whereas substances like milk and falling rain can be thought of as newly created matter, which, by a series of steps, can be crystallized into solid forms of cheese and ice.

In its solid form, matter is dense and nonreceptive, subject only to the influences of the earth (i.e. gravity, magnetism). As a liquid, matter is receptive and reflective. It can receive influences issuing from the stars and planets, so that new impressions can be fixed into it.[1] In its imponderable, fiery and airy state, it is, given that the other factors are right, greatly transmutable. Thus, man and stars can work into substance when it is liquid or volatile. Therefore, the alchemists, when carrying out their operations, studied the planets, their positions and aspects, carefully. By understanding these processes, the alchemists hoped to aid nature to complete its fore-ordained development of matter uniting with the spirit in a "chemical wedding" that would lead to health, wholesomeness and perfection of creation.[2] The search was blessed by the finding of medicine *(arcanum)* and the ability to transmute what is base into what is noble, such as heavy, dark lead into gold, the sun in its mineral form *(operis processio multum naturae placet).*

In this work the alchemists, having subjected themselves to various purifications (for, according to their thinking, like affects like), proceeded to subject matter to all sorts of operations in order to induce transmutations. The opera-

[1] Here belongs the idea that the fetus growing in the water womb receives the impression of the horoscope. Here, too, belong baptism and immersion rituals that rearrange people's souls in a new way.

[2] The words holy, whole, and healing have the same etymological root.

tions included calcination, congelation, fixation, solution, digestion, distillation, sublimation, separation, ceration, fermentation, multiplication, projection, blackening, vitrolizing, and so on. If gold had been transmuted, then with the right tincture, it could be multiplied. There are reputable testaments to the effect that this had actually been achieved.

This view of the nature of the material universe, especially the idea of the transmutation of elements, the concept of the four elements and the making of gold was scathingly ridiculed by Robert Boyle (1627-1691); and with the newer, enlightened scientists a new concept of matter started making its appearance. The great chemist Antoine Laurent Lavoisier (1743-1794) formulated the *law of the conservation of matter:* "Nothing is created, nothing is destroyed, everything is transformed." By the 19th century the concept of matter was well defined and posed little problem. Studied carefully by brilliant researchers operating with a modern scientific methodology and charted into the periodic table by D. I. Mendeleev, matter is seen as composed of atoms which combine into molecules, has mass and weight, occupies space and is subject to gravity, inertia, and the law of entropy (the second law of thermodynamics). After the original "big bang" (Kant-Laplace hypothesis) the law of entropy took over and now everything is seen as really in the process of winding down, like dust settling or a clock running down, until the energy is spent, the sun has burned out and life is gone. Life and spirit are seen as "epiphenomena" of this inevitable process. In agriculture, this meant teaching the peasants that plant processes are chemical reactions, animals are really machines, and that Liebig's theories could deal with inevitable soil depletion.

At this time alchemy was interpreted as the crude, superstition-ridden beginnings of chemistry, or as the confidence operations of gold-hungry swindlers. On the other hand, scholars such as Franz Hartmann and C. G. Jung saw only symbolism in alchemy that was projected into the world and really referred to spiritual striving or psychological processes.

Ideas, like immortals, do not die but emerge transformed. Alchemical concepts were developed further despite rejection and ridicule on the part of the new science. Samuel Hahnemann (1755-1843) founded *homeopathic medicine* which makes use of a number of alchemical concepts. Utilizing the principle that like works on like (similia similibus), Hahnemann took minute proportions of those substances, mainly plant derivatives, that when given in larger doses would produce certain symptoms of illness, and placed them in a liquid medium (water or alcohol) diluted 10:1, shaking them rhythmically for a long period of time. The solution, or tincture, would then be diluted again 10:1, again rhythmically shaken (D2), part this would be diluted again 10:1 and shaken (D3), and so on until a very, very dilute potion would be achieved. By shaking the liquid it would be potentized or made receptive to the forces working in the substance. At a certain point of dilution, the original substance is not even molecularly present (using the Lodschmidt formula), only the potentized water is left. Hahnemann was scolded as a quack, but the proof was in the pudding: healing was achieved in many cases where official allopathic and chemopathic medicine did not help.

The 19th century researcher Baron von Herzeele

published the results of some 500 experiments between 1876 and 1883 that indicated the transmutation of elements within organic substances. He showed that the ash content of certain minerals increases within seeds sprouted in distilled water. He asserted that plant organisms could transmute CO_2 into Mg, Mg into Ca, Ca into P, P into S, and N into K. Herzeele comes to the conclusion that "it is not the soil that produces the plant, but the plant that produces the soil," and "wherever calcium or magnesium is found in the soil, a living organism must have preceded it."[3] These ideas run counter to everything that modern chemistry believes, such as the law of the immutability of the elements, and, consequently, the publications were ignored until rediscovery by the mid-twentieth century.

When Rudolf Steiner was asked to hold his agricultural lectures in 1924 in response to the crisis in agriculture at the time, his recommendations and indications for preparations to aid the soil and compost smacked suspiciously of revitalized alchemy. He gave formulas for making preparations out of cow manure, quartz, and a number of herbs that were to be treated in various ways and then, greatly diluted, rhythmically stirred (potentized) to open them up to a number of in-streaming forces from the cosmos. With this arcanum the vegetation was to be sprayed, the soil, the composts and manures treated. If homeopathic medicine works for the microcosm, then it should work in the macrocosm, to heal the ailing earth organism. Steiner treaded on thin ice when he proposed in the agricultural course that the distant planets work through the silica in the earth to produce quality and form in plants, while the close

[3] Rudolf Hauschka, *Heilmittellehre* (Vittorio Klostermann, Frankfurt/Main, 1965), chap. IX.

planets (Venus, Mercury, Moon) create substance, mass, quantity in plants and animals by working through the earth's calcium. He speaks of transmutations that are occurring in the organic realm:

> I know quite well, those who have studied academic agriculture from a modern point of view will say: "You have still not told us how to improve the nitrogen content of manure." On the contrary, I have been speaking of it all the time, namely, in speaking of yarrow, camomile, and stinging nettle. For there is a hidden alchemy in the organic process. This hidden alchemy really transmuted the potash, for example, into nitrogen, provided only that the potash is working properly in the organic process. Nay more, it even transforms into nitrogen the limestone, the chalky nature, if it is working rightly.[4]

He states that "silicon, too, is transmuted in the living organism — transmuted into a substance of great importance, which, however, is not yet included among the elements at all."[5] In another place he makes the statement that the human organism would, if within a closed room where the air consistency is somewhat low in nitrogen, create its own nitrogen.[6] In earlier lectures (Dornach, 1923) he makes distinctions between earth substance that is being spiritualized and spiritual substance that is materializing.[7] The former are finely-wrought substances that have been thoroughly worked on by formative forces, such as the

---

[4] Rudolf Steiner, *Agriculture* (Rudolf Steiner Press, London, 1974), p. 98.

[5] *Ibid.*, p. 99.

[6] *Ibid.*, p. 48.

[7] Rudolf Steiner, *Man as a Symphony of the Creative Word* (Rudolf Steiner Press, London, 1970).

delicate plumage of birds, the dust on butterfly wings, the delicacy of flowers and the physiognomy of a person who has spent his life in virtue and thought. The latter are new substances that are fresh in the earth-sphere, such as mother's milk, egg yolks, and cow manure, which bring "spirit substance" to the earth. Elsewhere he talks of digestion as a process of the transformation of matter from the solid state by chewing it with the teeth, to the liquid state in the stomach, to the gaseous state in the intestine, and the sublimation of matter and creation of warmth beyond the intestinal walls. The feces themselves are a waste product of this process. The process is analogous to what happens when the plant grows from the solid root through the elemental phases and sublimates itself in flowering. On the other hand, the impressions of light and warmth that enter our senses condense in the body into form-building substance. Regarding the law of entropy, Steiner declares that it works in the purely mineral, physical world, but in the world of living matter, the opposite is true, energy is constantly being replenished by forces streaming from the sun. We see that this philosopher is at home with concepts of the appearance and disappearance of substances, the transmutation of substances, the use of rhythm to create and dissolve forces in substances, the use of homeopathic entities, and other alchemical concepts.[8]

[8] "It is a mistaken notion when from anthroposophical sides it is claimed that the bio-dynamic fertilizing techniques, as they were developed by Rudolf Steiner and so successfully carried out by his followers, are something completely new, something that has not existed heretofore. Those who claim this, simply do not know about alchemy and its essence, for otherwise they would know that the problem of fertilizing, of putrefaction, decomposition and combustion is actually the essential problematic of alchemy." Alexander V. Bernus, *Alchemie und Heilkunst* (Verlag Hans Karl, Nuremberg, 1969), p. 47.

What are we to make of these concepts and of what value are they? A Jungian psychologist might say that they are psychic projections onto nature, and, as such, they have value for the farmer and gardener, for as he stirs and sprays his bio-dynamic preparations over the land, he connects his psyche with the realm of his activity, creating a personal relationship to the land. It is, nonetheless, merely a subjective phenomenon.

Or one might realize that his approach makes sense phenomenologically. Just as the geocentric model of the universe makes sense in explaining the immediate phenomena of observable astronomic data, though actually the heliocentric model is the "correct" one, one can say that Steiner's system of concepts makes sense on the phenomenological level in that it can adequately describe what one sees, such as the sprouting and blooming annual cycle of vegetation, the sudden appearance and disappearance of bugs, the production of milk and manure, the stages of composting and so forth. But the question is; does it provide useful knowledge and does it make scientific sense? The success of bio-dynamic farms speaks for itself, and the concepts involved make a lot more sense now in the latter half of the century than they did in 1924.

The concept of the transmutation of elements started coming back with the discovery of the unstable transuranic elements which transmute into lead and other elements, while giving off rays and heat. The concept of the finality of solid matter has been shaken since Einstein's theorem $E=MC^2$ has been tested to show that matter can change into energy and *vice-versa.* The discovery of trace elements, or micronutrients, in plant nutrition gives some credibility to the effectiveness of minute homeopathic dosages (i.e. molybdenum is needed at a rate of only 10 oz per acre). The severe calcium loss experienced by astronauts in outer space raises questions about the appearance and disappearance of matter. For physics this is no longer a problem with the discovery of anti-matter (positrons, anti-protons, anti-neutrons), black holes and so forth. The collision of a positron and its counterpart, the electron, results in simultaneous disappearance, their masses reduced to zero. This annihilation of matter can be reversed in that gamma rays can turn into electrons and positrons. Fred Hoyle of Cambridge dispenses with the law of conservation of matter altogether, assuming that matter is being constantly created in space out of nothing "in response to the influence of other matter."[9] With the discovery of about 200 subatomic particles, modern physicists can no longer say what matter is. It has been dematerialized; it almost looks like the Hindu's *maya.*

In a more immediate sense, Steiner's indications are finding confirmation by a number of researches conducted by scientists such as R. Hauschka, E. Kolisko, E. Pfeiffer, L. Kervran, H. Spindler, P. Baranger, and others.

E. Kolisko and L. Kolisko carried out 16 years of far-ranging research on the effect of the bio-dynamic preparations, on cosmic influences on plant growth and on the effect of the use of homeopathic entities. The results verify Steiner's indications to a large extent.[10]

Rudolf Hauschka, long-time director of the research

---

[9] James Christian, *Philosophy* (Rinehart Press, San Francisco), p. 384.

[10] E. Kolisko, L. Kolisko, *Agriculture of Tomorrow* (Kolisko Archives, London, 1939).

laboratory of the Clinical Therapeutical Institute in Arlsheim, Switzerland and director of the WALA pharmaceutical company, became known primarily for his book, *The Nature of Substance.*[11] He took up some of Herzeele's findings, tested and verified them in the Arlesheim laboratory. Experimenting with cress seed, he placed them in measured amounts of distilled water into hermetically sealed ampules. In weighing the ampules carefully three times a day, he found that the weight showed increases and decreases, fluctuating with the rhythm of lunar phases, with increases during the full moon and decreases during the new moon periods. The results were difficult for Hauschka to repeat; he found, however, that with organically grown seed the results were somewhat more satisfactory. Perhaps the difficulty in repeating the experiment has to do with the nature of the subject under investigation, where often events occur together, but not causally (Law of Seriality described by Kammerer[12]); or, as Hauschka supposed, there are unknown factors involved.

The biologist Henri Spindler[13] discovered changes in the iodine level in the algae *Laminaria saccharina.* Within periods of 24 to 48 hours, he found that the iodine content varied up to a hundred percent, even though the algae had been kept in hermetically sealed containers. He also noted an increase of up to 15% potassium content in the algae. He concluded that organic matter might *not* be derived

---

[11] Rudolf Hauschka, *The Nature of Substance* (Vincent Stuart, Ltd., London, 1966, German original, 1950).

[12] P. Kammerer, *Das Gesetz der Serie* (Deutsche Verlag Anstalt, Stuttgart, 1919).

[13] H. Spindler, *Bull. Lab. Maritime de Dinard XXVIII* (1946) and *Bull. Lab. Maritime de Dinard XXXI* (1948).

from inorganic matter, but rather, that the mineral substances have been excreted from organic processes like the bark from a living tree. Spindler's research stimulated Professor Pierre Baranger of the organic chemistry laboratory of the École Polytechnique of Paris to check out Herzeele's work with the aid of modern equipment and procedures. After thousands of carefully run tests, he reports that there is indisputable evidence that plants are capable of the transmutation of elements.[14] After ten years of research with legume seed, Baranger verified that during germination manganese had disappeared while an equal amount of iron had appeared.[15] He concludes that there must be unknown energies in living organisms that can carry out these transmutations.

Louis Kervran in his book, *Biological Transmutations,* notes the numerous discrepancies found in the chemistry of living organisms. He notes the countless instances where matter seems to be created anew or transmuted from another substance. For example, herbivorous animals whose nourishment contains small amounts of nitrogenous substances, excrete more N than they take in; the opposite happens in carnivores. He notes the modification of the chemical composition of the soil due to earthworms; the increase in S, P, Mg, and Ca in dried fruit. His experiments show decrease in phosphorous in germinating lentils; increases in Ca in sprouting plants when calcium is lacking in the growing medium; and four times the calcium in hatched chicks than that originally found in the egg. Hens kept on a

[14] Pierre Baranger, "Science et Vie," (Nr. 499, April, 1959).

[15] Louis C. Kervran, *Biological Transmutations, trans. M. Abehsera (Swan* House Publ. Co., Binghampton, N.Y., 1972), p. 94.

calcium-free diet are capable of transmuting the potassium from mica flakes into the Ca needed for their shells. He notes that organic silica (as found in horsetail) aids broken fingernails and helps mend broken bones by transmuting into calcium. He concludes that organic life cannot be explained in terms of inorganic chemistry; that the law of entropy does not work for living organisms; that experiments performed on dead tissue or in nonrepresentative, sterile laboratory situations are not conclusive for living substances; he cautions against generalizations: "the transmutations are operations requiring a specific production of enzymes and a medium allowing the physiological development of cells, or microorganisms. One kind of plant will thus make a transmutation that another cannot make."[16]

The findings of these scientists help us understand how, at the agricultural research station in Rothamstead, England, an experimental plot could be cropped for over one hundred years and still come up with a steady, although low, harvest of wheat without fertilizer. Rain and wind-blown nutriments could not cover the loss of elements incurred with each harvest. Also at Rothamstead, a clover field was cropped two to three times a year for 17 years without fertilizer added:

> This piece of land gave cuttings so abundant that it was estimated that if one had to add what had been removed . . . (during the 17-year period) . . . it would have been necessary to dump on the field over 5,700 pounds of lime, 2,700 pounds of magnesia, 4,700 pounds of potash, 2,700 pounds of phosphoric acid, and 5,600 pounds of nitrogen or more than ten tons of

---

[16] *Ibid.*, p. 114.

> the products combined. Where had all these minerals come from?[17]

These researches also give explanation to some of the phenomena observed by E. Pfeiffer,[18] who noted that there is accumulation of copper in some legumes and grasses although the soils are devoid of it; that tobacco is rich in potassium when it grows in soil poor in potassium and vice-versa; that oaks rich in calcium (60% of the bark) grow in sandy, calcium-poor soil, that Spanish moss growing on wires accumulates numerous elements for its life functions which would be difficult to get out of the air or rainwater. Pfeiffer assumes that plants have a remarkable ability to accumulate these elements and concentrate them. Another assumption one can make is that plants are capable of creating these elements.

The study of the dynamics of fluids, of the sensitivity of water, was carried out by Theodor Schwenk. He shows convincingly that stirring and rhythmic shaking of water creates countless moving interfaces as the molecules move past each other at varying speeds. This "magnetizes" and sensitizes the water to substances dissolved in it and even to cosmic occurrences, such as eclipses and constellations.[19] His "drop method" of studying the characteristic forms of different kinds of water by letting it drop into glycerin, indicates that the characteristic drops are affected by cosmic phenomena. Similar studies by Giorgio Piccardi, of the In-

---

[17] Tompkins and Bird; *The Secret Life of Plants*, p. 246.

[18] Ehrenfried Pfeiffer, *Bio-dynamic Farming and Gardening* (condensed version by B. Rateaver, Pauma Valley, Ca., 1973, chap. 14).

[19] Theodor Schwenk, *Sensitive Chaos* (Schocken Books, N.Y., 1976) and *Grundlagen der Potenzforschung* (Verl. Freies Geistesleben, Stuttgart, 1972).

stitute of Physical Chemistry of Florence, confirm that water is affected by cosmic phenomena, such as the outbreak of solar eruptions, and proposes that these influences working through the water continue to work in living organisms.[20]

In conclusion, we can see that Steiner's holistic concepts take on ever more credence. Gardening involves the incredibly complicated alchemy of life, involving not just plants and animals, but the entire cosmos and the microcosm. The agriculture of today is not capable of taking all of the facts into account. It should begin by reexamining its philosophical foundations.

[20] G. Piccardi, *The Chemical Basis of Medical Climatology* (Thomas, Springfield, Ill., 1962).

CHAPTER VI
GOETHEANISTIC SCIENCE

One of the first modern thinkers who combined the newer empirical science with the holistic viewpoint of the ancients was J. W. Goethe, who is primarily known as the greatest German poet and author of the epic *Faust*. Yet Goethe considered himself equally a scientist and he added a number of discoveries to the annals of science, such as the discovery of the human *os intermaxillare*, a theory of color that differed from Newton's and pleased artists more than physicists, a concept of space, thoughts on the methodology of science in general, and studies on the metamorphosis of plants and animals.[1] Rudolf Steiner became well acquainted with the scientific works of Goethe as an editor of the natural science writings of the scientist-poet and revived Goethe's basic methodology under the name of *goetheanistic science*.[2]

Goethean Methodology and Epistemology

Goethe's ways of approaching and looking at nature are important considerations for us because many of the insights of bio-dynamics are based upon them. The author

[1] cf. Theodore Roszak, *Where the Wasteland Ends* (Vintage Books, N.Y., 1969). Chapter on Goethean science.

[2] Rudolf Steiner, *Goethes Naturwissenschaftliche Schriften* (Verl. Freies Geistesleben, Stuttgart, 1972).

came into contact with this approach when, as mentioned in the introduction, the beans suffered from aphids. Rather than rushing to spray with some organic insecticide, the head gardener beckoned patience as he squatted down by the beans, scratching his head, rubbing his chin, and mumbling to himself. He explained to his puzzled apprentice that he was looking for the correct concepts for what was happening to the beans and, after a while, stated that he would not do anything, for within a week the aphids would be gone by themselves. Later he explained that he had been trying to remember what previous crops had been there, what kind of fertilizer had been applied, what the weather patterns had been; in short, what conditions had existed earlier that could cause this infestation to come about.

The head gardener was solving the problem in a goetheanistic way. Goethean science relies on careful empirical observation and adds to it the proper concepts. Goethe rejects simplistic empiricism, which gives only an aggregate of isolated facts. He also rejects a facile rationalism that jumps to quick conclusions and sets up unprovable hypotheses. As he states *(Sprüche in Prosa):* "It is a bad thing that many observers immediately follow an observation with a conclusion and consider both of equal value." Or, "Theories are usually the impetuousness of an impatient intellect which would like to rid itself of the phenomena and replace them with images, concepts or just words." He rejects a science that can only garner isolated entities and tries to connect them by a series of hypotheses, plausible explanations, or rationalizations. Instead, one must let the facts, the contents of the careful empirical observation, speak for themselves and let them draw out of the observer's mind the appropriate idea. For it happens to be that every empirical object is incomplete; it is only half there, and it must be completed by its other half, the *idea* proper to it. The scientist, thus, in observing, does not just observe an external world available to his senses, but must observe the internal world of ideas streaming into him, in order to apprehend the totality of the phenomenon. Every empirical thing has its ideational aspect which is perceived only by the human mind as the inner form of the phenomenon. Whereas external perception gives individual entities, the internal perception gives wider connections, underlying ideas and principles. Perception gives us individual dogs, the internal perception gives us the class, or species, or "dogness." This approach differs from our ordinary scientific approach which tends to divide the world into the external world, which is real (objective) and the internal world of concepts, thoughts, symbols, which is arbitrary (subjective). The Goethean scientist considers only quickly drawn hypotheses subjective and, indeed, of little value, and the proper Idea belonging to the phenomenon as objective as is the phenomenon itself.

How does one arrive at the correct Idea that belongs to the phenomenon? Not by hypothesizing or postulating something that does not exist (such as metaphysical explanations), but by staying with the phenomenon, seeing it in one light and then another, observing the coincidental aspects *(Erscheinungszusammenhange)* that make up the whole, the gestalt. Then the mind can make the proper connections without straying into the fantastic and ungrounded, and concepts will arise that satisfy the mind's need for explanation.

In pursuing this holistic, phenomenological approach, the goetheanistic scientist tries not to distort the phenomena as they occur in nature by complex apparatuses and instruments, or by clever experimental methods that consider some factors "relevant" and others "irrelevant." All factors are relevant, and each manifestation is, on the phenomenal level, a unique one.[3]

Perhaps, as Goethe suggested, it takes a poet and an artist to understand this. The scientist needs an artistic, creative mind to understand the forms and creations of nature, to understand the ideas that properly belong to the phenomena. This by no means implies that an artistic science is less exact than experimental science.

For Goethe, nature is ordered and guided by divine reason[4] and man is to note the order, the basic ideas in nature, not project his theories and hypotheses into nature. This calls for a quiet, alert, meditative approach, rather than only an experimental approach that limits and tests segments of reality, but cannot fit the parts into an organic whole. Goethe expresses this in his Faust I (trans. Sir Theodore Martin):

[3] A similar understanding underlies the spagyric medicines of earlier centuries; to be effective a medicine had to be made new each time to fit the specific case of illness, the specific astronomical situation, the character of the individual, all these factors were considered relevant. Doug Boyd, in *Rolling Thunder* (Random House, N.Y., 1974), mentions similar considerations taken by native American Indian healers in regard to relevant and irrelevant factors: "Rolling Thunder offered us the idea that experiments do not cause things to happen. Events are caused by their natural causes. There is no experiment other than the real situation . . . How can 'science' make any valid test of American Indian medicine if it is too 'scientific' to include all the conditions of the real situation . . . the real situation includes the need for an unordinary result and the belief that the need will bring that result. It includes a certain attitude toward the sun and the earth and all of nature . . . Absent from the situation are skepticism and judgement . . . (p. 10).

[4] If the assumption of an order in nature is rejected as an unproven *a priori*, so can the assumption that chaos, or chance, dominates in nature be considered an equally unproven *a priori*.

He that would study and portray
a living creature thinks it fit
to start with finding out the ways
to drive the spirit out of it.
This done, he holds within his hand
the pieces to be named and stated
But, aah! the spirit-tie that spann'd
and knit them, has evaporated.

The "spirit-tie" is found not in dissecting the phenomenon, but by developing the appropriate ideas. Neither can instruments and devices replace the proper ideas:

Ye instruments, at me ye surely mock
with cog and wheel and coil and cylinder!
I at the door of knowledge stood, ye were
the key which should that door for me unlock.
Your wards, I ween, have many a cunning maze
but yet the bolts ye cannot, cannot raise
Inscrutable in noon-day's blaze,
Nature lets no one tear the veil away
and what herself she does not choose
unask'd before your soul to lay
you shall not wrest from her by levers or by screws.

A training seminar in the goetheanistic method is held in Dornach, Switzerland for young farmers and gardeners each year. It consists, among other things, of developing a sense of how nature forces artfully create their forms by painting natural forms, following them out with eurythmic body movements, and by continuous study of nature in its context. Nature is studied by daily walks along the same path each time. The participants are not asked to identify or name anything, but to primarily observe the "same" natural phenomena under the different circumstances of a rainy day or a clear day, in the light of dawn, at noon, at dusk.

A project assigned during one session was a tall oak tree whose three main trunks, which were covered by numerous sucker branches, tilted noticeably toward the north. South of the oak grew young pines to the height of a man. The question was posed: Why had the tree grown in such a peculiar shape? Rather than come up quickly with a hypothesis to be tested, the students were asked first of all to observe carefully and let one phenomenon lead to the next until the answer became clear. All the contexts were carefully noted. The soil was decomposed limestone, conducive to a beech/oak climax vegetation. Noting the direction of sunlight influx, it was an enigma why the top of the trunks grew towards the north. The numerous suckers in the trunks were counted to have about ten yearly growth segments. A count of the internodes showed the pines were about 12 years old. Soon the idea dawned that the forest

had been felled ten years ago, and only this oak by the path was left standing. Pines, not native to the area, had been planted in the clear cut. The oak had been shaded on its south side before the forest was cut, and thus had grown northwards. Sunlight had drawn the suckers out of the trunk now that it was no longer shaded by the other hardwoods. Similar deductions showed that the oak itself had been felled much earlier, causing three axial branches to make up its trunks. In this way, a mental image was created of how the peculiar shape of the oak had come about, how the landscape had looked a decade ago. A true idea had arisen by letting the phenomena speak, an idea that is true, and at the same time, goes beyond the immediate phenomena.

The faculty developed by this kind of thinking can be exercised by anyone. One can, for example, look at a sunflower seed and let it grow in the mind's eye and then take it back to the seed again, going carefully step by step. One can trace in the mind's eye the path that the food on one's plate took to get where it is. This is inducive to developing the inner perception of the phenomena without letting the mind drift into fantasies or abstractions. The gardener does this anyway each time he plants a garden and sees the garden grow before his mind's eye, foreseeing how it will look in midsummer, or in the fall. He does this when he plants little seeds far apart because he can imagine how much room the plant needs. (Beginners always plant everything much too close together.)

The Primal Plant or Ur-Plant

On a trip through the Swiss Alps and into Italy, Goethe noticed that plants of the same species which grew in his home country looked so different that one could be deceived into thinking one had a different species before one's eyes. (We can follow up the same observation if we take a plant such as the plantain and observe it growing with thin, pointed leaves on the dry hillsides and compare it to when it grows succulently and fleshy by the Oregon beaches.) From this Goethe developed the concept of a primal plant, or Ur-plant, as a basic theme that is played in a number of variations according to the circumstances. These circumstances, the various formative forces in nature, radically modify the plant's expression. This Ur-plant is not a phylogenetic or prehistoric prototype, but is present in all living plants. It is the appropriate idea that underlies the phenomena of all plants in their everchanging variation. Whereas the various manifestations are apprehended by the external senses, the Ur-plant is perceived by the mind. Both the empirical plant and the Ur-plant belong together to give us the whole plant.

The manifestation of the Ur-plant is modified by various elemental forces. The physiognomy of the empirical plant as it grows shows us what elemental and formative forces are at work, on one hand, but shows us the idea of the plant ever-anew on the other hand. As the Plant moves from seed to leaf to flower and fruit and back to seed, it is always changing, always in the process of "becoming," of expressing its being which is only comprehended by the inner senses. In characterizing the Ur-plant, Goethe sees the leaf as the basic organ, which goes through its various stages of metamorphosis from contraction to expansion, ever-changing and ever the same.

Thoughts like these lead the bio-dynamic gardener to the conclusion that if crops are not doing well, growing stunted

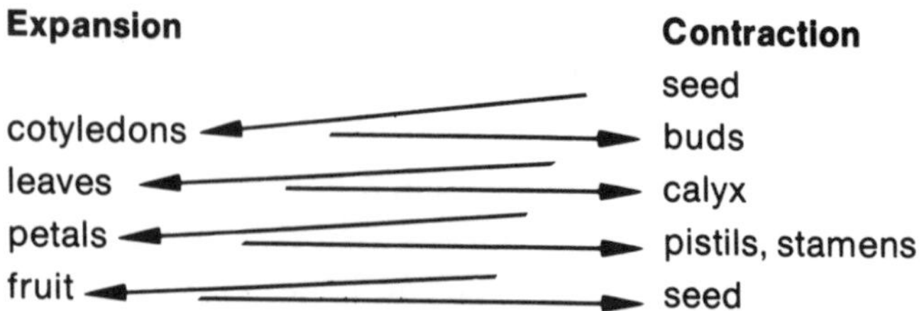

and subject to disease, the fault lies not so much with the plant as with the forces that work on the plant, the combination of formative forces (mineral, water, light, warmth) which give the Idea of the plant its concrete manifestation.

It is through understanding the idea of the plant, the Urplant, that works behind the manifestation, that Goethe could assert that the laws of mechanics are all right for the inorganic world, but for the world of living organisms other laws are at work. He delineated three laws that characterize living organisms, plants in particular. They are the laws of dynamic polarity, metamorphosis, and intensification.

1. *The law of polarity* shows that one of the major characteristics of plants is their dualistic nature. From the seed the plant grows geocentrically into the soil and heliocentrically into the air. Nowhere is something similar to be found in inorganic nature. The plant responds to the polarities of day and night, winter and summer, waxing and waning moon. Polarity is found in the "male" and "female" flowers, in the round, "cosmic" bud and the extended "terrestrial" leaf. Wherever one looks into the realm of organic nature, the archetypal polarities manifest themselves, such as in the green chlorophyll molecules and the red hemoglobin molecules, which are perfect mirror images of each other except that the hemoglobin has an iron radical

where the chlorophyll has a magnesium radical attached. A fascinating polarity exists between the plant and the butterfly. Do the eggs not correspond to the seeds; the quick-growing, segmented caterpillar to the quick-growing shoot that is segmented from node to node; then just as the plant folds itself into a flower bud, so does the caterpillar spin itself into a pupa to emerge in radiant color as a butterfly as the flower bud blooms into a flower. The butterfly's proboscis fits perfectly the flower chalice; and just as the one dies to lay eggs, the other fades to make seeds. Each step is thus exquisitely matched, as though one were watching a beautiful dance.[5]

In his meditative approach to gardening, the bio-dynamic gardener will look for such harmonies and symmetries; think of the roots when looking at leaf and flower, think of the opposites that make up the complete picture.

2. *The law of metamorphosis:* Living organisms do not grow by processes of mechanical addition or construction, they grow in pulsating rhythms, at certain points reaching a crescendo and continuing at a qualitatively different pace. Consider an ordinary weed. Who can predict, upon seeing the mere little seed, what kind of plant it will become? The seed does not just turn into a bigger and bigger seed, but it radically changes, metamorphoses; it breaks open, sends out a rootlet and two cotyledons. Again, the appearance of regular leaves could not have been predicted from studying the cotyledons. As new leaves form at the internodes, they remain pretty much similar, only being broader and rounder at the base and finer, more laced and pointed the higher the plant grows. Then, suddenly, another unpredictable change

---

[5] Gerbert Grohmann, *The Plant* (R. Steiner Press, London, 1974), p. 51.

occurs: the leaves totally metamorphose, turning into a corona of petals and sepals. Finally, a metamorphosis occurs in the fruiting and the creation of a new set of seeds. These metamorphoses occur rhythmically and in relation to terrestrial and cosmic factors. None of the stages are deductible from the previous level of organization. Each time a completely new set of phenomena appears, yet they are all part of the same plant organism passing into ever new manifestation.

The bio-dynamic gardener can watch if the metamorphoses are occurring in a normal fashion in his plants, or whether these processes occur too fast as in the shooting into seed of some plants, or too slowly as in delayed ripening. It becomes an heuristic exercise to study different plants in their characteristic development. Comparing the different *brassica;* we see that kohlrabi is really an exaggerated stem, broccoli and cauliflower are in the floral stage, collards and kales are fixated in the leaf stage, cabbages are really overgrown terminal buds, etc., each manifesting a stage within the whole metamorphic range of the brassica. Onions like to hover in the bud stage. Oak galls are a fruit induced by the sting of a wasp. The examples can go on forever.

3. *The law of increment or of enhancing intensification* is another characteristic of organic life discussed by Goethe. In the mechanical, inorganic world, systems wear down. The more energy is taken out, the less there is; parts wear out and depletion results. In the inorganic, physical world the second law of thermodynamics holds true. This is at the base of so much thinking in agriculture today; regarding weeds as competitors with the crops, insects as leaks in the energy system, fearing that the NPK continuously depletes

and must be replaced as one would do with a mechanism. Goethe saw nature in a different light. Life is not just wearing down and depleting, but it is building itself up and creating energy at the same time. The more life there is, the more life it can support. On a farm, for example, the more varied the number and kind of organisms are, the better the ecosystem will sustain itself. Maintaining a complex ecosystem is part of the reason for companion planting, for controlled use of weeds, for not getting hysterical about a few bugs, and for circulating animal manures within the system. There is a mazeway of subtle interaction and mutual support among all the organisms in such a farm, such that insects and weeds will not be a problem and overall vitality and quality will be enhanced.[6] Contrary to the thoughts of some radical vegetarians, livestock, in the right number, are not competitors with man for a limited amount of vegetation; instead they are valuable symbionts enhancing growth and health of the vegetation. By comparison, farms and gardens that practice monoculture create imbalances that will deplete the regenerative and enhancing potentials, will wear out the soil, and will experience weeds and bugs as competitors and incur heavy damage from them. We see here the mechanistic attitude turn into a self-fulfilling prophecy.

---

[6] The mutually enhancing effect of a great variety of organisms within a garden environment is part of the success of the French Intensive method as practiced by Alan Chadwick and his students.

CHAPTER VII
EVOLUTION

In order to get a better idea of the plant and animal organisms in relation to man and the cosmos, we will presently turn our attention to the idea of evolution. Striving for a more complete picture, we will consider not only the scientific inquiry of paleontologists, paleo-geologists, embryologists and prehistorians, but we will also look at the ancient documents of the wisdom and insights of philosophy. The scientist sees an evolution of matter; the Bible talks of a creation by the Divine Spirit; alchemical philosophers see both: matter is formed and worked on by the spirit to create a succession of forms, first in the macrocosm and then in the microcosm.[1]

[1] The three views need not be contradictory if their claims are examined in the right light. Two somewhat different accounts of the creation are given in Genesis Chapter 1 and Genesis Chapter 2. The first verses in Chapter 1 deal with the creation of the elements (physical world), then with the creation of the etheric, or plant world (1:11, 12) and, finally, the last to appear is the archetypal human conceived in the image of God. All this marks the first phase of creation, the creation of the macrocosm and the Idea of man. Genesis 2 speaks of the second phase of creation, the forming of the microcosm out of the elements and the in-breathing of the Spirit. Alchemists and kindred minds perceive in the process of evolution, the taking hold of the primal matter *(Chaos, hyle, prima materia)* by the creative Spirit *(eidos, forma)* and penetrating it with formative forces which leads to the creation of primitive life (pre-Cambrian); as the penetration proceeds, the astral forces appear amidst the ocean of etheric forces (Paleozoic to Cenozoic); and, finally, the Spirit re-creates itself microcosmically in the form of the human being (Pleistocene). As the scientist examines his evolutionary data stretching from the soft-bodied marine organism to homo sapiens, he is witnessing the involution-evolution of the microcosm out of the macrocosm.

We will examine this in detail by first looking at the animal world, comparing it to the plant world and then relating it to the human being. Using a goetheanistic approach, we will let the data speak, rather than merely impose an abstract scheme upon the data. Though nature does not "think" per se, it is ordered so that our thought can make sense of it. As we examine the data, we find that it suggests a guided development which we might call the evolution of the human microcosm out of the mineral, plant, and animal macrocosm. It is the flow of evolution itself that suggests the possibility of entelechy or, perhaps, teleology.

Older cosmologies operated with rigid, static hierarchies. The idea of progressive evolution is the great discovery of the 19th century, the century of Lamark and Darwin, which was a materialistic and biologistic age. Matter was considered primary; out of its molecular complexity life had evolved as an epi-phenomenon, and consciousness was a tertiary product of matter, like so much froth upon a wave. "The brain secretes thoughts like the kidney urine" (L. Buchner).[2] Shadows of these sentiments are cast into the 20th century as one can easily surmise when one opens up a botany text or a book on horticulture or agriculture. In this chapter we will examine the materialistic bias and try to show how the same phenomena can be explained satisfactorily in another manner.

The so-called occult evolutionists, such as Steiner and Blavatsky,[3] did not agree with the a priori assumption of the

---

[2] Michael Landmann, *Philosophical Anthropology*, trans. D.J. Parent (Westminster Press, Philadelphia, 1974).

[3] Theodore Roszak, *Unfinished Animal* (Harper and Row Publ., N.Y., 1975), chap. 6, "The Occult Evolutionists."

evolution of life and consciousness from dead matter. They turned evolutionary thinking around and saw matter as an end product of life, which itself was a creation of the Spirit. They envisioned an evolution from the highest hierarchies in a series of steps, of which only the last one, our present earth stage, consists of a material phase. The evolution passes from the spirit archetype, to the soul world, to life which finally crystallizes into matter. Most of Steiner's elaborate work concerns itself with such an evolutionary process involving plants, animals, and man in relation to the cosmos.[4]

Steiner is less concerned with the picture of evolution presented by fossilized bone fragments and teeth, as with the evolution of states of consciousness. As four main stages of universal world development, he identifies the "Old Saturn" state where consciousness can be likened to the cataleptic deep sleep such as found in the mineral world today, followed after immense spans of time by the "Old Sun" state with a consciousness equivalent to deep sleep like that of our plants; this was followed in the immensity of cosmic time by the "Old Moon" state with a consciousness like that possessed by animals today; and, finally, in the "Earth" state of evolution, wakefulness and rational self-consciousness,[5] after much preparation, came about. This evolution is not at an end, and higher states of consciousness are going to be achieved in further development. One can say that, in a sense, the minerals still live on "Old Saturn," the plants are still on the "Old Sun," the animals are still on the "Old Moon" and man has evolved "Earth"

---

[4] cf., Rudolf Steiner, *Outline of Occult Science.*

[5] An interesting etymological aside, the word "think" and "thing" are related. In the physical world we are "thinging" as we identify objects.

consciousness. The first three states of evolution occurred in the super-sensible realm, accessible only to the inspired seer, or to "spiritual science," which we have no way of counting or discounting. It is only the "Earth" period in its later phases that brings about physical manifestation, and is thus capable of being studied by the scientific method, using the five senses and logic. Only this fourth state is what our paleontologists and geologists can study; only the latter part is visible in the fossil record. What happened before that time is in the realm of cosmology, spiritual science, and the origin-myths of all the tribes and nations. It would take us too far afield to pursue these interesting topics, so we will proceed from where the fossil record begins.

Prior to the Cambrian, the fossil record becomes sketchy and science becomes highly speculative. There are, however, pre-Cambrian indications of primitive "plant-animal" organisms found in the "stromatolites" near the Great Slave Lake, Canada, and in the Gunflint Cherts of Minnesota and Ontario. Also, symmetrical, harmonious forms of organisms are found in the late pre-Cambrian Ediacara formations of Australia. Scientists in the 1920-30's (J.B.S. Haldane and A.I. Oparin) hypothesize a "dilute organic soup" composed of macromolecules of amino acids that were formed by the action of energy (cosmic rays, lightning) working into the water through an early atmosphere of hydrogen, helium, methane, and ammonia. The now classic experiment by S.L. Miller (1953) of synthesizing amino acids by reconstructing in miniature such an atmosphere, water, and energy charges, lends support to the "dilute organic soup" concept. From our perspective, we can say that we see here the *beginning of etheric forces taking hold of the primal matter:* entelechy starts working as an inner formative principle on physical substance, which by itself is subject only to deterministic causality.[6]

The pre-Cambrian with its soft-bodied filter sediment and deposit feeding organisms, who are like bits of intestine floating or sliding around through a nutrient medium, gives way to the Cambrian during which all but one phylum of invertebrate animals with preservable hard parts first appear. Animals and plants (algae) are now becoming clearly separated. Astrality begins to manifest itself slowly and cautionsly as the phyla start developing hollow inner spaces, as they evolve not just tissue that is turned outward toward the macrocosm, but endoderms and mesoderms which are separated from the macrocosm. In embryology this stage is marked when the little ball of cells, the *blastula* starts to indent, to involute, to form the *gastrula* that creates

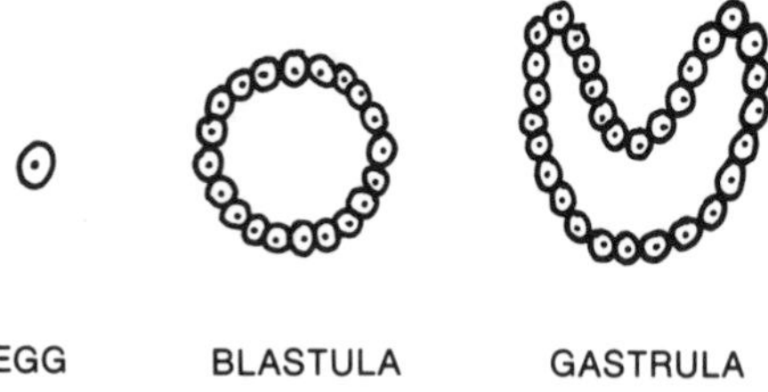

[6] The *prima materia,* which was predispositioned in the earliest phase of supersensible cosmic evolution on "Old Saturn" by the highest hierarchies, is now subjected to the organizing, ordering forces of the next hierarchy of the "Old Sun." A small picture of this is provided by the *Chladni figures:* Ernst Chladni "mounted a thin metal plate on a violin, scattered sand on the plate and found that when the bow was drawn across the strings, the sand arranged itself into beautiful patterns . . . By juggling around with powders of different densities and by playing notes with a wide range of frequencies, it is possible to induce a pattern to take on almost any form. It is interesting and perhaps significant that Chladni's figures most often adopt familiar organic forms." Watson, Lyall; *Supernature* (Bantam Books, N.Y., 1974), p. 90.

inner spaces where the inner organs can eventually form. This is a step that plants never make! Just as macrocosmically the protozoa are like sperms and eggs, and if they form rudimentary colonies like blastulas, so are the sponges, jellyfish, corals and grapholites macrocosmically at the stage of gastrula formation. Like most of the lower organisms, life is not centralized, but even if strained through a sieve they will regroup or regrow into a new organism. Specialized organs of blood, respiration, excretion and reproduction are absent, their function being performed macrocosmically. Their blood is the salt water of the ocean, their rhythms those of the tidal currents. Hard shells appear on the organisms by taking in calcium carbonate, silica, or calcium phosphate, but in their larval stage they retain the free-floating, soft-bodied modus of earlier phases of evolution. They begin to recapitulate their phylogeny, as the great biologist Ernst Haeckel would say. Reproduction is mostly asexual, by budding, parthenogenic, or hermaphroditic processes, indicating that the astral principle has only weakly manifested itself in these organisms.

By the time we trace the unfolding entelechy to the shells (brachiopods), snails (molluscs), annelid worms, starfish (echinoderms), and crabs (arthropods), we find much clearer organ development and the beginnings of nerve ganglia as astrality starts to manifest more strongly. Radial symmetry gives way to bilateral symmetry, so that orientation in space (up-down, frontback) becomes possible. The sexes start to separate and with this mode of reproduction rather than budding, mortality becomes reality. It marks life's entrance into the earthly dimensions of space and time. The arthropods are the first pioneers to venture out of the watery element into the light and warmth of the littoral.

Many of the descendants of these organisms remain little changed in the ocean for millions of years as reminiscences of earlier eras.

During the Silurian period, the creative entelechy takes hold of the phylum of chordates, specifically the fish, who at first appear as jawless *(agnathe)* bottom and suspension feeders without a solid inner skeleton but with bony, armor-like plates. In the Devonian period the limy substance of the bony armor starts to internalize to form partially calcified vertebrae and the incipient inner skeletons. During the upper Devonian the complex transition from a marine environment to a fresh-water environment is made. The rudimentary beginnings of kidneys, and a two-chambered heart circulating blood which contains about the same amounts and kinds of salts as sea water, are seen as an adaptation for an extramarine environment. Of these fresh-water fish, it is the lobe-finned, air-gulping fish *(crossopterygians)*, rather than the ray-finned fish, that slowly give rise to the carboniferous amphibians. The lobes are an extension of muscle tissue into the fins: We are now already at a point where the internalized forces start working actively outward. The amphibians mark the transition by chordates from the watery environment to the land. They now breathe with lungs, have a three-chambered heart and walk or hop on four legs. However, to get to this point, they recapitulate all the stages; they must return to the water to lay eggs, for the water is the womb; the male may grab hold of the female and deposit sperm as she sheds her eggs. The larva retraces all of its past evolution: blastula formation, gastriculation, bottom feeding, breathing through gills, until it can finally crawl to land in its adult stage. Frogs and toads have remained at this stage. Most rhythms are still determined by solar, lunar and planetary cycles. The etheric forces still work strongly in the amphibian, as seen in the rapid rate of reproduction, their greenish, plant-like coloration, and that like fish, many amphibians continue to grow their entire lifetime.

During the Permean, the involution of the macrocosm continues in the evolution of reptiles. No longer need reptiles go back to the water to reproduce, for they have developed the amniotic egg, a miniature ocean with "nutritive organic soup" in which the larva, or embryo, can develop. Now in reproduction the male and female are not just in proximity, but real coitus occurs with the development of organs of internal insemination. Reptiles can now radiate onto dry land where they meet Permean vegetation (gymnosperms) which is also capable of existing on dry land. The age of reptiles is the Mesozoic, during which the most varied forms are experimented with, from giant brontosaurs to flying pterodactyls. In the shadow of these mighty beings, the entelechy is working in the direction of birds and mammals. Birds, for the most part, leave the lower elements altogether and inhabit the lighter element of air. They liberate themselves further from the caprices of the macrocosm by beginning to develop warm blood. Unlike amphibians and reptiles, who depend upon the macrocosmic source of warmth, the sun, they internalize part of the sun's power in the form of a four-chambered heart and warm blood. Fertilization is internal, and the eggs are not abandoned as those of the reptile, but a nest (an external form of what later would be a womb) is built by cooperation of parents. The young are warmed externally by the parents as they brood and not left to the sun to hatch.[7] All this indicates a higher form of astrality incarnating itself in birds.

With mammals, the development taken by birds is carried further. By the time the placental mammals are reached, the placenta is a microcosm of what the macrocosmic environment of the ocean and littoral is for the lower vertebrates; it is a womb where the embryos are fed, warmed and protected. After birth, the mammal offspring are fed further by the mother's milk, a microcosmic recreation of the dilute organic soup of earlier evolution.

Organically and physiologically the involution of the macrocosm is complete with the advanced mammals. Sophisticated, specialized inner organs have taken over from the diffuse, generalized functions that clumps of cells perform in the hydras, sponges, and starfish. An inner limb system that gives structural support has evolved out of the limy seas by way of an external skeleton with bony plates and shells. A complex inner metabolism has evolved out of a loosely organized system of cells that floated within its nutrient substance. Reproduction has gone from unprotected gametes deposited into the womb of the ocean to the inner micro-ocean of the womb. The solar and lunar tides that determined the ripening and depositing of the gametes became estrus cycles and, finally, in the anthropoids, menstrual cycles that have separated and liberated themselves from direct lunar rhythms. An internalized rhythmic system of lungs and blood circulation has replaced the tides of the ocean. The external cosmic

---

[7] An African bird solves the problem by building a compost out of plant scraps and lets its heating hatch the eggs.

rhythms, though they still have their effects, do not so much determine the inner rhythms of the higher animals, as do the internalized sun, moon, and planets which have recreated themselves microcosmically as the major organs. Whereas the outer sun had to warm the amphibian and reptile, with mammals the inner sun of the heart and its blood circulation does the warming at a constant temperature of 37°C, a state at which water is chemically the most active. Theodore Schwenk points out the connection between ocean streams and the sun, and their correlation to the heart and the streaming of blood.[8] We can sense how the amoeba-like white corpuscles in the blood are kin to the protozoa of the oceans. Just as the planets move like a whirlpool about the sun, so are the organs of the microcosm connected to the heart by the streaming of the blood. The cosmic connection of the breathing-blood-circulatory system of the human organism with the sun is hinted at by the fact that, at the normal rate of 18 breaths per minute, we breathe 25,920 times each day, which equals one platonic year (the number of years required for the sun to go through the zodiac and return to its spring point). 25,920 days would equal about 70 years, an average human lifetime.

In advanced animals, impulses are received and given ever more by a centralized nervous system, rather than by the automatism of macrocosmic influences working on notochords and ganglia *via* cilia and antennae. With the in-

---

[8] Theodor Schwenk, *Sensitive Chaos*. In this outstanding work, Schwenk shows how in human and animal organs, the archetypal movements of fluids (water, air) recreate themselves in a solid form. The vortex-like structure of the heart, ear and intestines (pp. 84 to 93) remind one of the vortices of ocean currents, and these in turn of the great macrocosmic cortex of the planetary system.

creasing concentration of nerve function in the head (encephalization) of mammals, the entelechy is preparing organic life for its next major metamorphosis, the microcosmic manifestation of the Spirit itself.

Late in geological time, at the end of the Cenozoic, in the course of the Ice Ages (Pleistocene), the new impulse is given. Having worked its way from the formless *Prima Materia* through its manifestation of etheric forces in the primal seas, through its manifestation of astrality in the development from fish to mammal, now the Spirit itself works its way into the microcosm after the groundwork has been laid.[9]

With the *homo sapiens* the outstanding characteristic is not so much an advancement of specialized physical organs, but the developing of an inner world anchored in an increasingly larger cerebrum. Enclosed in the highly metamorphosed first segment of the spinal column, the brain undergoes explosive development. In the lower paleolithic tool use and manufacture, this inner, spiritual principle becomes manifest for the first time. In the use of fire by mid-pleistocene *homo erecti* we have the external picture of an internal process in man: the beginning of the in-dwelling of the Spirit, the "inner light." In the Magdalinian cave paintings showing numerous animals, we see the inner universe, lit up by the in-dwelling sun, step ever more into outward manifestation (just as with the muscles in the fins of the crossopterygians where the life force steps from inner to outer manifestation). The human spirit is leaving the "Atlantis" of the macrocosm.

---

[9] As Teilhard de Chardin would have it, the level of phyletization has been completed and the level of cephalization is commencing. cf. Teilhard, *Man's Place in Nature* (Harper & Row, N.Y., 1956).

The human being rapidly goes through all the stages of its evolutionary development (it recapitulates its phylogeny) as embryo, nursling, child and adolescent. Then its body is organically complete. The etheric forces that have brought the body into an upright stance and have given it energy to learn to walk and talk, are now freed for the use of the conscious life of the spirit. The spirit expresses itself in creativity, in speech and song: a long path from the silent fish to the chirping insect that resounds by mechanically rubbing its legs, to the mammals and birds who develop inner vocal chords, and, finally, to man, who not only produces sounds that have signal functions or are expressive of astrality, but whose sound can relate complex meaning, can conjure up the past as well as the future, can bless and curse, and can express worlds that do not exist anywhere in macrocosmic manifestation. With the human we have beings who can objectify the universe in thought, word, and deed; who can serve moral purposes beyond the immediate organic needs of eating, sleeping, reproducing, or self-preservation; and who can will and, to a large degree, determine their own future. Helen Keller, blind and deaf, was a great benefactor of humanity, a writer and humanitarian, whose indwelling spirit overcame severe organic handicaps. Beethoven was completely deaf when he composed perhaps the most beautiful work of music that humanity possesses. For an animal, on the contrary, that is sick, old, deaf or blind there is little inner light. It abandons life and returns to the macrocosm where its spirit dwells. Evolution is the chronology of the development of the microcosm out of the macrocosm. Every organism we meet is a reminiscence of a step taken. Our animal brethren have accompanied us many steps along the way, but have preferred (temporarily) to remain at one place or another faithful to the macrocosm, to the mother earth and heavenly father.

Plant Evolution

Having scanned the panorama of animal phylogeny, we must now ask: What is our relationship to plants? Plants, too, have progressed out of the primal "slime," from the early "plant-animals," the flagellates, bacteria, blue-green algae, to the humble, seedless vascular plants growing in the wet niches of the Devonian, followed in the late Carboniferous by primitive gymnosperms which could, by development of wind-pollination, colonize the dry land and, finally, to the flowering plants of the Mesozoic. Very early the sun laid claim to the germinal organisms that were to become the plant world, inducing the formation of chlorophyll and subjecting the plant to its form-giving forces.[10] Indeed, the plants in their growth and rhythm cannot be understood without taking the sun into consideration. As such, the etheric world finds full expression in plants: ever-growing, replicating segment after segment, silent, symmetric, and harmonious. As plants evolve further, their "organs" become more distinct and less generalized. In the tracheophytes true stems, vascular systems with xylem and phloem evolve and, with the flowering plants (angiosperms), distinct root, stem and leaf, flower and fruit formations appear, each with a specific relation to one of the four elements, earth, water, air, and light-warmth (fire). Except for plants such as algae, liverwort, and the

[10] The relation of plants and the form-giving forces of sunlight is illustrated by amorphous growth of potato sprouts in a dark cellar, by the mycelia of fungi in ne ground, or by blackberry vines in deeply-shaded corners.

sporophytes of the bryophytes which are dominated by the formative forces of the water element, the leaves and stems of mosses, ferns, horsetails, gymnosperms (pines, ginkgos) and grasses are parallel-veined or radial, as though they directly radiate the etheric sun energy back into space. With dicots, there are rounded leaves with netted veins so that the raying does not appear as direct, yet nowhere is the energy turned inward upon itself to form inner organs as in even the most primitive animals. Nowhere does gastriculation occur. The plant never internalizes astrality like the animal. The astral realm only touches the extremity of the plant in the form of insects that pollinate the flowers and worms that busy themselves at the root sphere. If insects eat up one's vegetables one can say that the astral sphere, represented by these animals, is pressing itself too heavily onto the plant. Something similar can be said when wasps sting oak or willow leaves causing fruit-like swellings, or galls. But even here the astral component is working on the plant from the outside. In the calyx formation of the flowers, the plant makes a feeble, albeit beautiful attempt at forming inner organs, but in so doing, it loses vitality and growth, dissipates itself in color, fragrance and pollen, and contracts itself into tiny seed in order to resume its vegetative growth, its proper habitus, later. Only in some poisonous plants and insectivorous plants can one say, by their animal-like signature, that astrality has entered the plant to a certain degree.

Let us look at the relationship of plants to astrality more closely. In his agricultural lectures, Rudolf Steiner, looking at the wider significance of the elements that make up most of organic chemistry, C, O, H, N, S, Ca, etc., identified nitrogen as the element that represents movement and sensitivity, and is the anchor of the world soul, or astrality. Protein-rich animal tissue characterizes, in its constant movement and sensitivity, this ensouled state, the astral body.[11] As Hauschka states,[12] the chemistry of plants is mainly a chemistry of C, O, H (carbohydrates, sugars, starches), except in flower and seed which encroach on the astral sphere, whereas the chemistry of animals is that of C, O, H, N (proteins). This is true very generally speaking; however, there are many important nitrogen processes in all plant cells. We must make finer distinctions. The plant's nitrogen is derived from animal excretions and bacterial metabolism in the soil. The roots absorb nitrogen as nitrate or ammonia, the plant combines these with organic acids to form amino acids which are then synthesized into true vegetable protein. It is found mainly in fast-growing tissue, and culminates in the flowers whose perfume and colors are results of further protein metamorphosis, and in albumen-rich seeds. In flower and seed the plant actually starts penetrating the lower levels of the astral sphere, the insect world. Otherwise we can observe the protein, the nitrogen substances, mainly in a flowing transit through the plant. This makes sense since amino acids are water soluble and hence readily mobile. The plant, surrounded by the air element (79% N_2) and the animal world (manures, insects) thus has nitrogen working on it mainly from the outside, and then working in the plants in transit. What happens when the plant, for one reason or another, holds up the

[11] When the animal sleeps, its awareness and movement decrease and, in that, it becomes more plant-like. One can say that the astral body leaves the physical and ether body during sleep, a condition that is more or less permanent in plants.

[12] Rudolf Hauschka, *Heilmittellehre* (Vittorio Klostermann, Frankfurt/Main, 1965), pp. 194 to 198.

flow of nitrogen through it, becomes possessive of it? It becomes animal-like, in one way or another, it attains a distorted astrality, it becomes poisonous, and it creates products of protein breakdown ranging from uric acid to cyanide. Since these plants do not have renal organs, these products often do not leave, but accumulate in the tissues of the plants. Most products of protein breakdown in plants are called alkaloids; their connection with astrality is obvious in that all have influences on the nerves, the soul life of man and animals, causing hallucinations, perceptual distortions, anesthetization, nerve paralysis, etc. Commonly known alkaloids are morphine from poppies, nicotine from tobacco plants, caffeine and strychnine from several species, atropine from poisonous black nightshade, mescaline from a cactus, coniine from the poison hemlock that killed Socrates. The ergot fungus (*Claviceps pururea*) contains several alkaloids and LSD, that caused madness and illness known as St. Anthony's Fire among medieval peasants. Many of the plants have bright scarlet, purple or black berries, strong smells that are often unpleasant, hair-like surfaces and unusual growing habits like nightshades and mushrooms. Poison hemlock has a pungent odor and purplish blotches on its stalks that look like symptoms of blood poisoning. Since they cannot retreat into the recesses of inner organs, many of these plants withdraw from the light ether of the sun into the recesses of the earth where strong poisons are produced, such as the mushrooms, which are very high in protein, the mandrake (*Mandragora officinarum*) whose narcotic roots take on humanoid shapes, the meadow saffron (*Colchicum autumnale*) and death camas (*Zigadenus venenosus*) who hide away most of the year in the earth. The insect-trapping carnivorous plants are another group of plants that has an unusual relationship to nitrogen. Here, too, we have the signature of astrality. The sun dew's (*Drosera rotundiflora*) secretory hairs have such an astonishing sensitivity that they can distinguish between the stimuli of an insect victim and a piece of gelatin. When the former lands on the sticky hairs, the tendrils move at 8 mm per minute. The Venus fly trap (*Diocea muscipula*) is much faster; it closes its trap in 0.01 to 0.02 seconds and then engages in protein digestion. The pitcher plant (*Darlingtonia*) has a strong animal signature: it is crustacean red, and a fishtail-like appendage hangs from its cobra-like head that makes up the funnel into which the insect falls.

The legume is another plant that has internalized some nitrogen processes. It, too, has corresponding signatures in its butterfly-shaped flowers, its rapid tendril growth, its habit of flowering while at the same time still vigorously growing, its fixing of atmospheric nitrogen with the aid of captive bacteria. Some of its members, i.e., locoweed, are poisonous. Pythagoras taught that the enjoyment of legumes as foods interferes with advanced thinking.

In the vein of this discussion it can be added that too heavy nitrogen fertilization of crops does pull the astral sphere into the plant region too strongly with the result of having aphids and insect damage.

Though we can say that the plant has evolved, we must say that it has done so within the realm of the macrocosm. It has no inner life with inner organs, senses, feelings, or voluntary movement. Even in the exceptions we have cited above, these qualities are highly rudimentary. The plant is entirely turned outward toward the cosmos. Plants are ecstatic" (M. Scheler).[13] The sun, moon and stars are their organs, not the heart, brain, liver or kidneys. That is why it is correct for the gardener to plant by the "signs" if he knows what he is doing. In a more immediate sense, the animal world represents the astrality of the plant. In the course of earth history we see plant evolution accompanied step-by-step by its animal "doppelgangers": marine invertebrates and algae, amphibians and the giant horsetails and club mosses of the Carboniferous, gymnosperms and dinosaurs of the Mesozoic, flowering plants and birds, mammals and butterflies. This goes into the finest detail: one need only look at the tomato hook worm and the tomato; or the yucca moth and the yucca plant; moth-pollinated flowers that open only at night; fly-pollinated flowers that smell of rotten meat and even trap flies for a day before releasing them (*Arum maculatum*); dead nettle which only takes bumble bees; bird-pollinated flowers with bright, contrasting colors and lack of scent; and there are even "bat-pollinated flowers. . . (which) have dull-colored flowers that open at dusk and have mouselike smells."[14] Since plants cannot move, many of these animals carry on vital functions for the plants, distributing nitrogen compounds, enzymes, and other substances. One can say the hormonal system of the plant is found outside in the animals.

---

[13] The word "plant-like" or "vegetative" designates an essential orientation toward the outside... In the case of plants, therefore, an ecstatic feeling or impulse is spoken of in order to indicate that they completely lack the capacity of animals to report organic states back to a center. Thus they lack completely a turning back of life upon itself, even the most primitive capacity of "reflection" or an ever-so-dim inner '"conscious" state. cf. Max Scheler, *Man's Place in Nature* (Noonday Press, NY, 1962), p. 11.

[14] Williams A. Jensen and Frank B. Salisbury, *Botany: An Ecological Approach* (Wadsworth Publishing Co., Belmont, Ca., 1972), p 507.

In the animal and human being, there are internal organs of digestion. The food is broken down by the teeth, worked on by enzymes and acids, and the energies liberated are absorbed by the little hair-like *villi* of the duodenum of the small intestine. Where does this process occur in the plant? We must look into the macrocosm: organic substance is broken down first by chewing insects, the teeth of the plant; then, it is worked on further by acids and enzymes given off by microoganisms in the soil rendering humus whose essence enters the plants through hair-like capillary roots. The soil is the intestinal content of the plant and the capillary rootlets are inside-out duodenal villi! The bio-dynamic idea of using the same herbs that cure upset stomachs and bad digestion as sprays on soils of afflicted plants begins to make sense. The trouble lies with the soil, not with the specific plant itself.

Where do we find the rhythmic system of the plant, the heart, the blood circulation, the rhythm of breathing lungs? Again we must look into the macrocosm. The plant depends on the day and night cycle of the sun for its rhythm; transpiration is directly linked to the sun. The yearly solar rhythm affects weather, precipitation, and thus the annual rhythm of plant growth. Its warmth is that of the sun. Its "blood," the green plant sap, is a mirror image of red blood, even to its chemical formula. The molecule for chlorophyll is the exact mirror of hemoglobin, except that the chlorophyll has a magnesium ion where the hemoglobin has an iron ion.[15] No chlorophyll can be formed, however, without iron being present, just as no blood can be formed without magnesium being present. Red and green are complementary colors, for if one stares at one too long, the

[15] Wilhelm Pelikan, *The Secrets of Metals* (Anthroposophic Press, Inc., Spring Valley, N.Y., 1973), p. 74.

retina compensates by producing its opposite. In the respiration of the animal and photosynthesis of the plant, we have a mirror image again, where oxygen as a "waste" product of the plant becomes the life element for the animal, and carbon dioxide, the "waste" product of the animal, becomes the structure-forming element for the plant. The plant takes in CO_2 and releases O_2; the animal takes in O_2 and releases CO_2.

Where is the calcinatious skeleton of the plant? It must be in the macrocosm of limestone rock and animal bones. Where are the songs, the varied sounds of the animal world, in the plant? They are still found in the macrocosm as the sound of wind, thunder, the chirping of birds and insects. Where are the reproductive organs of the plant? Botanists are quick to point to the stamen and ovary of the flower, but already Goethe was uncomfortable with this interpretation. The father of the plant is found in the formative forces streaming from the cosmos into the flower and seed; the mother of the plant provides the womb of the soil.

We can see in the plant a macrocosmic image of the human being. Man experiences himself as the center of being in the universe, as an "I am." The plant experiences the universe as its being. Its "I am" streams in from the periphery of the cosmos and from the earth. This is a significant distinction. Plato expresses this when he declares that the human being is a plant turned upside down with the roots reaching to the heavens and the branches to the ground.[16] We can interpret this concept of Plato's in the fol-

[16] Mircea Eliade, *Patterns of Comparative Religion*, pp. 274 to 275. Eliade also mentions the Hebrew Tree of Life, the *Otz Chiim*, which is an inverted tree, and Australian witch doctors who plant magic trees, daubed with human blood, upside down. In the *Bhagavad Gita* (chap. 15) one reads: "The rishis tell us of the tree Asvattha, heaven rooted, trunk below. Each leaf sets forth the Vedas. Who knows this, knows all."

lowing manner: Man has involuted, he has, in comparison to the plant, inverted his relationship to the macrocosm, has by this, evolved his own inner world, his relative freedom from the macrocosm. The animal stands half-way in between man and plant in this inverting process; even architecturally there is a link between the upright plant with its segmented stem, the animal with its horizontal backbone, and the human with his vertically upright backbone.

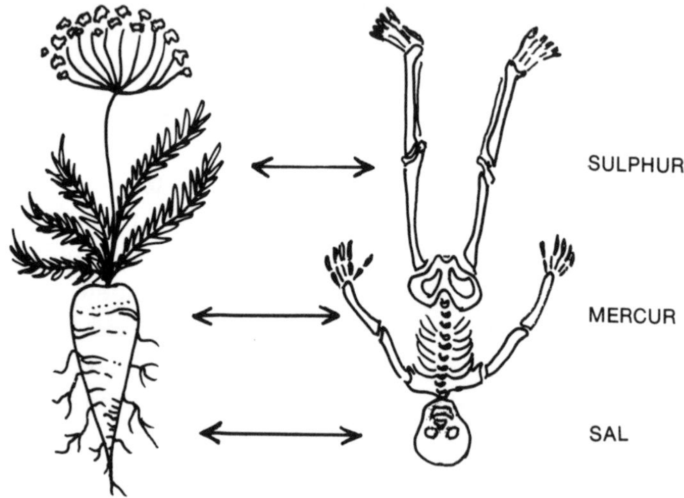

The plant is tied into the macrocosm: in its roots, the densest part, the *sal* processes dominate; in the leaves the *mercury* functions; and in the flowers the *sulphur* related to reproduction, to dissipation and sublimation of matter dominate. In the human being, the sal functions dominate in the head, the most concentrated part of the body; the lung and heart have the mercury functions of rhythmic mediation and circulation; the bowels and sex organs express the dissipation and sublimation in the form of digestion, odors, menses, and sperm production. This is why, in some forms of naturopathic medicine, the roots (e.g. horseradish) are used for ailments of nerves and head, leaves are used for lungs and heart (e.g. greens for blood) and flowers are used for digestive problems (e.g. camomile).

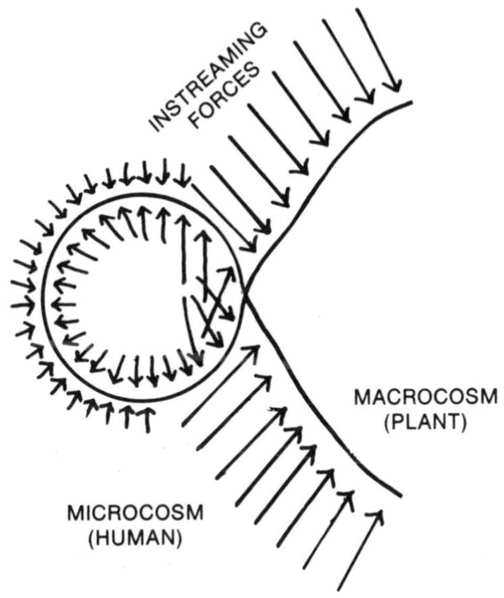

In all this, we perceive in the plant not so much an individuated being as in a higher animal, or in the human being, but a part of a larger macrocosmic process. We can see the plant world as an organ of the earth, having evolved with the earth organism as a whole. Grohmann calls the plant world the "light-sensitive organ of the earth."[17] Like

[17] Gerbert Grohmann, *Die Pflanze als Lichtsinnesorgan der Erde* (Freies Geistesleben, Stuttgart, 1962). When the plant photosynthesizes, it replaces the O_2 of the CO_2 with sunlight, letting the oxygen go. Thus, the plant fixes the sunlight which, when we eat a plant turns into inner light, by releasing it through oxidation.

the retina of our eyes, the plant's leaves, that 5 mm thin layer of foliage covering the planet, are composed of photosensitive tissue that take in the light forces streaming in from the cosmos and transmit them to the earth. Stories exist that the dwarves, who work in the dark recesses of the earth, perceive the sunlight not directly, but mediated by the plant through the roots.

Plants are part of the rhythmic system, the diaphragm of the earth organism. In the summer, the earth "breathes out" its plant forms and, in the winter, they return into the earth, into root and seed. In the winter, the earth perceives what the leaves and flowers have gathered during the summer.[18]

In another way, one can look at the plant as the mercury function of the earth. As a mercurial being, the plant grows, on one hand, toward astrality which it meets as flower in the insect world and, as root, it grows into the purely physical, mineral realm. It is the light-bringer to the dark mineral world and it is food for the animal (astral) world. The plant mediates between the two realms. By balancing out one-sidedness, it becomes one of the best sources of medicine.

In conclusion, we can re-emphasize that man is a microcosm: he has internalized the physical world in his body, the plant world in his etheric makeup; the animal world in his soul; and the spirit light in his "I am." The plant is present only as a physical body and ether body — its soul and spirit work on it from the outside; its essence is macrocosmic.

---

[18] This is expressed in the Greek legend of Persephone, the beautiful daughter of Zeus (the sky god) and Demeter (the mother earth), who is captured while picking flowers, by Pluto, the dark lord of the underworld and forced to marry him. She is freed by Hermes (Mercury), but by having eaten a pomegranate seed, she has to return each year to the underworld where during half the year she reigns with Pluto over the regions of the dead.

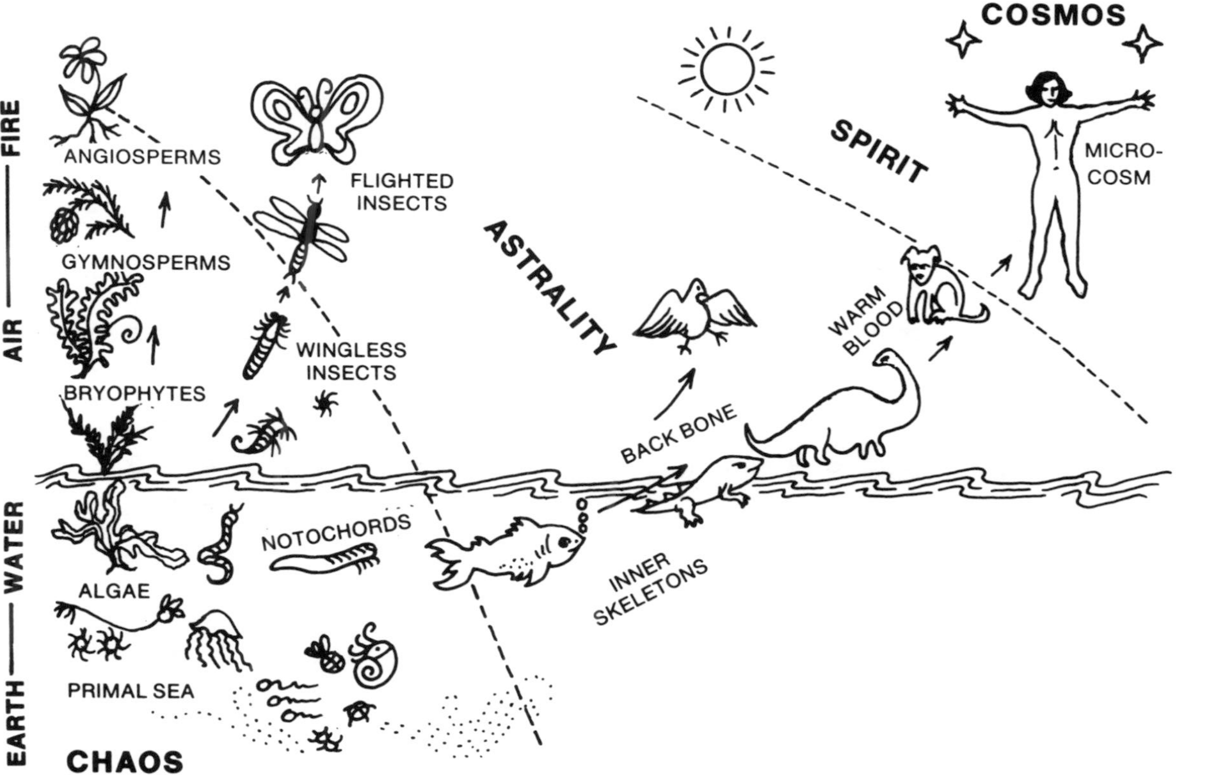
COSMOS
SPIRIT
MICRO-
COSM
FIRE
AIR
WATER
EARTH
ANGIOSPERMS
FLIGHTED
INSECTS
GYMNOSPERMS
ASTRALITY
WARM
BLOOD
WINGLESS
INSECTS
BRYOPHYTES
BACK BONE
NOTOCHORDS
ALGAE
INNER
SKELETONS
PRIMAL SEA
CHAOS

CHAPTER VIII
HEREDITY

Worried farmers called upon Rudolf Steiner to talk to them at Koberwitz because the continuing degeneration of seed varieties, the need to buy new strains of seeds every few years where previously the same strain had been kept for generations, and the mounting incidence of disease in livestock was an ever-increasing source of concern. The suggestion Steiner gave in response was to provide optimal conditions for the characteristic development of food crops and of animals. Good humus soil, made receptive to in-raying cosmic forces by the use of bio-dynamic preparations, would provide the living matrix in which the seeds of plants would retain their viability, quality, and other desirable traits. Similarly, animals fed on plants that were raised like this and kept in a way as befitted their type, would not have problems such as sterility, loss of vigor, or hoof-and-mouth disease. Given an optimal environment, the archetype of the species would be able to express itself in a healthy, vigorous fashion.

Plants and animals that are raised in a manner contrary to their basic constitution and needs will evidence devitalization of genetic substance in the course of several generations. In the same manner, increasing vitality due to corrective bio-dynamic measures is not immediately evidenced, but shown in subsequent generations, a factor making short-term study difficult:

> In the sphere of vitality . . . there is always the law of inertia. That is to say, it may not appear in the present generation or in the next, but it will in the third. The vitalising influence goes on beyond the first few generations. If you restrict your investigations to the present and do not extend them over several generations, you get a completely false picture. Then, when you observe the next generation but (only that) one, you turn your attention to quite other causes than the real ones, namely the feeding of the grandparent beasts. Vitality cannot be broken down at once. It is surely broken, but only in succeeding generations.[1]

Sir Albert Howard similarly notes the effect of unnatural habitat on the seed vitality of plants:

> A new set of facts suddenly fell into place: the running out of varieties, a marked phenomenon of modern agriculture, to answer which new varieties of the important crops have constantly to be bred — hence the modern plant breeding station — could without hesitation be attributed to the continued impoverishment of modern soils owing to the prolonged negligence of the Western farmer to feed his fields with humus. By contrast, the maintenance of century-old varieties in the East, so old that in India they bear ancient Sanskrit names, was proof of the unimpaired capacity of the plant to breed in those countries where humus was abundantly applied.[2]

Howard pointedly criticizes the Broadbalk experiments at Rothamstead, noting that wheat grown year after year for

---

[1] Rudolf Steiner, *Agriculture*, p. 164.

[2] Sir Albert Howard, *Soil and Health*, pp. 10-11.

nearly a hundred years on the same plot would probably have given out if no new seeds were procured from best outside sources to grow each season's crop.

> Had the harvest of each plot been used for re-sowing, in a very few years an important result would have been obtained. The effect of artificial manures, which we know is cumulative, would soon have begun to influence the stability of the variety itself and cause it to run out. In some period between twenty-five and fifty years the wheat would have collapsed.[3]

He goes on to note that in Nature there is "no running out of the variety and no necessity to supply new and improved strains, one generation follows another century after century . . . there is very little plant disease."[4] He states that a simple method for estimating the success of any method of farming is by seeing how disease-resistant crops are, and how normally and healthily livestock breed and reproduce.

Missouri soil scientist William A. Albrecht has reservations about plant and animal breeding. If the soil is alive and rich in humus, the plant will be able to express its genetic potential; if the soil is not in good heart then no genetic tricks will be able to bring about good plants:

> But in spite of the belief by some folks that we can select or breed legume plants, for example, to tolerate soil acidity, and wheat to resist smut, such beliefs rest on fallacious logic. It will not stand the common tests of *reducto ad absurdum*. If that reasoning is carried to its final conclusion, then we should be able to breed plants to tolerate starvation.[5]

---

[3] *Ibid.*, p. 75.

[4] *Ibid.*, p. 84.

[5] William A. Albrecht, *The Albrecht Papers* (Charles Walters, ed., *Acres, USA*, Raytown, Missouri, 1975), p. 258.

Hybridization seems to contradict the above, but Albrecht points out that before hybridization corn contained 10.30% of crude protein (1911), by 1956, the protein content had decreased to 5.15%. The same holds for other crops. Hybridization increased the yield measured in bulk, but the loss of protein and other qualities, and the increase in diseases and pests, show us that good soil husbandry is more important.[6]

Relying on long years of experience, the farmer Carsten Jens Pank feels that genetic vitality, the organism's life-carrying capacity, decreases when plants and animals are placed in unnatural environments (feedlots, hydroponics), leading to loss of vigor, health, and good reproduction. The immediate external characteristics of form and color might not change, but the vitality does. Despite hybridization of plants, the overall vitality is decreasing. "We have a moral obligation to at least maintain for those who come after us that which has been handed down by our forebears: the genetic continuity of our domestic animals and cultural plants."[7]

Other farmers express similar views. One oldtimer showed the author his potatoes. They consisted of a variety that had been taken off the market nearly thirty years ago, for it had lost vitality, subject to mildews. He surprised a government official with this healthy example of an "extincted" potato variety which he had grown for so many years in good soils and treated bio-dynamically.[8]

---

[6] *Ibid.*, p. 374.

[7] C.J. Pank, *Dirt Farmer's Dialogue* (B-D Press, Sprakers, N.Y., 1976), p. 127.

[8] Aside from the bio-dynamic preparations, Steiner gave indications for revitalizing potatoes by cutting single eyes with as little degenerate parent substance as possible, growing them in good humus, and planting them at the correct lunar phase. cf. L. Kolisko, *Die Landwirtschaft der Zukunft*, p. 347.

What is implied in the above is that our current methods of fertilizing heavily with NPK artificial fertilizer, using insecticides, herbicides, fungicides, hydroponics, hybridization, breeding experiments and other such methods that are hailed as the "Green Revolution" are a Trojan horse. The long run effect will be a devitalizing of the organisms we depend on for our foodstuffs.[9]

Is this correct or not? The scientific establishment and agribusiness, relying on neo-Darwinian or "synthetic" theories of genetics, vehemently disagree. There is no question, according to this point of view, that the extensive chemicalization of farming, the separation of food crops from animal manures, the use of feedlots and batteries, monocropping, spraying and dusting do not have any effect whatsoever on the genetic structure of the species involved. The idea that the environment can, in any directional way, influence genetic inheritance is labeled Lamarkism (the inheritance of characteristics acquired by interaction with the environment), a thoroughly disproved heresy.

Establishment Genetics

The modern neo-Darwinistic geneticist and plant breeder would say that the quasi-Lamarkian concerns of a Steiner or Howard, and the common sense pronouncements of ordinary gardeners and farmers are unfounded. Even though Darwin himself supposed that the environment might account for inheritable changes in species, ever since the pea-breeding experiments of Mendel were discovered,

[9] Questions can be raised whether the excessively protein-fed, artificially inseminated and overbred cattle will still be able to supply health-restoring manures for the soil.

it is known that there is no way in which the environment can influence the genes. If changes occur in the somatic cells, brought about by diet, accident, debilitation, or exercise, the effects have no bearing on the reproductive cells and on the offspring. The distinction between genotype, the genetic potential of the organism, and the phenotype, the outward expression of the genes, is made by Mendel. Genetic characteristics, he showed, are not lost or gained due to environmental influence, but due to random combinations of parental gene plasm. These traits are not blended together in fertilization, but are retained as segregated units that are sometimes dominant, or sometimes masked in the form of recessive traits which can reappear in homozygous combinations. The discovery of chromosomes as the location of the genes by Morgan, elucidates the physical basis of heredity, and adds more weight to the theory.

When August Weissman cut off twenty generations of rats' tails to show that what happens in the environment to the phenotype has no effect on the genotype, the Lamarkian ghost was laid to rest. The twenty-first rat generation had just as long a tail as the first generation!

The unraveling of the DNA code gives further support to this theory of the "splendid isolation" of the genes. The DNA, the macromolecules in the chromosomes of the cell nuclei, have the remarkable ability to duplicate themselves. They are the key to the ontogeny of the new organism. They code the RNA, which in turn, will key out the enzymes that build up specific amino acids and countless protein structures. The chain of causality is always from the DNA to the RNA to the protein, and never in the opposite direction.

Thus, the outside environment has no effect on the DNA. One can reason that if the environment had direct effect, then the species would prove very unstable, in continuous flux, helplessly adrift in capricious external circumstance. The isolation of the genes guarantees the continuity of the species and accounts for some of them, like the cockroach or ginkgo, not having changed for millions of years.

If the environment has no effect on the genotype, then how does evolution or change at all come about? The basic cause for change is *mutation,* which constitutes an accidental, random, nondirectional alteration in the chromosomes themselves, brought about by radiation, cosmic and ultraviolet rays, high temperatures, chemicals, by a "mistake" in the DNA replication in the sex cells, or by "cross-overs" and "deletions" in the random recombination of haploid gametes as they join to form the zygote.

These are changes in genotype, but they are purely accidental and indicate no purpose on the part of the plant or animal to try to change itself to fit better into the environment. Most such random mutations are disadvantageous, even lethal to the organism, so that the resulting phenotype will not be able to survive. Natural selection will weed out the unfit; they will not add the innovation to the gene pool. Only rarely, by chance, will there be an advantageous mutation that will spread itself throughout the population.

The mechanism is blind chance. There is no teleology and no entelechy. There is no volition on part of the species. We do not have to worry about the sensibility of species when we breed them by selection, culling, hybridization, inbreeding, cloning, and by trying to induce mutations by the use of cobalt radiation. We are merely taking over the blind workings of nature of inducing mutations where we decide which effect will survive in the gene pool for our advantage. As the well-known modern geneticist, Theodosius Dobzhansky points out, there is no archetypal or ideal species as Plato, Aristotle, or fundamentalist Christians assume. According to Dobzhansky, the "populational" thinking of neo-Darwinism has replaced such "typological" thinking.[10] Therefore, it is useless and meaningless to talk about degeneration, or of violating the plant or animal basic type. We are free to experiment in any way possible to produce new species or varieties. At the same time we need not worry about the impressions of the environment because the genes are not directionally affected by these. We can breed super-cows and super-vegetables, keep them in feedlots and plant them in chemically fertilized monocultures.

Breeding experiments, the production of hybrid corn, square tomatoes that ship well and can be machine harvested, strawberries at Xmas, and other such modern marvels show that the theory is correct.

It is out of the application of this theory that the fascinating advances of the Green Revolution have come. The production increases of western agribusiness brought about a reconsideration by the Russians of the Lamarkism furthered by the Soviet biologist T.D. Lysenko after Kruschev. Lysenko intended to improve the genes of crop plants by raising them repeatedly in specific environments and by grafting, so that the acquired characteristics could eventually be inherited. Lysenko, also stigmatized by

---

[10] Theodosius Dobzhansky, "On Genetics and Politics" in *Heredity and Society* (A.S. Baer, ed., Macmillan Co., N.Y., 1973), p. 31.

Stalinism, was not totally effective in showing that this could be done. He certainly did not get fast results.

Our modern biologists and geneticists are emphatic that the course outlined on the basis of neo-Darwinistic theory must be pursued to the point of genetic engineering if we are to "feed the starving millions."

Who Is Right?

Is there any validity in the statements by Steiner, Howard and others that there is degeneration or a loss of vitality due to modern agricultural practices? There is cause for concern:

> Since the advent of "miracle" hybrid seeds, the older seeds have, in many cases, been lost through neglect — ending a genetic continuity of many millenia. Agricultural researchers are experiencing great difficulty in acquiring stocks of native seeds for preservation programs. According to a recent United Nations report on genetic resources, "the older diverse (crop) varieties ... are sown no more; many of the wild relatives with which they maintained genetic interchange have been swept away."[11]

Seed banks set up are usually not capable of, or do not have the means for stemming, this genetic erosion. "The consequences of the loss of native seed germ plasm are staggering, when one thinks that within one short generation, human beings could throw away key evolutionary links in the food system — all in the name of progress."[12] Germ

---

[11] Wilson Clark, "U.S. Agriculture Is Growing Trouble as Well as Crops" (Smithsonian, January, 1975), p. 64.

[12] *Ibid.*, p. 64.

plasm has been lost that took generations of careful and loving selection by farmers and gardeners to develop. They were lost because they were unsuited to machine production; they were susceptible to newly appearing blights, insects, or disease that came in the wake of radically new farming practices. For example, about 75% of alfalfa and 90% of the clover breeding material has been lost since the turn of the century.[13] The result of the uniformization brought about by agribusiness, where hybrids have been selected for only one or two characteristics, is that our food plants are put on a very narrow genetic basis. The "miracle" wheat and rice of the Green Revolution, which is extincting locally-adapted native varieties, is completely dependent on high energy input in the form of chemical fertilizer, insecticides, irrigation and machinery. It is no wonder, then, if one calculates the energy input, that the yields are so fantastic at this point. The dysfunctional aspects of these developments, however, include the need for consolidation of land and capital, the forcing of peasants off the land and the consequent crowding of the cities by unemployed masses; besides the ecological abuse and the genetic erosion of crop varieties. The problems will multiply if the petroleum runs out. The further complication is that the new "miracle" seeds are degenerating, losing vitality, viability, and have to be replaced by plant-breeding stations every season. Which farmer or gardener of today still raises his own seed, adapted to the local climate, soil, or growing conditions and local taste choice?

The danger of a narrow genetic base was brought home

---

[13] Marguerite Gilstrap, *Seeds* (1961 Yearbook of Agriculture, USDA, Washington, D.C.), p. 26.

in 1970 when the high-yield hybrid corn crop was hit by a blight that knocked out 15% of the U.S. production. Frantic breeding of new seed in Hawaii throughout the winter stayed the catastrophe that time.

With the animals, which are selected for one or two traits, it is a similar story. Cows that are bred for fast-growing meat and dairy cattle for huge volumes of milk production become susceptible to all kinds of disease and sterility. One cannot breed cows for bigger udders and artificially inseminate them and expect, despite such intrusions into the sexual cycle, good fertility and easy birth.[14] Will the manure of such mistreated, protein-overfed cattle still have the healing, vitality restoring effect on the soil, or is this link of fertility also weakened?

The next question that needs to be asked is whether the gene plasm is totally isolated, not subject to the environment other than occasional haphazard mutations that might occur, or whether there might be a grain of truth in the inheritance of characteristics acquired from the environment. If so, environmental care takes on new importance.

There are cracks in the armor of neo-Darwinistic genetic theory. Lamarkism had been refuted with the demise of Kammerer's credibility and the fall of Lysenko. But no sooner had the Lamarkian hydra lost these two heads, then another one reared up under the name *teminism*. Howard Temin of the University of Wisconsin, as well as researchers at M.I.T. and Columbia, found experimental proof that cancer-causing viruses in animals, once they invade the host cells, produce their own hereditary DNA. Frederick Griffith, working with pneumococci strains, found

[14] E. Pfeiffer, *A Condensation of Bio-Dynamic Farming and Gardening*, pp. 39-41.

hereditary changes caused by the transfer of nucleic acids from one strain to another, a process referred to as *transformation*. This seems to indicate that the DNA does not live in as splendid an isolation as was supposed by orthodox theorists, and that the chain of effect from the DNA to RNA to amino acid is not necessarily a one way street.[15] It cannot be completely counted out that changes in body cells could, eventually working their way past all the filters and barriers by means of enzyme and hormone transmission, cause changes in the reproductive cells. There is also evidence of cytoplasmic inheritance separate from the DNA, such as the mitochondria that reproduce independently. When one considers the great number of known mutagens in existence today, the idea of the totally insulated germ plasm becomes less tenable. Numerous chemicals, rays and other hazards have been identified.[16] The more primitive organisms seem to be able to cope and adapt "intelligently"

---

[15] Possibly we can understand the concept of the splendid isolation of genes from a sociology-of-knowledge viewpoint, as a projection of the isolated and powerful position of researchers and ivory tower academicians of social prestige, who like to see themselves as effective in the world but not affected, as objective and not subject. Emphasis of "adaptation" to existing conditions, and a "survival" of the best adapters, seems to fit this line of thought that reveals itself as a projection of ideology into the bio-chemical realm.

[16] Mutagens, besides radiation, include a number of new chemical compounds, such as the fungicide captan, the plant growth inhibitor maleic hydrazide, the sweetener cyclamate, the food preservatives sodium nitrite and sodium nitrate, certain antibiotics, insect chemosterilants such as triethylene phosphoramide and trietheline melamine; agents used in methylating and ethylating phenols, amines and other compounds are ingested by organisms including human beings by way of air and water pollution, food preservatives, soft drinks, residual pesticides and medications. cf. James V. Neel and Arthur D. Bloom, "The Detection of Environmental Mutagens" in *Heredity and Society* (A. Bear, ed.), p. 44. The phenoxy herbicide 2,4,5-T sprayed widely on forests, cropland and roadsides to kill dicots, containing dioxin, effective in parts per trillion, has such mutagenic effects. cf. W. Boly, "Sweet Dioxin " (Oregon Times Magazine, Sept. 1977), pp. 39-42.

by genetic changes to debased environments, as with resistant germs, viruses, and insects. In plants and lower animals the strict distinction between reproductive cells and somatic cells breaks down anyway; all the somatic cells can function by budding to create new organisms. Koestler suggests that the "Weissmann barrier" against environmental effects is basically correct, but perhaps it is not an impenetrable wall, as much as a filter that lets select influences work on the germ plasm but otherwise maintains stability. It functions much like the mind which lets in only relevant stimuli from among all the potential stimuli.[17] This filter might be swamped by the excess of mutagenic chemicals thoughtlessly released into the environment. Koestler proposes that some of these changes are deliberately kept, others quickly eliminated. He quotes Waddington that "it may be unsafe to consider that the occurrence of directed (non-random) mutation related to the environment can be ruled out of court *a priori*."[18] There might, after all, be a guiding principle that gives intelligent direction to the development of a species. It is certainly hard to imagine the complex plant and animal species that populate the earth have arisen out of aimless, nondirected mutations. How could such diversified, intricate features as the eye, the egg, the seed, have come about? So many isolated factors must have mutated at once to make up the new organ or species, or the mutations must have been kept until there were enough to form the new structure (Ernst Mayr's "pre-adaptation"). Even if the necessary mutations were present at the same time,

---

[17] Arthur Koestler, *The Case of the Midwife Toad* (Vintage Books, N.Y., 1973), p. 130.

[18] *Ibid.*, p. 131.

they would not have constructed a complex organism, or as Waddington aptly states: "To suppose that the evolution of the wonderfully adapted biological mechanisms has depended only on a selection out of a haphazard set of variations, each produced by blind chance, is like suggesting that if we went on throwing bricks together into heaps, we should eventually be able to choose ourselves the most desirable house."[19]

If there were no entelechy or at least direction, why are we not comfortably adapted, rapidly multiplying one-celled organisms? Why bother becoming a multicellular complex? There is much validity in assuming, as Larmark, Bergson, and Nietzsche had thought, that "living things willfully seek their own ascending genetic change in obedience to a destiny that, once glimpsed, prescribes meaning of life on earth."[20] As Kammerer has it, evolution "is not the merciless selection that shapes and perfects the machinery of life; it is not the desperate struggle for survival alone which governs the world, but rather out of its own strength, everything that has been created strives upwards towards light and the joy of life, burying only that which is useless in the graveyard of selection."[21]

Kammerer, an eminent Austrian biologist, went as far as showing, in breeding experiments with a number of amphibians and the sea-squirt Ciona, that the inheritance of acquired characteristics is possible. As Koestler brilliantly

---

[19] Arthur Koestler, *The Ghost in the Machine* (Macmillan Co., N.Y., 1967), p. 127.

[20] Theodore Roszak, *Unfinished Animal* (Harper & Row, N.Y., 1975), p. 98.

[21] Arthur Koestler, *Op. Cit.*, p. 133.

documents,[22] Kammerer's experiments, in the beginning of the century, were fought in the most unsavory and unfair way by the neo-Darwinian establishment which could not allow the Lamarkian heresy to flourish. Kammerer eventually committed suicide when his experimental species had been tampered with to give the appearance of forgery. One problem with these well-documented experiments is that no one, up to now, has been able to repeat them, to get the amphibians to breed in unusual laboratory conditions, to produce the desired inheritable effects. Why can't they be repeated? Here we are confronted again by that factor X which perplexed Hauschka when he tried to repeat the experiments of the appearance and disappearance of matter. Perhaps the key to Kammerer is that he loved his experimental animals so much that he had a hard time bringing himself to kill any of them. One time, during a visit to a Moravian castle, he picked up a rare variety of toad in the garden and kissed it tenderly on the head.[23] Henceforth, he was known as the "Krotenkusser" — the toad kisser. He even names his only child, his daughter Lacerta, after the genus of pretty lizards, the lacertidae. It is perhaps this factor, this love for his experimental animals, that led to the remarkable, but as yet unrepeated, success with breeding for acquired characteristics. In a similar manner, Luther Burbank, George Washington Carver, and the Russian J.W. Mitchurin, who loved their plants, were able to achieve outstanding breeding results that have not been equaled. The inheritance of acquired characteristics has not been conclusively disproven, and the human factor of love and care,

---

[22] *Ibid.*, chaps. 4 and 5.

[23] *Ibid.*, p. 19.

the personal relationship that Steiner advocated, has not even been considered. Both Burbank and Carver, when asked the reason for their success, claimed that they communicated with the plants, and could not elaborate further on their methodology.

Are there archetypal patterns, or *leitmotifs*, for each species, akin to Plato's Ideas, Aristotle's entelechies, or Steiner's etheric forms which are plastic and adoptable within a certain range, but could be violated by constraining them in unnatural environments? Is there a "spirit" of the plant or animal that, when violated too often by excessive breeding experiments, by deprivations, artificial inseminations or dead soils, loses its joy of being, that withdraws slowly from manifestation, loses vitality and becomes "degenerate" or extinct? Is it possible that the spirit, the organizing intelligence, whose manifestation is this plant or that animal, is responsive to the human spirit, as most primitive peoples claim it is? Is it possible that Burbank's flowers and fruit trees, Carver's peanuts and Kammerer's salamanders responded to the warmth and love of these researchers?

Speciation has never been observed; it remains a theory. The countless fruitflies that have been subjected to doses of mutagenic X-radiations in the laboratories of H.J. Muller and T.H. Morgan did not produce new varieties, but only trivial and deleterious changes, indicating more the destruction of genetic potential than the creation of anything new. Neither were the mutations random, but specific kinds of changes (blindness, wing stunting, bristle change) occurred at definite rates. Pure bred (homozygous) blind flies suddenly had offspring with functional eyes again, as though there is a blueprint, an etheric model, that re-manifests itself after a time. Such blueprints, or ether bodies, are evidenced in the regeneration of lizard tails, the root and flower development from leaf cuttings, the regeneration of cut-up worms, a phenomenon that led H. Drietsch to the formulation of *vitalism* as a principle opposed to pure physicochemical causality. Even if we say that chromosomes with all the genetic material are found in each and every cell, how do these genes and chromosomes know when it is time to regenerate, and what part they should play?

Conclusion

We have voiced doubts about the practices resulting from modern genetic theory. What in Mendelian neo-Darwinism is based on sound logic and observation cannot be disputed; however, there are too many unexplained factors to permit raising the theory to the level of law. These are shaky grounds upon which to base our food sources.

The environment has a greater effect on the genetic vitality than is accounted for by the theory. Good husbandry and nurture require that an environment proper to the species be established and maintained, if degeneration and loss of vitality are to be avoided. The archetype of the organism must find an environment conducive to its specific nature in order to thrive and reproduce well. To deny the existence of the archetype and to change species by hyperbreeding and induced mutation will only accelerate genetic disaster. We can understand genes better if we think of them as anchors in the physical world of supersensible beings that constitute the essence of the plant or animal. By manipulation of the genes or by diminishing the environment of the genes, these nonmaterial essences will have an increasingly difficult time manifesting themselves. The essences, or supersensible archetypal forms, for our plants and animals are, of course, not available to the objective study by the scientific method because this method, limiting itself to external sensory data and mathematical, logical formulation, precludes such study. A meditative approach, a loving sympathy, a knowledge of the supersensible world as was part of all cultural traditions at one time, or a "spiritual science" as proposed by Rudolf Steiner, have an easier time understanding these things. A natural environment, good care and a loving, personal relationship to the creatures of farm and garden will, in the long run, provide better results than cold, mercenary practices hatched out in a distant laboratory.

To those who operate by the assumption that we live in a dead and meaningless universe given up to chance, we will let Goethe reply:

> The world of the spirit is not closed;
> It is your sense shut off,
> Your heart that's dead.

CHAPTER IX
A SUMMARY OF THE AGRICULTURAL LECTURES OF STEINER

The biological movement in farming and gardening had its beginning with Steiner's agricultural lectures and with the enthusiasm and dedication engendered among the participants of this course. Even though the lectures were admittedly hard to understand, experimental circles of farmers, gardeners and scientists were immediately formed.[1] Even after more than half a century, we can appreciate the newness of what was said at the time. It required study, not mere reading, and a background of practical agricultural experience to come to terms with the course and this is still true today.[2]

To summarize the contents, as is attempted here, is a difficult, if not impossible undertaking if one means to do these lectures justice. The reader first confronted with the course will perhaps have as hard a time of it as the first listeners because, essentially, a new world-view has to be grasped. The lectures begin to make sense when the world-view expressed in them is understood.

In the first lecture, Steiner points out that we must

---

[1] *Landwirtschaftlicher Impuls und Seine Entfaltung* (F.C.L. Schmidt. ed., W. Muller Verl. Birenbach).

[2] John Soper, *Studying the Agricultural Course* (Bio-Dynamic Agricultural Association, London, 1976).

proceed from a holistic point of view that takes all factors into account. Cosmic and tellurian factors are at work in all phenomena. The earth and the planets belong to the same system. Plants and animals are permeated by cosmic rhythms; so are human beings, where, however, the cosmic rhythms do not follow directly the cosmic phenomena, but have emancipated themselves by degrees (fever curves, menses, etc.).

He points out that there are two aspects of agricultural production, that of *quality* involving nutrition, aroma, clear metamorphic stages of fruiting and flowering; and that of *quantity*, related to the production of mass, bulk and also reproduction. Chemical fertilizer application supports only the latter process of creating bulk at the expense of quality. Quality is the result of the influence of the distant planets (Mars, Jupiter, Saturn) which work through the quartz (silica) of the earth's crust. 48% of the earth's crust is composed of this "inert" element. Quantity results from the workings of the lower planets (Mercury, Venus, Moon) through the calcium, potassium, sodium and their relatives in the earth. The faster-moving lower planets work more strongly into the annual plants, whereas the slow-moving, distant planets affect the perennial plants.

After opening with such a wide and unfamiliar perspective of linking the planets to the life of the earth, Steiner follows in the second lecture with the concept of the *integrated farm organism* (we would say ecosystem or biome, today), where plants and animals, soil and man operate like integrated organs within the total organism.

In a similar fashion, the earth planet is seen as an "organism" to which also the sun, moon and other planets belong. The soil, the surface of the earth, absorbs cosmic

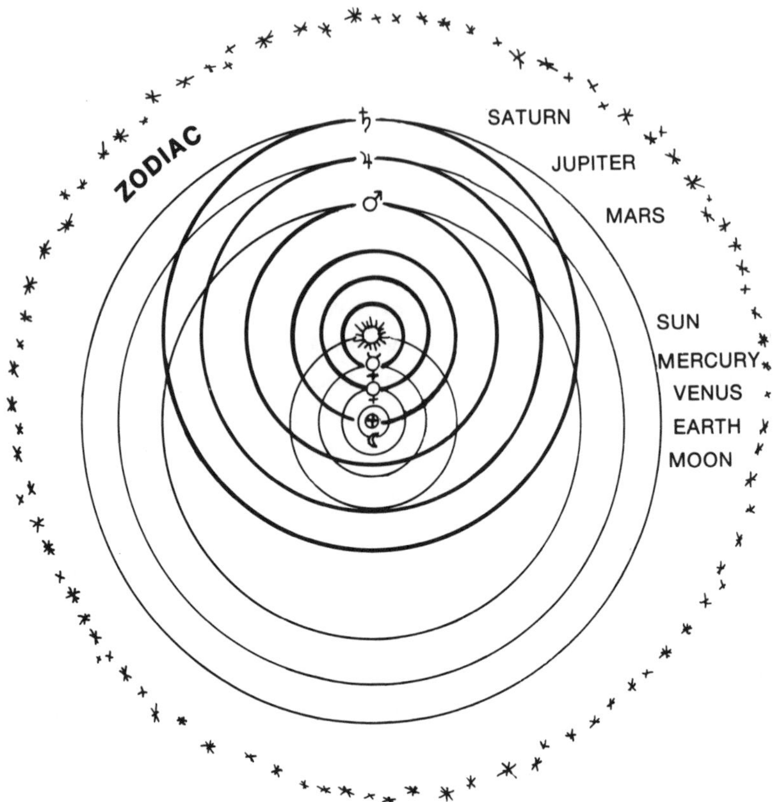

The distant and nearer planets seen in their geocentric and heliocentric orbits.[3]

forces and, by the use of silica, reflects them back into plant growth. Calcium pulls the atmospheric forces into the ground, affecting quantity production. The soil can be seen, as a diaphragm of the earth organism involved in these various exchanges. Clay works as a medium for the forces

---

[3] *Sternenkalender* (1971-72, Dornach, Switzerland), p. 58.

streaming in both directions. Earth, water, air and warmth are perceived to have different qualities when found above or below this diaphragm, the soil. Above the soil, air and warmth are "dead," while they are "alive" below the soil. Vice-versa, earth and water are considered to be living above the soil and dead below it. At first glance, these might be confusing concepts, but when one observes nature, one can see that warmth and air, fixed by the plant, enter the soil as living roots or as larva and worms, whereas mineral earth and water taken up from below the ground become part of living plant tissue above the ground.

The crystallizing forces radiate into the earth and water from the cosmos most strongly during the period from mid-January to mid-February, when, in the northern hemisphere, at least, the earth and water are the "deadest" and most receptive to the imprinting of cosmic forces. During this time, the plants, slumbering in thick-skinned seeds and tightly-packed buds, are neutral and self-contained. But when, later, the highly complex proteins of the seeds become a "little chaos" and fall apart in germination, these forces stream into the plants and imprint their form into the plants, as these plants build up their substance with the aid of humus. The cosmic forces reappear in the geometry of plant architecture, in their color and quality aspects.

In a profound foreshadowing of ecological thinking fifty years later, Steiner states that specific animals belong to specific regions of the earth and that they are in symbiosis with other life forms there. In providing the manures, they are tied into the soil processes with their digestive organs and, in turn, affect the vegetation. Thus, a healthy farm-garden organism must have just the right number of animals (cows, horses, sheep, fowl, etc.) to produce the right amount of manure to aid humus formation and maintain a healthy soil. Plant, animal and soil are an interacting unity.

The third lecture can be a breath of fresh air or a shaking of foundations for the biochemist, as Steiner discusses the life elements, carbon, oxygen, hydrogen, nitrogen and sulphur in Nature's household. Our current materialistic conceptions of these elements are inadequate. They are like snapshots of a person, not like the living person himself. The mesh of our conceptual net is too crude to capture the subtleties of these elements. Again, Steiner uses a comprehensive approach that goes beyond the charting of the cycles in nature of these elements. He tries to apprehend their essence, to meet the person, not the snapshot, by characterizing each element in the sum of its multifold appearances.

Carbon, that "black chap," is the *form-giving* element in organic nature. Using the carbon from the carbon dioxide taken in by photosynthesis, the plants build up their carbon framework (C-C-C-C-C-C) upon which the other elements become attached. When one burns a plant, the ashes consist mainly of carbon. Carbon's form-bearing potential is seen in the physical world in the diamond. In animals and man, in order to be free of the rigidity that characterizes the plants, CO_2 is constantly expelled by breathing, while the structure is provided by a calcium phosphate skeleton instead of a carbon framework.[4] Carbon, the form-giving

[4] Steiner suggests that the mysterious "Stone of the Wise" of the Alchemists is related to carbon respiration, where carbon has to do with the ability to translate images into form. Oriental breathing exercises include the retaining of the breath for a longer period of time than is normal, in order that the yogi may realize certain images.

element, is permeated by *oxygen,* the universal *carrier of life* (etheric). Without the carbon framework, the etheric would have no carrier. In the earth and inside organisms, the "dead" atmospheric oxygen becomes alive, activating light and warmth through oxidation. (The fact that our modern instrument-laden robots on the moon and Mars are searching for traces of oxygen is an acknowledgment of its function as life-carrier.)

Nitrogen, the element of universal *sensitivity,* is seen as a bridge between the life of forces and the spiritual archetypes. It is the element which provides the anchor for astrality (soul workings) in animals and man. In plants, whose tissues as carbohydrates, cellulose and lignin contain little nitrogen, the astrality works mainly from the outside. Nitrogen, the carrier of feeling, sensitivity, and movement, works in the soil in such a way that the soil can "sense" what is going on in the planet sphere, in the atmosphere and biosphere. The supposedly dull-witted peasant often knows intuitively what his plants or his soil need, for he picks up the nitrogen wafting up from a freshly ploughed field through his nostrils and comprehends, below the level of consciousness, what is needed for the farm. Like oxygen, nitrogen is "dead" in the air, but it becomes "alive" in the earth and inside organisms.

Whereas sulphur (L. sol=sun, ferre=to carry) has the function of carrying the spiritual forces into the physical medium, a process akin to sunlight being fixed into the plant, Steiner indicates that hydrogen, the lightest of the elements, dissolves forms, dissipates and carries substances back into the spiritual, nonmanifest form. All these elements are supported by the working of "greedy" calcium, that pulls oxygen and etheric forces into the ground, silicon, that rays outward cosmic forces, and clay, that works as a mediator between them. He goes on in this lecture to point out how each plant species has a specific function on the earth organism regarding these elements. For example, legumes are the organs for the in-breathing of nitrogen, supported by "greedy" calcium as shown by the fact that legumes need an alkaline soil.

The fourth and fifth lectures, the median point of the course, deal with central issues of farming and gardening, the maintenance of fertility. It is established that fertilizing is not a process of feeding the plant, but it means making the soil more alive so that the plant is not put into a dead medium. There should be no sharp division between the plant and the living earth. How does one achieve this enlivening of the earth? For one thing, the suggestion is made for raised beds of earth which are more easily penetrated with etheric forces. He likens trees to these raised beds, with each leaf and bud forming a separate plant. This principle has been made use of by the master gardener Alan Chadwick whose raised beds are also double dug, so that the "dead" air can enter the soil where it becomes alive. Mineral fertilizers are rejected by Steiner in favor of compost which is rich in etheric and astral elements. Mineral fertilizer cannot quicken the earth, it works only on the water; a statement that Lady Eve Balfour would agree with, claiming that "mineral fertilizer amounts to the art of making water stand upright."

Composts, made up of plant and animal residues, can be properly described as generalized living organisms which do not have specific organs but have vital energies circulating around within them. Like all living organisms, they should have a protective skin, they should not stink. If they do stink, a loss of life quality is implied, much as when sick animals develop bad odors. Slight amounts of lime should be added to the composts to soak up the excess etheric. It is the liveness, the quickness of the compost that is then imparted to the soil, whence it works into plants and into animal fodder, leading to the overall health of the farm organism.

A special preparation from cow manure is given at this point in the lectures as an enlivening measure. Cow manure, because of its rich etheric and astral forces, is especially suited for composting. A cow horn, filled with fresh cow manure, is buried in good soil over the winter. In the following season, homeopathic portions of its contents are stirred rhythmically in a bucket of water and then sprayed over the fields to aid root growth and foliage development. The horn is effective because the cow, with its elaborately developed digestive system, uses horn and hoof to ray back and intensify the digestive processes. Another preparation made from pulverized quartz, placed into a cow horn and buried in the ground over the summer, has the effect of making the plant more responsive to light and aiding the fruiting and flowering processes. This also is to be made by stirring a homeopathic portion in a bucket for an hour. Ideally, both preparations are stirred by hand with a birch broom, for this aids in creating the personal relationship that Steiner felt was so necessary to develop between the human being and the land.

In the fifth lecture, Steiner also points out that it is useless to inoculate the compost, manure, or earth with microorganisms, for they are not so much the cause of fertility as the symptom that life-forces are present. Not substances or bacteria are to be given to the soil, but primarily forces are to be transmitted to the earth and plants made receptive to them. These forces are not found by isolating substances in experimental situations and analyzing them microscopically, but are found by studying the wider connections of macrocosmic processes. In the rest of this lecture, Steiner prescribes preparations that can be placed into the amorphous body of the living compost like organs, to regulate its chemistry and make the compost especially receptive to the workings of the planets. These preparations are made from camomile, yarrow, dandelion, stinging nettle, oak bark and valerian.[5] It is in this lecture that the possibility of the transmutation of elements within the realm of living chemistry is suggested and the implication is made that the chemistry of living organisms transcends that which can be ascertained in the test tube.

The sixth lecture deals with the problem of weeds, pests, and so-called plant diseases. He discusses how strong lunar forces working through the water can influence weed germination and how, by passing the weed seeds, or insects, through a fire process and preparing a "pepper" of ashes which is sprinkled over the land, the pests will be discouraged. Cyclical recurrence of insect infestations is discussed. As regards plant disease, he points out how astrality can "slide down into the plant" impinging too heavily on it, causing mildew and insect damage. Vigor can be restored by a strengthening of the plant's etheric through the use of the preparations as "medicines." Sickness is something very different in the animal than in the plant organism, for

[5] These preparations will be discussed in detail in a later chapter in the second part of this book.

in the latter, astrality works from without, while in the former it works from within. Most illness is due to an imbalance between the astral and the etheric. Composts will strengthen the ether body in plants. When influences of the lower planets press too strongly onto the plant, spore-forming mildews and fast-breeding aphids appear, somewhat like premature fruiting and pollen production. These forces can be held at bay by the use of silica-rich horsetail (equisetum) tea spray.

The seventh lecture can be considered a classical statement on the ecological interconnections within the household of nature. We must see the plant, animal, mineral, insect and bird worlds as belonging together in one complicated system. They do not work on each other in crude causality, but there are multitudes of subtle forces (warmth, odors, etc.) to which the farmer and gardener must be sensitized. He must not only observe these interactions, but he must activate all senses, i.e. he must become clairsentient in respect to smelling. Animals, insects and birds must be understood as the expression of a landscape's astrality. The loss of one species in an area has many unfortunate consequences. He further points out the ill effects of monocropping and the importance of forest, hedges, and mushroom-harboring meadows to the farm organism. None of this can be successfully studied in the laboratory or on experimental parcels, for the effects must be understood in their entirety, the whole being greater than the sum of its parts.

The eighth and final lecture deals with feeding. Livestock need more than just bulk food that produces calories and fat. What the animal takes in with his senses as smells, air, sunlight and warmth is just as much a food that will have an effect on the animal as the food he eats. When these senses are satisfied and the cow is allowed to eat what its instincts command in the way of herbs and shrubbery-browsings, then the animal dung will have a special guiding and organizing effect on the plants. The manure will be of better quality, aiding the whole farm organism. The animals themselves will be healthier and more fertile. Animal dung should come from local animals where the same atmospheric and terrestrial conditions prevail, and beast and plant are geared for each other.

Though the course seems unusual in a number of aspects, it truly represents a pioneer work that has been a reliable guide to the many farmers and gardeners who have taken it seriously. The proof of the value of the outlook presented lies in the healthy and happy livestock, the steady high-yield and high-quality production of bio-dynamic farms and gardens.

Culture and Horticulture

A Philosophy of Gardening

PART II

Introduction to Part II

Whereas the first part of the book deals with modern ideas of organic and bio-dynamic gardening and delves into ancient cosmological concepts that have fallen into ill-repute with the changing of the times, finding gold underneath their corroded surfaces, the second part is more concerned with practical applications. Though we are talking about microorganisms and cation exchanges, the focus remains holistic, comprehensive and macrocosmic.

We begin with the great polarity, the *terrestrial factors,* mother earth, and *cosmic factors,* father sky, the sun-moon planets. Leaving the sphere of the elements, our attention is turned to the sphere of life, starting with *composting,* where life and death processes hold each other in balance, and how to prepare composts that will capture life forces and make them available to our plants. Then, the attempt is made to make natural plant sociology work for us in correct *companion planting* and proper *crop rotation.* The major *plant families are identified that we meet in the garden and the function of weeds* is explored. *Negative astral influences* in the form of *pests,* insects and fungi are discussed next, and natural *bio-dynamic medicines* and *preparations* are studied. Chapters on harvest, storage, seeds and seed production, herbs, hints on cooking, and on social aspects make up the concluding chapters.

CHAPTER X

TERRESTRIAL FACTORS: SOIL

Until recently, materialistic science thought of the soil as just a substance to hold plants up and to provide chemical building blocks for their growth. Recent experiments with *hydroponics,* growing plants in a watery medium without soil, seem to verify this theory. However, studies show that, besides the need for constant flushing and oxygenating of the liquid medium, the hydroponically grown plants steadily lose vitality and germination ability after a number of years. The chemicals are absorbed in an unbalanced manner by these hypertrophying plants. For the city dweller in crowded quarters, window sill, balcony or roof-top hydroponics might give pleasure and an occasional snack, but for larger scale gardening it is not to be recommended.

Before modern science came to view soil in terms of chemical constituents and mechanical processes, the soil was literally sacred. It was the Mother Earth from which all living forms sprang and to whom they all returned, eternally virgin, ever-fertile and receptive. Appearing in many forms and called by many names, she was worshipped in India as Prithivi, in Greece as Gaea, as Terra in Rome, as Dana by the Celts, as Siva by the Slavic people. We get an appreciation of how differently the peasant, his soul bound up with the soil for generations, related to the earth from a hymn of the Russian "Old Believers":

> The first mother is the holy Mother of God,
> The second is moist mother Earth,

The third, the mother who gives birth in pain.[1]

We understand the immigrating Sicilian peasant who brings with him a handful of his native soil. For the alchemist the soil was an expression of the amorphous *Prima Materia,* the ever-receptive chaos, capable of reflecting the forms projected upon it by the microcosmic and macrocosmic spirit. In primitive cosmologies the Earth Goddess is usually paired with the Sky God or is the groom's bride in a divine hierogamy. She is the *mater* (matter) that gives birth to the Father's offspring. Thus, agri*culture* becomes a sacred *cultus* (L. cultus=to tend, care); ploughing is the divine act of opening up the sacred womb.

The Phenomenology of Soil

In keeping with the goetheanistic approach, we should first let the soil impress itself onto our senses before we interject our metaphysical and theoretical considerations. What does the soil look like? Is it light or dark? How does it feel? Is it crumbly, gritty, greasy; has it fine or coarse texture? How does it smell? Does it have the good, plowed-earth smell? How much life is there in the soil and are there

[1]John Fletcher, *Russia: Past, Present and Future* (London: New Knowledge Books, 1968), p. 3. When the burden of carrying wicked humanity becomes too heavy to bear, the Mother Earth asks that she may be allowed to swallow them up. Christ answers:

"O Mother, Moist Mother Earth
Of all creatures thou art most in pain
By the sins of humanity thou art stained
Have patience yet a little while until I come again
Then thou, O Earth, shalt rejoice and skip
Thou shalt shine forth whiter than snow!
I shall change thee into a marvelous garden
Where beautiful flowers of Paradise shall bloom for thee!
O ye, my chosen souls rejoice."

earthworms? Do the weeds look healthy?

Usually, when we dig a trench, we notice a profile of soil layers called *soil horizons*. Generally, the top layer is simply loose debris, covering darkly-colored crumbly matter. The dark coloration is most often due to carbonaceous, organic matter. This layer is referred to as the *A-horizon*. This zone is most alive with microorganisms and is also referred to as the *edaphon*. The next layer, the *B-horizon*, is lighter in color and contains many suspended and dissolved organic silicate, clay, or iron particles. This is referred to as the zone of eluviation. Below this is usually weathered parent material called the *C-horizon*. It is important to familiarize oneself with the parent material, the bedrock, for this will tell a lot about the soil's needs.

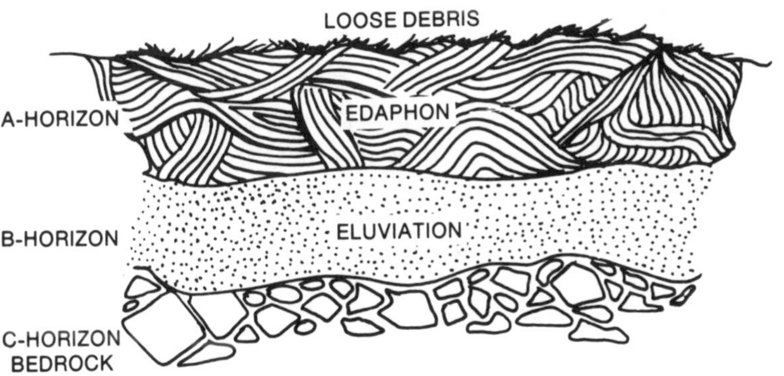

The climate, temperature, rainfall and topography are as important as the parent bedrock in the formation of the soil, so that only the general overall characteristics can be given here. Sandstone bedrock will give light, *sandy soils* that will heat and also cool quickly, have poor water-holding capacity, and poor nutrient-holding capacity. They are well aerated, drain well, and are easily worked. These soils readily transmit light and warmth etheric forces, so that carrots and potato tubers will do well in them. They provide a good basis for wine and herb cultures since light and warmth ether are related to quality and aroma. Granite bedrock,[2] a metamorphic-igneous rock, has a differential weathering rate, such that its quartz component weathers slowest, its mica component at a middling rate, and its feldspar component (orthoclase or plagioclase) is weathered the most quickly. The result is that the soluble minerals (Ca, Mg, Na, K) are soon washed out, while Si, Fe and Al accumulate. This leads to a sandy soil, that is acid and poor in nutrients, especially phosphorus. Limestone bedrock will produce soils rich in Ca, whose structure is usually good, and where life and chemical etheric forces (earth and water ether) work to produce good, quantitative yields. Legumes do well on these slightly alkaline soils.

If the parent material is clay, or shale, the derivative soils are heavy, compact, heat and cool slowly, hold much water and drain badly. Though they are hard to work and slow to get warmed in the spring, they have great potential for fertility, especially if supplied lime and organic matter, for their colloidal structure has a large surface area that can hold nutrient ions. When Steiner indicates that clay is a good transmitter of etheric forces, this should not be confused with poor draining and warming ability, rather, it refers to the potential of these soils for good quantitative and qualitative yields. Blue-grey clay indicates poor drainage (iron reduction), red clay indicates better aeration (iron oxidation), yellow indicates hydration and oxidation of iron.

[2]As found in Grants Pass, Oregon area.

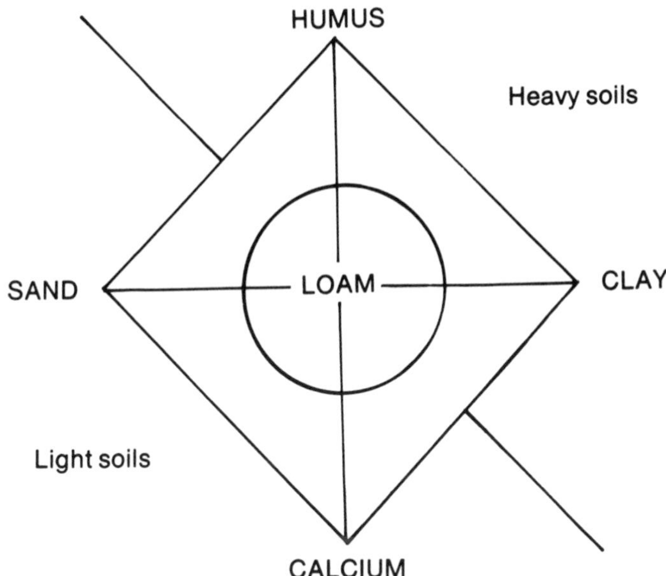

Humus refers to the organically derived compounds which give the soil a dark to black color due to the carbon contents.

A simple overview of the soil types is provided by the soil quadrant for classifying soils according to their humus, sand, lime and clay contents.

The closer the soil is to loam, the more each of the four types are represented in the soil, the more ideal it is for good growing conditions.

Texture of the soil refers to the coarseness ranging from gravel to sand (1/50" particles), to silt (1/500-12,000"), to clay (1/12,000"+).

Structure refers to the friability, crumbliness, tilth, or good heart of the soil. Its opposite is *compaction* and hard pan. Good structure is indicated when a handful of soil can be molded into a ball and hold its shape until flicked by a finger, causing it to crumble readily. Good structure is due mainly to mycelial growth and the gummy excretions of microorganisms found in humus. This humus in combination with inorganic colloids (clay-silicate colloids) forms the important *clay-humus complexes* that characterize rich, ripe garden soils. These clay-humus complexes, besides improving the tilth, have the ability to hold on to six times their weight in water, to hold the positively charged *cations*[3] (e.g. Ca, Mg, K, NH3, Na, etc.) and to buffer the soil against too much acidity or alkalinity. Whereas bacteria, humus, calcium, phosphorus and clay help create this desired structure or friability, the acid residues of artificial fertilizers in chemical salt form break down soil structure and clay-humus complexes. Deep plowing and heavy machinery have a similar effect in increasing compaction.

Acidity or Alkalinity (Percentage Base Saturation, pH), or the sweetness or sourness of the soil is indicated by the pH scale ranging from 1 to 14. Soils range from very acid soils

1	7	14
ACID, SOUR	NEUTRAL	ALKALINE, BASE, SWEET

of about a pH of 4, which is about the acidity of tomatoes, beer or grass silage, to a pH of 8, which is about as alkaline as sea water or eggs. Most plants prefer to grow in earth that has a pH of 6 to 7. Humus buffers the soil between 6 and 7. Wet soils are usually sour; they have low base saturation

[3]In the theory of atoms, a positively charged atom or group of atoms.

because the bases (Ca, Mg, Na, K, etc.) usually leach out in the rain, leaving an excess number of hydrogen ions that are the indicator of acidity. Sandy soils, peat-moss formations and the podsols of northern, wet climates furnish examples of this happening. In dry climates, as in southern California, the opposite happens – alkalinity increases and salts are deposited on the surface of the soil. Before indicator tests for pH came about, farmers could tell by looking at the weeds whether a soil was sweet or sour. The presence of sorrel, sour dock, buttercups, tussocks, hawkweeds, horsetails, knotweeds, cinquefoil and daisies usually indicates an acid soil; whereas alfalfa, sweet clover, burdock, coltsfoot, chamomile and others indicate a sweet soil.

The application of chemical fertilizer tends to acidify the soils so that the addition of large quantities of lime is concomitant with their use. Humus derived from careful composting, on the other hand, has such a buffering effect that the organic gardener does not have to worry about the pH at all. Humus and microorganisms buffer the soil by letting excess H ions go when the soil is too acid, and letting Ca ions go when the soil is too base. If, for the sake of a special culture, the gardener wishes to increase the pH, he can sweeten the soil by the addition of ground limestone or dolomite; or he can make the soil more acid by adding pine needle mulch, coffee grounds, oak leaf mulch, cotton seed meal, etc.

How Are Soils Created?

Soils are created out of the mother substance by the influence of cosmic forces working through fluctuations in climatic rhythms, temperature, rainfall, splitting and erosion. These forces are usually labeled *mechanical forces.* Secondly, there are *chemical forces* working in the life and chemical ether such as *hydrolysis,* when water works on feldspar forming clay; *hydration,* where the water combines chemically with other molecules; *oxidation,* where the oxygen combines with such minerals as Fe, Mg, Ti, Cu, etc.; and *carbonation,* where water combines with carbon dioxide to form carbonic acid in which lime, soda and potash become soluble. Most soil formation is, however, the direct result of *living* organisms working to create the proper living conditions for themselves. Roots and small soil organisms use a number of chemical forces (oxidation, reduction, carbonation) in order to modify the soil, and large roots and burrowing animals often act as mechanical forces.

We are essentially correct in following Hauschka and Herzeele in concluding that wherever there is soil, living organisms have preceded it, when we consider, for example, rocks freshly exposed in a rock quarry. Before long, lichens will appear on the bare rock, where they will thrive and spread. How are these plants able to survive these exposed, adverse conditions? From where do they get their nutrients? If we examine the lichen closely, we find two organisms, a fungus and an algae, living in a mutually beneficial association or symbiosis. The algae, containing green chlorophyll, can photosynthesize and create necessary sugars and starches for feeding itself and its partner. The fungus, in turn, provides a leathery covering for the algae that keeps it from drying out; it supplies the necessary minerals and transmits water to it. Where do these minerals come from? They are split by the fungus, out of the tightly-held molecular bonds of the rock structure, dissolved and transferred from the lithosphere into the biosphere. The lichens are capable of *chelation* (Gr. chela=claw, pincer), or of pinching the minerals off from the bare rock. The rock residues and older lichens, as they die off, become debris. Into this proto-soil the spores of mosses may fall. Mossy pads will form on the rock, assaulting it further with carbonic acids and other excretions. Older generations of mosses will form the substrata for next generations, creating a spongy mass that is able to hold water successfully. Soon, spores of more advanced plants, such as ferns, will find footholds. Gymnosperms and flowering plants will eventually find enough substance to gain a hold, developing strong roots that can crack the rock further. Small animals will now be added, who will supply nutrients to the plants at the same time that they feed on them. Here we have a picture of how soil is formed. We appreciate a little recapitulation of plant evolution in this.

A key factor is the chelating ability of plants, especially of the fungi. About 80% of the plant species live in a symbiotic relationship with a fungus that is associated with their root network. These root fungi, or *mycorrhizae,* make it possible for the great stands of conifers to find adequate nourishment in very poor soils.[4] Similar to this is the symbiosis between the legumes and the *rhyzobia* that helps bring nitrogen into nitrogen-deficient soils. If artificial nitrogen is

---

[4]This is one of the reasons, besides the direct health danger to man and beast, why spraying stands of forest with defoliants, as is done to rid the economically important conifers of their "competitor" species, is ecologically disastrous. The spray will likely kill off the mycorrhizae, which are very sensitive. The conifers, weakened by the loss of this symbiotic association, will become subject to insect damage, since the insect's function in the life-cycle is to destroy unhealthy tissues. The result will be the necessity of spraying not only artificial nutrients on the forests, but of resorting to the use of insecticides. All this spells profits for chemical companies but, on the other hand, ecological disaster.

supplied to the soil, the *rhyzobia* will not work. We see how plants actively work at creating for themselves the soil they need. Some plants function as accumulators and change the soil in one direction or another, e.g. daisies collect calcium in acid soils, horsetail collects silicon even in silicon-poor soils, orache collects salt, etc.[5] Upon their death, these plants will enrich the soil with these elements and change it correspondingly. Through their life activity, by fixing CO_2 and taking in sunlight, the plants penetrate the ground with their root masses and build light and warmth etheric forces into it. They modify the soil by retaining some elements and excreting others. They can do this against the diffusion gradient. The root masses are continuously growing and dying, constantly adding new organic substance to the soil. However, the roots are not alone in this soil-building process; animal manures with their complex enzymes are constantly modifying the plant growth, and an astronomical number of microorganisms in the edaphon support these living processes.

The Soil as a Living Organ of the Earth Organism

When we look at the microbial populations that inhabit the soil, we can in no way think of it as just a physical substance that obeys only the laws of inorganic chemistry and mechanical laws. In a teaspoon of good soil, there are literally billions of microorganisms carrying on life functions of continuous metabolism, respiration, reproduction, dying, excreting hormones and enzymes, exchanging cations and anions, responding to cosmic influences such as lunar phases and the daily and yearly solar cycles, and so on. The

[5]cf. E. Pfeiffer, *Bio-Dynamic Farming and Gardening*, pp. 91-103 and Bargyla and Gylver Rateaver, *The Organic Method Primer*, pp. 80-88.

complexity is so great, the factors are so multifold, that no scientist can hope to completely understand what is going on, and no laboratory can study all the interactions simultaneously. We see beyond the physical elements into the world of etheric forces when we look into the world of soil.

Soil organisms have the job of recycling the nutrients, regulating pH, aerating the soil, chelating minerals and eventually creating the crumbly, good-smelling earth that can support the vegetation. Furthermore, they decompose litter by reducing proteins and related substances to NH_4 and NO_3 that can be taken up by growing plants. Some produce sulphates, the only important form of sulphur utilized by higher plants. Some of the autotrophic organisms oxidize iron and magnesium, avoiding toxic build-ups in the soil, while still others can fix atmospheric nitrogen.

Soil organisms are somewhat arbitrarily divided into soil flora and soil fauna. We must look at them more closely in order to get a conception of how alive and active the soil is. There are approximately one billion (1,000,000,000) *bacteria* in a gram of garden soil. A bacterial cell has the ability to produce 17 million offspring in a day's time, and could produce, theoretically, a mass of protoplasm equal to the weight of the earth in a week's time. *Aerobic bacteria* need free O_2 for their respiration and are important in rotting and composting processes. *Anaerobic bacteria* can survive in the absence of free oxygen, as in liquid manures, and are important in fermentation. Some bacteria are *autotrophic,* deriving their energy from the oxidation of ammonium, sulphur, iron and other inorganic minerals, whereas *heterotrophic* bacteria derive their energy from metabolizing organic material by oxidizing carbohydrates, sugars, starches, etc.

With the bacteria we are at the bottom of the great Wheel of Life; here is the place where destruction and decay of organic substances can come to a halt before they reach total mineralization, and are reintegrated instead into the life cycle. Whereas some ammonifiers of the bacterial population break down the proteins into amino acids and ammonia, others (nitrosomonas bacteria) start the build-up cycle of oxidizing ammonia into nitrite ($NO2$), which, in turn, is oxidized further by nitrobacter into nitrate ($NO3$) at which point the nitrogen is readily assimilable by young seedlings for the eventual rebuilding of protein substances. This fascinating locus, where death and life forces verge on each other, will be studied more closely in the chapter on composting.

Soil bacteria work best when there is enough calcium (pH 6-8) available for cation exchange, so that calcium may pull the etheric forces into the ground. Organic matter is needed by the heterotrophic populations for food. Soil bacteria are most active on warm, balmy days when the temperature ranges from 70° to 100°F. Their need for water is similar to that of higher plants, i.e. the soil is not soppy wet, but is moist to the touch. Aerobic bacteria need free oxygen, found in pore spaces of the soil, to be effective; in adverse conditions of cold, heat, or drought they will form spores and rest until favorable conditions are restored.

Almost as numerous as the bacteria are the half-bacteria, half-fungi-like slime molds, or *actinomycetes*. These microorganisms are involved in later stages of decay, in the humification of organic residues, breaking down complex compounds such as cellulose, chitin, and phospholipids.

They are drought tolerant, but need a somewhat high pH (6 to 7.5), being absent below pH 5. Because one species of actinomycete is involved with the potato scab, potatoes are usually not limed. Their presence is indicated by the good "earth" smell of a freshly-plowed field or freshly-dug garden bed. Studies show that they produce antibiotic substances (Waksman), cleaning the soil of many diseases.

Fungi (mushrooms, molds, yeasts) are very important in the decomposing of organic material, and fixing NH_3 and other volatiles into their tissues by ingesting the products of bacterial decomposition. By chelating minerals, the fungi are instrumental in making nutrients available to higher plants. The various *mycorrhizae* (fungus root) extend the rooting system of some plants up to a hundredfold, supplying growth hormones (auxins), aiding phosphorus uptake, and making moisture available. Like actinomycetes, fungi are capable of producing antibiotic substances, such as the well-known penicillin and streptomycin, and thus performing the soil's neutralizing function of diseased and putrefied substances. The immense network of fine hair-like mycelia in some species gather together at times to make fruiting bodies that are recognized as mushrooms and toadstools. When fungi become too active, especially in the cool, rainy weather of the fall when the overall life forces are waning, fine sprays of silicon solution made from waterglass or from horsetail can be of help in the garden to overcome the problems of mildews or rots. In the spring, these silicious substances counter the damping off of seedlings, also related to a fungus.

Algae are soil organisms that have the ability to fix sunlight, but are of minor importance in comparison to the other microorganisms, except in rice fields where blue-green algae also fix N_2.

Roots should be included in the discussion of soil flora, for the rhizosphere is not radically separate from the other life forms in the soil. The rhizosphere harbors most of these organisms. A constant exchange of substances is occurring between the roots and the surroundings. The roots, continuously growing and dying, add food to the microorganisms. This is not an inconsiderable amount, either, for studies of rye and oat cover crops show that a single plant can grow three miles of roothairs per day, and up to 5,000 miles per season.

The *soil fauna*, ranging from protozoa to arthropods, are less numerous than soil flora, but they are important in the subtle chemical exchanges, in allelochemics, in that they fertilize the soil with their bodies upon death, and that they churn and aerate the soil. Microbes, amoeba, ciliates, flagellates and other *protozoa* live in wet films surrounding the soil particles. They are held in check by antibodies produced by the soil flora.

Of the worms, the *nematodes* (threadworms or eelworms) are important in helping to decompose matter and mix the soil as they feed on decaying materials. A few species that are predatory on soil fauna and some that are parasitic on higher plants, causing "root knot" or "stunt," might be a problem. Root knot occurs when there is not enough organic matter in the soil and the plants are weakened because of it. Rotation of crops, companion planting of French marigold *(tagetes)* and compost applications will solve the problem better than fumigation which is sometimes recommended but which harms other beneficial soil organisms.

Arthropods, mites, ants, insect larvae, and annelid worms such as the earthworms comprise the larger soil fauna that help aerate the soil and break down decaying vegetation. The earthworm is so important that it should be spelled in capital letters.

Earthworms

Darwin's last work, in which, as has been facetiously suggested, he tries to make up for the mischief of his evolutionary theory, deals with the earthworm.[6] His researches, showing the overwhelming beneficial effects of this unassuming creature, countered unfounded speculation in the 19th century about their possible harmful effects. Earthworms keep the soil in motion, mixing it vertically and horizontally, creating aeration and drainage. During digestion they humify organic matter, combining it with ingested clay colloids to form worm castings that are composed of clay-humus complexes, or *stable humus*. Stable humus is characterized by polymerized macromolecules whose nutrient ions are not washed or leached out, and an increased water holding capacity. Researchers show that worm castings aid the soil-building bacteria and actinomycetes. These castings, produced under normal conditions to the order of 12 tons per acre per year, contain 11 times the potassium, 7 times the phosphorus, 5 times the nitrogen, two and a half times the magnesium, and twice the calcium of the surrounding soil.[7] These nutrients, held

[6]Charles Darwin, *The Formation of Vegetable Mold* (1881).

[7]T.J. Barrett, *Harnessing the Earthworm* (Boston). Dr. Barrett estimates that with 8 to 10 earthworms per square foot, and 500,000 per acre, one can optimally count on 18 to 30 tons of transformed earth.

in stable form, are easily used by the plants as they need them. Where do the increases in nutrients in the castings come from? Are they derived from soil and mulch and concentrated by the earthworm, or is there a secret alchemy of transmutation at work? How many sacks of fertilizer would the farmer or gardener have to haul to equal this achievement? Whereas invertebrates excrete calcium into hard exoskeletons, earthworms are continuously excreting $CaCO_3$ as a slime as they move through the earth, which helps the soil maintain a pH that is within the range preferred by the plants. By regulating the calcium processes, the earthworm is instrumental in pulling life forces into the soil. He combines clay colloids, with the help of calcium, with the organic residues to form the basis for qualitative and quantitative plant growth.

Tending the earthworm population is as important a job as tending one's chickens and cows. Earthworms will starve in sterile soils. Organic matter derived from compost, manures, mulching or tilled-in cover crops is needed to feed them. An application of ground limestone or dolomite, but not quicklime which will burn them, and where clay is lacking in the soil, an application of powdered clay will be appreciated by these helpful creatures. The bio-dynamic preparation of valerian *(Valeriana officinalis)* made from an infusion of the flowers, when sprayed on the ground, will aid earthworm activity.

How to Care for the Soil

It cannot be stressed enough how important the soil organisms are for the organic gardener. They are aided by manure, composting, rotations, companion planting and mulching. They are harmed by excessive plowing, monoculture, burning of fields and soil sterilization, which reduces their overall number drastically, as well as diminishes the number of represented species. Pesticides, herbicides, fumigants and fungicides are even more drastic in their effects. Chemical fertilizer harms them by changing the osmotic balances and the pH of the soil. Residues of sulphates and chlorides from chemical fertilizer are harmful to them. Reduction of these organisms involves a loss of humus, the collapse of soil structure which negatively affects nutrition, aeration, temperature, pH and water-holding capacity. Much of modern agriculture has been concerned with these problems. Acidity of soils is dealt with by increased liming, which, if overdone, makes trace minerals (Fe, Mn, B, Zn, Cu) unavailable to the plants and can drive off nitrogen. Compaction is handled by building bigger machines for deeper plowing, chiseling the hardpan, or by the adding of vermiculite or plastic chips to aerate the soil. Lack of water-holding capacity of the soil is dealt with by various watering devices. A vicious cycle is evident in these practices.

For the home garden, the microorganisms are helped by the establishment of permanent *raised beds* that are not compressed by walking on them or running machinery on them. An expensive rototiller is not a necessity in a home garden. Neither is it necessary to spade the garden bed in such a way that the soil is turned over, for the subsoil is then brought to the top and many microorganisms die in the shuffling of their niches. The immediate effect is that the minute corpses of demised microorganisms will create a rush of fertilizing. In the long run, such a practice will wear the humus content down. If the soil is in excellent heart, then the *no-diggers* approach of some British gardeners or the mulching approach of Ruth Stout is recommendable. If the soil is not in good shape or one has more energy, then the *double-dig* method is valuable.

Permanent beds are best 4-feet wide (1,20m), for they can readily be reached from the foot-wide paths for easy planting and hoeing. Three-foot wide beds can be straddled for weeding or planting, but when one considers the number of paths needed, one finds inefficient usage of space. With foot-wide paths and three-feet wide beds, one fourth of the garden space is taken up by paths.

Simply stated, for double-digging,[8] the 4-foot wide beds

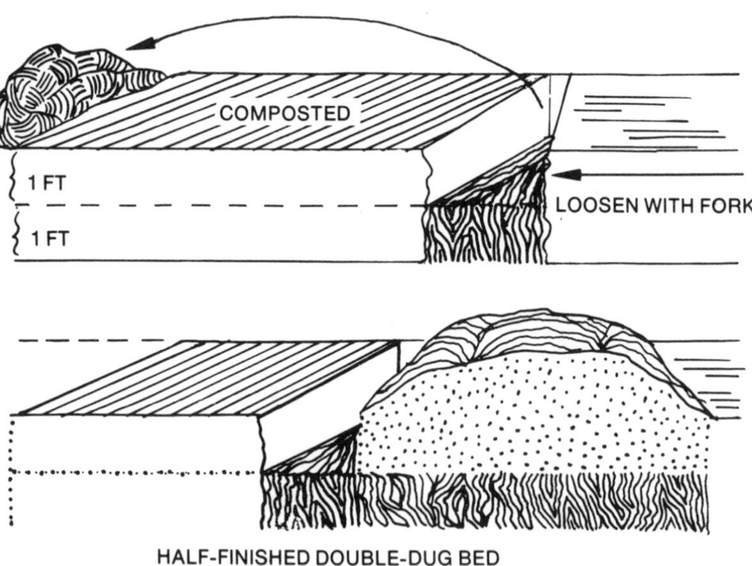

HALF-FINISHED DOUBLE-DUG BED

[8]c.f. John Jeavons, *How to Grow More Vegetables*, is a valuable guide in the proper application of the double-dig method.

are covered with compost. Then a trench, 1 foot deep, is dug at one end of the bed. The soil from the spade-deep trench is saved. Then, with a potato, or digging, fork, the bottom of the trench is loosened for another foot-depth. Then another spade's width is moved to fill the trench, creating a new trench. This is done without turning the soil, but simply moving it over. Again, the digging fork will loosen the bottom twelve inches. This work continues until the end of the bed, where the soil from the first trench fills up the last hole. This is hard work, but needs to be done only once or twice in the garden's history, because once the soil is aerated and composted, the microorganisms and worms will keep the bed in good heart. The effects of double digging are the enhancement of the activity of the soil organisms, better root respiration, and conservation of water by interrupting the capillary movement of water from one soil molecule to another toward the surface where evaporation occurs.

In the winter, the soil is protected by growing a *cover crop* or by *mulching*. All living organisms have skins, and everywhere in nature the ground is covered by leaf litter in the winter. The gardener will do well if he does likewise, for this will protect the edaphon, and earthworm activity will continue right up to the mulch layer. Earthworms and microorganisms will be fed throughout the winter. In the spring, when the mulch is raked away, a fine, dark layer of humified mulch, of new humus, will be found on the soil. Cover crops can be sown into cleared beds in late fall. The best combination is a grain and a legume, such as *rye* or *oats* with *Austrian pea* or *vetch*. The legume should be innoculated with the spores of rhyzobia, to increase their ability to fix nitrogen into the soil. The rye or oats, chosen as

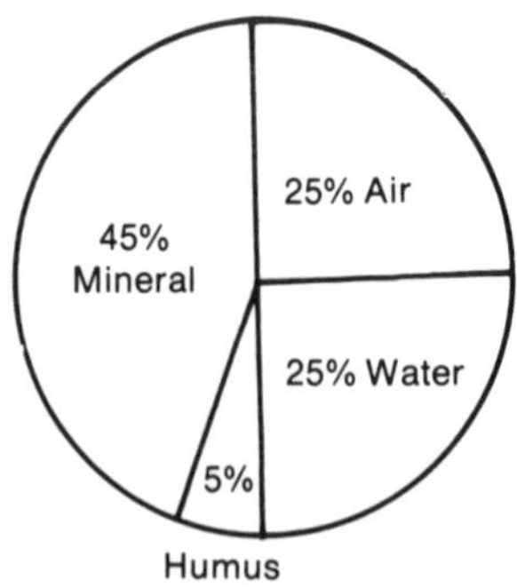

companion plants, grow an immense root mass which will fiberize the soil and add much organic matter to it. The roots continue to grow all winter long, except on the coldest of days, for the soil below the surface does not drop radically in temperature. In the spring, when the lush, tender stems and leaves are about 8 inches high, the green matter can be turned into the soil to feed the earthworms and to add fiber and organic matter.

By double digging, composting, cover cropping, mulching and other ecological forms of soil husbandry, the ideal soil composed of 45% mineral substance, 5% organic matter and 50% pore space (25% air, 25% water) will be achieved.

Soil air is important for the respiration of the roots and microorganisms. In compacted soils this air is diminished, the carbon dioxide from the respiration cannot escape, the plants become stunted and the soil sour. Soil water is found as *hygroscopic* water which is held tightly by soil particles or is chemically bound are not available to plants; as *capillary or cohesion water* which fills the pore spaces and makes up the main source of water for the plants; and as *gravitational or free water* which occurs in a saturated soil and is usually drained off. Good humus content will increase the water-holding capacity of the soil by several hundred percent.

In summary, we can appreciate the conception of the soil as a living organism, as the Mother Earth, the *Prima Materia*, ever-receptive to the influences of the ordering cosmic forces expressed in the rhythm of seasons, atmospheric conditions and climate. We see that the soil contains a physical aspect in the mineral contents, obeying mechanical and chemical laws; an etheric aspect in the humus and flora, obeying laws of the etheric world; an astral aspect in the fauna and the manures derived from the higher animals.

CHAPTER XI
NUTRIENTS AND FERTILIZER

So much emphasis is placed these days on mineral fertilizers that it is easy to forget that there are other important aspects to gardening. It is to the materialistic dogma emerging in the mid-19th century that one must look for the origin of this fascination with the basic nutrient building-blocks. The search for these substances cast shadows on other advances in farming and gardening. Already in 1809, A. Thaer discovered the significance of humus care and crop rotations.[1] It was the theory that nutrient depletion results from the harvesting of crops, as formulated by Justus von Liebig in 1840,[2] that set the ball rolling toward an understanding of the chemical nature of plant nutrition. Liebig's *Law of the Minimum* showed that crops often fail because they are limited by the deficiency of a single nutrient element. One could pour on as much lime, potash, phosphorus compounds and other nutrients as one would like, but it would help the failing crops little if the deficiency was, say, nitrogen. The analogy is that of a barrel whose staves are broken at different lengths; the barrel will hold only as much water as the shortest stave permits. In the illustration, the limiting factor would be the potassium. The water level of the barrel would be representative of the crop yield.

---

[1]A.D. Thaer, *Grundsatze der Rationalen Landwirtschaft* (1809).

[2]Justus v Liebig, *Chemie und ihre Anwendung auf Landwirtschaft und Physiologie* (1840).

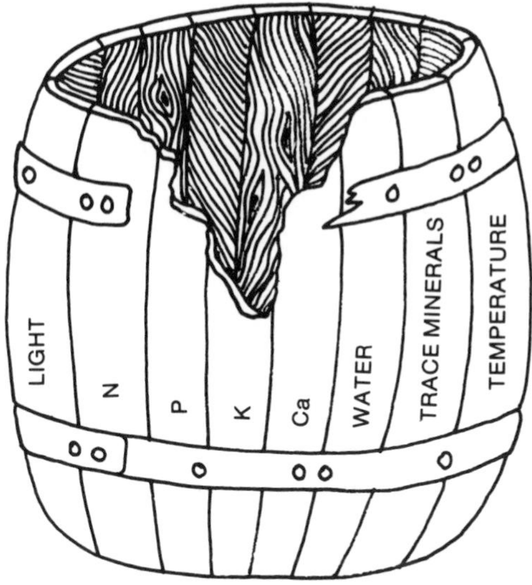

Following Liebig, the ash contents were examined for the percentage and weights of nutrient minerals present, and then computations were made per acre, or per hectare, regarding how many pounds of nutrients are removed from the soil with each harvest. From this, it was calculated how many nutrients would have to be replaced. A herculean task it turned out to be, leading to the fear that humanity would soon starve if the chemical artificials could not be found to replace these nutrients.[3] This gave impetus to the building of chemical fertilizer plants.

At this time, Julius Sachs and W. Knop developed

[3]This fear, of course, still exists today in the minds of most agronomists. Seen from a comparative, socio-cultural perspective, one can understand how an age under the spell of the Second Law of Thermodynamics, that feared that the sun would eventually burn itself out, would have similar fears in other areas. We are most surely dealing with projected fears generated in a culture that operates on rapid consumption of a nonrenewable fossil energy base, coal then and oil now.

methods of water culture, or hydroponics, in order to get a better test of nutrient requirements, enabling them to elicit at what point the deprivation of an element produces characteristic deficiency symptoms in a plant. Their research established the need for a cluster of elements in the lower range of the periodic table, the so-called *macro-nutrients* (C, O, H, N, P, S, K, Ca, Mg). This orientation and work has continued into the 20th century. Ever more elements were found to be necessary for plant growth, some in the minutest quantity; so minute, in fact, that due to impurities in the growing media, they had escaped earlier researchers. These *micro-nutrients,* or trace minerals, include Fe, Mn, Cu, Zn, B, Mo, Na, etc. The number of needed elements keeps increasing. Recently, for example, it has been discovered that tomatoes need minute traces of silicon. So far, at least 60 elements of the 92 natural elements have been found in plants, but there is no indication as to how essential they are.[4] The picture is complicated by the fact that different plant species have different needs. The testing continues; one can imagine that eventually all the elements are going to be considered essential.[5]

Micro-nutrients are difficult to handle; they cannot be easily put into a fertilizer because in excessive amounts they become toxic. Micro-nutrient availability has become more

---

[4]Frank B. Salisbury and Cleon Ross, *Plant Physiology* (Belmont, Ca.: Wadsworth Publ. Co., 1969), p. 192.

[5]The concern with essential and inessential plant nutrients has its analogy in the Darwinian postulation concerning inessential vestigial organs, or "survivals" of earlier evolutionary phases. 187 such survivals have been identified for homo sapiens (toes, wisdom teeth, appendix, tonsils, etc.). By now, the list of inessential organs has drastically diminished. Hospitals no longer have a "tonsil day" on Friday afternoons for the youngsters.

problematical because livestock have been removed from farms and homesteads, and the manures that contain and recycle these minerals in a biologically assimilable form are not there for the soils. Only in isolated instances has the deliberate application of micro-nutrients been of great value, as in Australia where many acres were made productive by the addition of molybdenum. In most cases, there is danger of over-application. Deep-rooting hardwood trees will pull trace elements out of the substrata, and make them available in the leaves that are shed in the fall. A compost of deciduous foliage, manures, rinsed sea weed, and fish emulsion is all that is needed to restore all the trace minerals to the garden soil. The organic gardener does not have to worry further about trace minerals. Most of them, as Steiner suggests in his *Agricultural Course*, are a free gift of the heavens, supplied by wind and rain. The hydroponic method for finding out the essentiality of trace minerals must be questioned also, for it is not representative of any garden bed or field.

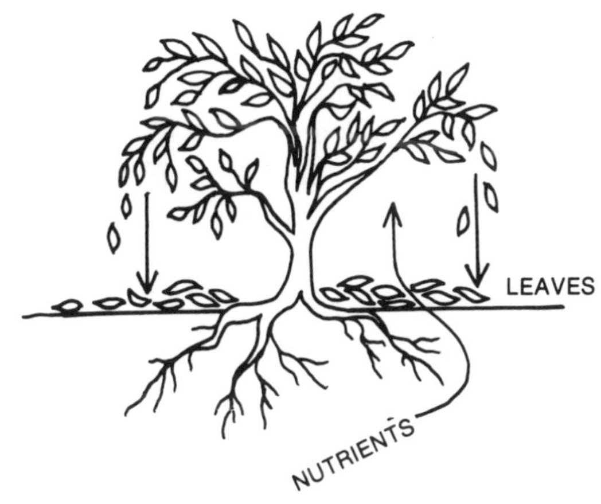

The crude, materialistic outlook is more difficult to maintain as time goes on. The simple barrel analogy, the Law of the Minimum of Liebig, is not quite correct, for plants can substitute, at times, other elements for those that are lacking. At times there can be a partial replacement of K by Na, Ca by Sr, Mo by V, Cl by Br, and probably others.[6] When there is a good supply of N in the plant, it can take up phosphates and sulphates more easily.[7] Mitscherlich (1909) pointed out that an increase in any one of NPK will increase growth, even if one of the macro-nutrients is deficient. That is, if all the other factors are in order, the deficiency symptoms are eased. Aside from all these considerations, however, it is not a matter of simple test tube chemistry. Other factors play a major role: humus level, light intensity, temperatures, water availability, type of plant grown, type of fertilizer and others. Liebig's experiments were done in exhausted soils where test tube equations work. He himself was one of the first to indicate that the soil is not the equivalent of the test tube or laboratory, and emphasized the need to build humus and use manure.[8] Though he is hailed as the "father" of chemical agriculture, in his later writings (which have been shelved), he warns against chemical fertilizers.

Much of modern agriculture consists of a complicated calculus of suitable fertilizer-combination formulas, soil tests, nutrient-requirement charts of plants, application-timing schedules, and charts on the mixability of fertilizers,

[6]Ross Salisbury, *Plant Physiology*, p. 193.

[7]*Ibid.*, p. 201.

[8]Justus v. Liebig, *Chemische Briefe* (1859).

distinguishing those which can be mixed and stored and those which must be used right away. Similar formula juggling occurs with pesticides, herbicides and fungicides which, as we have seen, follow of necessity in the steps of chemical fertilizers. Gardeners are much impressed with this scientific jargon. Impressive pseudo-cabbalistic numerology is passed between gardeners: "I've been using 16:16:16," an old neighbor proudly told the author. It sounds so scientific and smart.

Indeed, once the soil is lifeless to such a degree that it responds like a laboratory retort, one must resort to such magic. There are many possible mistakes that can be made. For example, most NPK salts will leave the soil too acidic. Lime is copiously applied to bring up the pH, but this makes the trace minerals (Fe, Mn, B, Cu, Zn) unavailable, and can drive N off. Chemical nitrogen fertilizers, when used excessively, cause poor root development (marble potatoes), poor flower and seed formation, groundwater contamination (Decatur, Illinois)[9] and accumulations of nitrites in leaf greens. Sulphate of ammonia is acid, water soluble so that it leaches out, kills earthworms and microorganisms and can damage germinating seed. Urea can damage germinating seeds and is quickly volatilized. Calcium and sodium nitrate clump together and are hard to handle. Superphosphate ties up iron as insoluble ferric phosphate; it also ties up calcium and aluminum. Potassium chloride raises the salt content of the soil. The mixing of fertilizers presents a problem; when, for example, lime is mixed with ammonia fertilizers, it drives off the N. Superphosphates should not be mixed with nitrates and chlorides. Antagonisms exist

---

[9]Bird and Tompkins, *Op. Cit.*, p. 197.

between ammonium and K, Ca, Cu; between nitrate and P; between P and Mn, Zn, Cu; between Ca and P, Mg, etc.[10] The examples of complications can go on. No wonder one needs a college education to know how to garden!

To study this is interesting, no doubt, but is not actually necessary for successful farming or gardening if the humus is maintained, and the soil organisms are allowed to take over some of the work load. When the soil is made alive by the use of composts, manures, green manures, slow-working mineral meals that can be chelated by soil flora, catch crops that keep nutrients from being leached out, mulching, and other biologically sound means, then there is no need for such chemical juggling. If mineral substances are to be used, they should work, as Steiner suggests, as they do in Nature herself.

On the other hand, one cannot be dogmatic about avoiding the use of chemical fertilizer altogether, even Sir Albert Howard recommended at times the use of "suitable artificials." One must just be very sure of what one is doing. A nitrogen fertilizer, e.g. urea, can be used in a compost of sawdust to bring the carbon-nitrogen ratio closer, to speed up the rotting by supplying the bacteria with the nitrogen they need for their metabolism. Elstrup Rasmussen writes of using limited amounts of superphosphate and potash salts in combination with manures on the sandy podsol soils of his bio-dynamic farm in Denmark, in order to aid the development of legumes.[11] Similar methods were tried in Guatemala, in combination with the Clinico Bernhorst's efforts,

[10] C.J. Pank, *Dirt Farmer's Dialogue,* p. 79

[11] Elstrup Rasmussen, *Lebendige Erde* (Darmstadt: May, 1962).

to achieve an adequate nutritional standard for the Indian population on their poor soils. These supplementary minerals are used in combination with legumes, especially in the warmer climates, and primarily with manures in the colder climates, or, preferably a combination of both. The criterion is always the livening-up of the soils, the improvement in plant quality and animal health. It is especially the artificial nitrogen fertilizers that are to be avoided.[12]

Just as one may, under special circumstances, use artificial fertilizer, depending on specific conditions, so also are there times to be cautious about "natural" or "organic" fertilizers. Stockyard manure created by unhappy, sick animals that are injected with antibiotics, chicken dung from chicken concentration farms that is sprayed with pesticides, and sewage sludge from big cities that has accumulations of heavy metals which people flush down their drains (Co, Cu, Zn, Mg, Cd, Pb, Hg, As, Mo, etc.) belong to this group.[13] Some natural rock meals that supply P or K might contain fluorides in larger amounts.[14]

In any case, one should handle fertilizing intelligently, even organic fertilizing. The fertilizer should be tailored to the individualized farm-garden organism and its specific needs in regard to climate, soil type, time of year, and kind of crops. A personal relationship to this farm-garden

---

[12] Ibid., p.78

[13] The author's own experience with steer manure placed in water to make "Russian tea" for fertilizing heavy feeders during the growing season was that the "manure" immediately colored the water an unnatural brown, indicating that the substance had been artificially colored to make it look like good compost. Needless to say, the stuff did not ferment. It is a similar story with a bag of "chicken manure" which took two years to break down.

[14] Koepf, Pettersson, Schaumann, *Bio-Dynamic Agriculture,* p. 117.

organism must prevail over abstract or generalized schemes of fertilization, be these chemical or natural. It is with correct composting that one cannot go wrong.

The Major Elements Involved in Plant Growth

Most of the bulk of the vegetation is composed of carbon, oxygen and hydrogen, making up about 98% of plant substance. As important as NPK and other nutrients are, they make up relatively little of the plant. Carbon is derived from the carbon dioxide of the air, oxygen and hydrogen from the water and most, but not all, other nutrients are derived from the soil.

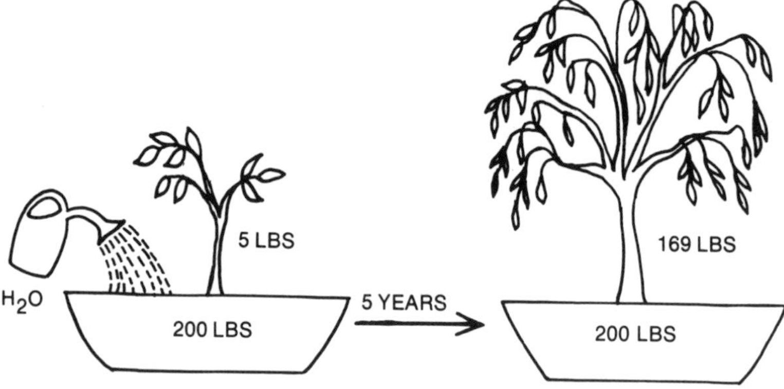

Van Helmont (1577-1644) conducted the classical experiment of planting a 5 lb. willow sapling in a basin containing 200 lb. of soil. For 5 years he gave it nothing but rainwater. After these 5 years, the tree weighed 169 lb; and how much did the soil weigh? It was still nearly 200 lb., having lost only 2 oz. This should make it clear that there is more to plant growth than juggling various chemicals; that there are important factors of water management and the influence of the formative forces coming from air, light, and warmth involved.

As discussed elsewhere, the physical elements in the plant can be understood as the anchor for forces that are working upon the plant from various cosmic regions. We have discussed carbon as the anchor for the form-giving forces, oxygen as the anchor for the life-giving forces, nitrogen for the receptiveness of impressions, and hydrogen for the force that takes life forms out of manifestation. In the same light we can see all the rest of the elements as transmitters of forces of one kind or another.

Generally, in plants, the order of the amounts of elements present in a scale from the most prominent to the least, goes from the carbon to oxygen, to hydrogen. At much smaller frequency are found nitrogen, then potassium, then calcium, magnesium, phosphorus, silicon, and so on to some sixty elements. This order of representation is not a passive mirror of the soils, which are composed in the order of oxygen, silicon, aluminum and so on.

In bio-dynamics, *silicon,* which in orthodox agriculture is barely considered, is understood as a transmitter of forces of warmth and light.[15] Silicon helps plants to ray into themselves these important formative forces, creating quality, aroma and flavor. Because of this ability, it counteracts fungal diseases which are related to cool, moist weather and to excessive nitrogen concentrations which increase the water contents in the leafy tissue.

Silicon is present in about all plants, but especially in the

[15]This is most likely why blackberries grown along dusty roads are the sweetest; they are dusted with fine particles of Si.

grains and grasses, found mainly in the sheaf and spelt. It makes straw stiffer, so that it does not lay down in a thunderstorm; it makes it more difficult for pests, aphids, and fungi to penetrate the tissues.[16] Silicon, which makes up 48% of the earth's crust, is not highly reactive in its inorganic state as quartz; "an aloof gentleman," Steiner calls this element. It must find its way into organic compounds in the form of silicic acid (H_4SiO_4) to work organically. Silicon effectiveness can be increased by the bio-dynamic cow horn preparation (501), in which mountain quartz crystals are pulverized and buried in the ground over the summer in a cow's horn, so that microbial activity works on the silicon. This, finely diluted, is sprayed on the foliage of maturing, flowering, fruiting, and seeding plants to increase the quality. Studies show that NPK fertilizers create an effect similar to that of plants grown under moist, shady conditions, whereas silica preparations increase the effectiveness of warmth and light.[17] Silica-rich waterglass (sodium silicate) solutions (2%) and horsetail tea *(Equisetum arvense)*, sprayed on plants, are effective against mildew and aphids. Quartz sand sown with carrots and other *umbelliferae* increases the light-absorption of these plants, creating better quality.

---

[16]Due to excessive chemical fertilization the amount of silica in plants, especially in grains, has diminished by about 30% ash-content analysis in the last 90 years. The result is poorer keeping and baking quality in bread and a decline in the nutritional quality of bread. Thatch roofs, common for farmsteads around the North Sea, once lasted about 30 years; now, because of the poor quality of the straw, they last, at the most, 15 years. cf. Nicolaus Remer, *Lebensgesetze im Landbau* (Dornach, Switzerland: Phil.-Anthrop. Verl., Goetheanum, 1968), p. 38-62.

[17]Koepf, Pettersson, Schaumann, *Bio-Dynamic Agriculture,* chap. 9; also, Manfred Klett, "Untersuchungen von Licht-und-Schatten-Qualitat" (Darmstadt: Biologisch-Dynamischer Land und Gartenbau II, 1973), p. 178.

Whereas silicon works with the imponderables of light and warmth, *calcium* works more with the ponderables. Contrary to silicon, it is highly bio-chemically reactive and involved in the metabolism of soil and plant. Lime furthers soil bacteria, especially nitrogen-fixing bacteria in legumes. It aids soil structure, opening up heavy, clay soils; it neutralizes excess acid, balances potassium and sodium in plant sap, thus decreasing viscosity. It also works as a mediator of cosmic forces originating in the subsolar planets. One can lime too much, driving off the nitrogen and locking up many trace minerals. For this reason, quicklime should be avoided; ground limestone and ground *dolomite* is preferred. Dolomite contains *magnesium,* which is essential in chlorophyll development and in the activation of a number of enzymes. All plants need magnesium and fruit trees, tomatoes, and vegetables growing in sandy or peaty soils need a lot. If sulphur is needed, *gypsum* (calcium sulphate) can be applied. Usually sulphur does not pose a deficiency problem; in industrial areas it is brought in by the rainfall. On the alkaline soils of the arid South, calcium is supplied by gypsum application, because it causes an acid reaction, with the sulphur turning into sulphuric acid. In the compost, gypsum favors the fungi, but decreases the cellulose-digesting bacteria.

Any substances that are needed in the garden are best worked sparingly into the compost instead of dumping them directly onto the soil. In the compost, the microorganisms can work on them and tie them into the structure of the humus molecules.

Bio-dynamic farmers and gardeners are more interested in processes and forces than in the substances themselves and have developed their herbal preparations as guidances for these processes. The yarrow preparation harmonizes the sulphur metabolism, the oak bark and chamomile preparations guide the calcium processes. (See chapter on TEAS, PREPARATIONS AND BIOTIC SUBSTANCES). These special preparations are also added to the composts.

Our attention now turns to nitrogen, phosphorus and potassium, the NPK of the commercial fertilizer formula. In the generalized plant, the phosphorus works mainly in the fruit and flower development; nitrogen works on leaf development, as seen in its effect on greens and spinach; and potassium works on the roots.

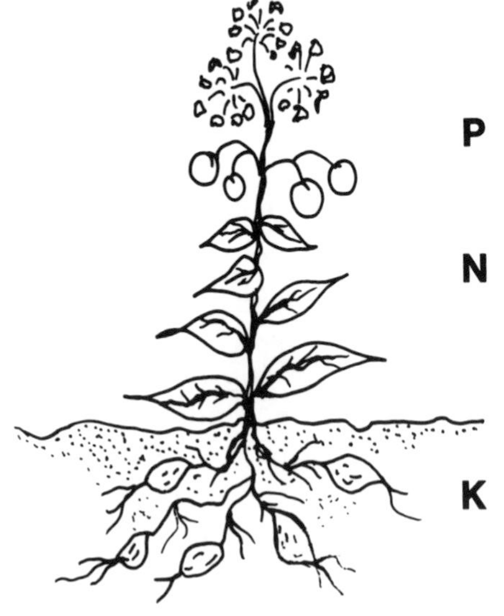

Nitrogen, as one of the major plant "foods," is always best applied in organic form from manures, composts, cover crops, and possibly feather-, horn- and hoof-meal, and fish scraps. Both liquid manure and solid manure of animals contain large amounts of nitrogen.[18] The liquid manure should be fermented in vats or storage tanks that are stirred daily to supply the liquid with oxygen and it should be treated with nettles, B-D preparations, old compost, or Pfeiffer's compost starter to stabilize it. (See COMPOSTS AND LIQUID MANURES.) Legumes, innoculated with the spores of nitrogen-fixing bacteria[19] before sowing, and grown as cover crops or fallows, increase the nitrogen supply. These nitrogen-fixing bacteria can accomplish this task at ordinary pressures and temperatures, compared to the 1,000 lb. pressure and the 6,000 calories needed per kg. of nitrogen fixed by industrial processes.[20] Sewage sludge might work as a nitrogen source on individual farmsteads or in China, but in mass consumer societies the sludge has too many toxic residues.

Nitrogen lack is indicated by plants that are tough, spindly, and from which the older leaves turn yellow and drop off. Excessive nitrogen is shown by rank, lush, green growth and too much leaf and stem growth but poor root and flower-seed formation. Aphids, insects, and fungi appear, as if wanting to soak up the excess nitrogen. Cows do not like fodder grown under these conditions.

Phosphorus, needed for good flower, seed and fruit development and sugar metabolism, is best derived from

---

[18]A horse gives 9 t manure per year; a cow, 11 t; a hog, 3 t; a sheep ½ t; 100 hens give 7 t, which equals 280 lb. N, 250 lb. P, and 140 lb. K. The NPK ratio of rabbit manure is 2.4-0.62-0.05; of chickens, 2.3-1.8-1.8; of turkeys, 1.3-0.31-0.41; cow urine, 5.-0.05-8.4, and cow solid waste, 5.-5.-1.6.

[19]Sold commercially as NITROGAN.

[20]Some people feel that legumes are hard on the soil. This is due to the fact that increased yields also lead to increased consumption of P and K, which are not supplied by the legume.

powdered rock phosphate or colloidal phosphate, both of which are added to the compost where organic acids and chelates break them down into forms usable by plants. Chicken and other bird manures are good phosphorus sources. Lupine and vetch, used as mulch or cover crop, gather P. Bone meal is a good source of P, and the bones chewed by one's dog or from the soup kettle can be burned in the fireplace, then pulverized and added to the compost. The bio-dynamic preparation 507, made from the squeezings of valerian flowers, helps soil and compost regulate the phosphorus metabolism.

Lack of phosphorus becomes evident when plants will not mature, show reddish-purple discoloration on leaf veins and stems, and the seeds are defective. In corn, or maize, this is indicated by irregular rows of kernels. In tomatoes, the underside of the leaves turns purple.

A nice little vignette of the transfer of phosphorus in nature appeared a long time ago in a Hartford newspaper:

> For the purpose of erecting a suitable monument in memory of Roger Williams, the founder of Rhode Island, his private burying ground was searched for the graves of himself and his wife. It was found that everything had passed into oblivion. The shape of the coffins could only be traced by a black line of carbonaceous matter. The rusted hinges and nails, and a round wooden knot, alone remained in one grave; while a single lock of braided hair was found in the other. Near the graves stood an apple tree. This had sent down two main roots into the very presence of the coffined dead. The larger root, pushing its way to the precise spot occupied by the skull of Roger Williams, had made a turn as if passing around it, and followed

> the direction of the backbone to the hips. Here, it divided into two branches, sending one along each leg to the heel, when both turned upward to the toes. One of these roots formed a slight crook at the knee, which made the whole bear a striking resemblance to the human form. There were the graves, but their occupants had disappeared; the bones even had vanished. There stood the thief, the guilty apple tree, caught in the very act of robbery. The spoilation was complete. The organic matter, the flesh, the bones, of Roger Williams, had passed into an apple tree. The elements had been absorbed by the roots, transmuted into woody fibre, had bloomed into fragrant blossoms; and more than that had been converted into a luscious fruit, which from year to year had been gathered and eaten. How pertinent, then, is the question, "Who ate Roger Williams?"[21]

Potash, or potassium, needed mainly for good root development, is found in greensand (glauconite), which also contains Fe, Si, Ca, P and trace minerals, in granite dust, in woodash coming from hardwoods especially, in hog manure, in seaweed, bracken fern, vetch, and alfalfa used as mulch or compost. The bio-dynamic dandelion preparation (504) helps regulate the potassium processes in compost and soil.

Lack of sufficient potash is indicated by the edges and tips of leaves looking dried and scorched and by stunted plants. Nubbin corn, fruits that are soft and ripen unevenly, carrot leaves that curl, and beet roots that taper are exam-

[21]Dorman J. Steele, *A Fourteen Weeks Course in Chemistry* (New York: A.S. Barnes & Co., 1868).

ples of potassium lack. Sufficient K is needed to ward off root-infecting organisms.

In concluding this chapter on mineral fertilizing, we can say that the main concern is to make the soil as alive as possible. It takes compost, animal manures and legume cover crops to do this. To this are added minerals with low solubility: basalt flour, greensand, dolomite, rock phosphate and other "conditioners" and natural fertilizers which can be made available by microorganisms. A careful study of one's soil and crops will indicate when, what and where these should be applied. Each farm and garden, each crop, climate and time of year has different requirements. For this reason a *soil test* from a soil test kit or the agricultural extension agent, is only an indicator. In a gram of living soil there are thousands of simultaneous chemical reactions occurring in fractions of seconds. This is enough to indicate that no fixed statements can be made. The nitrogen content is lower in the spring than in the summer, and in the morning than later in the day. The phosphorus and other elements fluctuate during the course of the year in living soils. Soil tests are more important on lifeless soils than they are on soils with good structure. Simple tests can be made by growing cress seeds *(Lepidium sativum)* in pots containing the soils and composts to be tested, and making observations on germination speed, growth pattern and general appearance of the plant on a comparative basis.

CHAPTER XII
COSMIC INFLUENCES

To assume that what comes to pass in the wide expanses that surround the earth planet has little or no effect on the life of the earth, is the legacy of the world-view that described planets solely as dead physical matter held in orbit by purely mechanical forces, and held that the stars, as infinitely distant suns, could not possibly transmit anything across the vacuum of space. This legacy is still a cornerstone in the thought of such laboratory scientists as the majority of biologists who work on the "biological clocks." They claim that these clocks only appear to be affected by cosmic rhythms, but try to show in laboratory test cases that they are endogenous, adaptive mechanisms intrinsic to the bio-chemistry of some species. The chemical base or the mechanism of the clock itself has, as yet, not been isolated. Apart from mechanical, photoenergetic influences derived from the sun and moon, our planet appears to be a hermetically-sealed space capsule run by intrinsic machinery.

In contrast, the sages of all the peasant and gardening societies have never doubted the influences of forces stemming from the cosmos, which control the seasons and influence plant, animal and man alike. These influences were not seen as mere mechanical forces, but experienced as powerful, personified beings that could be appealed to and dealt with in various ways. Calendar-makers and specialists, able to interpret seasons and celestial events, were employed by all these peoples.[1] In this way, the ecologically appropriate action could be taken when the signs were right. The Tukano of Brazil, for example, know that when the Pleiades dip below the horizon in the evening after sunset it is time to plant the crops just in time for the seasonal rains. When Sirius started to appear on the horizon just before sunrise, it was time for the fertile mid-summer flood of the Nile Valley, marking the start of ancient Egypt's agricultural year. The European peasant's rules for sowing, planting, harvesting, animal husbandry and herb gathering, going back to ancient Babylonian, Chaldean and Egyptian sources, are of the same order. Agricultural rules relating to astronomical phenomena are recorded by the Romans Plinius (23 A.D.) and Virgil (70-19 B.C.). The countless sky, moon and sun deities of tribes and nations throughout the ages, each demanding certain taboos, rituals, feasts and proscriptions are considered by current anthropologists not so much superstitions, as functional ways of adapting to specific environments.

In the West, with the change of calendar and the influence of the Enlightenment, the planetary gods were shorn of their powers and dethroned. Only the most backward peasants clung stubbornly to a tradition which degenerated into superstition and eventually lost its empirical base. What was at one time a functional belief system came in time to be relegated to the velvety parlors of "of-

---

[1]Biblical support of these beliefs is given by Genesis 1:14, "And God said: Let there be lights in the firmament of the heaven to divide the day from the night; and let them be for signs and for seasons and for days and years." Also, Eccl. 3:1-8, "To everything there is a season and a time to every purpose under the heaven. A time to be born and a time to die; a time to plant and a time to pluck up that which is planted, . . . etc."

ficial" occultists, esotericists, and astrologers. It was safely relegated to those with a leaning toward mystery and the obscure, whose nerve had failed them in the "brave new world." As the crisis of culture deepens, more people are drawn to these topics, while at the same time, there lingers in the minds of some farmers and gardeners the feeling that there must be more to the plant and animal world than is taught in the agricultural extension courses. The current situation finds a revitalized interest in the beliefs of astrology and moon-sign planting. A symptom is the recent book by Louise Riotte, *Planetary Planting.*[2] The book, which generally contains good gardening information, starts out with Chapter 1, entitled: "Why Believe?" The point that we are trying to make here is different. One need not merely believe anymore, or intuitively follow archaic tradition, because clear evidence is accumulating quickly that the earth is not a sealed mechanism running its course, but an organism that is open and responsive to the influences streaming in from the cosmos.

Basic Geocentric Astronomy

A distinction must be made at this point between *astrology* and *astronomy*. Astrology, as used by those who cast horoscopes, is a belief system that is based on the way the planetary motions and the equinox appeared about two thousand years ago. Most astrologers never look at the sky, but consult ancient charts to work their horoscopes.[3]

[2]Louise Riotte, *Planetary Planting* (New York: Simon & Schuster, 1977).

[3]Some astrologers feel that this system is justified, for at the time of the birth of Christ, the human soul had evolved out of its immediate intimate relationship with the external universe, so that the astrological data refer to the microcosmic universe with its inner constellations, not to the macrocosmic universe with its outer constellations.

Astronomy is concerned with what the sun, moon and planets are doing at this point of time in relation to the constellations of the fixed stars. Whereas academic astronomy takes a *heliocentric* perspective, taking the sun as the center of its model with the earth and planets orbiting about this glowing star, we prefer to use a *geocentric* perspective. After all, we live on the earth and not on the sun. Whereas a heliocentric conception might be easy to think, the geocentric is available to our direct experience. Likewise, the plants in our gardens experience the cosmic forces from a geocentric perspective as they stream into the atmosphere. As they spread their leaves, these light-sensitive organs do not experience the sun heliocentrically.

Geocentrically, we have our feet firmly on the ground. Our garden becomes the center of the universe. When we look up into the sky, we perceive the overawing cosmic rhythms of day and night. The sun lights up the day, rising in the east and setting in the west. In the yearly cycle the sun has a low point on the horizon, characterized by the shortest day, the winter solstice, and a high point on the horizon characterized by the longest day, the summer solstice. Between these points there are days when the day and night are of equal length, the spring and fall equinox. These four points mark the cardinal points of the year, which are celebrated by feasts and rituals in nearly all societies. The cycle of vegetation, animal migration, rutting seasons, the seasons of sprouting, growing, flowering, fruiting and dormancy are synchronized with this overall yearly cycle.

The night time sky contains the stars and planets. Following the Greek geocentric tradition, we include the sun ☉ and moon ☾ among the seven visible planets. The planets (Gr. planetes=wanderers) move pretty much along the same

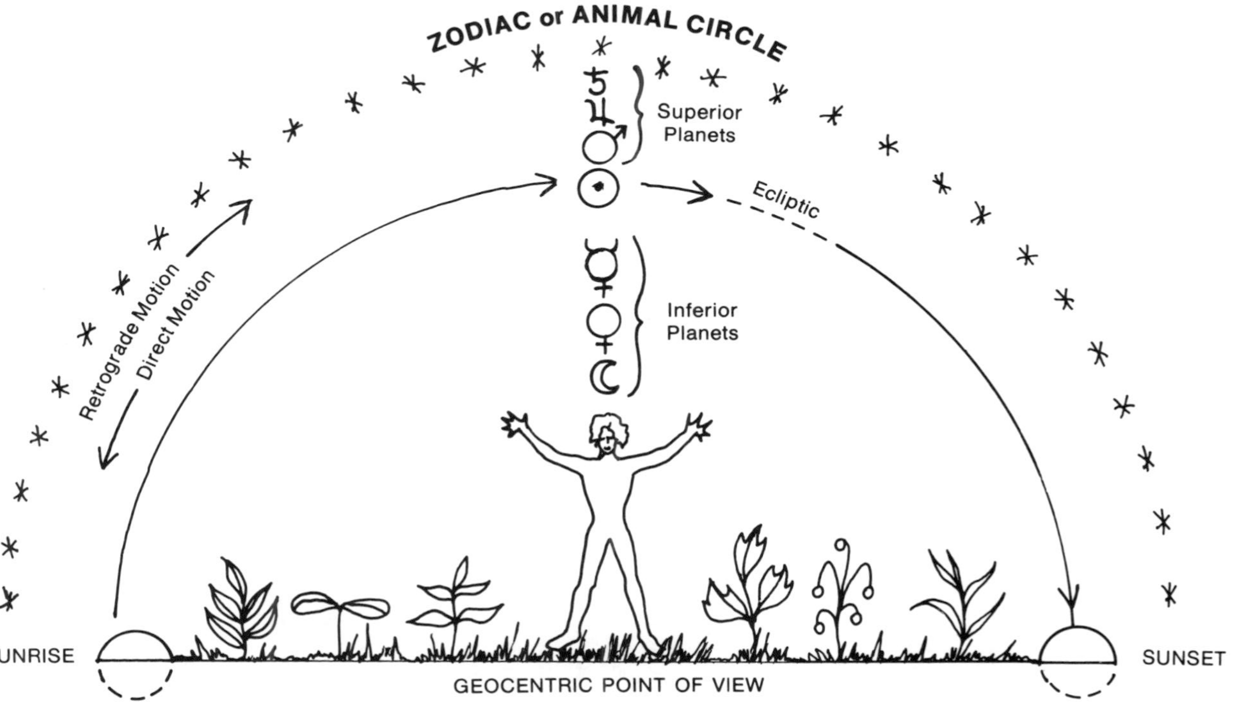
ZODIAC or ANIMAL CIRCLE
Superior Planets
Ecliptic
Inferior Planets
Retrograde Motion
Direct Motion
SUNRISE
SUNSET
GEOCENTRIC POINT OF VIEW

plane as the path of the sun, the *ecliptic*. Their movement along this plane can be clockwise (retrograde) or counterclockwise (direct). The movement occurs against a background of *fixed stars*. This ribbon of fixed stars is divided into 12 regions, each 30° wide, that make up the animal circle, or *zodiac*. The whole heavenly vault moves in clockwise motion, so that we can talk about the rising and setting of the stars as a whole.

A picture of this would be a clock and, indeed, the clock is an abstraction of the basic movements of the sun (big hand) and the moon (little hand) through twelve hours (signs of the zodiac). The great cosmic clock includes not just two hands (sun and moon), but also Mercury ☿ and Venus ♀ that are always moving near the sun and thus appear as the morning or evening stars. The clock includes the distant planets, Mars ♂, Jupiter ♃, and Saturn ♄. Each of these is moving at its own speed relative to the zodiac. Sometimes the planets Mercury, Venus, Mars, Jupiter, and Saturn reverse their movement and move backwards (in retrograde). It takes the sun a year to go through the zodiac and return to the spring point at equinox, which is in Pisces.[4] The moon is, of course, much faster and completes the journey around the zodiac in 27.32 days; Mercury swiftly runs its course in 88 days. Venus needs 225 days. Mars has a sidereal period of nearly two years, Jupiter, approx-

[4]The spring point itself is in retrograde (called the precession of the equinox), so that it is moving approximately every 2,200 years into a new zodiac sign. It is now moving from Pisces into Aquarius, which is why people are singing about the "Age of Aquarius." Jesus was born at the beginning of the age of Pisces, and before that was the age of the Ram, a time when sheep were considered to be proper sacrifices. The Platonic World Year (about 26,000 years) is the movement of the spring point through all the 12 signs.

imately 12 years[5] and the old man Saturn requires nearly 30 years to journey around the zodiac. If we imagine the clock with these seven hands, moving backward and forward against the zodiac positions, we must also imagine the clock itself revolving in a daily motion from east to west.

This by no means exhausts the movements that occur in the visible sky. The moon has other rhythms than the *sideric*

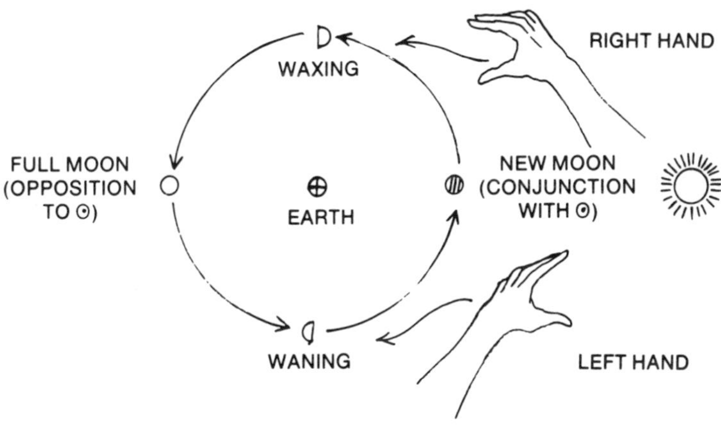

[5]The 12-year cycle of the East Asian calendar of years is based on this Jupiter period. These 12 years are known as the year of the rat, ox, tiger, rabbit, dragon, snake, horse, sheep, monkey, cock, dog and boar.

rhythm, which marks the 27.32166-day cyclical (27 days, 7 hours, 43 minutes) journey to the same place (sign) in the zodiac. Most obvious to the sky-watcher are the four *lunar phases* or *quarters* of the moon, the *synodic month,* alternating between conjunctions with the sun (new moon) and opposition to the sun (full moon). The first quarter, the new moon, or waxing crescent moon, gives way to the second quarter, or gibbous waxing moon, which is followed by the third quarter or waning gibbous moon and, finally, by the fourth quarter, or waning crescent moon. This cycle lasts about 29.531 days (29 days, 12 hours, 44 minutes). When looking at the moon, one can tell if it is waxing or waning in the following way: If the curvature looks like that of the right hand, it is a waxing moon; if it looks like the left hand, it is a waning moon.

Another lunar cycle is the *anomalistic month,* where the moon alternates between *perigee,* closest to the earth, and *apogee,* farthest from the earth. This cycle of 27.555 days is caused by the elliptical orbit around the earth, involving a distance variation of 40,000 km or 16,000 miles.

The *draconitic month,* or lunar nodes, caused by the moon's wobbling about 5° above and below the sun's path (ecliptic), is a cycle of 27.212 days. When the moon dips below the ecliptic, one speaks of the moon's *descending node* or dragon's tail ☋. When the moon rises above the sun's path, one has the ascending node or dragon's head ☊. It is at these nodes that a sun or a moon eclipse is possible.

A fifth lunar rhythm is the *tropical month,* lasting about 27.32158 days. Just as the sun in its yearly cycle has a northern and a southern tropic, its lowest and its highest point on the horizon, so, also, does the moon, except that it does not take a year but only 27 days. In almanacs this is referred to as the moon's *descension* ☊ and *ascension* ☋. These points usually occur in the sign of Scorpio-Saggitarius and Taurus-Gemini.

As one can see, these varying lunar periodicities make for a complicated astronomy. The rhythms are close, but not synchronized. Just for two rhythms to get back in step, the synodic and the siderial moon for example, takes 18 years 7½ months. The rhythms that we reckoned for the moon can be described for the other planets also. For example, the Mayan calendar was based on the phases of Venus.

The complexity of these rhythms *in toto* has the result that the conditions of the heavens are never exactly the same. They are always somewhat different, although their orbits and cycles are orderly. We see then, that the analogy of a clock is not quite justified, for in the clock we have a finite system, where events are repeatable, whereas in cosmic conditions we have an infinite system. The heavens never go back to an exact original starting point, a fact which makes a perfectly accurate calendar impossible. This makes the analogy of an organism, with its rhythmic life, much more appropriate.

For scientists, research on lunar and planetary effects becomes a hot iron, since the factors are innumerable and no experiment is exactly repeatable. One cannot say to the moon: "Wait a minute, could you repeat this?" or say to the planets: "You are insignificant variables; we will not consider you in this experiment." It is safer for such a scientist to infer an endogenous system of biological clocks and intrinsic mechanisms to explain plant and animal life, while considering the whole cosmos an "irrelevant variable"! However, evidence points in other directions — to those that indicate cosmic influences. The farmer and gardener can be assured when he plants his crops in the right seasons and in the right signs and phases, that there is something to it.

Dimensions of Time and Space

All of life is rhythm and pulse. Death is the cessation of rhythm. The rhythms of living plant and animal organisms are in synchronicity with, or permutations of, cosmic rhythms. These living pulsations, be they circadian, monthly, annual, 4-year, 8-year, 9-year, or other cycles, all have some cosmic counterpart. In plants and in lower animals these rhythms are in direct phase with the cosmic phenomena, whereas in the higher animals these rhythms are obscured by the fact that internalized rhythms and impulses are provided by the inner cosmos of the inner organs and endocrine system.

The rhythms of life (growth, petal movement, assimilation, etc.) are expressed as manifestations and demanifestations in material space. Organic forms, but also some inorganic forms such as crystals, are images of cosmic forms and forces sculpted into matter. Flowers and leaf nodes show spiral relations that are mathematically equivalent to the ratios of the movement of planets as seen from a geocentric point of view. Organic forms, such as spirals, vortices, radial symmetry, bilateral symmetry, and the combinations and allometric permutations thereof, are archetypal, hinting at sympathy with planetary orbits, galactic whorls, lunar phases and other cosmic occurrences.

Given these analogies of rhythm (time) and form (space configurations), one can postulate a connection of some sort between organic life and cosmic influences. The connection could be one of causality, in which the cosmic force causes the organism's response. It is easy to imagine how organisms, in their life functions, can vibrate with the wide range of electromagnetic energy that constantly bombards this planet from outer space. Such energy reaches from the extremely short gamma- and x-rays, through the ultraviolet, the visible spectrum, the infrared to the long radio waves. We see the effect of lunar gravity on water, causing the tidal behavior of seashore fauna; and the plants with their green tissue are photo-receptive like our retinas, monitoring the instreaming visible light from the cosmos.

On the other hand, the relation between the cosmic phenomena and the terrestrial counterpart might not be one of causality, but might be one of synchronicity, both of them the expression of a deeper-lying archetypal factor.[6] Time and space have been separated analytically in western thought. Primitive thought, such as found among the Hopi Indians,[7] makes no such distinctions. For them, every time has its space and every space has its time. Though time and space are principally connected manifestations, we will treat them separately in our discussion of cosmic influences.

Time and Cosmic Rhythms

The most common and simplest rhythm is the daily (circadian, after F. Halberg, 1960) movement of the sun (solar

---

[6]The lunar nodes at which eclipses occur are regarded by peasants as unfavorable and only the most important work is done at this time. The author's experience concerns a lunar eclipse in Scorpio, May 28, 1975. While watching the spectacle, the temperature dropped so that the beans and tomato plants froze. The temperature drop was not necessarily causally related to the reddening, darkening moon in Scorpio, but it did occur synchronically.

[7]Benjamin Lee Whorf, *Language, Thought, Reality* (1956).

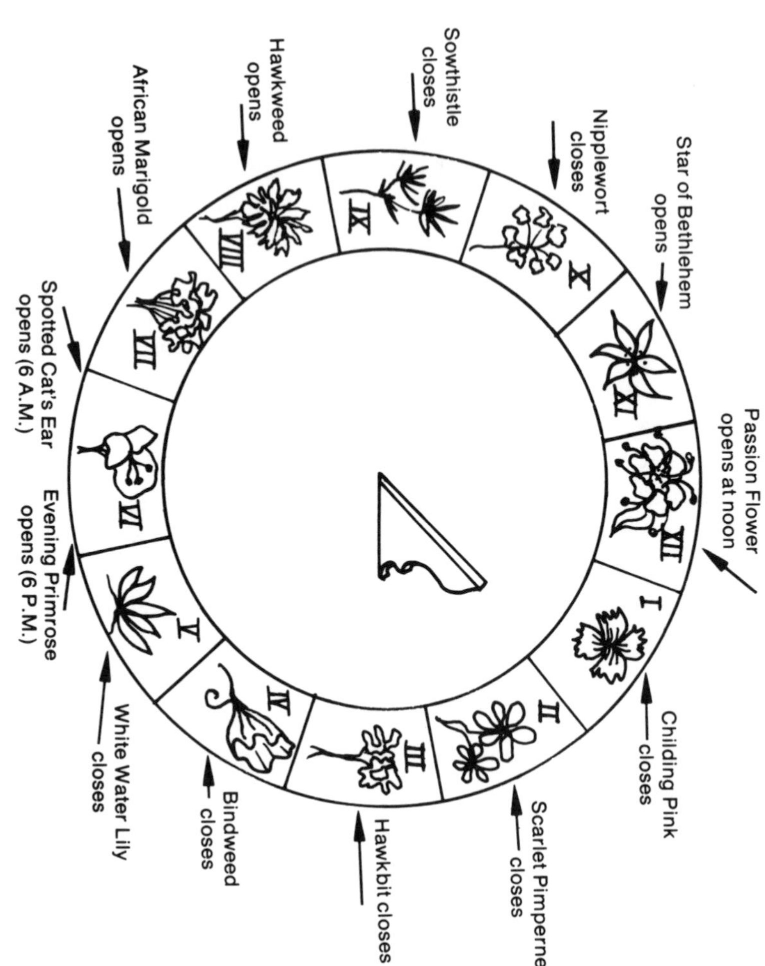

Passion Flower opens at noon
Star of Bethlehem opens
Nipplewort closes
Sowthistle closes
Hawkweed opens
African Marigold opens
Spotted Cat's Ear opens (6 A.M.)
Evening Primrose opens (6 P.M.)
White Water Lily closes
Bindweed closes
Hawkbit closes
Scarlet Pimpernel closes
Childing Pink closes
XII
I
II
III
IV
V
VI
VII
VIII
IX
X
XI

day) or the revolution of the heavenly vault (sidereal day). This rhythm profoundly affects all life, including one-celled organisms. It includes the daily opening and closing of flower petals, and the movement of leaves in some plants, such as the bean, into nightly vertical sleep positions and horizontal day positions. These daily rhythms are so accurate that, in the 18th and 19th centuries, flower clocks were planted in gardens where it became possible to tell time by the opening and closing of the petals.[8]

Wachsmuth describes the daily bipolar rhythm in plants. A period of concentration around 3:00 AM, characterized by maximum cell division, auxin production, starch accumulation in the lower plant parts and a minimum of sap excretion, gives way in the morning to the opening of leaves into the daytime position with increases in assimilation, respiration and secretion. In the afternoon at 3:00 PM, there is maximum glucose production and cell enlongation, which gives way in the evening to starch accumulation in the lower portion of the plants after they assume sleeping positions.[9]

A ten-year study by Frank A. Brown, Jr., of Northwestern University, shows a daily metabolic cycle in potatoes.[10] Brown shows that there is a peak metabolic activity in potatoes at sunrise, at noon and in the evening. This cycle follows yearly fluctuations; while in January the noon peak is the greatest, in mid-year it is less significant, and in the

---

[8]Ritchie R. Ward, *The Living Clocks* (New York: Alfred A. Knopf, Inc., 1971), p. 48.

[9]Gunther Wachsmuth, *Erde und Mensch* (Dornach, Switzerland: Philosophisch-Anthroposophischer Verl., 1945), chap. VI.

[10]F.A. Brown, "Hypothesis of Environmental Timing of the Clock," in *The Biological Clock* (New York: Academic Press, 1970).

fall, the morning peak is the greatest. "The metabolic pattern varies systematically with the celestial longitude of the earth as it makes its annual journey around the sun."[11] He concludes that geomagnetic and electromagnetic forces seem to be at work, which are, of course, affected by the planets. Other studies show a time awareness in cockroaches which scavenge at night, and in fruit flies which hatch only in the early morning hours when moisture (dew) exists. Even human beings show circadian rhythms, which are upset when a jet trip crosses time zones.[12]

Lunar rhythms, which work mainly through water, are effective in all organisms.[13] Most organisms are composed mainly of water, and all organisms go through an amorphous zygote stage, in which these forces can be especially influential. Instruments have been developed that are so sensitive that they can measure lunar tides in a tea cup. Researchers find that it is harder to sterilize water during the full moon. Plinius writes in his Natural History that it is best to sell fruits picked before the full moon because they will be plumb full of water, but for one's own use, it is wise to pick fruit around the new moon period for they will keep

---

[11]*Ibid.*, p. 32.

[12]The entomologist and electronics specialist Philip Callahan, in *Insects and How They Function* (New York: Holiday House, 1971), chap. 10, distinguishes chemo-receptors for olfaction, located mainly in the mouth parts and legs of insects, from the sensilla of the antennae which function like dielectric antennae that are receptive to electromagnetic wavelengths, ranging from radiowaves, through infrared, visible, ultraviolet, past X-rays, to the high energy gamma-rays. The dielectric antennae of insects are perfectly constructed to receive and amplify such short wave radiation as light, infrared, and short-millimeter radiation bands. There is no reason to assume that they are not affected by cosmic influences.

[13]Agnes Fyfe, *The Signature of the Moon in Plants (Die Signatur des Mondes im Pflanzenreich,* Stuttgart: Verl. Freies Geistesleben, 1967).

better. He states that it is best to castrate animals or prune trees during the new moon to avoid excessive bleeding. Modern scientists find this to be true also.

Frank Brown, in a study of fiddler crabs, finds, besides the diurnal cycle of color change, a lunar rhythm of 12.4 hours, timed exactly to the lunar tides. Oysters, which open their shells at high tide and close them at low tide, when transported from the East Coast to Evanston, Illinois, changed their rhythms to what the tides would be there, if the seashore were in Illinois.

Lunar rhythms are especially evident in the lower animals, particularly in the reproductive cycle. The timing by these animals is sometimes awesome. The grunion, or smelt, of California, ride the last flood tide wave onto shore to deposit eggs and sperm in the sand and ride the first ebb tide wave back out into the sea. Two weeks later, the next tide that is equally high, is the exact moment when, at the crest of the tide, the larvae hatch to be swept out into the sea. Similarly dramatic, the female paloloworms of the South Pacific rise to the ocean surface at an exact time at dawn when the moon reaches its last quarter in November, where their egg-laden tails break off and float. Immediately all the males rise to the surface where their sperm-containing hind quarters also break off.

In relation to fertility, Eugen Jonas of Czechoslovakia found that in the human female the ability to conceive coincides with the lunar phase when she was born. From this insight, a nonchemical birth control method was developed which is claimed to be 98% effective.[14] Weather, rainfall cycles, barometric pressure, changes in the magnetic field and

[14]Schroeder and Ostrander, *Psychic Discoveries Behind the Iron Curtain*, chap. 26.

other phenomena have been correlated with the moon. Police officials, bartenders, and caretakers of mental patients also tell of the effects of the moon on the human psyche.

Planets are the source of powerful radio waves, and each planet leaves in its wake a tail of electromagnetic disturbances. We can easily assume that the planets, other than the moon and sun, have an effect on the earth. One such effect is the 11-year sunspot cycle found by Sir J. Herschel. Sunspots occur when planets are in conjunction or opposition to the sun; that is, when they form one gravitational arc that has an uneven pull on the corona of the sun. The effects include icebergs off of Iceland, good vintage years for Bordeaux, drought patterns in India, the shift of flowering dates of some plants, earthquakes and others. There are 35-year and 85-year rhythms superimposed on this 11-year cycle.[15] An 8-year precipitation cycle has been related to Venus. George Unger, in his laboratory at Dornach, Switzerland (1971), using the drop-method investigation of fluids developed to indicate water quality, shows the effects of the constellations on water. Measured quantities of fluids to be tested are dropped into glycerine, creating characteristic drop patterns. The glycerine is so sensitive that the characteristic drop patterns are disturbed slightly when conjunctions and oppositions occur.[16]

An interesting observation was made by Joachim Schulz in investigations of beech nut harvests. Beech trees bear

---

[15]Ellsworth Huntington, *Mainsprings of Civilization*, "Cycles, Rhythms, and Periodicities" (New York: Mentor Books, 1962), Chap. 24, p. 459.

[16]The impressionability of water to cosmic influences has also been shown by the research of T. Schwenk, *Sensitive Chaos* (1976).

heavily about every six to eight years, according to records kept since 1799. The irregular quantity of the harvests is not dependent only on the climate and weather, since the whole species in various locations bears well during good years despite climate variations. This seemed to be random behavior. In the years 1948 to 1951, Schulz was able to correlate the harvest patterns with Jupiter, Mars and Saturn positions in various constellations. On this basis he set up probable harvest predictions to the year 1985. G. Wolber and S. Vetter reinvestigated this in 1971 and found the predictions verified.[17] Other investigations on planetary influences by L. and E. Kolisko show that the crystallization of certain salts in the laboratory are affected by the positions of the planets.[18]

Corresponding to the sidereal rhythms of the plants are the growth rhythms of the plant families. The rapidly-growing herbaceous annuals are linked with the fast-moving subsolar, or nearer, planets. This places most

SIDERIAL CYCLE	28d	88d	225d	I yr.	2 yrs.	12 yrs.	30 yrs
PLANET	☾	☿	♀	☉	♂	♃	♄
	(monocots)		(dicots)				
PLANTS		ANNUALS		BIENNIALS		PERENNIALS	

[17]G. Wolber and S. Vetter, "Samenjahre der Rotbuche und Planetenstellung im Tierkreis" (Dornach, Switzerland: *Sternkalender* 73-74, 1972).

[18]Kolisko, *Landwirtschaft der Zukunft* (1939), p. 72.

monocots under the influence of the moon and Mercury, and the dicot herbs with Venus and the sun. Biennials and shrubs are related to the two-year rhythm of Mars, perennial herbs and hardwoods to the 12-year cycle of Jupiter, and most of the conifers to the long-enduring cycle of Saturn.[19]

The preceding might seem to be somewhat simplistic, analogical thinking; but, in keeping with the goetheanistic approach, we will make note of the analogies of simultaneously appearing phenomena before jumping to conclusions. Here we are perhaps not dealing with the law of causality, but with the law of synchronicity. In the next section on plant forms, other factors will become evident which show that the correlations indicated are perhaps not quite as arbitrary as they at first appear. We are only touching on the subject of rhythms and their correlation with cosmic phenomena here. There are undoubtedly other rhythms, ranging from cycles of glaciation (250,000 years) to very short-term rhythms occurring within organs or cells which can be correlated in frequency curves with various short wave patterns derived from the cosmos.

It is the studying and understanding of such rhythms in their relation to the etheric formative forces that underlies the rhythmic preparation of homeopathic medicines, and of the stirring of liquid manures and bio-dynamic preparations.

Forms and Shapes

All life is rhythm (energy) and matter is temporarily frozen energy. The archetypal patterns of organisms in-

[19]Ernst Michael Kranich, *Die Formensprache der Pflanze* (Stuttgart: Verl. Freies Geistesleben, 1976), p. 168.

dicate rhythmic movements that have temporarily taken on physical form and substance. Formative forces are indicated by crystal formations in frost flowers, snow flakes, tension lines in cooling liquids, hexagonal honeycombs, and others which Steiner indicated as vector lines originating in the region of the earth-distant planets. Hard as it may be to prove by conventional means, it is certainly a probability that can be visualized by means of projective geometry.[20] These hard-lined forces, originating in outer space and working through the earth into crystal formation, are akin to the "earth" etheric forces. The formative forces of "water" and "air" express themselves in flow patterns, spirals and vortices. They are seen in whirling galaxies, cloud formations as photographed from space satellites, wind and ocean currents, whirlpools, the shells of snails, the hair whorl on the back of the head (cowlick), the calyx of flowers such as the morning glory, the spiral placement of leaf and bud around the stem, seed placement as in sunflowers, all the way to the double-helix spiral of the minute DNA molecule.

Water and air etheric forces reveal themselves in concentric rings found from the rings of Saturn, to tree rings, to water disturbed by a thrown pebble, and equally archetypal

[20]Organic forms can be explained not only from inner concentric forces, but also, by outer tangential forces. Just as a sphere can be explained in geometry as the end points of all radii, it can equally well be seen as having been molded plastically from without by all the possible tangent planes. These tangent planes that fill the universe invisibly can be labeled "etheric, or counter space." In a similar fashion, the sun, which is usually seen as a radiating center, can be seen in its opposite as a suction force, as the center of a vortex around which the planets rotate. Mathematics in this direction have been done by L. Locher-Ernst, *Projective Geometrie* (1940); George Adams, *The Plant Between the Sun and Earth* (Stourbridge: 1952); and Olive Whicher, *Projective Geometry* (London: Rudolf Steiner Press, 1961).

are reflections and bi-polarities found in higher organisms and in magnetic fields. Another form of primal energy is seen in such raying, outpouring energy as that of the raying sun, the primitive radiolaria and other planktons, the radial symmetry of horsetails and other primitive plants. Such archetypal forms and patterns are found in the whole range of nature, from the telescopic to the microscopic universes.[21]

Leaf arrangements (phyllotaxy) occur in opposites (one-half around the stem to the next leaf), in thirds (one third around the stem to the next leaf), or in spirals of 2/5, as in blackberries where one has to go twice around the stem to arrive at the fifth leaf which is directly above the original one. Others have the ratio of 3/8, 5/13, 8/21, 13/34 and so on.

Similarly, the flower petal arrangement and seed placement patterns of such plants as the composites reveal spirals that intersect clockwise and counter-clockwise, according to the above-mentioned ratios. These ratios are not random, but form a mathematical progression that was discovered by the Renaissance mathematician Leonardo da

[21]See also Nathan Cabot Hale, *Abstraction in Art and Nature* (New York: Watson-Guptill Publications, 1972).

Pisa, also known as Fibonacci, after whom this Fibonacci sequence is named.[22] A further point of interest is that the ratio between any two numbers in the series (after the third) approaches that of the Golden Ratio, or Golden Section (1:618).[23]

The existence of the Fibonacci sequence in the arrangement of leaf and flower spirals indicates well enough how "God ever geometrizes" (Plato), but the astronomer Joachim Schulz has pointed out that this sequence is also found in the movement patterns of the visible planets as perceived geocentrically.[24]

The force of the sun pulls the vegetation upward (heliotropism), giving it the vertical tendency. Just as the planets move in and out of conjunction with the sun and cross the ecliptic above and below, so do the buds, leaves and flowers move about the vertical stem of the plant, mirroring the mathematical relationships that hold sway in planetary movement. Schulz tries to show how the opposition and two-fold symmetry in plants relates to the moon, which alternates from full moon to new moon. The path of Mercury reveals three loops (retrogressions) and six yearly

---

[22]The Fibonacci sequence is also found in the logarithmic spirals of the chambered nautilus, the curvature of mountain sheep horns, elephant tusks, winter rosettes of plants and other organic phenomena.

[23]The Golden Ratio, a key to the universe since Pythagoras, is found in the intervals of music (monochord), mollusk shells, the genealogy of drone bees, as well as in works of art such as the proportions of the sculptures of Phidias, the ratios of the pyramid of Cheops, and others. Gustav Fechner found this ratio in windows, architecture, books, crosses, playing cards and other objects that are intuitively held to be well-balanced and harmonious.

[24]Joachim Schulz, "Blattstellungen im Pflanzenreich als Ausdruck kosmischer Gesetzmassigkeiten," *Lebendige Erde* (Darmstadt: 1973), Bd. II, p. 267.

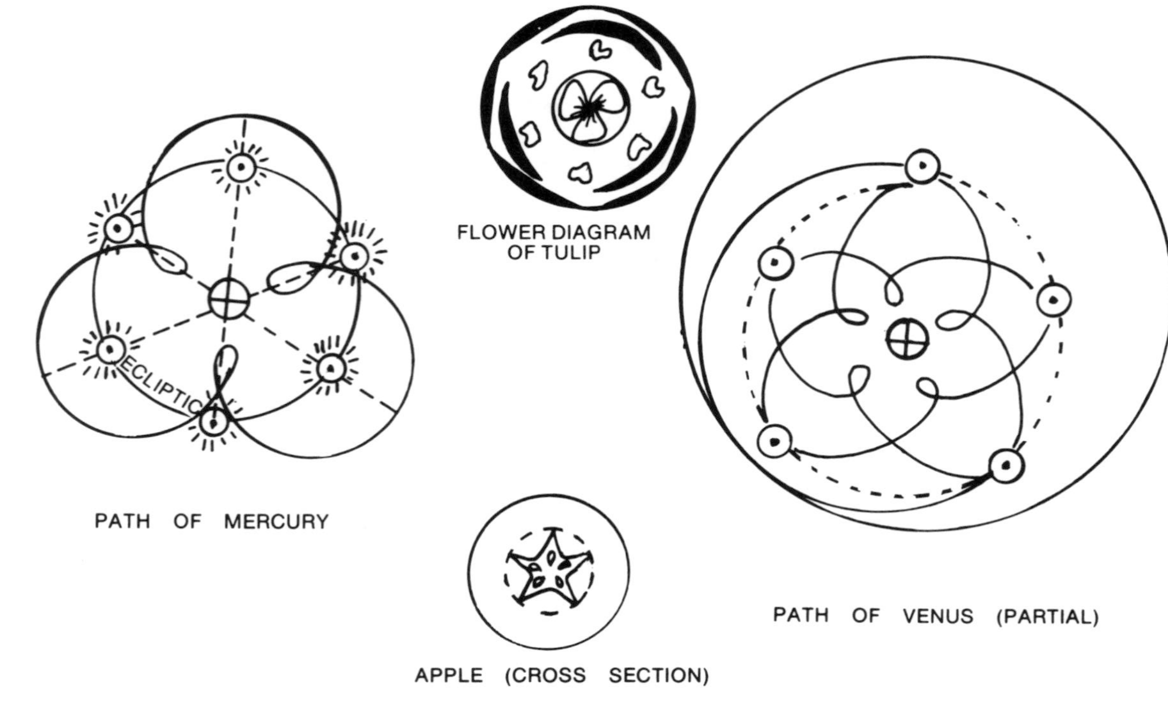
ECLIPTIC
PATH OF MERCURY
FLOWER DIAGRAM
OF TULIP
APPLE (CROSS SECTION)
PATH OF VENUS (PARTIAL)

conjunctions with the sun, three above and three below the ecliptic. Moon and Mercury symmetries are found permeating the world of the monocots, the lilies and grasses.

Venus forms five loops (retrogressions) below the ecliptic in eight years, dividing its path into five parts; much like the bud and leaf placement of the five-sided blackberry stem, going around twice to get to the same place, creating the next ratio of the Fibonacci series, 2:5. A picture of the geocentric perspective of Venus' path looks like the core of an apple and characterizes the geometry of such plants as the *Rosaceae*. The spiral configuration of Mars approaches a 3:8 ratio, as found in the leaf placement of the *Cruciferae*. Most dicots prefer either the Venus ratio of 2:5 or the Mars ratio of 3:8 for their leaf or flower placement. The Jupiter ratio of 5:13 is found in many composites and in the figworts *(Scrophulariaceae)*. The Saturn ratio of 13:34 is approached by some conifers and can be counted in the placement of scales in the pine cones (e.g. *Pinus pumilion* and *P. montana*). The even higher ratios in the sequence are extremely rare, found only in fossil plants, or in primitive plants such as mosses and club mosses. For the higher planets, the ratios only approximate those of the plant geometry because these patterns are never closed patterns, but show slight progressions *(Spirodistichia)*.

A methodologically more sophisticated work, building upon Schulz, is the book by E.M. Kranich,[25] who analyzes a number of plants in morphological detail and relates their growth processes to similar structural relationships found

---

[25]Ernst Michael Kranich, *Die Formensprache der Pflanze* (Stuttgart: Verl. Freies Geistesleben, 1976).

among the planets. He relates the rooting process to the moon and the vertical growth to the sun. The leaves and flower petals, as they diverge from the vertical stem tendency, are an image of the movement of Mercury and Venus bilaterally to the sun, as experienced from a geocentric position. Anther and pollen formation relate to Mars, fruit formation to Jupiter, and seed formation to Saturn.[26] He details the studies with careful botanical obser-

---

[26]These observations also coincide with older color schemes which attribute the colors of the rainbow to the superior planets. The colors range from the red of Mars, through the yellow of Jupiter, to the blue of Saturn. Green, the color of the vegetative plant, is the color of Venus in connection with the sun. Mercury is said not to have a color as such, but consists of a sheen. The moon is identified with the subterranean color of silver, and the sun with gold, both beyond the range of the rainbow.

vations and flower diagrams.

It is not possible to go further into correlations between morphology, phyllotaxy, and geometry of plants and the geometric movements of planets within the limits of this exposition. These studies do establish the possibility of connections and partially vindicate some of the older planetary designations of plants, such as those of Culpeper.

All plant species, from primitive radially-symmetric mushrooms to complex fruit trees, have characteristic patterns. A whole gestalt dominates each species, giving it its overall characteristic form. When, for example, leader branches are removed on trees, another branch takes over to keep the characteristic gestalt. Scientists have succeeded in culturing the entire plant out of one cell, regardless of whether that cell has been taken from the root or from the leaves. This indicates that there is a "blueprint." It is hypothesized that this blueprint is found in the cell as the DNA code of the chromosomes. We advance the contention that the DNA provides the physical substrata upon which the formative forces, deriving from etheric space, from the periphery of the earth, can find expression; or as Poppelbaum expresses it:

> The "blueprint" of an organism does not result from the chemistry of the various components of protein, etc.; it images an extra-spatial order that gives form and position to the organs and also determines the earthly-cosmic layout of the organism as a whole. The enzymes, hormones, etc. that move about in the organisms are not shaping causes; rather, they are mere indicators of the relationships in the form-field at a particular spot. The total structure of the living being

> proceeds from the superspatial form that is developed in etheric space.[27]

Loss of the geometry-creating, rhythmic impulses of the formative forces leads to death. Interference with the flow of these forces produces a loss in geometry, or harmony, as in the so-called callus growths, plant tumors, and destruction by means of insects and disease.

George Adams, in an exposition of projective geometry, *Physical and Etheric Spaces,* talks about manifold streams and influences flowing together from the cosmos. "At the place where they interpenetrate, there arises by their interplay (it is a *qualitative* interplay, but its effect is at the same time spatial) the etheric organ as a whole. These currents from the universe are the cosmic parts, the etheric member of the organ. The organ as a whole is therefore

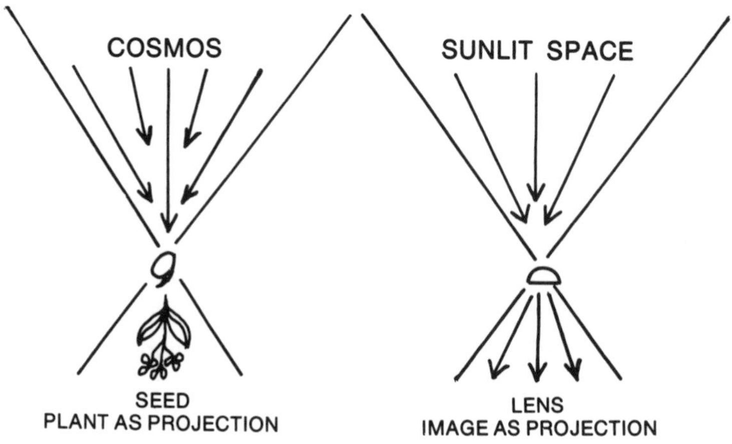

[27]Hermann Poppelbaum, *New Light on Heredity and Evolution* (Spring Valley, New York: St. George Publ., 1977), p. 15.

smaller than its parts. This is an absolutely real process, perceptible to supersensible consciousness . . ."[28] We can clarify this by looking at a seed. The forces working on the seed from the cosmic periphery are as much a part of the plant as the visible members of the plant. In its manifestation within space and time, the plant is diminutive, whereas etherically the plant is greatly, though not visibly, expanded.

The illustration suggests that the plant is a projection of cosmic forces focused by the seed point, in analogy to the sunlit space that is focused by the lens of the eye to provide a retinal image as a projection. Steiner, and later Grohmann, conceive of plants as the eyes of the earth organism, open in the summer and shut in the winter.[29]

Practical Application

Having attempted to establish the possibility of cosmic influences upon plant life, it now becomes a question of practical concern about how to use these forces. If they are always present, how can one do anything about them? The gardener can amplify or tone down these forces in his work. He can create "relationships and disrelationships of plants as they are governed by the Revolutionibus of the whole ordinance of the government of the sun with the primum mobile, the secundus mobilus, the stars that we can see and the ethereal world that we cannot see."[30] How can this be done? It is done primarily by sowing one's seeds, working

---

[28]George Adams, *Physical and Etheric Spaces* (London: Rudolf Steiner Press, 1965), p. 23.

[29]Grohmann, *Die Pflanze als Lichtsinnesorgan der Erde* (1962).

[30]Alan Chadwick, Bio-dynamic conference in Los Angeles, 1974 (recorded by Steve Dinkowitz).

the soil, and planting the seedlings at the right times. We do this automatically with the solar cycle, which is the most obvious. The lunar cycles are less obvious, but just as important.

In order to plant by cosmic rhythms correctly, one must learn to identify the astral phenomena, such as the sign in which the sun, moon and the other planets are found, the phases of the moon, the conjunctions and oppositions. A good astronomical calendar that indicates all the necessary data *correctly* and a good book on the constellations, or a movable star chart will be of help in learning. Secondly, it is important to keep note of the sun's position, the sign, phase, node, ascension and descension, and the apogee and perigee of the moon in one's garden diary day by day. In this way, a good scientific record can be kept indicating correlations over a number of years between nature phenomena (the appearance of certain bugs, the first and last frost dates, rain periods, etc.) and celestial phenomena. In the same entry, the garden work that is done each particular day should be noted. Such a record, if kept up diligently over a few decades, will be a valuable aid in understanding a number of cycles and patterns that have bearing on the farm and garden.

The solar cycle: Most of us have an idea when to plant in the spring and to harvest in the fall, although the author had students from California who wanted to plant watermelon and other warm weather crops in November. One has to plant early enough in order to get a crop. Cold weather plants can be planted before the *frost-free date,* whereas warm-weather loving plants must be planted after the frost-free date. (See chapter on the GARDEN CALENDAR.) For biennial plants, which include many of our vegetables, such as beets, cabbages, kales, brussel sprouts, carrots, celery, etc., during the first year the vegetative growth takes place, and a cold period *(vernalization,* T.D. Lysenko) must be passed through for the plant to bloom and make seed the following year. This is important for gardeners who want to make their own seed.

Photoperiodism (Garnerr, Allard), or the ability of plants to perceive and respond to differences in the length of day and night, is related to solar cycles. *Long-day plants,* such as most garden plants (beets, lettuce, poppy, carrots, radishes, spinach, and others) flower when the days get longer and start to exceed 12 hours. These are plants that flower into the summer. This explains why radish and spinach go to seed in the summer. *Short-day plants,* originating mostly in the more southernly latitudes, need shorter days for flowering and will start to flower in late summer and fall as the sun's arc narrows; they include tobacco, corn, hemp and cosmos. *Day-neutral plants,* such as shepherds purse, chickweed, tomato and sunflower, do not have any special preferences.

Lunar cycles: Lunar cycles are very handy in our attempt to create "relationships and disrelationships" with the Revolutionibus. The moon works through the water. Since most organisms consist mainly of water, it is little wonder that there is a noticeable effect. The most important lunar rhythm to work with is that of the moon phases (synodic moon). Anyone who has sprouted alfalfa seeds for salad, or closely watched the garden by comparing a new moon to a full moon, notices accelerated growth during the full-moon period, especially if it has rained. It is best to sow or plant in the second quarter, or a few days before the full moon. Root crops can be planted in the third quarter. The fourth quarter is a rest period in the cycle during which weeding and pruning can be done. The first quarter is characterized by slow but steady growth.

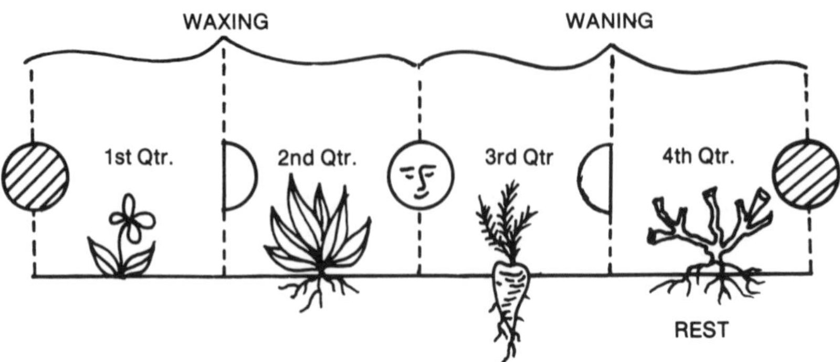

Fifteen years of experiments with wheat, barley, and oats were carried out by L. Kolisko.[31] A large number of seeds were sown during different lunar phases with other variables, such as soil-type, water, and fertilizer, held constant. Exact measurements carried out on weight, length of roots, leaves, and internodes produced curves that showed maximum growth always occurring in the waxing 2nd quarter moon. Another series of tests showed that sprouting is best 2 days before the full moon. Comparisons made between plants (carrots, tomatoes, peas) planted 2 days before the full moon, with controls planted 2 days before the new moon, showed that full moon sowings had significantly larger harvests and grew better than the controls. Plants sown in the advantageous phase surpassed those plants sown in the new moon, even when the latter

[31]Kolisko, *Agriculture of Tomorrow*.

were put into the ground 2 weeks earlier. Vegetables sown around the full moon were juicier, whereas those sown at the new moon periods were found to be drier and "woodier." Some plants are exceptions to the rule; potatoes and legumes can be planted during the new moon phase.

The lunar phases are not the only consideration for planting by the moon. The zodiac sign in which the moon finds itself (the sidereal moon) is also important. Older, now decadent, traditions give each sign of the zodiac a specific value regarding barrenness, fertility, moisture or dryness, and masculine or feminine traits.[32]

Maria Thun, continuing investigations carried out in Europe by F. Rulni and H. Schmidt on the effects of phases, nodes, and eclipses, found that differences occurred in test plots of radishes despite the weather, crop rotation, fertilizer, seed, lunar phases and planetary conjunctions.[33] Taking a hint from G. Wachsmuth about the formative forces and their relation to the zodiac, Maria Thun set out to sow equal amounts of radish seed daily into little ex-

---

[32]Traditional correspondences are as follows:
Aries (Ram), the head, is barren, dry, fiery and masculine.
Taurus (Bull), the neck, is fertile, moist, earthy and feminine.
Gemini (Twins), the arms, is barren, dry, airy, and masculine.
Cancer (Crab), the breast, is fruitful, moist, watery, and feminine.
Leo (Lion), the heart and back, is barren, dry, fiery and masculine.
Virgo (Virgin), the bowels, is barren, moist, earthy and feminine.
Libra (Scales), the hips, is semi-fruitful, moist, airy and masculine.
Scorpio (Scorpion), the loins, is fruitful, moist, watery, and feminine.
Saggitarius (Archer), the thighs, is barren, dry, fiery, and masculine.
Capricorn (Goat), the knees, is semi-fertile, moist, earthy and feminine.
Aquarius (Water Carrier), the calves, is barren, dry, airy, and masculine.
Pisces (Fish), the feet, is fruitful, moist, watery, and feminine.

[33]Maria Thun, "Komische Wirkungen im Boden und Pflanze im siderischen Mondrythmus" (Dornach, Switzerland: *Sternenkalender,* 1974).

—*Work on the Land and the Constellations* (Peredur, G.B.: Lanthorn Press, 1977).

perimental plots, while noting the sign in which the moon was to be found. After about four years, the typology became clear. Radishes sown in the "earth" signs showed good root development, those sown in the "water" signs showed abundant leaf development, those sown in "air" and "fire" signs tended to bolt and seed well. The typologies were amplified by always sowing earth sign radishes from seeds obtained from earth sign radishes, and taking seeds from water sign radishes to sow on water sign days, etc. Even the working on the beds and harvesting was done on the respective sign days. Other experiments with potatoes, cereals, and fodders were carried out along with the radish experiments for nearly three decades. Professor von Boguslawski, of the University of Giessen, Germany, investigated the claims of Maria Thun and found them scientifically sound, sending U. Abele to do a Ph.D. dissertation on the subject. As a result of this research some of the older rules are vindicated. Thun also found that the typology is clearer on organically fertilized soil.

One aids root crops when they are sown in Taurus, Virgo and Capricorn; flowers are best planted in the air signs of Gemini, Libra, and Aquarius; leaf crops are aided by the water signs of Pisces, Scorpio, and Cancer; and fruits do best in the fire signs of Aries, Saggitarius, and Leo.

As to the tropical month, whether the moon is in a high sign (Taurus) or a low sign (Scorpio), tradition has it that there is an increase in vitality when the moon is in ascension, which is good for grafting because the juices flow better in stem and leaves. When the moon is in descension, it is good for the roots, for transplanting and hedge trimming, at least the Swiss peasants swear by this.

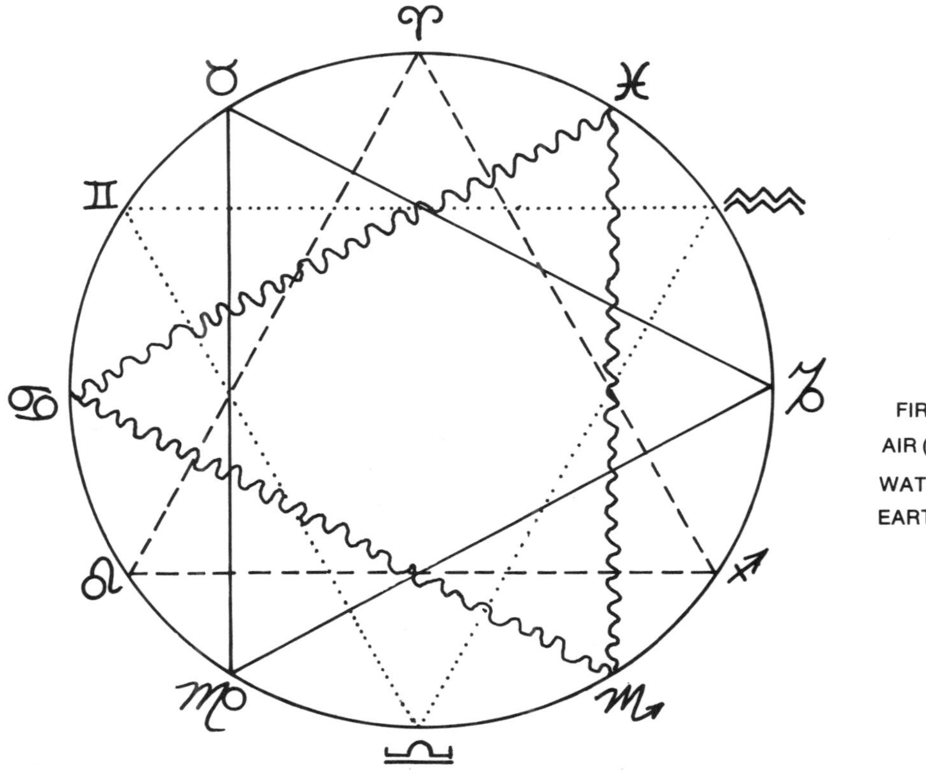
FIRE (FRUIT)
AIR (FLOWER)
WATER (LEAF)
EARTH (ROOT)

Apogee, the distant moon, tends to further bolting in plants sown on these days, which is good for seed crops. Potatoes like to be planted at apogee. Plants planted in perigee tend to be more subject to pests and mildew. In general, it is a good practice not to do major planting or sowings on either Ag or Pg. The same can be said of the lunar nodes, when the moon crosses the ecliptic; that it is best not to do any major gardening work on these days. Maria Thun has found verification for most of these old customs in her research.

As for the planetary influences, there is evidence that insects are affected in their habits by certain conjunctions and planetary positions in the zodiac. There has been little research on this. Rudolf Steiner makes mention of burning insects and pests in certain planetary constellations in his *Agricultural Course.*

In conclusion, it may be said that planting at the right phase and sign can be one of the many factors that lead to successful gardening. The good soil must be there, for it is the soil with its teeming life that is mainly receptive to these influences. If all the other factors are handled well, the crop rotation, companion planting, good soil husbandry, composting, and good watering, then the planting by the signs will be an extra plus. By itself, astronomical gardening does not guarantee a great garden; by the same token, if a good planting day has to be missed because of weather or of other commitments, it will not be, in itself, catastrophic.

CHAPTER XIII
ATMOSPHERIC FACTORS

Moderating, transferring and mediating between the great polarity of the terrestrial factors and the cosmic factors are the forces of wind and water, the climate, weather, sunshine and rain that make up the *atmospheric factors.* Included are the following:

1. *moisture,* involving humidity, rain, hail, sleet, snowblankets, dew and fog.
2. *wind,* involving strength, direction, seasonal variation, and local breezes.
3. *air pressure,* involving barometric changes.
4. *the light climate,* involving cloud covers, angle of sunlight, length of days, and shadows cast by buildings, trees, and hills.
5. *temperature,* involving temperature averages, extremes of day and night, extremes of seasons, and frosts and chills.

All of these factors are intimately involved with how the garden grows. The gardener must be very aware of these factors for they will determine to a large extent when to plant and harvest, when to water or cultivate, when there is danger of aphid or mildew infection, and what the quantity and quality of the produce will be like. Entries should be made into the garden diary for each of these factors, providing a valuable record after a number of years that gives predictability for the local situation. To aid in the observations and recordings, simple instruments can be used, such as a *thermometer* for temperature measure-

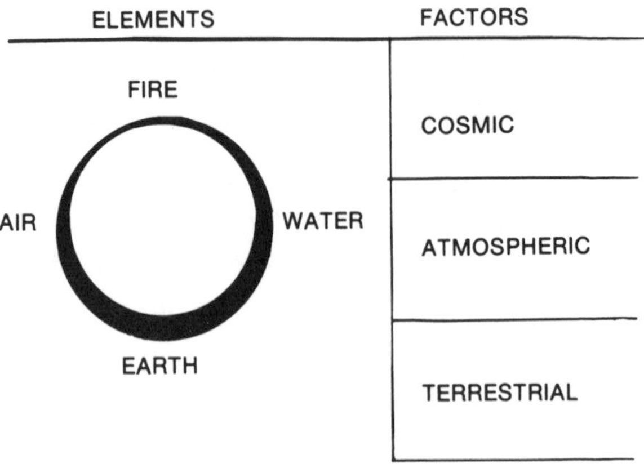

ments in sunny and shady locations, a *weathervane* for showing the wind direction, a *hygrometer* to measure humidity,[1] a simple *anemometer* which is a whirligig that indicates the speed of the wind,[2] a *barometer* to give information on the air pressure, the highs and lows, and a *rain gauge* which shows the amount of precipitation. The position of the sun in the zodiac, the place on the horizon where it rises and sets, a measure of the angles of the sun's rays, and a charting of the procession of shadows across the garden and other observations belong in the diary next to entries concerning composting, cultivating, planting, fertiliz-

[1]Simple hygrometers are made from a human hair with a weight for a pointer suspended from it. Peasants in Europe use a little "weather house" which shows Hansel and Gretel when the weather is fair and an old witch when the weather is poor. Other devices include frogs in jars with a ladder to climb up and down on, twisted ropes which coil and uncoil with changes of humidity, and fir twigs.

[2]Simple, homemade weather monitoring instruments are recorded in *Weather (New York: Life Science Library, Time Inc., 1965), pp. 160-170.*

ing and rotations.

Nature observations, hints by "old timers" and local folk sayings provide a rich storehouse of information. Farmers tell that animals in the barn are nervous and cows hold back on their milk when there are impending changes of weather and that aches and pains in the joints and old wounds mean the same thing. All animals, because of their more immediate contact with nature, give indications regarding atmospheric conditions, if one can read them. Especially insects, which are still very closely tied into the macrocosmic processes, reflect the weather and even predict it. When gnats and mosquitoes dance high in the air, the weather will stay fair, but when they fly low and bite, the weather will change. Bees are nervous when the weather changes, sting when it is humid and windy, strip the pollen off their legs to fly home faster when there is a storm on the horizon. Yearly forecasts can be made by observing bee larvae; when the brood is large there will be a sunny year, good for fruits and flowers; when there are few larvae, the year will be rainy and cool. Ants are interesting to watch in similar respects. Woolly bear caterpillars, which are often seen crossing the roads in the fall, indicate the kind of winter to follow. If the brown band around the caterpillar is broad, the winter will be mild; if it is narrow, the winter will be harsh. Crickets are regular thermometers; they chirp faster when it is warmer and proportionately slower the cooler it gets. Some observant old timers can actually tell the degrees Fahrenheit by counting the chirps in a certain way. Similarly, spiders, besides being useful bug catchers, are good weather forecasters. When the little spiders hatch in the spring, it is a sure sign that warm weather is coming; when spiders weave fine nets, there will be a spell of good weather; when they build nests it is a sign of coming cold, and when they weave thick strands, it will be cloudy or rainy.[3]

Mindful observation of the plant world gives good hints to the gardener regarding seasons and weather. Each step of the season is marked by its particular phenomenon in the flowering world. In southern Oregon, it is a sure sign of spring when the hazelnut blooms, the miner's lettuce, slender toothwort, plums and others start flowering. This early flowering is followed by the shooting stars, the ragged star flowers, camas, grass widows, and others. Successive flowering continues until mid-summer is graced by the sun-like St. John'swort, to be followed in the fall by asters, chicories and others. Watching the natural flowering patterns is a surer way of knowing at which point the season stands than relying on abstract numerical dates. For predictions of the coming year, the greening of the oak is compared to the greening of the ash tree. If the oak greens before the ash, the summer will be wet; if the ash comes out before the oak, the summer will be dry.

Other natural phenomena can be helpful. In the Grants Pass area of Oregon, the weather starts to milden in February, making it possible to put out peas and spinach, but the last frost can be as late as the beginning of June. Newcomers to the area are usually fooled into putting their summer gardens out way too soon, only to find that a succession of unexpected frosts kills them off. The seasoned gardeners know that only when the mountain tops are free of snow is it safe to put out corn and tomatoes. A planting

[3]Quatremer-Dijonval, who was incarcerated in a spider-infested dungeon in 1787, when the Prussians invaded Holland, made an intensive scientific study of these creatures at that time, and verified these rules.

rule going back to the Iroquois in the Midwest, not planting corn until the leaves of the white oak are about the size of squirrels' ears, holds only conditionally for this region.

Cloud formations, the colors of sunrise and sunset, wind directions, rising and descending fog and other natural phenomena ought to be studied by the gardener for each local area.

Magical Weather Control

Since weather is an important factor to all people, especially agricultural and horticultural societies, propitiation of weather deities and spirits, and magical weather control was (and is) universally practiced. In western culture, notwithstanding, there is a long tradition of lore regarding weather. Germanic tribes propitiated Thor to ward off giant elemental beings of frost and ice with his thunderbolt, and to send fertile rain for the boor's swidden. Wodin was seen with his wild warriors sweeping through the winter storms on his gray steed. Zeus was the thunderer, cloud gatherer and rainmaker for the Greeks. Iris brought the rainbow, Poseidon the storms of the sea, Zephyr brought the moist, mild west wind, Boreas the cold north wind, Notos the dry south wind, and Apelides the east wind. Helios was the sun god and Apollo the god of light. These and other gods, lesser spirits and elementals were accountable for the changing phenomena in the macrocosm, as well as the changing moods and passions within the microcosm. Because of this macrocosmic-microcosmic kinship, the human being, in the form of a priest, sorcerer, or magician could approach the spirits and deities that operated behind the phenomena. He could beseech them as a priest and pray for rain, the cessation of rain, for warm weather or the cessation of a heat wave, or he could work as a theurgist, as a magician, and compel the weather deities to act according to his wishes.[4] He could work for the welfare of the suffering community, or like Shakespeare's witches in *Macbeth,* create harmful winds and storms. We still speak of a spell of weather, of a rain spell or a spell of sunshine. Spells were originally woven by chants, songs, or the casting of sacred symbols, such as runes, or water into fire.

Ethnographic research shows that public rainmakers are universal, making rain by the imitative magic of sprinkling water to imitate clouds, drumming to imitate thunder, dressing in dark colors to look like rain-laden clouds, and other practices, while the community sings and dances for rain.[5] Men cut their arms or bleed animals for sacrifice and in imitation of the rain. Often weather rituals are carried out in stark nakedness, or in garments of foliage. If these rituals are of no avail, the recourse is often taken by threatening or abusing the saints or gods associated with weather control. To stop rain, its elemental opposite, fire, is used. Torches are thrown in the air or at the clouds. Wind is controlled by the imitative magic of blowing, or summoned by the clapping of hands. English sailors still tie three knots into their handkerchiefs and hope to release the wind by untying the knots. Christian hymnals contain prayers and songs beseeching God to send rain and protect from ill weather.

---

[4]Christ reveals himself as the master of the macrocosm and microcosm when he calms the storm on the sea of Galilee and the fear in the hearts of his followers.

[5]On the Howerth Farm in Grants Pass, Oregon, a rain dance was held when the February waxing moon was in Pisces, a good water sign, to alleviate the severe 1977 drought. A chanting, praying, dancing group gathered for the conjuring. Indeed, despite the weather bureau's prediction for continuation of the dry weather, it rained the next day.

A modern scientist cannot but help consider these practices to be superstition born out of ignorance, as attempts at control based on faulty pre-scientific premises (Frazier), or as rituals that function psychologically to relieve anxiety (Malinowski). For the scientist who counts as real only the objective world of logic and the senses, this must be the right conclusion: weather is something we can't do anything about! If, on the other hand, one considers moods and states of mind as real and effective as physical things, then one can appreciate the possibility of a sympathy between people's hopes, desires and frame of mind and the external state of nature. Perhaps what once were effective means of channeling energies through rituals have at this time in our evolution become empty superstitions, in a time when the intellect overshadows our other human faculties. Many gardeners are almost intuitively aware that there is more to weather than just mechanistic processes. Remembering our discussion of the plant as a macrocosmic being, we can think of the climate with its changing moods of weather as part of the plant's wider nature, as vectors of formative forces working on the visible expression of the plant, just as the storms of passion, the hot and cold temperaments, the moods of joy and gloom reveal themselves in the physiognomy of the human microcosm. Could there be a subtle sympathy between the temperaments of people and the weather phenomena? In light of the recent weather irregularities and calamities, perhaps these standpoints ought to be reconsidered.

Working with the Micro-Climate: Practical Aspects

Even if we are not able to significantly affect the macroclimate, the overall weather patterns, there is a lot we can do to create micro-climatic conditions that are conducive to good plant growth. We shall deal with practical considerations for warmth, light, watering, frosts and wind protection.

Light and Warmth

It is best to choose a sunny location for the garden. Light and warmth, in interaction with the plant's water, produce the sugars, starches, oils and fragrances that account for the flavor, good keeping quality, and resistance to disease.[6] In planning the garden space and layout, one should watch the sun over its year's path to see how the shadows of houses, trees and hills are cast. Warm weather crops should be put into the sunniest part of the garden.

If one's terrain is hilly, it is important to know the warming pattern and the angle of the sun on the hill. At a 90° angle, the sun is much more intense than at a 45° angle. The southwest of the hill is the hottest and driest, while the northeast side is moister and cooler. The east slope is cooler because the dew has to dry in the mornings before it can warm up. Hillsides are usually slightly warmer than valleys because at night cool air moves downslope. Because frosts are more severe in valleys, and light radiation is not quite as intense, it is a good idea to put fruit trees on slightly higher grounds, on southern slopes. As for the ground itself, dark humus absorbs warmth faster and keeps it longer, whereas light soil (sand) reflects the light and absorbs less heat. A light background for reflection of light is made use

---

[6]The atmospheric factors of light and warmth in combination with water bring out the colors of the rainbow as well as in the blooms, indicating the mediation between the light (cosmic forces) and the dark (terrestrial forces).

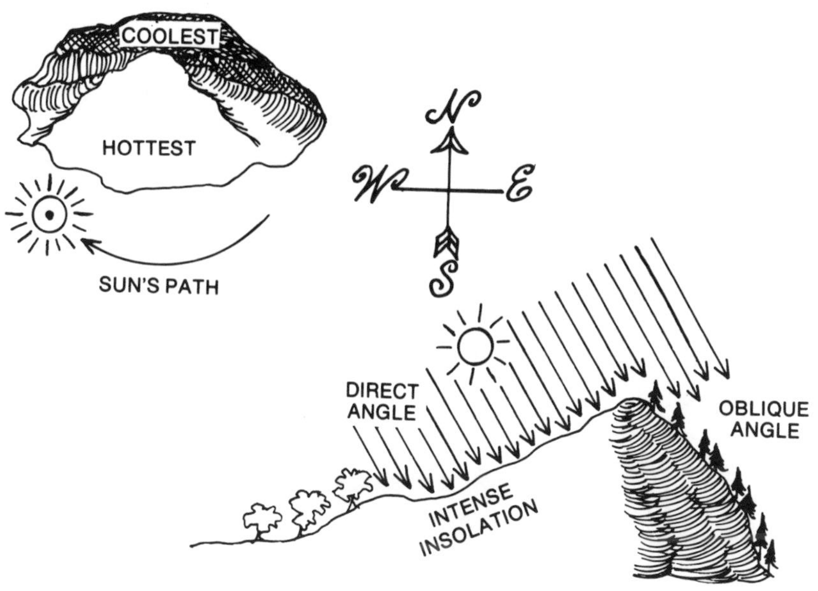

of in trellises for fruit grown next to house walls.

Frosts

Old Jack Frost is usually a problem in the spring, just when the plants are still small and tender. In the early spring the ground is still cold and only its surface warms during the day. At night the little amount of stored-up warmth is given off, radiating into space, while cooler air rushes in to replace the warmer air. This is especially a problem in drier climates, where the daytime temperatures might get fairly high (70's), and because there is little water to hold the moisture, the night time temperatures become cold (20's).[7] In southern Oregon, where heavy logging has reduced the ameliorative effect of forest vegetation, the daytime-night-time temperature difference in the spring months amounts to over 40°F. Moister soils, although they heat slower, will keep the warmth longer than dry soils, and they take much more cold before the frost point is reached. For this reason, one cultivates a little later in the spring, so that the soil does not dry out so much. Shrubbery, groves and hedges, or a nearby pond or river raise the humidity and give some frost protection. A clouded sky reflects back the heat given off by the ground, so that on overcast days no frost can be expected.

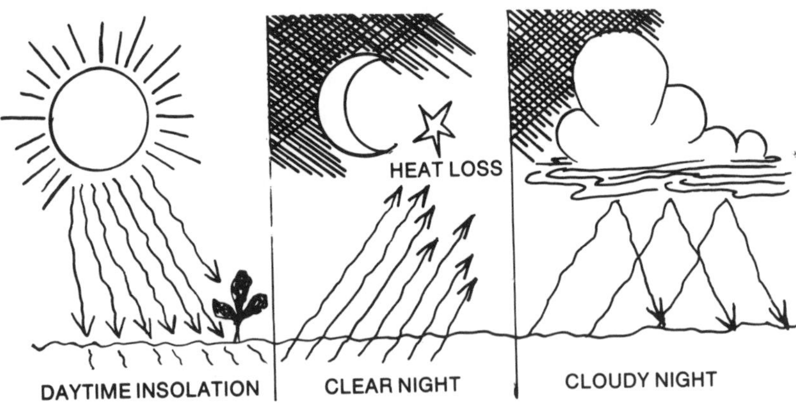

[7]It is the difference in air moisture that accounts for the fact that in the desert one can go into the shade to cool off, whereas in the humid Midwest, the shade offers no relief from the heat. Though it takes 4 to 5 times the heat to warm a quantity of water by one degree than it takes for an equal amount of air, the water will hold the warmth much longer.

Since cold air flows like a river, following the path of least resistance, it is a good idea to study the flow patterns and the low areas where the frost settles. This flow of cold air at night will continue as long as there is snow in the mountains. At dawn, one can literally see the advance of white patches, the footsteps of frost giants as Nordics would say, as the cold moves down into the valley. One can deal with the cold flow by not putting the garden in a very low area, but on slightly higher ground. One can either block the flow with a wall or a hedge, or one can make sure that the frost is not impeded as it moves past. The main thing is to prevent it from settling. One can create the equivalent of a protective cloud cover by setting up plastic tunnels over one's beds in the spring. These are opened during the day, and closed at night. In orchards, smudge pots are used for similar purposes, or ventilators are set up to keep the air moving. Turning one's sprinklers on during the coldest hours at night will keep the frost from harming the plants, because as long as there is fresh water coming to be turned into ice, the temperature of the leaves will not dip below the freezing point. It is also a good idea not to mulch until the frost danger is past, so that the ground can sufficiently warm up.

In short, what one has to watch for, especially after a cold front has passed, is a clear sky, dry, windstill air and dry, cool ground. Given these factors in early spring, one can expect frost.

In the fall, the first frost will kill most of the warm-weather plants such as tomatoes, eggplants, peppers, beans, squashes, etc. One can extend the season somewhat by the use of plastic tunnels and spraying the bio-dynamic preparation made from valerian. (See PREPARATIONS, TEAS AND BIOTIC SUBSTANCES.)

Air and Wind

The gardener should be familiar with local wind directions and velocities. He should know what kind of weather the major winds bring. Does the southwest wind bring warmth and rain, while the northeast wind brings cold and clear skies? Are there cool evening breezes from the hills or from bodies of water?

If wind sweeps too swiftly across the garden plot, several problems result. Wind cools, dehydrates and removes the carbon dioxide which is needed by the plant for sugar production. Carbon dioxide, which is slightly heavier than normal air, hovers above the ground among the foliage layers, having been given off by the respiration of soil organisms, from whence it is absorbed by the pore openings of the leaves. With adequate wind protection the crops will be a week ahead of time, and production will increase by about 10%. Wind protection is best provided by hedges, shrubbery or lattice fences. Hedges are not havens for vermin, but provide shelter for useful animals such as toads, garter snakes, birds and weasels which eat mice and gophers. A hedge can shelter bee hives, provide nuts and berries and bean poles or tomato stakes. To make a hedge denser, one should trim it. Gooseberries, red and black currants and other berry bushes can function as a windbreak as well. In a new garden where there has not been time for a hedge to establish itself, the tall crops on the border of the garden can give wind shelter (Jerusalem artichokes, corn, runner-beans, peas, for example).

Hedges and fences should have about 40% permeability, just slowing the wind, but not stopping it. An impermeable barrier, such as a wall, creates turbulence farther on that

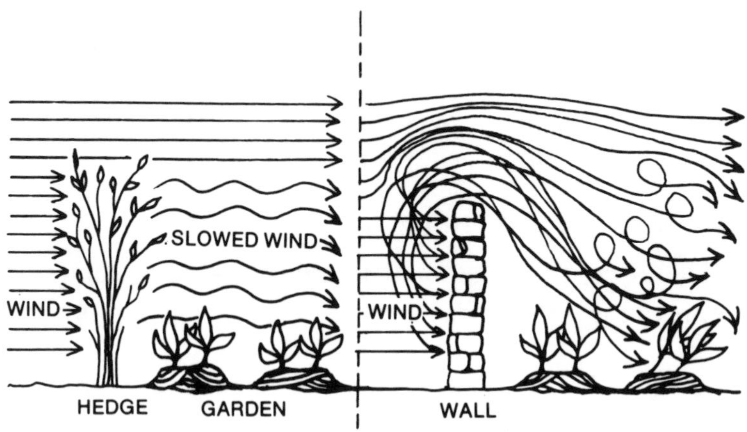

can be destructive.

Water

The gardener must know the rainfall patterns of his region and the water-holding capacity of his soil. In southern Oregon, the year divides itself into dry summers and wet winters. One can have problems of water-logging during part of the season, and dryness during the other part. If water-logging becomes a problem, it is a good idea to set up a *drainage system* by laying tile pipes or open trenches that empty into a lower area. If there is no lower area to empty into, it is profitable to dig a pond. A pond will keep a more steady humidity level which moderates temperature extremes; one can raise fish and ducks in it, and use it as a water source for one's plants. Raised beds are a help, also, where the soil is soggy in the spring planting season. Roots need air pockets; they can drown in water-logged soil.

One might have collecting tanks or barrels to catch rain water from the roof. Rainwater collected during a thunderstorm is rich in nitrates, and collected during a full moon period is rich in the formative growth forces that are connected with the moon. Water of this nature is preferred over tap water or city water for watering the garden.

Dry-Weather Gardening

During dry weather, or drought conditions, one can improve the water utilization of one's crops in a number of ways.

1. *Double Digging* is a means of enlarging the rooting zone, so that cultivated plants can more easily grow into the deeper, moister levels of the ground. The loosened soil interrupts the capillary action of water molecules as they move upwards in the soil, where they eventually evaporate on the surface.

2. *Compost* increases the soil's clay-humus complexes. A clay-humus molecule holds six times its weight in water, and retains up to 900% of the moisture compared to sand. Its electrostatic charge holds on to 4 molecular layers of water which are not given up to gravity or the sun's evaporative pull, but are made available to the plants when their transpiration rate makes it necessary. It is shown experimentally that plants lacking in nutrients need more water; they have to transpire more water to get the equivalent amount of nutrients that plants in rich humus soil would be getting. It is for this reason that during droughts organic gardens stay green, while those relying on artificial fertilizer instead of compost wither and die.

3. *Mulching* is the equivalent of bringing an overcast day to the level of the ground; the evaporation is greatly reduced. Ordinary mulch can reduce evaporation about 50%, whereas straw, which reflects light, can reduce evaporation

70%.

4. Create *wind-shelters*, such as hedges or fences, which will decrease the amount of evaporation caused by the wind.

5. *Watering practices* involve watering less often, but more thoroughly. In the spring it is important to keep the seedlings from drying out and more frequent watering is recommended, but after midsummer the watering should occur less frequently. Many people spoil their plants by turning on the sprinklers every day. Such plants respond by making a shallow root system, and as soon as the top layer of the ground dries, they begin to look wilted, waiting for a new shower. It is better to train the plants to root more deeply by watering less, but then to soak the ground thoroughly so that the deeper zones become moistened also. After such a soaking, the garden should be mulched to keep the evaporation rate down. If no mulch is available, it is advisable to *dry mulch* by hoeing after each sprinkling or irrigation in order to interrupt the evaporative pull by interrupting the capillary movement of the water molecules. This is how the Pueblo Indians are able to grow gardens in the desert. After each rain, the whole village races to the fields to start hoeing.

Watering should never be done in the noonday sun, but at night or in the mornings, for the cold water on warm leaves creates a shock for the plant. The leaves of the plant, physiologically set for the hot sunny day, are traumatized by the sudden shower of tap water. As a result, the plant hesitates in its growing, and this blockage of energy flow becomes a signal to insects and slugs to start eating. Some people become worried when the leaves of beans, squashes and other plants droop in the late afternoon, thinking it is time to water. Actually, the plant organisms are just adjusting to the hottest part of the day, protecting themselves from excessive transpiration. If done right, one need not water more than once, twice or three times during a month, depending on soil and location. One of the best times to water is *just before* the full moon, so that the lunar forces can work on the vegetation through the water.

Cool-weather loving plants, the potatoes, cabbage family, beet family and carrot family, do not mind overhead sprinkling, but the warm-weather-loving plants, especially the tomatoes and beans, are sensitive to having their leaves wet. For the latter, *soaker-hoses* and *drip-irrigation* are recommended.

The soil should have the wrung-out sponge feeling all the way down to the root tips. One must make sure to water deeply enough. For experimental purposes, one could dig a hole to get an idea of the watering depth and amount that is right for one's soil. Faulty watering is one of the greatest causes for garden failure. In the midwest, where the land is blessed with a weekly thundershower, this is no problem.

6. The *close spacing* of plants as recommended in the French intensive method of gardening helps shade the ground and reduces evaporation. The plants are grown so that the leaves touch each other, and select plants are harvested from the bed to keep the green canopy.[8] This method might be of merit in arid climates, but in the author's estimation, the crops are too crowded, preventing the archetypal form of each plant from coming into expres-

[8]Jeavons, *How to Grow More Vegetables.*

sion.

7. Choosing *drought-resistant varieties,* as advertised in some catalogs, might be helpful.

Mulching and Ground Covers

A final consideration for maximizing the microclimate of one's garden ecotope is to mulch between the rows. Each kind of mulch has a different effect. *Straw* mulch cools the ground, which is recommended for members of the cabbage family and other cold-weather-loving plants. *Hay* mulch feeds the soil organisms, as does straw, to a lesser extent. *Paper* mulch will do in a bind, but is messy because it blows away easily. *Plastic* sheets warm the ground and might be good for giving strawberries, tomatoes, eggplants and peppers a start, but they inhibit air circulation, causing anaerobic soil reactions. Black plastic keeps longer than clear plastic and warms more efficiently, but all plastic is difficult to get rid of. Burning it causes air pollution. *Pine needle* mulch is very acidic, and is not recommended except for strawberries and azaleas. *Oak leaf* mulch discourages slugs, but like most leaves, it is slightly acidic. *Fresh sawdust* will rob the soil of its nitrogen until it is finally broken down. Mulching primarily saves water, but it also prevents weeds by depriving them of light. A six-inch mulch cover practically eliminates weeding and hoeing, while feeding and protecting the soil. Mulch buffers the soil, so that the hiatus between the atmosphere (air and light) and the soil (earth and water) is not so abrupt, making it possible for earthworms and microorganisms to work to the very top layer of soil. Mulch feeds the earthworms. Mulch keeps the soil from crusting over after a rain, which lets the soil breathe and keeps the lettuce and strawberries from being splattered with dirt.

One problem with mulch is that it might shelter slugs, but with proper watering practices, such as not sprinkling every day, this should not be a problem. Slugs are the worst problem with *clean cultivation* (where weeds are destroyed and no mulch is given), where living plants are attacked. Since slugs prefer wilted greens, the right kind of mulch might even lure them away from the crop plants.

For further ideas about mulching, *The Ruth Stout No-Work Garden Book* makes for interesting reading.[9]

In this chapter, we have touched upon the so-called atmospheric factors, and indicated how we can modify and meliorate some of the extremes of temperature, water and wind, by creating beneficial microclimates that make the garden into an oasis.

---

[9]Ruth Stout and Richard Clemence, *The Ruth Stout No-Work Garden Book* (Emmaus, Penna.: Rodale Press, Inc., 1971).

CHAPTER XIV
COMPOSTS AND LIQUID MANURES

Composting (L. compositum=something put together) is the deliberate putting together of any number of organic substances for the sake of rotting them in such a way that a high-quality natural fertilizing agent, a medium of micro-organismic life, can develop. We must distinguish between the (1) *ingredients* and the (2) *processes* of composting itself; both must be carefully attended to if the end product is a good stable, permanent humus.

In Nature's "Wheel of Life," composting occurs on the bottom of a cycle, where death processes are turned back into life processes. The cycle starts in the spring, when seeds, lying dormant in the soil, are awakened to life by water and increasing warmth. Quickened vegetative growth characterizes the vegetable kingdom from spring until mid-summer, when the rapid buildup of carbonaceous substance comes to a halt and increasingly the impulse toward flowering and subsequent seed formation is given. Older leaves start yellowing and dying off; they are chewed and shredded by insect populations, as the overall annual *break-down cycle* picks up speed. Finally, in late autumn, fallen leaves and stems litter the ground as mulch, and the break-down cycle continues as bacteria and fungi metabolize the carbohydrate substances. By spring, this mulch is broken down and metamorphosed into humus as the *buildup cycle* of vegetation commences anew.

We get a grand picture of the rhythm of life and the inter-connectedness of soil and plant when we contemplate how

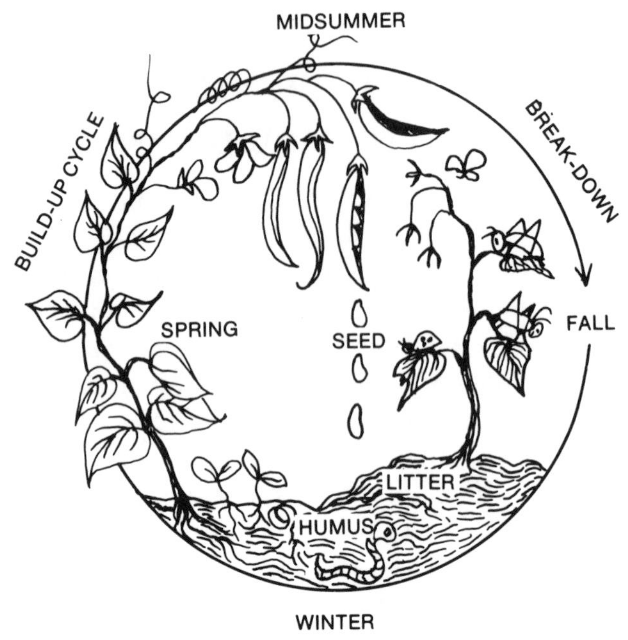

THE WHEEL OF LIFE

the plant during half of the cycle grows as lush vegetation, and during the other half of the cycle separates into a tiny germ, the seed or bud, on one hand, and litter and mulch on the other hand, to be finally reunited in the spring when the seed grows out of the living forces of the humus. Animal substances, manures, urine, secretions and corpses work into this cycle of life and death.

In biologically sound organic farming and gardening, building soil by composting is the key. In nature we observe composting processes at work all the time as decaying leaves, litter, dead animals, tree stumps and other remnants of life whose etheric forces have left them or been weakened, are being putrefied, rotted, decayed or fermented. Some gardeners feel that it is important to copy these processes exactly. This is done by mulching continually or letting the mulch rot on the ground as time goes by. This kind of "composting" is very much like nature does it. There is nothing to be said against this practice; however, building a compost pile and conducting a guided decomposition process is lending nature a helping hand. Composting is bio-dynamics *par excellence,* for here one is neither letting nature take its course, nor is one violating nature's principles, but one is aiding nature, speeding her up a bit, and guiding the changes in such a way that it is beneficial for the garden organism.

The art of composting is very ancient. The Roman Plinius wrote about it, the 11th century Arab scholar Ibn al Awam discusses it, alchemists practiced it to find the secrets of transmutation and peasants have practiced some form of composting for quite some time. In the West this tended to be the dung heap, where manure, carcasses, scraps and stall bedding was thrown and left to rot. These were reeking piles that lost much nitrogen to the atmosphere due to denitrifying bacteria and anaerobic putrefaction. In the Orient, more careful management of compost has been practiced for centuries, making it possible for large families to survive on two to five acres. Here, everything organic, weeds, human excrement, animal manures, pond dredgings and sod were composted in special composting sheds that formed part of the cluster of buildings that made up the farm-stead.[1] Roofed-over manure piles were also found in Swiss farm-steads.[2]

Compost science and care was neglected in the decades following the advent of chemical farming and the displacement of animals from the farms, of horses by tractors, of cows, chickens and hogs into feed lots. This development has a serious ecological impact and puts the permanent fertility of the land into question. The organic agriculture movement has re-emphasized the importance of composting (e.g. Sir Albert Howard's Indore Method), and biodynamics in particular has added valuable scientific data to the art of compost making, by analyzing ingredients, composting stages, kinds of special compost for specific crop needs, and providing preparations made from herbs to guide the decomposition in the most favorable way. (See chapter on PREPARATIONS.)

Compost Ingredients

Any organic substance can be composted. There are different types of composts that can be made from different materials for different purposes. Common garden compost can be made from garbage, weeds, manures of domestic animals, leaves, paper and sod. The ingredients should be mixed as well as possible; this is even better than layering the ingredients. Chopping the materials as finely as possible with a silage chopper or *shredder* can be of great advantage, especially when dealing with such ingredients as

---

[1]King, *Farmers of Forty Centuries*, p. 212.

[2]Hauser, *Bauernregeln*, illustr. p. 64.

sunflower stems, cabbage stalks and other tough haulms. The cost of a compost shredder could be shared by a neighborhood or garden club.

Of great importance is the *carbon-nitrogen ratio* (C-N ratio), the relative amount of carbon to nitrogen, of the compost materials. Sawdust, which has 500 parts carbon to 1 part nitrogen, is said to have a wide ratio, whereas sludge, which has a ratio of 6 parts C to 1 part N, is said to be close. An ideal C-N ratio at the start of the composting process is about 30 to 1 or 25 to 1. After the compost starts working, it will lose volume due to the escape of carbon dioxide and water vapor, which brings the end product close to an ideal of 15:1 to 20:1 ratio. If one has substances such as sawdust,

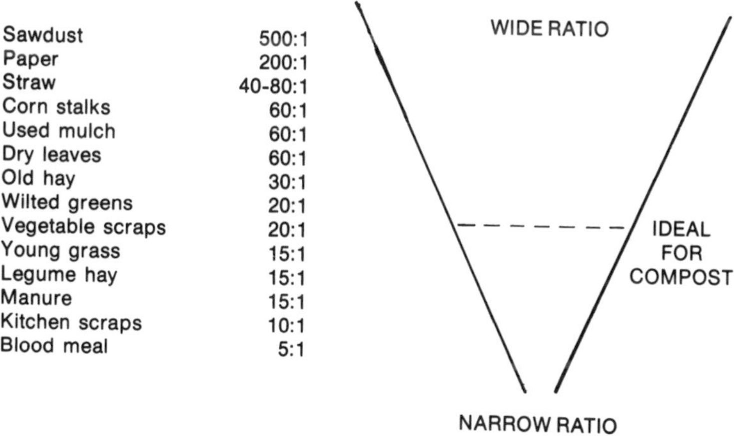

paper, straw or leaves which have a wide C-N ratio, then one must balance this out with substances having a narrow ratio in order to approach the ideal of 25-30:1 C-N ratio. This is done by adding manures, guano, blood meal, bone and horn meal, wool, feathers, urines, chicken manure, pig bristles, slurry, and even hair sweepings from a barber shop.

Fresh sawdust might even be treated at first with artificial nitrogen (e.g. urea, ammonia sulphate) to narrow the C-N gap and help bacteria break it down. After such a predigestion, the sawdust pile can be reworked into a regular compost. This is one of the few instances where artificials might be cautiously used.

Too close a C-N ratio at the beginning of composting leads to nitrogen losses, which can be detected by the smell of ammonia. This also attracts flies. Composts properly prepared should not have strong odors.

Too wide a C-N ratio slows the composting considerably. If lack of sufficient nitrogen is coupled with low temperatures and too much moisture, an acid, peat-like end product, resembling the peat in northern climates, results.

Besides the ingredients that furnish the C-N ratio, other substances are added to the compost. *Earth,* at the most 5% to 10%, can be mixed in to aid the earthworms and humus formation. *Clay* that has been pulverized can be sprinkled among the layers of compost materials. When examining a clay-treated compost, one finds that most of the earthworm eggs and young earthworms are active near the clay particles. *Lime* or calcium, preferably in the form of dolomite or ground limestone, should be dusted among the layers of the compost every once in a while, as though one were dusting a cake with powdered sugar. This is a better way of adding lime to the soil than broadcasting it directly onto the ground; in the compost it becomes tied into the permanent humus molecules and facilitates the cation exchange. The right amount of lime keeps the compost from souring and discourages flies. Too much lime must be avoided for it will drive off the ammonia and, because of its alkaline reaction, discourage the ammonia-absorbing compost fungi. Cellulose-digesting bacteria, on the other hand, need the presence of some calcium. *Wood ash,* which supplies potassium and minerals, should be finely laced throughout the compost. Like lime and clay powder, it should not be put into the compost in large clumps, for then it forms caustic lye (potassium hydroxide) when moistened. Ashes from coal fire contain too much sulphur to be of good use. Ashes from plastics, colored, glossy paper, and chemical stuff should not be used in the compost. *Granite flour,* basalt flour, green sand, rock phosphate, colloidal phosphate, and other amendments are put into the compost in the same way.

There are a number of *compost-starters,* or compost-activators, on the market. Rodale is of the opinion that they are not really needed, for the bacteria and spores of micro-organisms are everywhere in the ground, air and water, so that the pile, given the correct C-N ratio, will take off by itself.[3] This is generally true, although Pfeiffer's bio-dynamic compost starter, containing bacteria isolated from the bio-dynamic preparations made from herbs, brings the right kind of bacteria into play, so that the rotting will proceed favorably.[4] Pfeiffer compares the starter to yeast added to bread. One can mix the flour and water and then leave it ex-

---

[3]J.I. Rodale, ed., *The Complete Book of Composting* (Emmaus, Penn.: Rodale Books, Inc., 1975), p. 137.

[4]B-D compost starter available at the Pfeiffer Foundation, Threefold Farm, Spring Valley, N.Y. 10977. See TEAS, PREPARATIONS AND BIOTIC SUBSTANCES.

posed to the air to catch wild yeast spores that will ferment and raise the dough, but what an awful taste! Yeast must come from a select strain to make good bread.[5]

Old compost is an excellent starter when sprinkled into the new heap. *Russian tea,* or a fermentation of cow dung in ten parts water; *Chairman Mao's compost starter,* made from a four to one dilution of urine; *nettle tea* or *nettle ferment,* made by brewing nettles or fermenting them in rainwater; or a ferment of *comfrey* leaves *(Symphytum officinale),* when added to the compost, help to get the proper rotting processes started.

When, Where and How to Set Up the Compost

It is best to have a permanent composting area, centrally located in the garden for easy transport of materials. The compost should be placed on the bare ground and not on wooden or cement platforms, so that bacteria from previous piles can infect it and earthworms can travel into the subsoil and back into the compost. The compost should not be put into a pit, and certainly not be trampled down, for that would result in *anaerobic* decomposition, in putrefaction and fermentation, with the result of an inferior end product. Nitrate-producing bacteria need plenty of oxygen, since they are *aerobic.* Therefore, the composts should be somewhat loosely piled on top of the ground, where the pile can be kept moist, but not water-logged, which would encourage reducing organisms. The materials are shredded as finely as possible to increase the surface areas for the bacteria to work on.

The composting site should be either shady or roofed

[5]Pfeiffer, *Condensation of Bio-Dynamic Farming and Gardening,* p. 22.

over in warmer, drier localities. Elderberry, hazelnut, birch and alder make ideal compost shade trees for their leaf and root exudates aid in the decomposition processes. In cooler climates, composts should be put into wind-sheltered, sunny areas. It is well worth protecting the compost with a layer of black plastic, which keeps the compost from drying out during a dry spell, and, on the other hand, keeps the nutrients from leaching out during a rainy season. Evaporating moisture will condense underneath the plastic and percolate and circulate through the pile. A roofed-over compost place also protects from drying or leaching.

Windrows about four-feet high, six-feet wide, and as long as necessary, are the best shape to give to the composts. In this way, a "critical mass" is achieved, for the bio-chemical reactions to take place. If the compost pile is too small, it will not heat and decompose properly; if it is too large of a pile, then the inner layers will still be raw, besides being deprived of air, while the outside mantle will have already broken down.

Like any living organism, the compost must have a skin to keep the gases, such as ammonia and methane, and other products of metabolism from being dissipated. A mantle of peat, sawdust, straw or other nitrogen-poor substance will not let the odors, which are really fertility in volatile form, pass into the atmosphere. Underneath, the compost might be bedded upon straw, hay, peat or a similar absorbant substance if there is a chance of runoff of liquids.

For smaller gardens, a wooden composting bin, or a roll of wire mesh, make good composting devices. Fresh material is pitched into the top, while finished compost can be scooped out of the bottom.

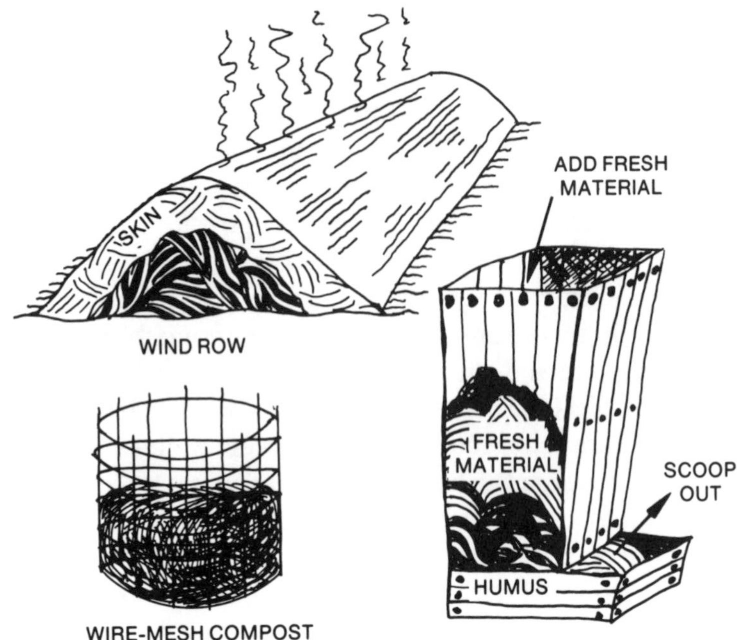

Special Composts and Manures

There are a number of composts other than the ordinary garden compost that is made from available weeds, leaves, and kitchen scraps. Special composts for legumes can be made from clover or some other legume sod that is composted together with manure for a year with some lime added. This method, developed by N. Remer, can be used to fertilize legume fields and pastures. It produces a special virulence among the *rhyzobia* and will stimulate nitrogen-fixation.[6] A tomato compost can be made from old tomato

[6]Remer, *Lebensgesetze im Landbau.*

plants, together with soil and manure. This is good fertilizer for tomatoes, which have a narcissistic predilection for growing on their own rotted remains. A special earthworm compost is made from shredded paper, straw, and manure with clay powder added.

Special composts can be made for specific purposes from various animal droppings. In general, it can be said that the part of the plant upon which an animal characteristically feeds is best fertilized by the manure of that species. *Hog manure* is rich in potash, and when well-humified, is best applied to root crops, especially potassium-hungry leeks, celeriac and potatoes. The hog is primarily a rooting animal, feeding on roots which it digs up.[7] Composted *horse manure* is light and will lighten

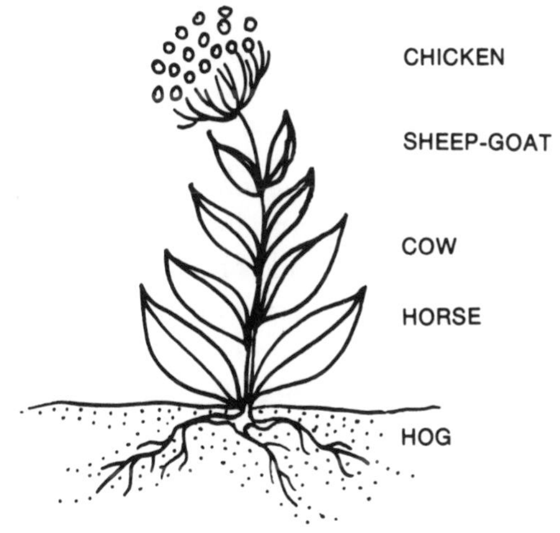

[7]Pigs are de-natured if not allowed to root or if rings are put through their snouts to prevent this behavior. In France, the rooting ability is put to good use by training pigs to dig up truffles.

heavy, clay soils. Horses feed primarily on foliage and grass; consequently, their manure aids leaf and foliage development. Horse manure, which is rich in ammonia, will heat steadily for a long time. This makes it ideal for use in hot beds for raising seedlings in the spring. For a home garden, or even a larger garden where no greenhouse is available, this is a good way to start plants. (See chapter on the GARDENING CALENDAR.)

Cow manure is the best manure that can be used for composting purposes, as is evident by examining the long, complicated digestive organism of this beast. Cud-chewing ruminants like the bison or buffalo made possible the humus-rich prairies, which became the bread basket of the world.[8] Were it not for the sacred cows, India would be in much worse shape than it is. These cows are not competitors, as some western technocrats believe, but they live in symbiosis with human beings, eating weeds and roughage that could not otherwise be utilized and returning milk, draft power and manure. This dung amounts to 700 million tons annually, half of which serves as fertilizer and the other half as fuel (the thermal equivalent of 27 million tons of kerosene, 35 million tons of coal, or 68 million tons of wood).[9] In countries of the cooler latitudes, cows are one of the mainstays of fertility, because with high rainfall and low temperatures, the soils become leached and acidic, leading to podsols and peat formations. The cows, inside

---

[8]It is not just our superior agrarian technique which makes bumper crops in the wheat belt possible as the USDA ethnocentrically suggests, but the stored-up fertility of soils where the buffalo ranged for millenia that creates bigger crops than are attainable on soils worked for up to four thousand years.

[9]Marvin Harris, *Cows, Pigs, Wars and Witches* (New York: Vintage Books, 1975), p. 19.

their warm organisms, carry a microbial flora and fauna that break down, ferment, and digest cellulose, proteins, carbohydrates and other such substances that might be done externally in the soil in the warmer latitudes, but here must be done inside the animal organism. The intestinal microorganisms help to bind the nutrients into the manures so that fertility can come to the acidic, starved northern soils.

When one looks at the ruminants, one finds four-chambered stomachs. In the first two chambers, the rumen and the reticulum, chewed plant material is stored and fermented. Bacterial flora by the billions are involved in this pre-digestion. Fiber and roughage cause regurgitation of the food and a further chewing of the cud. Bacteria and protozoa secrete enzymes (cellulase) which break down the glucose-yielding cellulose. Complex acid-base relationships permeate the digestion process. Amino acids, vitamin B12, and fatty acids are synthesized by these microorganisms for the cow. No other animal can make such good use of roughage. Feeding grain, Peruvian sardines, offal, and nitrogen-rich alfalfa to cattle is violating their basic nature and will make these animals sick (scuttles, milk fevers, mad cow disease, etc.) The alimentary tract is richly endowed with nervous tissue, monitoring the digestive process the whole long distance of the alimentary canal. It takes eighteen days for this process to be completed.

It is appropriate to compare the complexity of the cow's digestion to that of the human brain. Whereas in primate fashion our senses are turned outward to the world at large, the seemingly dull cow has its senses turned inward, into its digestion, "meditating" on the forces and energies that are fixed into the vegetable kingdom and liberating these forces during digestion. No wonder the cow is sacred in India, for besides its utilitarian uses, it is the very image of a consciousness turned inward upon itself in deepest meditation. With this in mind, is it any wonder that cow dung, cow manure, has a special healing value for the soil and makes the best compost material imaginable?

It is one of the greatest sins of our time to have severed the cows from the land and placed them into concentrated livestock operations, to have deprived the human being of his association with this beatific beast, and to have chemical salts replace their valuable manure. An average feed lot of 25,000 cattle produces 650 tons of manure daily; its removal is expensive and its storage causes runoff-pollution problems.

Cow manure compost is one of the best for the gardener to acquire. It is best to get the manure from cattle that are fed on local fodder, for the cow's digestive processes produce manure that is hormonally and enzymatically geared to the specific needs of the soils on which the fodder was grown.

Rabbit manures, rich in nitrogen, are good for foliage, stem and shrubbery development. Chicken, pigeon, and other *bird manures* are good for seeds, flowers and fruits, because their manure is rich in phosphorus and complicated *indole* compounds (auxins involved in flower and ovary formations). It is on the perimeter of the generalized plant, on the border of the macrocosmic etheric and astral planes, that the chickens feed as they peck for seeds and scratch for worms and grubs. In this, they feed on the opposite end of the plant from the rooting hogs; they are far enough apart on the food chain that hungry hogs are not adverse to devouring chicken droppings.

Chicken manure, which is sticky, wet, and odorous, is hard to compost. It is best made into a liquid compost by mixing it into ten parts water and letting it ferment in a barrel. This potent brew should be stirred every day. It is ready in about six to eight weeks and makes an excellent liquid fertilizer for the heavy feeders that are to flower, fruit and seed, such as tomatoes, corn, okra, squash or cauliflower.

Sheep and goat manure are excellent for increasing the quality and aroma of fruits and the oil content of herbs. Sheep manure helps the mint family members *(Laminaceae or Labiatae)*, so that it is a good idea to graze sheep in large mint fields where they clean out the weeds and, because of their manure, increase the essential oils of the mint. One can appreciate how sheep and goats fit into the ecology of the Mediterranean region, such as Provence in France, where olives and world-renowned culinary herbs are grown. Other plants rich in oils and etheric oils (e.g. terpineols, phenols, ketones, aldehydes), the mustard oils of the *Cruciferae*, the oils of hemp, flax and other herbs are aided by this manure.

Manures are composted like other substances, with the addition of small amounts of earth, clay, lime, wood ash, rock flours, as well as straw, hay, weeds, or other vegetable matter. For heavier manures, such as cow or hog manure, special care has to be taken to bring air into the compost pile. This can be done by mixing it with straw and other light materials, tossing it with manure forks into a pile so it does not clump as much, or, on farms, setting the manure spreader on "stationary" and running it through onto a pile.

Composted manures aid the garden crop by creating ideal conditions for the edaphon and feeding the soil life, not just by feeding the plant itself. Growing in such a living medium, the plant expresses itself truer to type; the stages of metamorphosis, the rooting, foliage unfolding, flowering and fruiting are more clearly defined. The increased vitality of the plant helps ward off disease and insect troubles.

Liquid Manures

Liquid manures, used in the watering of the heavy-feeders during the growing season or as compost activators, can be made from a number of substances that are placed into a barrel of rainwater or pond water at a ratio of 10:1 and left to ferment for a number of weeks. *Stinging nettle* liquid manure is rich in iron needed for the chlorophyll-formation of green leaves, and helps in the humus buildup of the soil. *Cabbage leaf slurry* aids the sulphur metabolism of the soil. *Comfrey, rich in various minerals (Ca, K, P, Ma) and vitamins, makes an effective liquid manure.*[10] *Chicken and pigeon dung,* as well as *cow pies* can be fermented in water and used for special feeding purposes; the bird slurry for flowers and fruits, the cow manure for aiding root development in general.

Liquid manures, which involve anaerobic fermentation, produce strong odors (sulphur, ammonia and swamp gas smells). To keep the odors at a minimum, it is advisable to stir daily to bring air into the brew and to inoculate with old compost, compost starter, or shredded stinging nettle to help guide the fermentation processes in the right direction. Some gardeners put a floating layer of peat moss, chopped straw, or sawdust on the slurry to absorb the fumes.

---

[10]Gardeners at the abbey at Fulda, Germany, suggest using this comfrey slurry to feed tomatoes. cf. Abtei Fulda, *Comfrey, Was ist das?* (1972).

In the summer, the inch-long sluggish, fat *rat-tailed maggots* of the hovering flies (genus *Eristalis*), which feed upon decaying liquid substances, will develop in these potent brews as an indication that the liquid is biologically ready to be used.

The Composting Process

Just watching what one puts into the compost as ingredients is not enough to ensure its success. The ensuing process itself must be carefully monitored. One can compare this process to the digestion of animals, which is a process similar to composting. The same kind of fodder, such as clover and grass, can be given to a goat, rabbit, horse, or cow. Though the input is the same, the output is different because of dissimilar digestive processes involved. Each will come out with its characteristic manure. Involved are different lengths and shapes of the digestive apparatus, different intestinal flora and secretions, and different time sequences involved in the digestion (18 days for cows, 4 days for horses, etc.). Cow manure is heavy with its distinct, aromatic smell, pig manure is heavy and sour smelling, horse manure is light and gives off ammonia vapors, sheep and goat manures are dry and have their characteristic shape, and so on. In the same way, the compost can end up as a nitrogen-poor, peat-like substance, heavy, dark humus high in ulmic and fulvic acids, or any range in between, depending on how the decomposition has proceeded. In an extreme case, one can lose most of the substance of the compost into the air if the break-down cycle is not accompanied by the buildup cycle, if the bacteria metabolize the carbon into carbon dioxide, the nitrogen into ammonia and

N_2, and the hydrogen and oxygen are given off as water vapor.

For achieving *guided decomposition*, the four elements earth, water, air, and fire must be in a balanced relationship. *Earth* is the solid matter, including the 5% of soil mixed into the compost and the mineral amendments. Too much earthy substance slows the composting processes down. *Water* involves the critical moisture content which is needed by the bacteria in their metabolism. Especially in the earlier composting stages, enough water must be present. The right amount of water is indicated when the compost has the feel of a wrung sponge; when squeezed, it moistens the surface of the hand, but no drops come gushing out. The gardener must keep a check on maintaining this kind of moisture content. Handling the *air* element involves making sure that the compost is not packed too tightly (a shredder helps here), so that oxygen is available for the aerobic bacteria, and keeping one's nose alert to the possible loss of ammonia. The *fire* element involves the initial heating process of the compost, which might reach temperatures of up to 140° to 160° Fahrenheit.

When the composting activity deviates into the direction of the lighter elements, when the compost is too dry, too loose, or has lost moisture during the initial heating phase, it will develop a musty smell, white mildew, and an unusually large number of pill bugs or sow bugs *(Amadillidium vulgare).* If the compost deviates into the direction of the heavier elements, if it is too wet and too compacted, then it will putrefy, develop strong odors, turn black and slimy, and maggots (fly larvae) will appear as the characteristic animal. If the compost is centered and balanced among the elements, then the smell is pleasant, almost like perfume, the

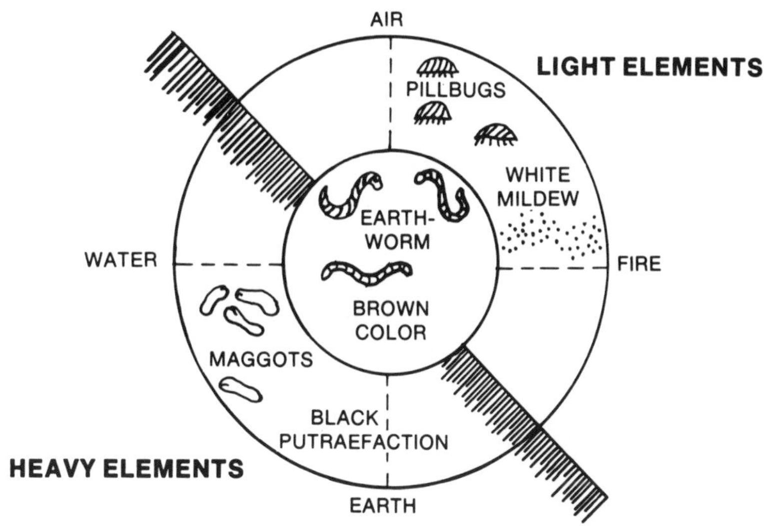

color is rich brown, and the characteristic animal is the manure or compost worm *(Eisenia foetida)*, a close relative of the earthworm. This earthworm species is much more efficient at humifying organic material than the pill bug which works in a drier medium.

In bio-dynamic agriculture, the decomposing processes and the buildup of new substance is not left to circumstance, but special preparations made from common herbs (dandelion, oak bark, nettle, yarrow, chamomile, and valerian) are placed into the compost to guide the processes. This is discussed in detail in the chapter on TEAS, PREPARATIONS AND BIOTIC SUBSTANCES.

The compost carries out life functions and goes through distinct stages. In that sense, we can talk of the compost as a living organism, not the specialized organism of advanced animals, but a very generalized organism like primitive sponges or algae in which the life functions are not centralized. Like all living organisms, it does best when given its characteristic shape, that of the windrow in this case, and a protective membrane, a skin of straw, peat moss or plastic so that the vital odors do not escape. Only composts whose processes have gone awry develop odors, just as only when animals are sick do they develop unpleasant smells.

There are three life stages to this generalized organism, somewhat in analogy to man's lively childhood, adolescence and ripe old-age. The first stage (Stage I) is the *bacteria-fungus stage.* This is still part of the overall breakdown cycle in the revolving "Wheel of Life." Proteins are broken down by bacteria into amino acids and finally ammonia. Carbohydrates are broken down into simple sugars, organic acids, and carbon dioxide. Other compounds are similarly broken down. If this bacterial breakdown were to continue, the organic compounds would be reduced to inorganic substances such as free carbon dioxide, atmospheric nitrogen, sulphur, oxygen, hydrogen, etc. This does not happen, for the buildup cycle meshes right into the breakdown of the original organic substances. The buildup cycle proceeds with fungi, which eagerly ingest the free ammonia and rebuild in their mycelia the amino acids. Stage I is characterized by the generation of much heat given off by energy liberated during metabolism of thermophilic organisms. When one sections a compost at this stage, one can see how the bacteria eat their way into the center of the

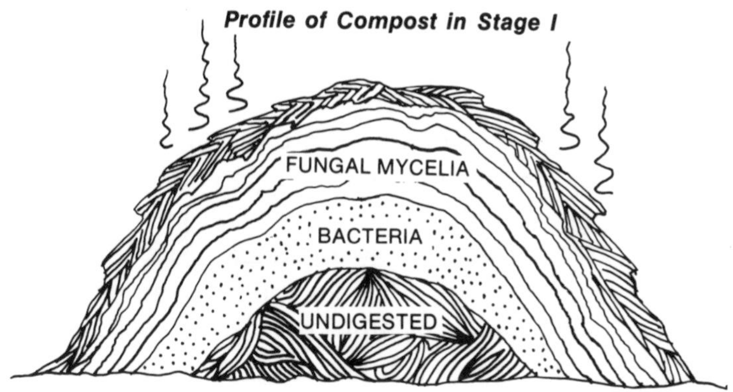

pile, and how they are followed immediately by the whitish mycelia of the fungi which absorb the gases given off. During this stage, the moisture content is critical and must be monitored by the gardener.

The second phase in the compost's life cycle is the *earthworm stage* (Stage II). During this, the adolescence of the compost, the heating has reduced, the heat-loving bacteria have formed spores and the fungi have predigested the organic substances for the earthworms and actinomycetes to work on. If stage I has not gone completely satisfactorily, with undigested, putrid or dry sections in it, this is the time to turn the compost for a brief recapitulation of stage I, causing a brief reheating. If stage I has been completed successfully, no further turning of the compost is necessary.

The earthworms now proceed to mix the organic substances which the fungi have predigested with small amounts of clay in the presence of calcium, within their organisms. In doing so, the polymerized carbon-chains are reconstituted in the form of clay-humus complexes, which absorb cations such as calcium, ammonium, magnesium, potassium, sodium and others.

The as yet little understood clay-humus molecule is more than a simple anion, but also coats itself with phosphates, sulphates and nitrates. In other words, this macro-molecule becomes a sponge for nutrients. Whereas stage I compost would interfere with the growing process of plants, stage II compost can be used already as mulch or as fertilizer for such heavy feeders as cabbages, corn, okra, pumpkins, squashes and melons. At this point of development a number of arthropods, such as centipedes, millipedes and predatory metallic looking carabid beetles start to settle the compost.

For young seedlings and for root crops such as carrots, beets, oyster plants or parsnips, it is better to wait for the compost to reach the *stage of ripeness* or maturity (Stage III), the stage of the humus bacteria and actinomycetes. It is during this stage that the compost turns into good, crumbly, fragrant, humus earth. Nitrates and saltpeter, which are needed by root crops and young sprouting plants are made available by organisms that further oxidize the nitrogen substances.[11]

The speed at which the compost goes through its three stages depends upon extraneous factors such as climate,

---

[11]As there is no coincidence that the words *human* and *humus* are related, and the Bible reminds us that from dust we came and to dust we shall return, we can appreciate the significance of the analogy of three stages of human life, childhood, adolescence and adulthood, to the three stages of humus development. In the first stage, the compost breaks down and completely rebuilds its substance. Humus is a new product, not just rotted organic material. In an analogous fashion, the child, during its first 7 years, will completely exchange its inherited physical substance to build up a new body, signaled by the loss of the milk teeth. The next seven years of the child are a ripening out process until puberty, and the years from puberty to the legal age of 21 at which stage the child is considered mature (L. maturus=ripe). The "salt of thinking" then developed is analogous to the nitrate salts of the compost.

temperature, the size of the pile and the kind of ingredients. The quickest composts, such as Miss Bruce's Quick Return Method or the University of California Method, succeed in making compost in two weeks under ideal conditions.[12] Quick-rotting materials that are shredded to increase the surface area, a narrow C-N ratio supplied by fresh grass clippings, legumes, manure and amendments such as bird manure, blood meal, fish meal, or cottonseed meal, and maintenance of the right quantum of moisture and air by frequent turning result in a usable fertilizer in the shortest time possible. The product basically only goes to stage II, before the earthworms enter. It is doubtful that the clay-humus molecules that account for creating permanent fertility result from this speeded-up process. Quick composts seem to be symptomatic of our age of instant success and instant gratification. The quick composts make good top dressings, and feeding for heavy feeders, but like sheet composting, they do not lead to a permanent buildup of fertility. Ripened composts that have taken six months to a year are more stable. Some composts can even take up to four years and be fitted into four-year fertilizing cycles.

Human Wastes

Human excreta has been used extensively by agricultural people in Asia, Meso-America, Africa and elsewhere. In China, every bit of night soil is collected and turned into fertilizer by fermenting it in pits or composting it. In East Asia, contractors are paid for the privilege of collecting the night soil of the cities, which they in turn sell to the peasants, and privies along country roads are set up so that the traveler

[12]Rodale, *The Complete Book of Composting*, pp. 91-93.

might benefit the farmer with a bit of fertility.[13] Most of these wastes are fermented anaerobically and the slurry is eventually applied to the crops by long-handled dip buckets after a heavy rain. In dry, arid climates, night soil is dried and pulverized, and then is mixed into compost for turning into humus.[14]

In much of the Western world, such practices were not entirely unknown. The runoff wastes of barn and latrine were collected in large pits and utilized by the peasantry who spread them with "honey wagons" and "honey buckets," to fertilize the pastures and fields in late fall or in spring. American pioneers planted fruit trees over outhouse holes when these were full to supply nutrients to the growing tree. With the increased urbanization of the industrial age, disposal became ever more of a problem, and the findings of L. Pasteur and R. Koch about the existence of pathogens in excreta (Anthrax bacilli, tuberculosis bacilli, salmonella, and viruses) led to the development of the sanitary flush toilet. Subsequently, the western world flushes millions of tons of basic fertilizing nutrients into rivers and oceans, while relying increasingly on chemical fertilizers. King cites figures of 5,794,300 pounds of nitrogen, 775,600 pounds of phosphorus, and 1,825,000 pounds of potassium that are produced per annum per million population which, if not returned to the land, are flushed into the ocean.[15]

What about the utilization of human feces and urine in

---

[13]F.H. King, *Farmers of Forty Centuries*, p. 19.

[14]*Ibid.*, p. 257.

[15]*Ibid.*, p. 194.

smaller gardens? Generally, gardeners have not had the need to utilize human excrement because of availability of other manures and organic substances. Bio-dynamic practitioners have avoided the use of human excreta, except within the circulation of matter of the closed, self-sustaining farm organism. Most organisms avoid their own excretions. Cows and horses for example will not eat the grass that sprouts lusciously around their own droppings, but the cow will eat where the horse droppings have fertilized and the horse will cherish the grass benefited by the cow dung. Between the excreta and the consumption of food, a number of conversions and natural cycles must intrude. In the wake of the First World War, when bio-dynamics was pioneered, fertilizer was dear, and raw sewage had been used on the fields surrounding the larger cities, such as Berlin, to close the fertilizer gap. The resultant vegetables, especially the cabbages, had an awful taste. It was then realized that human wastes cannot be used immediately as they are. If, however, they are fully composted, and perhaps passed through other organisms, then they are perfectly good sources of nutrients. Bio-dynamic farms, visited by the author in Switzerland, collected barn runoff and latrine runoff in large cement containers. These containers are treated with the bio-dynamic preparations and stinging nettle cuttings to help them ferment in the right way. The stench of such anaerobic decomposition is avoided by floating a six-inch layer of shredded straw, peat moss or sawdust. The tanks, when filled, are left for two to four years to ferment, while another tank serves as a collecting tank. The resultant slurry is distributed over the pastures, where it completes its cycle by being used by soil organisms and plants. The plants are fed to cattle who close the biological cycle by producing milk.

For smaller gardens, the cycle must be different. The Findhorn garden made use of human wastes in its early stages by emptying night buckets together with straw onto the compost heaps and letting it go through regular decomposition. This seems to have been satisfactory, though it is not such a long cycle.[16] John Todd of the New Alchemy Institute reports of a longer cycle involving a number of organisms to purify sewage. A series of pools are set up through which the sewage circulates. Aquatic plants are grown in the first pool, which are fed to aquatic insect larvae, which feed fish, which in turn are fed to chickens, which in turn feed the humans again. The final runoff is used to irrigate tree crops and lawns.[17]

Composting toilets,[18] such as the Clivus System, the Van der Ryn System, or the Könemann closet,[19] are worth investigating. In any case, a thorough composting process and a long biological cycle must be made use of in order to get the best and most sanitary results. The composting can be done either aerobically, as when dried sludge is composted with other ingredients and goes through a good heating process, or when anaerobic digesters are used which produce methane that can be utilized to fulfill other

---

[16] *The Findhorn Garden*, The Findhorn Community (New York: Harper and Row, 1975), p. 15.

[17] John Todd, "A Modest Proposal: Science for the People," in *Radical Agriculture*. ed. Richard Merrill (New York: Harper and Row Publ., 1976), p. 272.

[18] Clarence G. Golueke, *Biological Reclamation of Solid Wastes* (Emmaus, Penna.: Rodale Press, Inc., 1977), p. 106.

[19] Ewald Könemann, *Düngerstätten, Kompost und Düngersilos* (Berlin: Siebeneicher Verl., 1941).

energy needs, as well as resulting in a fertilizer of sorts.

Humus

The desired end product is, of course, *humus* composed of long-chained molecules which act as a sponge for nutrients and water. Good humus is covered by four molecular layers of water held by excessive electrostatic charge. It has 900% the water-holding capacity of sand. This water becomes available to the plant when it needs it. Humus creates good structure or tilth, and keeps the soil from compacting. The clay-humus complex produces steady fertility. Since it binds the nutrient ions in its macromolecular structure, it is not subject to losing them by volatilization or leaching. Humus is the home of soil organisms, who are a fertilizing factor themselves because of chelation and by adding their bodies to the stock of nutrients when they die. Humus warms the ground more quickly in the spring. Studies show that humus stimulates the sugar production in plants[20] and leads to better oxygen utilization. It results in better seed germination. Vitamin, protein, gluten and carotene contents increase in plants grown in humus as opposed to those grown in soils salted with synthetic NPK. Humus buffers the pH, maintaining the degree of acidity-alkalinity preferred by plants.

There can be no doubt about the central importance of proper humus management to the wellbeing of farm and garden and to man and beast. In view of the fact that in the short span of the last one hundred years, some 60% of the world's humus reserves have been lost, and that the cost of

---

[20]Maria Linder, "Compost," in *Acres, U.S.A.*, April 1975, Vol. 4, No. 5, p. 18.

supplying chemical fertilizers will go up as energy shortages increase, humus management becomes ever more urgent; and composting is the right way to go about it.

CHAPTER XV

COMPANION PLANTING, CROP ROTATION AND WEEDS

It is a basic understanding of organic and bio-dynamic gardening that Nature is an interacting whole. Every part has an effect on every other part. Why should plants growing next to each other in the garden bed not follow this principle? Many gardeners have observed such mutual influences. Scientists have been slow to study these effects because the current scientific methodology has great difficulty isolating and locating the exact interactions and chemicals involved. As we have seen, a similar problem exists in the study of lunar and planetary influences on plants; it is nearly impossible to separate the significant from the insignificant variables and to repeat the exact conditions in experimental settings.

Nonetheless, few scientists deny such interrelationships among plants, and a fledgling field of synecology, plant sociology, and allelochemics (the study of the effects of plant excretions on one another) exists. Research done in the 1930's has been mentioned by Pfeiffer.[1] A pioneering effort on the subject has been undertaken in a booklet called *Companion Plants* by Helen Philbrick and Richard B. Gregg.[2] It is admittedly a primer, not a scientific treatise, but it is useful for the gardener since it lists all the entries in

---

[1]Pfeiffer, *Condensation of Bio-Dynamic Farming and Gardening*, p. 91.

[2]H. Philbrick and R. Gregg, *Companion Plants* (New York: Devin-Adair Co., 1966).

alphabetical order. A similar book has been written by Louise Riotte, *Companion Planting for Successful Gardening.*[3]

What are the reasons for companion plant effects? Different species are accumulators of different substances that are vital within the whole ecology. We all know how legumes function as accumulators of nitrogen, creating beneficial effects for plants growing beside them or following them in rotation. Other plants have other functions within the organic totality. For example, daisies, broom, buckwheat, dandelion and chamomile accumulate calcium, even if growing in calcium-poor soil. Henbane, thornapple, and valerian specialize in phosphoric acid. Foxglove collects Fe, Ca, Si, and Mg. German chamomile collects K and Ca; horsetail is an avid collector of Si; yarrow collects K, Ca, and Si. The list goes on indefinitely.[4] Measurements are hard to specify because some plants increase the percentage of elements with age as the plant grows; others decrease the percentage. Hauschka indicates rhythmical variation during the year and during the lunar cycles. Conditions of the soil substrate influence the chemistry of plants, so that, for example, tobacco is rich in K when it is grown in soil poor in K and vice-versa. Furthermore, the study is complicated by suggestions of elemental transmutations, as researched by Kervran, Hauschka, and Spindler.

---

[3]L. Riotte, *Companion Planting for Successful Gardening* (Charlotte, Vermont: Garden Way Publ., 1975). *The Organic Gardening and Farming Magazine* has published several lists of companion plants, incl. Feb. '77 issue. William H. Hylton writes of "The Companionable Herbs" in the *Rodale Herb Book*. Other good sources for companion plant lists are B. and G. Rateaver, *The Organic Method Primer;* John Jeavons, *How to Grow More Vegetables* (Palo Alto, 1974); Koepf, Petterson, Schaumann, *Bio-Dynamic Agriculture* (1976).

[4]B. and G. Rateaver, *The Organic Method Primer,* chap. 5, p. 78.

Plants are not passively at the mercy of their environment, but actively engaged in selecting and rejecting nutrients, sending root hairs throughout the soil and then dying back, altering the soil in the process and providing specific conditions for the myriad of microorganisms, which in turn alter the chemistry of the soil. These biological processes make use of mechanical laws such as diffusion, osmosis and so forth, but much of it occurs contrary to purely mechanistic laws, just as plant growth itself counters the law of gravity. As the great Dutch botanist Hugo de Vries pointed out in 1905, the chemical combination of the plant does not conform to that of the soil or water in which it grows, and sometimes the variation in two adjacent plants is very great.

Not just the elements are accumulated and given off by specific plants, but also complex compounds such as amino acids, hormones, enzymes, auxins, growth inhibitors and others, not all of which have as yet been discovered. These biotic substances are given off into the surroundings of the plant as the perfume or pollen of the flowers, as essential oils by the leaves, by excretions of the roots, by the discarding of dying plant tissue and they are carried in insect droppings or by insect go-betweens, as is the pollen by the bees. Sometimes the quantities given off are minute, occurring in homeopathic dosage or at the rate of trace minerals. A few years ago, such incredibly small quantities would have been scorned as ineffective, but now it is known that some elements, even when removed to a distance, have an effect on the living organism of a plant.[5] Plants, especially herbs, as they give off minute substances that alter soil flora

[5]Pfeiffer, *Condensation of Bio-Dynamic Farming and Gardening*, p. 95.

and other plants, work within the ecology of the soil much like the endocrine glands within the microcosm of the animal organisms, by regulating metabolism, reproduction and other life functions by minute chemical programmers. Since we are dealing with a macrocosmic process, the effects are not as compact as they would be in a more specialized organism. The companion effect can be created by purposeful planting of certain species next to each other, or, sometimes, by the administration of herb teas and ferments to the soil. Companion plant effects are probably more widespread than we realize. One need only look at fields, meadows and forests to realize that some species prefer to grow with specific others, fitting together like pieces of a jigsaw puzzle. Up until the dawn of ecological studies, our biological science labored under the assumption that the first law in nature is the struggle for survival and the survival of the fittest. We have seen that this dog-eat-dog idea is more a projection of the conditions created by industrialization and class struggle, than it is a true understanding of biology. Why should plants not have evolved for mutual benefit? As the conservationist Joseph Cocannouer shows so effectively, even weeds, having evolved right along with horticultural practices, often have beneficial companion effects; they are not just mean competitors for nutrients.[6]

Flowers make good companion plants, also, besides adding beauty to the vegetable garden. The suggestion has been made that flower saps keep predators alive when pests are in low supply. The predators of sugar-sap secreting

---

[6]Joseph A. Cocannouer, *Weeds, Guardians of the Soil* (New York: Devin Adair Company, 1964).

aphids are kept around the garden by having flower nectars available.[7] Borders of aromatic herbs keep hungry insects away from crop plants, possibly because the fragrance masks the odor of the other plants. Other companion plants distract the insects from the crops.

As Alan Chadwick points out concerning the effects and influences of plants upon one another, here, too, it is the craft of the gardener to create "relationships and dis-relationships" by planting some plants together and avoiding others.

Many native horticulturists have been aware of companion planting and have incorporated it into their agricultural lore. F. H. King reports examples of "multiple crops" in the Far East, such as wheat, windsor beans and cotton, or alternating rows of beans and millet.[8] Other examples are cited in ethnographic accounts, but much more research could be done in this area. Famous are the combinations of the American Indian companion cropping of corn, beans, squash, often with amaranth and a number of weeds that served as soup greens. The anthropologist Clifford Geertz tells of the almost "uncanny imitation" of the natural ecosystem of many swidden horticulturists: "The swidden plot is not a field at all in the proper sense, but a miniaturized tropical forest composed mainly of food producing and other cultivates."[9] Of the Tsembaga of New

---

[7]William H. Hylton, "The Companionable Herbs," in *The Rodale Herb Book*, p. 225.

[8]F. H. King, *Farmers of Forty Centuries* (Emmaus, Pennsylvania: Rodale Press, Inc., 1911, reprint).

[9]Clifford Geertz, "Two Types of Ecosystems," in *Environment and Cultural Behavior*, ed. A. P. Vayda (Garden City, New York: Natural History Press, 1969), p. 14.

Guinea, anthropologist Roy Rappaport writes about the use of companion and succession planting that results in maximum utilization of sun energy by the leaves, protection of soil against washing out even on hillsides, discouragement of insects, and the availability of alternative food supply if one crop does not yield. The jungle-like atmosphere is recreated when he writes: "A mat of sweet potato leaves covers the soil at ground level. The taro leaves project over this mat; the hibiscus, sugarcane and pitpit stand higher still, and the fronds of the banana spread out above the rest."[10]

As a final example of interplanted gardens, we read the description of a typical Guatemalan garden as seen by a botanist:

> The garden I charted was a small affair about the size of a small city lot in the United States. It was covered with a riotous growth so luxuriant and so apparently planless that any ordinary American or European visitor accustomed to the puritanical primness of north European gardens would have supposed (if he even chanced to realize that it was indeed a garden) that it must be a deserted one. Yet when I went through it carefully I could find no plants which were not useful to the owner in one way or another. There were no noxious weeds, the return per man-hour of effort was apparently high. . .[11]

He goes on to describe the great variety of plants complete with fruit trees, shrubs, flowers, vegetables and bee hives,

---

[10]Roy A. Rappaport, "The Flow of Energy in an Agricultural Society," in *Scientific American* 225, p. 121.

[11]Edgar Anderson, *Plants, Man, and Life* (Boston: Little, Brown, and Co., 1952), p. 137.

stating that though it was on a slope, there was no problem of erosion because of the intertangled root systems, pests and diseases were checked because individuals of the same plant species were separated by other plants, and there was high efficiency in terms of production per pound of vegetables and fruits per man-hour per square foot. "In terms of American or European equivalents the garden was a vegetable garden, a medical garden, a dump heap, a compost heap, and a bee yard."[12]

The bio-dynamic, French-intensive method of gardening as taught by Alan Chadwick has reintroduced such high energy gardening into the temperature latitudes.[13]

A Few Good Companion Plant Combinations

Since other books have been written on the subject, only a partial listing of companions is made here. These were gathered by observant gardeners and gleaned from tradition.

Cabbage grows good with bush beans, is aided by border plantings of dill and chamomile, and when interplanted with hemp *(Cannibas sativa),* it has less problems with the cabbage moth. Fall cabbage will do well when preceded by early potatoes.

Beans grow well with almost everything, especially cucumbers, strawberries, early potatoes, cabbage, and celery.

Celery and any member of the umbellifer family, such as carrots, parsnips, hamburg parsley, and celeriac, will

[12]*Ibid.*, p. 140.

[13]Jeavons, *How to Grow More Vegetables* (1974).

grow well with any member of the lily family, such as onion, shallots, garlic and leeks. Carrots and leeks grown together will discourage carrot fly and onion fly. Carrots are good to grow after flax, which loosens the soil. A combination of onion, lettuce and carrot makes an excellent early bed.

Corn combines well with beans, squash and cucumbers.

Cucumbers grow well with corn and lettuce.

Herbs make good companions for all vegetables. Stinging nettle increases the volatile oils of mints.

Kohlrabi grows well with beets and onions.

Leek grows best with celeriac or celery, because both like potash fertilizer and require the same amount of care. Woodashes and composted pig manure provide K.

Lettuce does well when interplanted with carrots, radishes, strawberries or cucumbers.

Onions are good with beets, lettuce, beans and any member of the carrot family.

Peas grow well with radishes, carrots, cucumbers, spinach, and turnips.

Potatoes grow well with beans, cabbage and peas. A border of horseradish and hemp is beneficial.

Radish likes nasturtium, chervil and peas.

Spinach grows well with strawberries.

Swiss chard can be interplanted with cabbage and endives.

Tomatoes like New Zealand spinach, parsley and basil as a ground cover. They also grow well near a row of asparagus.

Turnips grow well with peas.

Some plants do *not* make good companions. The vegetable Florence fennel is unsocial and likes to have the bed all for itself, although the author has grown good carrots among the fennel. Carrots do not like dill. Onions do not go well with peas and beans. Potatoes become stunted when sunflowers or Jerusalem artichokes are grown with them, and they do not like cucumbers.

Surprisingly enough, often what tastes good together when cooked into a meal also makes for good companion planting. For example, good food or planting combinations are beans and savory; beets and onions; cabbage and dill; carrots and leeks; corn and beans (succotash) or peas; tomatoes and parsley or basil; lettuce with carrots, onions and radishes; horseradish and potatoes; etc. Of course, this rule, like so many other rules in gardening, cannot be absolutized.

Intercropping

Intercropping is similar to companion planting in that several species are planted into the same bed, but the purpose is less that of mutual symbiotic effects than that of maximum utilization of garden space. A main crop, such as cabbage, bush beans, squash, etc., that takes a long time to mature is interplanted with quick-growing, quick-maturing crops, such as loose-leaf lettuce, kohlrabi, radishes, garden cress, or spinach. The secondary crop will be harvested before the main crops spread out to fill the space, or they are hoed into the ground as green manure. Another kind of intercropping is practiced when a tall growing crop is grown with a low, crawling plant which will provide ground cover, spinach under tomatoes, or squash underneath pole beans.

The *staggering* of crops refers to making sowings or plantings of the same species at different times of the year, such as lettuce and radishes which can be sown out every month before it gets too hot. This can be worked into a system of intercropping and companion planting.

The gardener must keep good records in his diary of each of these sowings, in order to work out the best combinations and rotations for his particular situation.

Crop Rotation

Just as companion planting is in keeping with the natural plant associations, so crop rotation makes use of the principle of natural *plant succession.* A landslide or a freshly bulldozed plot will quickly be settled by fleabane, nightshade, docks, mulleins, Queen Anne's Lace and other annuals and biennials. These first-aid plants hold the soil and keep it from being washed or blown away, working much like scar tissue on a body. Next in the succession are the tightly-matted thorns and brambles guarding the ground, warning us, "sorry, you cannot go through here now; but here, don't be angry, have some berries!" Amidst the shade and protection of the brambles, trees make a start, quick-growers like willows or cottonwoods, or, in drier areas, manzanita and sugar pine. Many decades later the climax forest reestablishes itself. Such is a natural succession, as one might find in Oregon.

In the garden the induced succession is not as elaborate, but it, too, follows its own laws, involving crops and weeds. An abundance of nasty weeds, or of a singular species of weed, tells us that the soil has been treated one-sidedly. The weeds are a sign that the earth wants a change to redress the one-sidedness.[14] Lambsquarters will take over land that is tired of potatoes, for instance. A season of weeds makes a good fallow to restore a balance, a practice made use of in the three-field system of the Middle Ages.

There are several rotational plans that may be followed by the gardener. One is to identify the *heavy feeders,* consisting mainly of leaf crops (e.g. cabbage, lettuce, Swiss chard, spinach, celery, leeks, corn, cucumbers, squash and nightshades such as tomatoes, eggplant, peppers); the *soil improvers,* consisting of nitrogen-fixing legumes (peas, beans, broad or fava beans); and the *light feeders,* consisting mainly of root crops (carrots, beets, parsnips, hamburg parsley, rutabaga, turnips, onions, Jerusalem artichokes). The rotational cycle starts with heavy feeders planted in freshly fertilized soil (compost in stage II or III). After they are harvested the soil is given a rest with a leguminous crop which fiberizes the soil and restores some of the nitrogen. Then the light feeders may be sown in, with a dressing of very ripe compost (stage III), to complete the cycle. A weed fallow, or a crop of completely unrelated plants such as a bee pasture of phacelia, flax or buckwheat, which are not ordinarily in the rotation, may follow; or the cycle can be started again immediately.

Another plan of rotation is similar but starts from different considerations. In order that the entire four-fold plant finds expression in the garden so that the four ethers are harmoniously balanced, one should plant root, leaf, flower and fruit-seed crops. A bed starts out in the first season with *leaf crops* which are mainly heavy feeders, fol-

[14]E. Pfeiffer, *Weeds and What They Tell* (Springfield, Ill.: Bio-Dynamic Farming & Gardening Assn., 1976).

lowed by *flowers* which are beautiful and easy on the soil, followed by *seed and fruit crops,* including legumes, and, finally, in the fourth season, followed by *root crops* which include most of the light feeders. In essence this method is not much different from the first one mentioned, though it may be easier to remember.

One more consideration enters the planning of functional rotations. One must know the plant families to which the crops belong, so that members of the same family are not planted on top of one another. Family members tend to have the same nutritional needs and would wear the soil one-sidedly if planted in succession. It is surprising that out of the many thousands of plant families, only a mere dozen or so have chosen to let themselves be cultivated by man. The following is a list of some of the common vegetables and the family affiliation.

Families of Cultivated Vegetable Plants

I. Monocots

1. *Grasses (Gramineae)* include the staples upon which the civilizations of the world are built such as wheat, barley, oats, rye, millet, and rice. Of importance for the gardener are Indian corn *(Zea mais)* and oats and rye that are grown with vetch or peas as a winter cover-crop.

2. *Lily family (Liliaceae)* includes onions *(Allium cepa),* garlic *(A. sativum),* leeks *(A. porrum),* chives *(A. schoenprasum)* and asparagus *(Asparagus officinalis).* In folklore, plants of this family are considered pure and sacred. Their innocence is shown by the white of the flowers, so that Gabriel is shown holding a lily at the Annunciation. Liliaceae do not make wooden parts, indicating that

they have not descended into matter to the degree that the red, thorny rose has, which was thought of as their opposite during the Middle Ages. These plants can take cold weather. Leeks and asparagus are heavy feeders.

II. Dicots

1. *Crossbearers, or Mustard Family (Cruciferae),* named after the flower petals which arrange themselves in a cross, are cold weather plants, heavy feeders who like plenty of moisture, and include the following members: The *cabbages (Brassica)* spring from a Mediterranean weed *(Brassica maritima),* hence their ability to tolerate a "seashore" environment of a "salty" soil, fairly fresh manure and lots of moisture. Thanks to their content of mustard oils and sulphury essences, the brassica do well in northwestern Europe, a region with so little sunshine that the indigenous people have evolved light skin, blue eyes and fair hair in response. All through this region are eaten kale, sauerkraut cabbage, head cabbage, red cabbage, savoy cabbage, collards, cauliflower, broccoli, brussel sprouts, kohlrabi, turnip *(B. rapa)* and rutabagas, or swedes *(B. napobrassica).* From the Far East are added pe-tsai and pak-choi *(B. chinensis).* Other crossbearers include the horseradish with its pungent root *(Cochlearia Armoracia);* the scurvy grass *(Cochlearia officinalis)* which makes an excellent spring tonic; the garden radish *(Raphanus sativus);* garden cress *(Lepidium sativum)* used as a soil and compost tester; the water cress *(Nasturtium officinale)* and mustard *(Sinapis alba)* that is used for its seeds or grown for greens. One is amazed at the plasticity of this family; from root through stem, leaves, bud, flower to seed, every part

The Archetypal Brassica

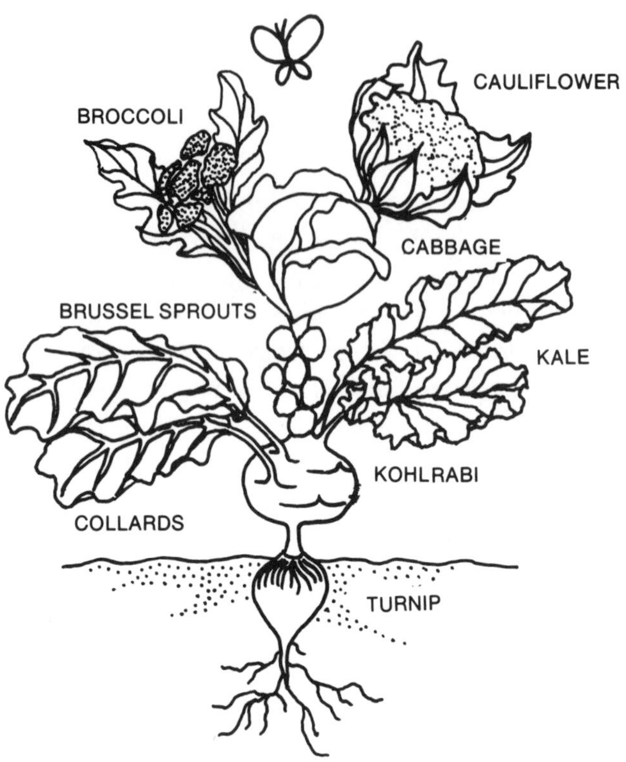

has a use for man. Common garden weeds of the cross-bearers include shepherd's purse, charlock, penny grass, bittercress, wild radish and others.

2. *The Pea or Butterfly-flower Family (Leguminosae)* includes the beans *(Phaseolus)*, many of which, such as the lima, kidney, navy, pinto, blackeyed, wax and scarlet runner *(P. multiflorus)*, originated in the gardens of the American Indians; the broad, fava, or horse bean *(Vicia faba)* which, like vineyards, was carried wherever the Roman army went;

and the soybean *(Glycine max)* from China. The leguminosae include the pea *(Pisum sativum)* found already in the neolithic lake-dwellings in Switzerland; the snow peas; the garbanzos or chick peas *(Cicer arietinum)*;[15] the vetches *(Vicia)* that make good winter cover-crops; and the clovers which feed out livestock and bees.

Legumes are characterized by astrality that penetrates through the plant into the roots where the nitrobacter form. Unlike most other plants that reach the culmination of their growth when flowers indicate contact with the astral realm, the legumes continue growing while below, at the same time, they are flowering and making seed. Most plants which have astrality reaching so deeply into their organization would become poisonous, like many nightshades, but legumes turn it into usable protein. Pythagoras warns, however, that the enjoyment of legumes will create insensitivity to subtler forms of thought,[16] and in the Bible Esau sells his birthright for a pot of lentils, indicating that the enjoyment of legumes has its effect on the psyche (astrality) of the human being also.

3. *The Carrot Family (Umbelliferae or Apiaceae),* a family that gives us some of our important root crops, herbs and medicines, is characterized by its openness to light etheric forces. Slender stems that radiate into numerous branches which, in turn, radiate into myriads of tiny flowers (umbels), are accompanied by lacy, feathery leaves whose

[15]The great Roman poet Tulli became known as Cicero, because of a prominent wart the size of a chick pea (ciser).

[16]The French call dumb people "haricots" (beans), the Germans say that a dullard is as "dumb as bean straw," and the English label the same "full of beans."

substance seems to have melted away in the sun. The light seems to shoot through the plant, creating bright, fragrant roots that are rich in vitamins and sugars. Such is the characteristic of the carrot (*Daucus carota*); the parsnip (*Pastinaca sativa*); hamburg, or root, parsley (*Petroselinum crispum*); celeriac, or root celery (*Apium graveolens*); and also the fragrant stems and foliage of the Florence fennel (*Foeniculum sativum*); celery stalks (*Apium rapaceum*); dill (*Anethum graveolens*); chervil (*Anthriscus cerefolium*); parsley (*Petroselinum sativum*); herb fennel (*Foeniculum vulgare*); and lovage (*Levisticum officinale*). The numerous seed herbs, containing essential oils, include coriander (*Coriandrum sativum*); anise (*Pimpinella anisum*); caraway (*Carum carvi*) and others. The root of the angelica (*Angelica archangelica*), or angelwort, has such vitalizing medicinal properties, that the folklore of many nations considers this plant to be sacred and a protector from many evils. Most of these plants are light feeders and can take cool weather.

The umbellifers include also some strongly poisonous plants, such as the poison hemlock, or hellock (*Conium maculatum*), whose infusion was the death drink of Socrates; water hemlock (*Cicuta maculata*), fool's parsley (*Aethuas cynapium*); cow parsnip (*Heracleum lanatum*) and others that the gardener ought to recognize for they can occur as weeds in the garden.[17] The wild carrot, or Queen Anne's Lace, is a common weed of this family.

4. *The Goosefoot Family* (*Chenopodiaceae*), providing leaf and root vegetables, is involved in sal processes as

---

[17] For reference on poisonous plants, see Walter Conrad Muenscher, *Poisonous Plants of the United States* (New York: Macmillan Company, 1958).

indicated by the fact that these plants collect salts and sugars. The chenopod family includes red beets (*Beta vulgaris esculenta*); Swiss chard (*Beta vulgaris cicla*); sugar beet (*B. vulgaris altissima*); mangle (*B. vulgaris*); spinach (*Spinacia oleracea*); orach (*Atriplex hortensis*), which has a salty taste; and Good King Henry (*Chenopodium Bonus Henricus*). Lambsquarters and saltwort are weeds belonging to this family.

5. *The Nightshade Family* (*Solanaceae*), which includes the potato (*Solanum tuberosum*): the tomato (*Solanum lycopersicum*), the eggplant (*Solanum melongena*); the chiles, peppers and paprikas (*Capsicum*); the ground cherries, or husk tomatoes (*Physalis*); and the tomatillo (*Lycium pallidum*) used to make green taco sauce, have derived, for the most part, from the warmer regions of the Americas. These often rank-growing plants with their colorful fruits indicate an eagerness on the part of the plant to take astrality into itself. This is indicated by the fact that some of our strongest psychotropic poisons and alkaloids are derived from the nightshade family, such as tobacco (*Nicotiana tabacum*): black and bittersweet nightshade (*Solanum nigrum, S. dulcamara*): and the inevitable ingredients in the witches brew, the thorn apple (*Datura stramonium*), belladonna (*Atropa belladonna*) and the black henbane (*Hyoscyamus niger*). A common weed is the horse nettle (*S. carolinense*) which is poisonous. Even the potato when it is green contains solanin, a poisonous alkaloid. A flower of this family, the petunia, which is not poisonous, has been used as a companion plant for potatoes.

The first potato was grown in Europe in 1588 by the botanist Celsius. In a sense, the potato marks the beginning of the age of materialism in Europe, at which time the gentry forced the peasantry to grow potatoes because they seemed so much larger than the traditional grains. The Irish were forced to grow potatoes to feed the burgeoning industrial cities. Failures of the potato monocrops in Europe, especially in Ireland, caused millions of peasants to settle the New World.

Except for potatoes, which originate in the cool, foggy slopes of the Andes, most of the nightshades prefer warm weather and are heavy feeders.

6. *The Gourd Family (Cucurbitaceae)* is at home in a warm, moist atmosphere with rich soil. It includes many gourds, melons *(Cucumis melo);* cucumbers *(Cucumis sativus);* pumpkins *(Cucurbita pepo);* squashes *(Cucurbita specis);* watermelons *(Citrullus vulgaris),* originating in Africa; and the prolific zucchini *(C. pepo)* developed by the craft of Italian horticulturists.

7. *The Composite Family (Compositae)* blesses humanity with numerous flowers, medicines and foods. The composites represent the culmination of the evolution in dicots with their complex flower heads, which are composed of many individual flowers, finely arranged into a head. Each little flower is complete, yet it is part of a greater whole, so that it could well symbolize to humanity a harmonious society. The vegetables of this family include all the lettuces *(Lactuca sativa);* the summer endive *(L. sativa lonifolia);* the winter endive *(Cichorium endivia);* the sugarhat *(Cichorium);* and the witlof *(C. intybus);* furthermore, the sunflower *(Helianthus annuus);* the Jerusalem artichoke *(H. tuberosus);* the globe artichoke *(Cynara Scolymus);* the cardoon *(C. cardunculus)* which is an edible thistle; the oyster plant, or salsify *(Tragopogon porrifolius);* the

Spanish oyster plant *(Scolymus hispanicus);* and the black salsify *(Scorzonera hispanica).*

This family includes the dandelion, chamomile, and yarrow that are medicinal herbs and are used in the biodynamic preparations. It includes such medical plants as the arnica *(Arnica montana),* a tincture for wounds; the mugwort and wormwood *(Artemisia vulgaris and* A. *absinthium);* tarragon *(A. dracunculus);* marigold *(Calendula officinalis);* and many others. Common weeds of this family include the groundsel *(Senecio vulgaris);* the giant burdock *(Arctium lappa)* and the common burdock *(A. minus);*[18] all thistles *(Cirsium* and *Carduus)* belong to this family, as does the sowthistle *(Sonchus);* the hawkweed *(Hieracium);* the goldenrod *(Solidago);* the asters *(Aster);* fleabane *(Erigeron);* dog fennel, field chamomile and pineapple weeds *(Anthemis* and *Matricaria);* the ragweed *(Ambrosia);* the frenchweed *(Galinsoga);* wild lettuce, or compass plant, which sets its leaves in a north-south position, and numerous others.

The preceding plants constitute most of our vegetable species. Other families that have made minor contributions include the *buckwheat family (Polygonaceae)* which provides us with rhubarb, buckwheat, and sour dock, as well as knotweeds, smartweeds, docks and sorrels; the *morning glory family (Convolvulaceae)* which supplies us with sweet potatoes, yams, beautiful heavenly blues and pearly gates, and the bindweed; the *mallow family (Malvaceae)* provides us with okra or gumbo as a vegetable, besides mallows and

---

[18]The Japanese have bred an edible burdock called *takinogawa.* (Seeds are available at Nichol's Garden Nursery, 1190 North Pacific Hwy, Albany, Oregon 97321.)

hollyhocks; the *nettle family (Urticaceae)* includes stinging nettle, hops, hemp, as well as mulberries and slippery elm; the *pokeweed family (Phytolaccaceae)* is responsible for poke greens; the *carpet weed family (Aizoaceae)* provides New Zealand spinach; the *amaranth family (Amaranthaceae)* provides the pigweed whose crop of nutritious seeds Rodale is trying to introduce to North Americans. Most of our fruits and berries, the blackberries, raspberries, cherries, plums, apples, strawberries, quinces, and rose hips belong to the *rose family (Rosaceae);* although the goose berries and red and black currants that grace the borders of our gardens belong to the *saxifrage family (Saxifragaceae).* Most of our herbs, which are important in the garden, though they are not vegetables, belong to the *mint family (Labiatae)* and include mint, garden sage, oregano, marjoram, thyme, rosemary, basil, lemon balm, bergamot, savory and others.

Weeds

Like the insects, weeds have caused a lot of thoughtless reactions, providing targets for misplaced fixations about cleanliness. Some "gardeners" are fanatic about keeping weeds out of the garden, as though they were dread enemies and use strong herbicides that not only wreck the garden ecology, but prove to be adverse to human health, as well. This paranoid attitude even finds its way into the literature where, for instance, it is written of the sheep sorrel *(Rumex acetosella):*

> Sheep sorrel is a communist. It waves the red flag wherever it moves in, and it moves in wherever it finds the democratic grasses struggling against adverse con-

> ditions. Small though it is, its snakelike rootstalks crawl under and among the grass roots and send up new "reds" among the grass bunches.[19]

Often a xenophobic attitude is revealed, as when a naturalist writes of noxious weeds as aliens that have been naturalized.[20] These aliens must be dealt with in a drastic way, for they are suspected of harboring plant pests, lowering the economic value of the crop, "their rank growth and unsightliness" is a "perpetual nuisance in turf," they are a safety hazard, poisonous, and cause hay fever.[21] The latter statements are from a popular textbook of horticulture.

Viewed objectively, what are weeds? They are the primary succession of plants where the soil has been disturbed. Usually, they are followed by grasses or brambles. They are indicators of poor soil, showing the observant gardener whether his soil is getting too poor, too acidic, too compacted or too alkaline.[22] Weeds do not, for instance, drive the grass out of a pasture; they merely come in and fill the gap when the soil will no longer support the grass. Thus, weeds are symptoms and not causes of our problems. Spraying for weeds is, again, putting the cart before the horse. Weeds will appear in abundance only if the conditions are right, the seeds lay dormant in the soil until such a time. For example, the fireweed and some fleabanes sprout

---

[19]Edwin Rollin Spencer, *All About Weeds* (New York: Dover Publications, Inc., 1974), p. 83.

[20]Eugene N. Koxloff, *Plants and Animals of the Pacific Northwest* (Seattle: U. of Wash. Press, 1976), p. 184.

[21]Jules Janick, *Horticultural Science* (San Francisco: W. H. Freeman & Co., 1963), p. 259.

[22]E. Pfeiffer, *Weeds and What They Tell*, pp. 11-17.

only after a fire has gone over the ground, others germinate when the land has been plowed, and some germinate only when there are specific planetary constellations.[23] "Analyses of soil in fields have shown that a square foot of soil down to the depth of plowing may contain 7,000 viable seeds representing a number of species."[24] These seeds are waiting for specific conditions before they will grow. By maintaining good soil husbandry, these weeds need not be a problem at all. If the soil does go out of kilter, it might even be a good idea to include a fallow of weeds to restore a balance of the soil organisms and soil nutrients.

Joseph Cocannouer, in his *Weeds: Guardians of the Soil,* speaks of weeds as a blessing in disguise. Weeds are deep-rooters; they explore the depths, breaking through the plow sole so that the weaker roots of the domesticated species may follow, providing them with a larger feeding zone. Weeds, because of their deep-rooting systems, pump up nutrients that have been leached out. They fiberize the soil, countering compaction. During rainy or windy seasons they hold the soil against erosion. They help bring water to the topsoil by the capillary action of water molecules along their roots. They aid the organisms of the edaphon through exudations and chelates. When harvested, they enrich the compost with minerals and nutrients and, in the pasture, they provide sources of vitamins for livestock, resulting in fewer veterinarian bills. Following the lead of F. C. King, Cocannouer suggests letting select weeds grow in the gar-

---

[23]Maria Thun, *Work on the Land and the Constellations,* p. 21: "There is very high weed germination from a soil that is worked when the moon is in Leo."

[24]Rexford Daubenmire, *Plant Communities* (New York: Harper & Row, 1968), p. 170.

den to serve as "mother weeds" for domesticated crops. Mother weeds, such as sowthistle, lambsquarters, annual nightshade, ground cherry or ragweed, will let the roots of the domesticates grow alongside into the deeper horizons, making water and nutrients available to them. Other weeds can be hoed and left as green manure, while still other weeds, such as purslane and chickweed will provide a living mulch for the taller crop plants.

According to Alan Chadwick, healthy weeds, properly managed, create an aura of vigor and health in the garden. He sows as a cover crop a mixture of fava, vetch, sow thistle, rye, groundsel, scarlet pimpernel, veronica, plantain, and others.

According to Robert Rodale, there is experimental evidence that weeds act as insect controlling factors. In a South American study it was shown that weeds among corn reduce the leafhopper by 40 to 53% and the cutworms by 68%.[25] This, of course, involves the principle of companion plants.

Weeds also aid the soil fauna. Dying root and leaf parts feed the earthworm and the channels left by the deeper roots provide passage tunnels for the earthworms as they travel from the higher to the lower horizons of the soil.

Bargyla Rateaver lists the following companion plant effects of weeds in her *Organic Gardening Primer*:[26] Weeds that are soil improvers because they either absorb excess salts and bind them organically or they fiberize the soil, include goldenrod, nightshade, ragweed, purslane and

---

[25]Robert Rodale, "Making Enemies into Friends," in *OGF Magazine (Feb. 1977), p. 58.*

[26]Rateaver, *Organic Gardening Primer,* p. 91.

shepherd's purse. Weeds that hold the soil against erosion include ragweed, pigweed, and clovers. Weeds that attract earthworms and aid the soil with root exudates include stinging nettle, plantain, dandelion and thistles. Other weeds work directly as companion plants, such that bindweed helps corn; nettle and yarrow improve the volatile oils in herbs; jimson weed helps pumpkin; lambsquarters and sowthistle aid cucumbers and melons; mustard is good under grapes; dandelion helps strawberries; nettles aid the tomatoes; pigweed *(Amaranth)* is good with all the nightshades (potato, pepper, eggplant and tomato); purslane is a good mulch for corn; whereas sowthistle, yarrow, dead nettle and valerian are good for all vegetables in general.

Thus it makes good sense to know one's weeds and use them in a dynamic way. It is mainly during the spring sowing that the germinating weeds must be kept in check, so that they do not smother the crop plants. This is done by working the soil about two weeks before planting, letting the weeds sprout, then cultivating again before sowing in the seed. Regular hoeing during the early growing season and hand picking within the rows will keep the weeds down between the rows. After the cultivated varieties are strong enough, one can mulch and the weeds should not be a problem. If they are a problem, then the soil is most likely one-sided in an unhealthy way. The few weeds that make it despite mulching, should be welcomed as mother weeds or as edible weeds. Grasses, which form a succession to the weeds, must be kept out of the garden, for they feed in the same rooting zone as the domesticated species and can be real competitors.

Instead of chemical warfare, flame throwers, and

hysterical reactions, one can enjoy the weeds and even eat most of them, as Ben Harris suggests in a book called *Eat Your Weeds.* Cocannouer writes that many Indians made no linguistic distinctions between weeds and "good" plants, so that the Indian women cultivated the weeds as pot greens and medicines right along with the vegetable crops. The eating of weeds has a long tradition. The stomach and intestinal contents of the Tollund man who was preserved in a Danish bog after having been sacrificed to Odin some 2,000 years ago, shows a last meal consisting of a gruel made from barley, linseed, camelina sativa, knotweed, and many different weeds associated with cultivated land, including bristle grass, dock, black bindweed and chamomile. The Grauballe man, another iron age sacrifice preserved in the peat muck, contained a spring-time menu of clover goosefoot, buttercup, lady's mantle, black nightshade, yarrow, wild chamomile, smooth hawks-beard and nearly sixty others.[27]

Good, common, edible weeds that are found in most gardens include burdock (*Arctium lappa*); curly dock (*Rumex crispus*); dandelion (*Taraxacum officinale*): lambsquarters (*Chenopodium album*); milkweed (*Asclepias*): peppergrass (*Lepidium*); purslane (*Portulaca oleracea*), which used to be grown as a vegetable in cloister gardens; sorrel (*Oxalis*); sowthistle (*Sonchus oleraceus*): pigweed (*Amaranthus*); plantain (*Plantago*); chickweed (*Stellaria media*); wild mustard (*Brassica arvensis*); gill-over-the-ground (*Glechoma hederaceae*): and many others. Some of these are eaten raw in salads, some must be cooked and others have only some

---

[27] P.V. Glob, *The Bog People* (New York: Ballantine Books, 1975).

edible parts. It goes beyond the scope of this book to go into further detail. Care must be taken to identify also those weeds, such as the hemlock, that are poisonous.

CHAPTER XVI

INSECTS AND OTHER BEASTIES

There is much paranoia these days about the multitudes of six-legged, eight-legged, or thousand-legged fellow inhabitants of our earth. The appearance of a few bugs in the garden often causes a hysterical reaction, even to the point recently reported in a newspaper of a gardener who sprayed so much that he was found dead among his cabbages from a self-inflicted overdose of chemicals. Hysterical spraying is just another sign of people alienated from the actual workings of nature. It amounts to a fear reaction that leaves little room for calm observations.

This fear is fed by the chemical industry which sells a $700,000,000.00 product annually. Pesticide sales rose by 169% from the years 1952 to 1968 in America.[1] Vested interests fan the hysteria through mass media by showing defoliated fields and forests, by computing fantastic projections of the reproductive capabilities of insects,[2] and suggesting clever sayings such as "The only good bug is a dead bug," or "Raid kills 'em dead." Entomologists working with the chemical companies write chilling reports in a clinical language that, covertly or overtly, gives way to the most life-

[1]V. G. Dethier, *Man's Plague: Insects and Agriculture* (Princeton, New Jersey: Darwin Press, Inc., 1976), p. 86.

[2]For example, that a single pair of flies, if unhampered, would have offspring so thick that it would form a tightly-packed sphere of flies 96 million miles in diameter (more than the distance to the sun) within a year's time, is reported in the Life Nature Library, *The Insects* (New York: Time: Life Books, 1968), p. 108.

negating, sadistic fantasies that man is capable of. Echoes of Cotton Mather and other puritanical fanatics are conjured up in such statements as, "It is either us or the insects!"

The attitudes toward the insect are those of total war; and it seems to be a war that mankind is losing, although he is winning some battles. Insects are, indeed, becoming more problematical. Species that have hitherto not been a problem suddenly become pests, and others are becoming immune to new poisons almost as fast as they are produced.

What are the facts? The cost of insect damage is not as great as it is made out to be. The millions of dollars assessed as insect damage are exaggerated because they include the cost of preventative spraying, research, equipment, advertising and distribution, not the actual damage of the insects to the crops. Little has been done to realistically estimate the real impact of the insect. As we know, the spraying itself is a factor in increasing insect damage because the natural predators that keep pests in check are greatly reduced and the pest, which recuperates more rapidly, has a free go of it.

More extensive damage to crops is done by mildews, rusts, molds, and adverse weather conditions than by insects. Dethier writes that the "black mount of the Third Horseman of the Apocalypse, Famine, rides in many guises, but he is not an arthropod."[3] Although insect pests are increasing due to monocultures, crops grown outside of their natural habitat, destruction of ecological balances and increased transportation, "evidence that insects compete

[3]Dethier, *Man's Plague,* p. 73.

seriously with us for *food* is unconvincing. Weather, plant pathogens, and complex socioeconomic factors are the principle agents that threaten our food supply."[4]

A Glimpse at History

People's relationship to bugs has not always been as fearful as it is today. With the exception of locusts, there is little record of insect infestations in the past.[5] When locust swarms appeared, whether in the ancient Mid-East or in medieval Europe, they were seen as punishment by God.[6] Many times they appeared in conjunction with other plagues such as flood, drought, pestilence, and famine. The recommendations for insect control in these cases were penance for the sins committed.

Some writers cite the prophet Joel as evidence that insects always have been a major problem to the grower:[7]

> That which the palmerworm hath left hath the locust

[4]*Ibid.*, p. 73. It goes without saying that insects can cause consternation when one sees trees defoliated by moths and grasshoppers eating the garden bare. Epidemic diseases have certain insect vectors: fleas are links to bubonic plague, mosquitoes to malaria, lice and mites to typhus, flies to typhoid and dysentery. Our aim, however, must be not to rush into a hysterical reaction at the sight of a few bugs.

[5]*Ibid.*, p. 57.

[6]For example, in Exodus 10:12-19, Moses is commanded to stretch out his hand over the land of Egypt, "for the locusts, that they may come upon the land of Egypt and eat every herb of the land, even all that the hail hath left." When the Pharaoh finally repents. "The Lord turned a mighty strong west wind which took away the locusts and cast them into the Red Sea; there remained not one locust in all the coasts of Egypt." In this account in Exodus we read of lice plagues (8:16), fly plagues (8:21), frog plagues, red algal blooms, and human and animal deaths; in other words, we have an account of ecological disaster in the Nile Valley.

[7]e.g. Cynthia Wescott, *The Gardener's Bug Book* (Garden City, N.Y.: Doubleday, 1964).

> eaten; and that which the locust hath left hath the cankerworm eaten; and that which the cankerworm hath left hath the caterpillar eaten. (Joel 1:4)

However, we are dealing here with a prophet's warning, and he includes droughts, earthquakes, fires, war, the sun turned to darkness, and the moon turned to blood in subsequent verses, in order to bring the people back to the path of righteousness, at which time, the Lord promises to "restore to you the years that the locust hath eaten, the cankerworm, and the caterpillar, and the palmerworm, my great army which I sent among you" (Joel 2:25), then, "ye shall eat plenty" and swords will be beaten into plowshares and spears into pruning hooks. In pre-modern times, the relationship of man to the little beasties has been one ranging from delight, to awe, to reverence and respect. According to Nahuatl tradition the red ant brought mankind corn, being commanded by the gods to find food for humanity. The Iroquois say that the locusts put their orenda (power) to work by chirping to control the summer heat for the ripening of the maize.[8] Similar connections were made by Italian and German-Swiss peasants: "In agosto quanda canta la cigala dicono, e segno che il panico e il granturco maturano bene." (It is said when the cricket sings in August, that the millet and corn ripen well.) "Wenn die Grille im September singt, so wird das Korn billig." (When the cricket sings in September, the grain will be plentiful.)[9]

Sir James Frazer cites examples of magical propitiations

[8]W. D. Storl, *Shamanism Among Americans of European Origin* (U. of Bern, Switzerland: Dissertation, 1974), p. 112.

[9]Hauser, *Bauernregeln*, pp. 407-408.

of the insects by peasants.[10] Estonian peasants will not let a child kill a weevil, admonishing: "The more we hurt him, the more he hurts us." Weevils are given a fine name and are buried or put under a stone with a corn offering. Transylvanian Saxons guard against leaf-flies by shutting the eyes and scattering three handfuls of oats in different directions. To guard the field against bird, insect or beast, the sower goes over the field imitating broadcasting with the empty hand, saying: "I sow this for everything that flies and creeps, that walks and stands, that sings and springs, in the name of God the Father, etc." A garden is kept free of caterpillars by the German peasant woman by walking at night all around the garden dragging a broom, not looking behind, while saying: "Good evening, Mother Caterpillar, you shall come with your husband to church." All the while the garden gate is left open. Frazer tells that the Sea Dyaks of Sarawak catch vermin such as grasshoppers, put them on a tiny boat well-stocked with favorite food, and float them down a stream. If that does not work, a model crocodile is set in the fields and offered food, rice wine and a chicken; it is then hoped the crocodile will devour the crop pests. In the Balkans and the Mid-East, bugs such as locusts and beetles are buried and a funeral is held for them. In Syria, when caterpillars invaded field or vineyard, "the virgins were gathered, and one of the caterpillars was taken and a girl made its mother. Then they bewailed it and buried it. Thereafter, they conducted the "mother" to the place where the caterpillars were, consoling her, in order that all the caterpillars might leave the garden."[11]

---

[10]Frazer, *The Golden Bough,* pp. 614-616.

[11]*Ibid.*, p. 616.

In the Middle Ages, insect prevention was based on prayer, but once they became a problem, they could be taken to court. Regulations were written by a Burgundian how to carry on legal procedures against grasshoppers:

> A court would be convened upon written request, a judge appointed, and a prosecuting and defense lawyer assigned. The prosecutor would present the case against the grasshopper and demand that they be found guilty and burned. The defense would argue that the demand was illegal because first the grasshopper had to be requested to leave the country within a specified period of time. If at the expiration of this period they had not left the proper sentence was excommunication.[12]

Some jurists at that time argued for the rights of the birds who would suffer at the extradition of the grasshoppers. In Berne, Switzerland, caterpillars were excommunicated by the archbishop and banished in 1479 and in Lausanne, maybugs were banished for their behavior in 1493.

In many instances bugs were not considered in a negative sense at all, as children's rhymes and peasant sayings indicate.[13] Some bugs were sacred to humanity. To the Egyp-

---

[12]Dethier, *Man's Plague,* p. 105.

[13]Baby Bye, here's a fly
We will catch him you and I
How he crawls up the walls
Yet he never falls!

I believe with six such legs
You and I could walk on eggs
There he goes on his toes
Tickling Baby's nose.

or: Buzz-Buzz was a jolly fly, full of life and gay
You could hear his merry dance at the dawn of day

tians, the scarab beetle, rolling a ball of dung, was a sacred symbol of the sun being moved across the heavens. The hornet was a war symbol, as was the fly, of which an amulet was given to brave warriors for their courage and impudence in battle. When the seven grasses bloom in the fall, the Japanese catch or buy crickets and other insects and place them in little cages. At a certain ceremonial moment, the little prisoners are freed and fly at the light of the many paper lanterns chirping to the delight of all the participants.

In most cultures insects are seen as omens sent by the gods. Some insects, like the lady bird, or lady bug, are held in high esteem, called "vaches a Dieu" (God's cows) or "Bete de la Vierge" (the Virgin's beast) by the French, "Marienkaefer" (Mary's chafers) by the Germans, and "Himmel-guegerli" (Heaven watchers) by some of the Swiss. Folklore sees in bees and ants symbols of wise industry, selflessness, and prudence.

What Is an Insect?

For Darwinists, the insect, like man, is a parasite on vegetation, and is, therefore, a competitor with man for limited food resources. A different picture reveals itself when we operate with the understanding of nature as a superorganism, when we see that the insect has its definite place in the *scale naturae,* and plays an important role in the wheel of life.

Up and down the windowpane, in the soup tureen
Buzz-Buzz was the dearest fly you have ever seen.

from J. L. Cloudsley-Thompson, *Insects and History* (New York: St. Martin's Press, 1976), p. 127. The author remembers visiting farms in Europe as a child where the flies settled as thick as raisins on the cakes. The farmer's wife just shooed them away when serving the delicious yeast cakes. No one seemed to mind.

Insects and other invertebrates are part of the macrocosmic breakdown cycle, the cycle of demanifestation in the wheel of life. This is evident when we see ants, carrion beetles, and maggots break down organic tissue where the life force (or etheric body) which provides the structure and form, has left the organism at the mercy of the chaotisizing forces of dead matter. This is evident in the blow fly maggots which eat gangrenous tissue, while at the same time secreting allantoin that helps heal wounds faster. We see this in the appearance of wire worms in soils that have uncomposted organic substances in them, such as newly turned over sod. Even the beautiful bees and butterflies help dissipate the flowers by carrying off pollen and nectar before the flower dies back and returns to seed. Life would not be possible if it were not for the armies of insects breaking up dead or dying plant and animal tissue, so that bacteria and fungi could recycle them for new growth.

Plants that are eaten by insects, especially if the damage is heavy, are already weak or dying; their etheric forces are ebbing low. Any gardener will have observed that it is precisely the weak and sickly plants, probably at the end of the bed where the compost did not reach, that are devoured by the bugs. In the same way, farmers will notice that it is the runty, weak animals that are most infested with lice, ticks and other vermin. With unbending instinct and persistence, the insect world will attack and devour that which is not fit for life. This helps us realize that an insect infestation is not the cause of our problems, but the symptom. Plants that need to be protected by insecticides are unhealthy and unhealthful to begin with; their deficiency in life force is transmitted to the animal and man who feed upon them. Our work as gardeners must be to maintain the life force in plants, in order to avoid insect troubles.

The gardener's main duty is to see that this vital flow of the etheric forces goes on uninterrupted from seed and seedling, through the vegetative growth phase, through the flowering phase, and finally, to the fruiting and seeding stage.

The insect "doppelganger" accompanies the metamorphic stages of the plant all along, from egg to its own vegetative larval growth, to the bud-like pupa, and finally to the flower-like adult. Like mirror images these two kingdoms of nature indicate their relationship, as is poetically expressed by the idea that the flower is an earth-bound butterfly and the butterfly is a liberated flower.[14] Though some bugs are general feeders, many are associated with one characteristic plant of their own, such as the cabbage looper with the brassica, the bean weevil with beans, the carrot caterpillar with carrots, the colorado beetle with nightshades, or the pretty monarch with the milkweed. The proboscis of butterflies and the nectar-filled chalice of the flower, together, form a symbiotic whole; and so it is with many plants and insects. Only abstract, alienated thinking can conceive of an insect-free garden, or fantasize about the "eradication" of insects. An insect species that gets out of control and seriously harms a crop is only an indication of an existing imbalance in nature. There is some evidence that insects are needed by the plants upon which they feed; their droppings containing trace minerals, hormones, and other substances synthesized in their bodies

[14]Philbrick, *Bug Book*, p. 120.

that are of benefit to the growth of the plants. Studies show that some plants can lose up to 30% of their leaf mass without much lessening of the yield.[15]

In a healthy situation, the insect larvae will feed upon older leaves that have been shaded out and are yellowing. Others feed upon mulch and litter. Only if the ground is bare will some insects (or slugs) consume the entire plant. Only if the whole plant is unhealthy will the whole plant be attacked. A healthy plant protects itself with numerous exudates that are becoming known to organic chemistry as alkaloids, glycosides, terpenes, tannins, alcohols, esters, acids, saponins, steroids, carotenoids, and others. Sickly or weak plants do not manufacture enough of these substances.

Another way of looking at the insect and invertebrate world is to see it as the lower level of the working of astrality in nature. The border between the manifested etheric (the plant world) and the manifested astral (the animal world) is where the insect meets the flowering plant and the worm meets the dying root. Here the plant loses its true characteristic; it dies or dissipates itself. In the flower petals the etheric vitality of the green leaves and shoots has been sacrificed; the plant falls apart into pollen, perfume and seed. Bee, butterfly, moth, bumble bee and others help to dissipate the plant into temporary nonmanifestation by dispersing the pollen and nectar. Approximately 85% of our domesticated plants depend on insects for pollination. We would be in a sad state of affairs of these proverbially industrious beasties were not at work. This is something

[15]F. Lawson, cited in Rodale's *Organic Plant Protection*, p. 56.

humanity ought to consider with all its dusting, spraying and fumigating.

Even general feeders, such as locusts or gypsy moths which appear in plagues, fall into the role of dematerializing organic substance that is low in life energy.[16] They appear at their worst during droughts, unseasonal weather, and other environmental disturbances, when the etheric energy of an entire region is at a low point. That this is so is shown by the fact that locust plagues are associated with other disasters, such as droughts, famines, bubonic plagues, pestilence, etc. as recorded in Asia, ancient Egypt and medieval Europe.[17] Sometimes these disasters are related to cosmic rhythms that superimpose themselves on the etheric of the earth.[18]

Another way of looking at the insect is in terms of the old teaching of the four elements. The insect, when its metamorphosis is complete, goes through the four elements in its life cycle, starting from an earth-egg stage (often a saline solution concentrated in an egg, buried in the ground), to a

---

[16]Sudden outbreaks of bark beetles that leave dead trees in the forests of Oregon and keep the foresters puzzled are the result of radical disturbance of the etheric forces. The author has observed that such insect damage always occurs after bulldozers and construction equipment, spraying, or gangs of precommercial thinners have gone through the forest with chain saws. Here again, the beetles are not the cause of the trees dying, but merely an indication that the life forces have declined.

[17]Cloudsley-Thompson, *Insects and History*, Chap. 9, "Famine, Hysteria, and the Dancing Mania," p. 178.

[18]For example, the *Brückner Cycle* averaging 35 years, associated with disturbances in weather, including warm, wet winters and dry, cool summers, coincides with cycles of insect pest maximums (for Europe, 1700, 1740-1743, 1780-1783, 1815, 1850-1853, 1880-1883, 1920-1924), which in turn coincides with peak emigration periods due to ruined crops (e.g. three wet years led to fungus favoring conditions of the Irish potato famine). cf. Ellsworth Huntington, *Mainsprings of Civilization* (New York: Mentor Books, 1962), pp. 461-463.

water-larval stage (succulent, mobile larva, often living in a liquid medium), to an airy-pupa state (a cocoon exposed to air and light) and culminating in a fire-adult stage. The goal of the insect is to grow into elemental fire. Its affinity to the fire element is shown in the attraction that the flame and light have for the adults of many species; it is shown in the luminescence of some, and in the nuptial flights of bees and ants in the sunlit springtime air.

In the old elemental teachings, earth and water are connected with the coming into manifestation, whereas fire is connected with the going out of manifestation, with the sulphur process that involves the disappearance from the visible world. The insects, with their affinity for the fire element, work as an astral fire upon the etheric world of the vegetation. Just as physical fire takes wood and other combustible substances out of manifestation, so the insect, working on living or near-living substances, takes the plant or animal that has lost its life force out of existence. In peasant imaginations insects have been associated with the "fire-spirits" or "salamanders." The skaldic poets of the North tell of Loki, a fire god, being able to change himself into a fly.[19] Many cultures associate destructive insects with demonic forces that return "cosmos," the orderly and structured world, to the "chaos," the amorphous and unstruc-

[19]A Norwegian legend connects pestering insects with the fire element in the following way: Long ago, there existed a terrible dragon that flew over the land breathing fire and spewing fumes. His body was made of shiny, slippery scales. The archangel Michael, in the form of the knight St. George, fought the dragon and slew him. However, the scales of the monster's body began to turn into flies, lice, fleas and other pests that fly in the air, while out of the flesh maggots and grubs crawled into the ground. The legend clearly associates the pests with the Dragon of Chaos, and with the devouring element of fire. cf. Dan Lindholm, *Wie die Sterne Entstanden* (Stuttgart: Ver. Freies Geistesleben, 1973), p. 24.

tured world.[20] In Goethe's *Faust,* Mephistopholes reveals himself as the lord of insects and the son of Chaos. He is the doppelganger of man, just as the insect is of the plant. Perhaps one of the reasons for the irrational fear people have of insects, of the fire beings, is that they are often associated with death. Even butterflies have been linked to death; the adult slipping out of the chrysalis likened to the soul leaving the body. Also bees, associated by early Rosicrucians to selfless service and selfless death, must die when they sting in defense.

The fundamental idea of bio-dynamics is to channel energy into positive developments, and not to squander the energy fighting what is deemed negative. Instead of poisoning insects, this positive direction calls for good composting practices, crop rotation, planting by the signs, companion planting and good garden care in order to deal with the insects. The insects will still be there, but will pose no problem. On the other hand, to put energy into fighting the negative is severely frustrating. Ever since the advent of powerful insecticides and other sophisticated methods of fighting insect pests, the problems have gotten worse.

It seemed such a simple solution when, as a side-product of war-related research, chlorinated hydrocarbons and organo-phosphates were discovered to poison all the pests. Instead, we have poisoned our environment, our fellow birds and mammals and ourselves. The bugs were able to mutate and adapt to every poison devised, becoming

[20]A Mohammedan legend tells of a locust that fell to the feet of the Prophet. Upon its wings was written: We are the army of the Great God and we lay 99 eggs; if the number of these is completed to 100, we shall eat the world and what there is in it.

resistant to the point where some species even thrive on the poison. Predators that keep the "pests" in check are instead wiped out or greatly reduced because, for one thing, they accumulate more toxins being higher up the food chain. After insecticidal application, it has been noted that other insect species, formerly harmless, become pests.[21] Profits of agriculturists have been shrinking because of the great cost of insecticides, and yet the crop losses to insects increase despite (because of) ever heavier doses.[22]

New pests of which there is no historical record about being very detrimental at earlier times have been cropping up in increasing numbers. In the U.S. in the last two centuries, the Colorado beetle, hessian fly, cotton weevil, screw worms, grasshoppers, army worms, gypsy moth, chinch bug and others have become a problem. This is due to unecological cultivating practices, monocropping, the transport of insects and crops out of their natural environment, the destruction of natural predators, as well as the synergistic effects of chemicals in the ecotope. Herbicides have been shown to trigger pest outbreaks; for example, the infamous 2,4,D sprayed on corn increased the corn borer larvae and made the moths more fertile.[23] Fertilizer imbalances brought about by the application of synthetic NPK fertilizer cause insect problems. This is tacitly admitted by the perpetrators of the Green Revolution, whose "miracle" crops only survive with the application of massive doses of poison. Especially nitrogen is problematical. As Steiner indicates in his

---

[21]Dethier, *Man's Plague*, p. 119.

[22]*Ibid.*, p. 119. Estimated crop losses in 1904 were 11%, in 1968 13%.

[23]*Organic Plant Protection*, ed. Yepson, p. 22.

Agricultural Course, nitrogen is the carrier of world astrality. Healthy plant growth depends upon a proper balance between the etheric (in part manifested by the sugars and carbohydrates) and the astral (in part manifested by proteins and amino acids). Excessive nitrogen application draws aphids and mites, while too little draws other bugs to devour the sickly plants. Phosphorus deficiency increases white fly and spider mites.[24] Modern fertilizing techniques have decreased the amount of silicon content in plants, especially in the cereals. Silicon in the tissue makes many plants insect-resistant and unappealing to insect mandibles.

The need for large and quick profit has misled many a farmer and gardener to the use of strong poisons against these beings whose function merely indicates unhealthy processes already present. Instead of turning to the wisdom of a loving, organic agriculture, further black magical practices are being devised. These include bacteriological warfare, the breeding of radiation-exposed sterilized insects that will not be able to produce viable offspring when released to mate with fertile partners, the use of "juvenile hormones" that retard the larva and prevent it from ever reaching maturity, new and more insidious poisons, the use of lights and scents (pheromones) that lure, trap and destroy multitudes, or genetic manipulation. Even with these new methods, there are indications that the insects are mutating and adapting, and that there are most likely other unforeseen, harmful effects on the rest of nature. The entomologists and chemists involved remind one of the

[24] Ibid., p. 26.

sorcerer's apprentice, whose every solution to the basic problem creates new problems.[25]

Perhaps the Bible is right when it considers insects (locusts) to be sent by supernatural agencies in consequence of having erred from the path of life. The suggestion is made that insect pests are stopped by repentance (L. repensum=to reconsider) concerning the way mankind has been carrying on its business.

Materialistic science cannot really understand the insect. The tremendous adaptability to adverse conditions brought about by DDT, arsenic and other poisons indicates a great biological "intelligence." Despite very costly efforts to eradicate pests, not one species has been eliminated successfully. Who has not been amazed at the rapidity with which aphids can suddenly populate a cabbage or bean patch? Already as it is born, parthenogenically and viviparously, the young aphid has embryos of several hundred more developing inside itself.

Consider the marvelous architecture of the hexagonal honeycomb, the paper wasp nest, the air-conditioned termite hills in Africa; consider the uncanny camouflage of the walking stick, the tomato hook worm which looks like a rolled up tomato leaf, or moths that look like old yellowed leaves; consider the tachinid fly larva that slowly eats its caterpillar host from the inside, making sure that no vital organs are damaged until it has completely hollowed it out and is ready to slip out.

---

[25]One is reminded of a science-fiction movie of the 1950's showing an invasion from outer space by ominous-looking space capsules that land offshore. The air force quickly bombs the invaders, but the strikes are of no avail. The capsules open and robot-like creatures invade the land. They seem to get more energized after every attack against them. Just as it is about to be decided to use nuclear weapons on them, it is realized that these invaders are not to be destroyed by force. Every use of force against them increases their power. It is with flowers and songs that the monsters are finally vanquished.

Some insects seem to have established their patterns hundreds of millions of years ago, and some have found a niche for themselves only yesterday, such as the drugstore beetle, which can live in bottles of arsenic and other poisons for years as its favorite habitat. What overwhelming intelligence is there in the social insects, in ants, bees and termites, as they divide into social bodies of egg-laying queens, armies of workers, fighters, nursemaids and other functionaries. This remarkable adaptability of insects cannot be explained merely by microscopic or chemical analysis of individual bugs. We do our observations more justice when we consider once again the notion of an organizing genius for each species, that guides and directs each insect as part of a concerted whole, much like the cells and organs of our bodies are subject to an overall structural, functional gestalt. That this organizing intellgence exists beyond the make-up of the single individual insect is seen in the single ant removed from its colony as it errs haplessly about until it dies. A hive or a colony of social insects might be analogous to an organ for the "individual" that marks the genius of the species. At this point, we once again reconsider the idea of supersensible "group souls" or "grandfathers" that are spoken of in the lore of most native peoples. With this in mind, perhaps we can find a better way of dealing with insect problems.

Insect species are still very macrocosmic beings. They have not condensed and centralized into a single body with centralized organs. Considerations of this nature show us that killing an insect is not of the significance that killing a bird or a mammal is. It is more like pruning plants or cutting hair or fingernails. It is not a deeply-incarnated astrality, let alone a self-conscious ego that is killed, but a being with very diffuse macrocosmically-rooted soul functions whose essence is found in supersensible realms.

Beneficial Insects[26]

Estimates of the number if insect species vary. There are several hundred thousand species, of which 90% are considered beneficial. Of the remaining 10%, only a small portion qualify as serious pests. Some so-called pests might cause slight scarring of the fruit rind, causing cosmetic damage which, however, in no way diminishes the quantity or quality of the food.

Pollination is one of the most important functions of insects. All of our fruits (citrus, apples, pears, strawberries, cranberries, etc.), most vegetables (melons, squashes, eggplants, peppers, carrots, etc.), corn, cotton, tobacco, and the clovers which feed our livestock depend on insect pollination. Some insects are specialized to pollinate only one or a few species, such as the fig wasp, the figs. The rosaceae are pollinated by bees, the legumes by bees and bumblebees, night-flowering plants by moths, umbellifers by flies, bugs and wasps.

We are dependent on insects for honey, beeswax, silk, shellac, and various dyes and medicines.

Many insects, and other arthropods, are important as predators and parasites that keep populations of potential pests in check. Entomophagous insects include the dragon and damsel flies that eat mosquitoes, ladybug beetles that eat aphids, and wasps (Vespidae and Sphecidae) that eat caterpillars and grasshoppers. Lacewings (whose larvae are known as ant-lions) eat aphids, various hemiptera eat caterpillars, praying mantises eat grasshoppers and any other

---

[26]Donald J. Borror and Dwight M. DeLong, *An Introduction to the Study of Insects* (New York: Holt, Rinehart & Winston, 1972), p. 657.

bug they can get their *tarsi* on, tachinid flies parasitize other bugs by laying eggs in them, and so on.

Carrion beetles, dung beetles, dung flies and others function as scavengers, removing diseased and obnoxious substances. Ants, termites and beetles turn dead logs into humus for the forest. Soil insects are important in churning, aerating, and adding organic residues to the soil. Some species keep weeds in check. Most insects are food for the animals that delight our senses, the fish, the frogs and lizards, the birds, skunks, moles, shrews and hedgehogs.

Finally, the aesthetic delight of delicate butterflies and moths, the shiny, metallic glimmer of beetles, and the songs of crickets and katydids in the summer must not be forgotten.

With this in mind we can appreciate the need for caution when it comes to indiscriminate spraying or poisoning. Even organic, bio-degradable insecticides should be used with caution, if at all.

Practical Application

Most bio-dynamic gardeners are not much concerned with insects, for seldom do they become a problem. Biodynamics works on a preventative, prophylactic basis. Once again, it is the practice of conscientious composting, companion planting, rotation, planting at the right cosmically determined moment, and the use of bio-dynamic preparations that maintain the balance. A healthy garden *must* have bugs in it, at least a thousand different species. One can even admire the squash bug and take delight in the cabbage butterfly without panicking.

Pest damage is kept low by ensuring smooth, steady

growing from seed to harvest. This involves proper watering, avoiding droughts or sudden cold showers during the heat of the day, for that would shock the plant and interrupt the flow of vital energy. Planting in the proper season and sign implies making cosmic energies available to the plants. Composting guarantees the kind of nutrient release that will not be excessive or too slow, making for harmonious growth of insect-resistant plants. Companion planting consists of picking varieties that grow well together, as well as planting flowers and herbs that keep insect levels lower. Flowers and herbs on the border of the garden plot help mask odors attractice to insects, according to one theory, and flower nectar keeps predators alive when pests are in low supply.[27] Garlic is such a companion for many crops; nasturtium is good with squash for protection against white fly and wooly aphids; beans and potato rows alternated keep both bean beetles and colorado beetles down; carrots alternated with leeks or onions keep the carrot fly in low frequency; cabbage is aided by hemp, mint, thyme, sage and other herbs in repelling bugs; marigolds keep nematodes from infesting the soil (nematodes or eelworms, are mainly a problem in soils with insufficient organic matter); savory aids beans, basil helps tomatoes, and so on.[28] Certain *catch crops* such as soybeans, calendula, radish (for flea beetle) and tomatillo attract bugs that will keep the other plants relatively free.

Besides companion plants which add color, fragrance

[27]Flowers also attract bees, whose positive astrality disposes the astrality of pests which is not so positive. Beekeepers find that beehives near the gardens tend to keep the pest population lower than expected.

[28]William H. Hylton, "The Companionable Herbs," in *The Rodale Herb Book*, p. 254.

and beauty to the garden, one can create optimal conditions for other predators of insects, such as birds, amphibians, reptiles and some mammals. It takes keen observation and becomes a lifelong study to see the intricate ecological connections that exist in the garden. In the chain of nature, the birds eat at the extremities of the plant; they eat seeds or bugs from the crown of the plant and scratch grubs and worms from the foot of the plant. Some birds tend more to the side of the seeds, such as seed-eating sparrows and pigeons, others are purely insectivorous, such as swallows and woodpeckers, whereas most are omniverous, varying their diet between seed, berry and bug. Most of our beautiful songbirds are strongly insectivorous. To lure these creatures into the garden ecotope, bird feeders, baths, and shelters must be provided.[29] Various seeds and suet (for woodpeckers and chickadees) can be fed. Birdhouses can be made easily.

Hedges not only keep chilling and desiccating winds from blowing across the garden, but make for ideal bird shelters. A hedge can feed the gardener as well as the birds. Elderberries make good tea from the blossoms and wine and jam from the berries. Hawthorn, roan, rose, blackberry, mulberry, chockecherry and other berry bushes provide teas or jams, or both. Hazelnut hedges bless the gardener with filberts. One can plant hedges of hackberry, dogwood, barberry, viburnum and others that are of aesthetic appeal and keep the birds from some of the prized domesticated berries. Even wild patches of evergreens or blackberry thickets are useful for nesting areas for our feathered helpers, or as shelters for toads, garter snakes, turtles and skunks, all of

[29]*Organic Plant Protection*, Chap. 12, p. 145.

which are avid gobblers of bugs. Toads like to live in the moist atmosphere of the compost pile. From the magnitude of their droppings, consisting of hundreds of chitinous skeletons, one can ascertain how beneficial they are. If new toads are procured, it is a good practice to leave them in their cages in the garden for a few days, for they need some time to acclimate themselves; otherwise they will start hopping back to where they came from. Garter snakes like to patrol the garden, keeping insect populations at a minimum. Some gardeners let bantam hens, ducks and geese range in the garden but might lose a lettuce or tomato, or two, in the process.

All these procedures and precautions, aided by some hand-picking, should be enough to prevent any major insect problems in the garden. If for some reason, however, there is an infestation, the gardener ought to investigate thoroughly and study the problem closely before reacting with poisons. Even organic poisons kill beneficial predators and upset the biological balance. With the aid of one's garden diary, one should recall the weather conditions, type of fertilizer used, type of crop, constellation of planting date or outbreak, preceding crop rotations and other vital data that might indicate what led to the outbreak. One might also study the life habits of the pest to see how one can cope with it in the simplest way.

Ecological interconnection must be understood before any drastic action is taken. Sometimes people find holes in their cabbages or tomatoes with an earwig, pillbug or even an earthworm in it, promptly declaring these hapless creatures guilty. Real observation would show that they merely sought shelter in these cavities, feeding on the droppings left behind by the slugs which ate the holes in the first place.[30]

During adverse conditions, when plants are likely to be befallen by a bug, or in the early stages of an infestation, nonpoisonous teas and preparations can be given to strengthen the plants. Helen and John Philbrick, in *The Bug Book*, provide a number of such recipes.[31]

Compost water, manure teas, and comfrey or nettle ferments aid weakened plants in regaining their life forces. Stinging nettle ferment or tea slightly changes the makeup of the plant sap, so that the plant does not taste as good to

---

[30] The need to understand ecological networks is illustrated by a slug infestation in a Swiss garden. Clean cultivation was practiced for a number of years and the slugs could be hand-picked without much problem. Over a period of three years the slugs became unmanageable. What had happened? City water had been made available to the garden at reduced rates, and consequently an elaborate overhead sprinkling system was installed to make the watering easier. The continual moistness of the ground not only aided the slugs, but watering during the heat of the day weakened the plants and made them more susceptible. Besides the large red slug (*Ario ater*) and the little milk slug (*Agriolimax reticulatus*), the edible "escargot" snail (*Helix aspera*) was present. A garden worker of French background, delighted at the presence of the escargot, set about diligently collecting jars of them to turn into sauces and gourmet delights. After picking the Helix snails, the slugs became worse, nearly unmanageable. What had happened? The escargot, or Helix, eat the white, translucent eggs of the slugs wherever they find them. By now the problem was out of hand and the gardener resorted to poisons, which were immediately effective, of course, but apparently killed the hedgehogs that lived in the hedge on the garden's edge. Slugs are one of the favorite foods of the hedgehog. The gardener concluded that slugs, like fate, are something that nothing can be done against, and went elsewhere. What should have been done instead? The watering should have been managed better, using mulch to preserve the soil moisture, instead of continuous overhead sprinkling. Providing mulch would have given the slugs something to eat besides the plants on the clean cultivation plots. The hedgehogs should have been encouraged with saucers of milk to frequent the garden. Planks should have been laid in the rows as traps under which the slugs hide by day. Deep containers filled with beer could have been used as lures into which the slugs would fall and drown. The escargot should have been partially conserved.

[31] Helen and John Philbrick, *The Bug Book* (Charlotte, Vermont: Garden Way Publishing, 1974).

the bug as before.

Only as a final measure, if all else fails and it is a matter of saving the crop, might one resort to poisons. Most insecticides can be grown right in the garden. Plants from which insecticides can be made include beautiful flowers such as pansies, marigolds, asters, chrysanthemums, petunias, cosmos, nasturtium, coreopsis, and herbs such as feverfew, wormwood, coriander and garlic.[32] Most of these flowers can be dried, pulverized for dusting or brewed into a tea. Tea mixed with old-fashioned soap, such as green soap, to make the poison stick longer to the leaves, will do the job.

Bio-degradable insecticide sprays and dusts made from tropical plants can be purchased. These include derris (rotenone), which kills all cold-blooded animals such as toads, frogs, snakes besides insects, pyrethrum, ryania, and tobacco (nicotine). These poisons can be combined with soap for adhesion. If used, they should be used selectively, not applied in a blanket, indiscriminate fashion.

Importing predators, such as praying mantises, trichogramma wasps, or lady bugs is probably not necessary. Often they will not stay in the garden, and usually there should be enough natural predators in the area, unless mindless spraying has severely decimated the predator population.

It should not be necessary to use such radical means as viral (e.g. nuclear polyhedrosis) and bacteriological (e.g. Bacillus thuringiensis) means. Light traps and electrocutors are to be avoided, for they lure insects from the surrounding countryside and often friendly or harmless bugs

---

[32] *Organic Plant Protection*, p. 113; *The Basic Book of Organic Gardening*, ed. R. Rodale (New York: Ballantine Books, 1974).

are destroyed *en masse* this way. The use of pheromones, hormonal control (juvenile hormones) and putting bugs through blenders and then spraying seem unnecessarily cruel. Such practices probably work to shock the "genius" of the species, and will most likely have unforeseen repercussions. It goes without saying that the synthetic sprays that are carcinogenic or mutagenic, that kill friendly insects, birds and mammals, contaminate soils, ground water, and mother's milk should be avoided altogether.

For more specific information about any of the insect controls, the reader is advised to consult the literature of the Organic Gardening Movement (Rodale Press) and of the BIO-DYNAMIC Farming and Gardening Association (P.O. Box 29135, San Francisco, CA 94129-0135).

Fungus, Virus and Bacteria

Fungi (mildews, rusts, smuts, molds), bacteria (rots) and viruses (mosaic, leaf curl, yellows) are signs of environmental disturbances that weaken the flow of vital energies in plants. Fungi and bacteria are saprophytes that take hold of tissues whose life is declining. The disturbances are often weather induced. Dry weather followed by wet, drizzly weather is ideal for fungus infections. At such times the ground is often still dry, but the moist air induces the stomates or pores of the plant to open, so that fungus spores can easily grow into the weakened plant. Artificial fertilizer, such as sulphate of ammonia, which releases nitrogen too rapidly, as opposed to steady-release compost, creates softer tissues which rupture and dissolve more easily when atmospheric conditions favor fungi and bacteria. Low silicon content, correlated with artificial fertilizer, makes it easier for mildew infection.

Prophylactic measures include healthy soil that can deliver nutrients and water steadily, care in watering and mulching to prevent soil moisture from fluctuating, and compost application which aids the mycorrhizae, which as Waksman and others have shown, give off antibodies that can be absorbed by the roots of the crops. Thinning plants to the proper distances, so that they have access to sunshine and air, keeps many fungi in control.

On rainy, cool days it is a good idea to spray the plants with horsetail tea and a 2% waterglass solution, whose silica content helps to bring light to the plant tissues. Chamomile tea, milk, dilutions of sulphur, solutions of garlic juice and a tea made from chives inhibit mildew on cucumbers and other plants. Damping off of young seedlings in seed-beds can be prevented by spraying chamomile tea, horse-tail tea, and mixing peat moss into the bedding soil.

Fungi, bacteria, and viruses related to fluctuations in weather and other environmental factors are generally more detrimental to plants than are the insects.

CHAPTER XVII
THE GARDEN CALENDAR

The seasons express themselves differently in the diverse locations and altitudes of the country. Most garden books and almanacs have general information that is fairly safe to follow. The monthly indications given in the "Organic Gardening and Farming Magazine," the *Calendar of Organic Gardening,* and the voluminous *Encyclopedia of Organic Gardening,* all put out by the staff of Rodale Books, divide the United States into general climatic zones, giving hints for month by month gardening activity.

The gardening calendar discussed here is based on data collected locally in the Rogue River Valley area. Other parts of the country will have similar, but not exactly, the same seasonal distributions. The *frost free date* in spring, the first frost in the fall, the thaw out after a winter freeze, the length of the growing season, the average yearly temperatures, the relative amount of cloud cover and rainy days compared to sunny days, each of these factors will be different from location to location. It is best to ask the old-timers in areas where one is a newcomer.

In Southern Oregon the year divides into a dry, sunny, warm season that lasts from the end of May into October and a cool, rainy, cloudy season that starts with the protective fogs in November and lasts on and off until May. The sunny season is ushered in by concerts of frogs and a parade of the most beautiful spring flowers. As the summer proceeds it gets progressively drier. As madrone and manzanita shed their bark and previous year's leaves, the woods are alive with the metallic rustle of locusts and desiccated leaves. Thunderstorms are rare and do not bring the relieving moisture as in the mid-West, for example. The cold, rainy season, coinciding with the half of the year when the moon makes a higher arch in the heavens than the sun, brings an abundance of lunar vegetation, including many mushrooms that are the gourmet's delight (boletes, milky caps, russula, coral mushroom, puff balls, and hallucinogenic psilocybin mushrooms), and lichens and algae that coat the oaks in their winter garments. There is an echo of early spring when the rains start, with grasses, chickweed, miner's lettuce and dandelions turning green and lush until frost nips them.

There is never the long, hard freeze and continuous blanket of snow that makes it impossible to dig in the ground in the winter, as in other parts of the country. In February, as the days noticeably lengthen, it is already possible to put in one's first crops (peas, snow peas, broad beans, rocket, spinach, onions). Yet, the frost-free date is still a long way off. As long as the white shimmer of snow stays on the mountains, it is not safe to put summer crops out. Many a newcomer has been fooled by the mild weather interspersed with rain, lasting from February to April and May, into putting summer crops in, only to see his tomatoes, eggplants, peppers, beans, and squash limp and black after a frost has passed in the morning. Frosts lasting to the end of May and into June make gardening tricky in this region, and the dry conditions of July, August and September make it even more difficult. It is no wonder that the native Indians, the Takilma, preferred hunting and gathering to horticulture, for they could not make use of such techniques as irrigation, sprinkling, or setting up protective plastic tents. Indians in the more hospitable Midwest, East and Southeast were, on the other hand, master horticulturists.

In the spring, *raised beds* help to warm and drain the soil more quickly. The winter cover crops (legume-grain combination) will have gotten high enough by February-March that they can be turned in and still have plenty of time to rot and feed the earthworms before the summer crops go in. After mid-summer solstice, it is important to concentrate on the watering and mulching to cut down water evaporation. Usually the fall weather is mild and lasts a long time, so that it is easy for the winter garden to get a good start. (See Appendix I, WINTER GARDENING IN OREGON.)

The following is a month by month description of how the gardening year might proceed in the Rogue Valley Area.

JANUARY: Prune fruit trees and berries in late January. Feed your bird friends wild bird seed mixes and include suet for the hairy woodpeckers and chickadees. Build bird shelters.[1] It is a good time to plan the year's garden crops and rotations, to read garden books and catalogs, and to order whatever seeds one might need.[2]

FEBRUARY: On drier days in February one can prepare the double-dug beds for sowing the first crops. Toward the end of the month, fava or broad beans, snow peas, pod peas, corn salad or maches, onions, shallots, gar-

---

[1]A number of good books on the market are worth consulting for helpful hints on how to attract and care for garden visitors, including *Attracting Birds to Your Garden* by the editors of Sunset magazine, Lane Books, Menlo Park, Ca.

[2]For good reading on seed catalogs, seed companies, good gardening book lists, and other helpful hints, consult *The Green World, A Guide and Catalog,* by Stone Soup, Ltd., A Berkeley Windhover Book, N.Y., 1975.

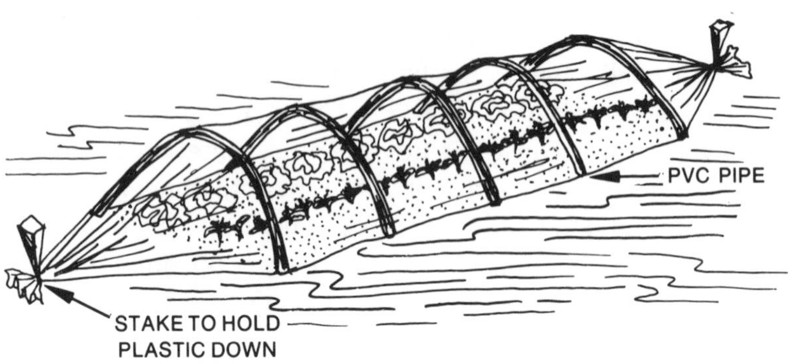

den cress, and radishes should be already sown. Local gardeners pick George Washington's birthday (Feb. 22) as the day to sow peas. Pea beds can be interplanted with early lettuce, spinach and radishes, with the tall peas on the north or west side of the bed and the short peas on the south side of the bed for better light utilization. The peas and fava beans should be inoculated with nitrogen-fixing bacteria spores.

These new plantings can be protected from frost by stretching clear plastic tents over them. These tents can be supported by a frame of PVC pipe, which is the cheapest material to use. Care must be taken to air the tents out in order to prevent mildew, to uncover them when the sun is shining to prevent cooking the seedlings, and to cover them over on cold, clear nights. If it gets really cold, an extra layer of plastic, blankets, or straw can be placed over the tent.

SHORT PEAS
TALL PEAS ON TRELLIS
SPINACH
LETTUCE CRESS
LETTUCE OR RADISH

EARLY BED

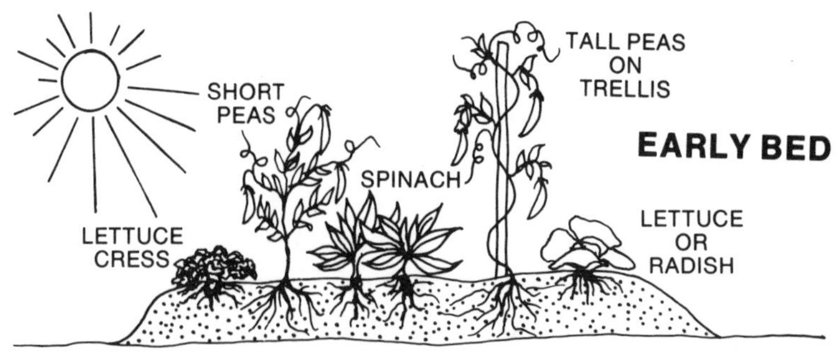

SUMMER SOLSTICE
ST. JOHN'S TIDE
JUN
JUL
FROST FREE DATE
MAY
AUG
SUNNY SEASON
Sunny
Hot
Dry
EASTER
SEP
APR
SPRING EQUINOX
FALL EQUINOX
MICHAELMAS
OCT
MAR
Rainy
Cloudy
Foggy
RAINY SEASON
FEB
NOV
JAN
DEC
WINTER SOLSTICE
CHRISTMAS

THE YEAR

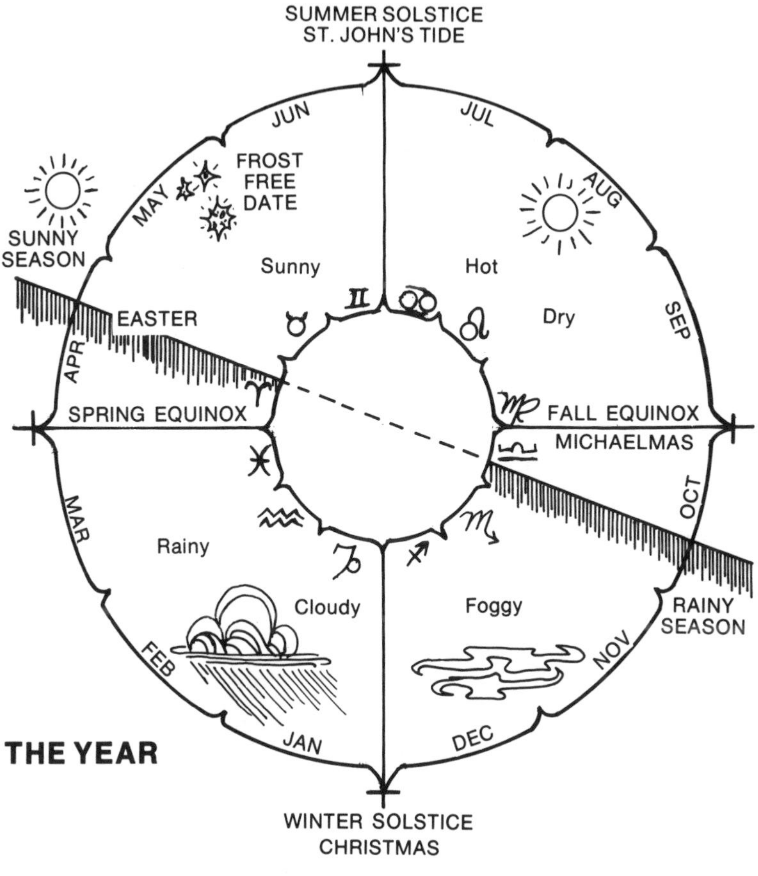

Milk jugs filled with hot water can be put under the tent. Water gives off its warmth slowly enough to prevent freezing.

The winter cover crops can be turned over and left to rot. Root crops that are still in the ground from the previous season (carrots, oyster plant, beets, hamburg parsley, parsnips, celeriac) are imperceptibly getting ready for new sap flow in their biennial cycle, and can be removed to a root cellar to keep them from getting too stringy and tough too early.

MARCH: In early and mid-March the following plants can be sown into carefully prepared soil of the *cold-frame:* summer cabbage, broccoli, cauliflower, collards and other members of the cabbage family; lettuce, Swiss chard, onions, leeks, celery, celeriac and endive. The cold frame, composed of a sifted mixture of good soil (1 part peat, 1 part sand, 1 part ripe stage III compost, and 2 parts good garden loam), is framed with boards and has a lid made from storm windows or stretched plastic. Most gardening books give directions how to build it.[3] Into this cold frame the seeds are sown into little patches of one or two square feet, for later transplanting. The seedlings need good care after they germinate. They must be kept watered, weeded and thinned so that they do not crowd each other. A light sprinkle of horsetail-chamomile tea to keep them from damping off is recommended each week. The cover should be closed at night and lifted slightly to dry them and circulate the air during the day. Like all the umbelliferae,

---

[3] *Encyclopedia of Organic Gardening,* ed. Jerolme Olds (Emmaus, Pa.: Rodale Books, Inc., 1975), pp. 201-205.

celery and celeriac take a long time to germinate (3 weeks), so that patient weeding and gentle watering of the soil are needed. Celeriac seeds are so small that mixing the seed with fine sand is recommended, then sowing the mixture to space the seeds more evenly.

From mid-March toward the end of March oyster plant, dandelion, orach, beets, carrots, kohlrabi, mustard, parsley, hamburg parsley, parsnips, turnips, and rutabagas can be sown out. Slow-germinating carrots can have a few lettuce or radish seeds mixed in to mark the rows. The row distances vary; most seed packets and garden books give recommendations and directions. The rows should be spaced wide enough to be able to cultivate with a hoe or a pendulum hoe. It is recommended that the bed be worked two weeks before the sowing, so that weed seeds will have had time to sprout and can consequently be destroyed by hoeing and raking. After the sowing of the rows, the bed must be hoed to prevent the soil from crusting, to facilitate carbon dioxide/oxygen exchange, to stop the capillary movement of water molecules upward, and to keep weeds from overtaking the crop plants. This is done regularly, but especially after rain or watering.

In March one can still put out more peas, corn salad, onions, spinach and one can sow asparagus for later transplanting.

March is also the time during which potatoes can be put into the ground. St. Patrick's day, the patron saint of the Irish whose fate is so tied up with this tuber, is a good time to plant the potato, providing the moon is in a good position. The potato, a very lunar plant, is best planted near Apogee and in the earth sign of Taurus. Scorpio and

Cancer do not make for good potatoes. Like legumes, they can be planted in the new moon.

Like most staples, such as rice and corn, the potato is surrounded by magic and ritual.[4] It seems that almost every gardener has his own procedure as to how best to grow potatoes. Some swear by mulch, some by hills, some by planting them in tires, but in any case, an old saying goes that "the dumbest farmer has the largest spuds."

The method used successfully by the author involves preparing the soil with a good rotted manure and a wood-ash dressing and spraying bio-dynamic preparation 500, the horn-dung preparation. The seed potatoes are laid into the window sill for a week to green out. On the day of planting, the seed potatoes are cut into sections containing an eye each. Each eye forms a new plant. These sections are dipped in hardwood ashes to cauterize the fresh cut and to provide them with the potassium they like. The cuttings are then laid in rows two feet apart, at a distance of a foot and a half within each row. The soil is raked over the rows, forming a ridge. As soon as the first leaves appear, more soil is raked over the ridges, leaving just the top leaves exposed. In the summer, the potatoes are heavily mulched. As soon as they flower, the first potatoes can be dug up for eating (late June) and when the foliage finally dies back in September, the field can be cleared and the potatoes stored in the cellar.

At the end of March, toward the beginning of April, a *hot bed* can be put in, if there is no greenhouse available, for

[4]Peruvians placed stones in the ground to increase the number of potatoes, and every peasant society honored the last potato dug as the "Potato Mother."

growing the seedlings of tomatoes, tomatillos, peppers, eggplant, okra, New Zealand spinach, Malibar spinach, and cucumbers and squashes. The hot bed is made by digging a bed three or four feet wide, to a depth of three feet. Two feet of fresh horse manure is packed in and soaked with liquid manure, animal urine, slurry, or sludge. A five inch layer of peat moss covers the manure to absorb ammonia and methane which might otherwise escape and injure the young seedlings. A foot of good garden loam, a mixture like that which went into the cold frame, is put on top, into which the seeds for the spring crops are sown. The sides are boarded up and glass or a stretched plastic cover is put over the seedbed at an angle toward the south exposure to catch and collect the sun's warmth. In this way the seedbed will be heated from above and below. The horse manure mixture heats steadily and gently for about six weeks, a fact made use of by alchemists who cooked their concoctions in horse manure.[5] All the rules relating to the cold frame must be observed here, too: gentle watering with slightly warmed water, careful weeding, thinning to space the seedlings, airing the bed, and covering during cold nights. A system like this demands constant, daily attention, but it will be much cheaper than buying pony packs at a store or nursery, and it will give good seedlings which can be set out after the frost free date has passed. The squash, zucchini and cucumbers, if they are grown in the hot bed, should be placed into *peat-pots* to make the transplanting less traumatic for them.

During March, also, certain perennials such as asparagus,

---

[5]"A dragon springs therefrom which, when exposed in horse's excrement for 20 days, devours his tail till naught thereof remains," from a Greek alchemical poem, Holmyard, *Alchemy*, p. 159.

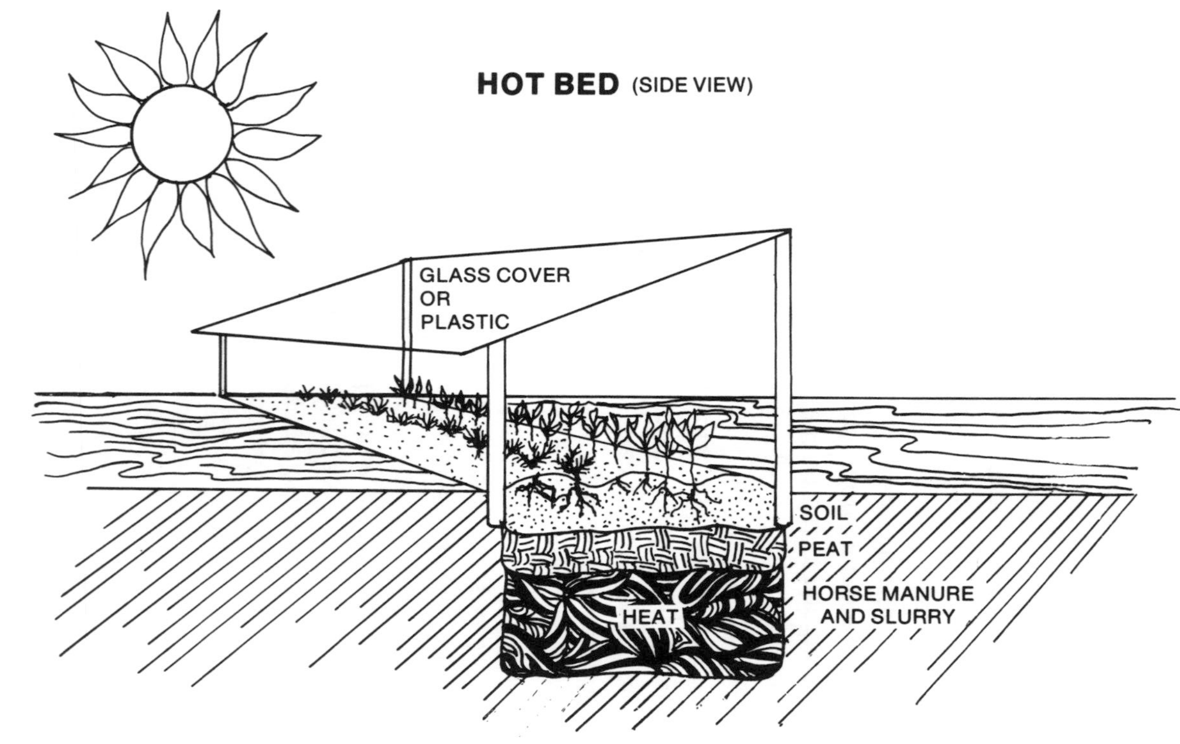
HOT BED (SIDE VIEW)
GLASS COVER OR PLASTIC
SOIL
PEAT
HORSE MANURE AND SLURRY
HEAT

horseradish, pokeweed, rhubarb, Jerusalem artichoke, and comfrey can be planted along with hardy herbs such as nettle, chives, lavender, sage, hyssop and others. Chamomile can be sown at this time in slightly alkaline soil.

APRIL: In April much of the work that has been started in March continues. More sowings of the hardy plants can be made. The cold frame and hot bed need special care, as do the composts. Easter season, determined by the full moon after equinox, is known to be the most fertile time of the year, when the land is greening with astonishing vitality. Some old timers put in special Good Friday gardens.

MAY: Very hardy plants such as the cabbages, broccoli, cauliflower, endives, lettuce, Swiss chard, and leeks can be planted out a couple of weeks before the frost free date. Toward the end of May one ought to be eating some snow peas, pod peas, perhaps some fava beans, besides spinach, nettle, lettuce, onion greens, cress and radishes.

JUNE: By now, as midsummer, or St. John's tide, approaches, forces of light and warmth streaming in from the cosmos make it possible to put out the warmth-loving plants. Transplanted from the hot bed into the regular garden beds are tomatoes, okra, New Zealand spinach, Malibar spinach, eggplants, peppers, ground cherries, tomatillos, cucumbers and squash. At first it might be a good idea not to mulch so that the ground can warm up some more, but later, mulching is essential. At this time the celeriac needs to be planted out; any earlier would not endanger its survival, but would adversely affect its tuber-forming ability. Tender herbs such as basil, savory, marjoram, rosemary or nasturtium are sown out at this time.[6] Beans, corn and summer

[6]See the *Rodale Herb Book* for exact indications.

lettuce can be sown directly into the ground. The early pea and spinach beds can be cleaned out now and more room for the summer plantings made. Strawberries should be thinned and mulched now, and the runners transplanted to a new bed. It is also high time to stop cutting rhubarb and asparagus so that they will have a chance to acquire strength for the next year.

JULY: Mulching and correct watering are the concern now. Tomatoes should be trained up stakes, so that the fruit will not rot on the ground. The suckers should be cut off, so that most of the energy of the tomato plant goes into the main shoot and the tomato fruits. Similarly, cucumbers should be trained up chicken wire fences to that they do not sprawl all over the ground and can be picked without moving the vines when they get ripe; usually it is because the vines are unnecessarily moved that the cucumbers become bitter. The cold frame is needed again by the end of this month to sow out fall cabbage, cauliflower, kale, brussel sprouts, broccoli, sugar hat, lettuce and endives. These seedbeds must be kept moist and shaded by lattice, burlap, or cheesecloth. For more winter vegetables, carrots, turnips, kohlrabi, rutabagas, chinese cabbage, hamburg parsley and beets can be sown in any beds that are still unoccupied. A more shaded location, good humus, sufficient moisture, and special care might alleviate some of the problems of seed germination at this time of year. Often it is necessary to re-sow these rows because of poor germination. Melons must be thinned to keep them from crowding each other. Zucchini must be cut continuously so that it will keep producing. Now is also the time to sow out Florence fennel, so that it will grow big, bulbous leaf bases that make delicious fall and early winter eating.

AUGUST: The July work continues in August. By mid-August the plants in the coldframe can be planted out into the fields. These plants must receive a scoop of good compost, be watered and mulched immediately. This is the time to cut and dry many of the herbs, just before they bloom. (Except the ones from which the flowers are desired, such as chamomile, for example.) The best plants can be marked for saving for seed. By now, an abundance of fresh food will bless the gardener.

SEPTEMBER: There is still time to plant sugar hat, corn salad (maches) and spinach for fall and winter. Cover-crops can be sown out wherever there is room. Putting them in at this time of year ensures a good, lush growth before the days get too cold; and the birds, still having plenty of other food to eat, will not be so tempted to scratch up the seeds. Garlic cloves can be put in. Most of the other work consists of harvesting the summer crops, this being the time most traditional harvest festivals were celebrated.[7]

OCTOBER, NOVEMBER: With the passing of fall equinox, or Michaelmas, the jungle-like profusion that characterized the summer garden is gone. Jack Frost and other such elemental beings might be appearing soon, so it is wise to get one's plastic tents ready to put up in case of a cold night. Valerian spray can be used on tomatoes to extend their frost hardiness. Jerusalem artichokes, having finished blooming, are now harvestable, but are left in the

---

[7]A hint from an old gardener (Alice Hackett) on how to tell if the watermelon is ripe: "Thump it. If it sounds like your head, it is too green; if it sounds like your gut, it is too ripe; but if it sounds like your chest, it is just right."

ground over the winter, unless it is an exceptionally cold one. Toward the end of November, it is advisable to put leaf and straw mulch over the winter crops that stay in the garden soil, to protect them from later frosts and light freezing. Strawberries, asparagus and rhubarb rows are now mulched with old, rotted manure. As the beds are cleared and leaves raked up, composts are built that last through the winter. These composts are fed during the winter with garbage and various manures. They should be sufficiently humified in the spring for use.

DECEMBER: This is a good time to relax, eat pumpkin pie, and count one's blessings. The compost should be watched, so that the rains do not leach them out. The twelve days of Christmas, from Christmas to Epiphany, used to be taken as oracles for the coming year; each day represents the consecutive months of the year. How the weather and the moods are on each day is a foreshadowing of the coming season.

This cursory description of the gardening year is by no means complete. Each landscape, each farm-garden organism, as well as each year has its own particular character. Some years this or that crop will do very well, and another year rather poorly. Each year has a distinct weather pattern and the kinds of bugs, birds or weeds will be slightly altered. There can be no exact how-to-do-it manual, as in the mechanical sciences.

In the winter months when the garden rests in the mind of the gardener, as well as in the form-giving forces of the Cosmos, we can awaken the intuitive sense and pictures of imagination that are as important in gardening as the tools and the practical manuals are. We can let the coming year pass before the mind's eye and, while looking back on the store of experience of past years, plan the manifestation of the garden in its next season.

CHAPTER XVIII

TEAS, PREPARATIONS AND BIOTIC SUBSTANCES

We have seen how very alive the soil is with its billions of churning, breathing, metabolizing organisms. Like all living organisms, the soil is sensitive to a number of influences. Chemical fertilizer, insecticides, fungicides, herbicides, and even the exhaust fumes of farm machinery sprayed on the soil in very fine doses will have an effect on the soil organisms. If the soil is healthy, it can buffer the adverse influences and draw on eutrophic influences, buffer the pH, the moisture, mediate between cosmic and terrestrial factors, and thus provide a living, healthy medium for plants to grow in. Plants, as we have seen, do not end at the tip of their roots or leaves, but are intimately connected with all that goes on in the surrounding soil. Plants cannot be sick by themselves, rather sick plants are registering disturbances in the environment of the plants.

If the plants are ailing, then medicines can be used to lead the soil back into its life-supporting state and to strengthen the plants. Since similar biological, bio-chemical processes go on in the soil and plant macrocosmically as go on within the human or animal organism microcosmically, the use of such medicines makes sense. Such medicines are infusions, decoctions, macerations, and extractions made from herbs or manures, which having gone through living processes, work more gently on the soil than would chemical salts.

The bio-dynamic preparations help to restore abused soil

over the years, and to maintain healthy soil. They can be used prophylactically for various problems. "Preparations create conditions under which plant and soil become sufficiently sensitive to react to and absorb the incoming stream of life from the cosmos."[1] The preparations are not "food" for the plants, but facilitate the work of etheric forces. They are not the usual compost starters, although they stimulate compost organisms, and Pfeiffer bases his compost starter ("PayBac") on the soil bacteria that accumulate on the preparations as they are made. The preparations are the "dynamic" part of bio-dynamics.

How the Preparations Are Made

The preparations, arbitrarily labeled 500 through 508 by the same research group that provided the name "bio-dynamics," are based on indications given by Rudolf Steiner in his fifth agricultural lecture.

Preparation 500, the *horn-dung preparation:* Fresh cow manure is packed into the horn of a healthy cow that has fallen to the butcher's knife. In the fall, the horn is buried in good soil two feet under the ground and left until spring. After having spent the winter in the ground, the horn is taken out; the dung, by this time, is well-rotted and gives off a pleasant smell. One uses a pinch of this horn dung, about as much as a pea's size, and puts it into a normal sized bucket of lukewarm rainwater. This is then stirred for one hour, preferably with the hand. The stirring is done in one direction until a funnel is created in the water, reaching to the bottom of the pail; then the direction is abruptly

[1]John Soper, *Studying the Agricultural Course* (Clint, 1976), p. 43.

changed. Again a funnel is created, then the direction of the vortex is changed again, and so on. Preparation 500, which aids rooting processes and terrestrial forces, is then sprayed by a knapsack sprayer onto the ground that is to be planted, onto the prepared beds. A whisk broom can be used if a sprayer is not handy. The best time for the spraying is in the late afternoon.

Preparation 501, the *horn-quartz* preparation: Quartz rocks, preferably quartz mountain crystals, are pulverized. The resultant powder is made into a paste by adding rain-water and then it is inserted into a cow horn. The horn is buried in good soil about two feet deep and left in the ground throughout the summer to be excavated in the fall. Again, a peppercorn-sized portion is used for stirring rhythmically in a bucket of water for one hour. This preparation, which aids the light-and-warmth-transmitting cosmic forces, is sprayed in the morning directly onto the leaves, flowers and young fruits. It should not be sprayed on seedlings and seedbeds.

Preparations 502 to 507 are mainly used for preparing the compost to develop certain processes, break down quicker and retain and amplify energies that might otherwise be lost.

Preparation 502, *yarrow blossoms:* Moistened yarrow (*Achillea millefolium*) blossoms, gathered in spring, are packed into the bladder of a deer stag or hart. The bladder is hung into the sun over the summer and buried into good soil over the winter. The contents, dug up in the spring, will aid the compost to regulate potassium and sulphur processes.

Preparation 503, chamomile blossoms (*Matricaria chamomilla*): Chamomile blossoms are gathered in the summer. They are moistened with chamomile tea shortly before they are stuffed into the small intestine of a freshly butchered cow, made into little links of sausages and buried into good humus in the fall. They spend the winter in the ground in an area where the meltwater of snow is accessible to them. The chamomile preparation helps regulate the calcium processes in the composts.

Preparation 504, *stinging nettle (Urtica dioica):* The nettle is buried in the soil for the duration of a whole year, preferably enclosed in a mantle of peat moss. It aids the humification of the compost.

Preparation 505, *oak bark (Quercus robur):* Scrapings from the outer rind of the oak bark are placed into the skull cavity of a domestic animal such as goat, sheep, or cow. The skull is left whole. The oak bark is put in through the foramen magnum. The skull is buried in the fall into a ground that has water percolating through it, as for example under a leaking drainpipe. The contents are usable in the spring. This preparation works on the calcium processes and contributes to making plants disease-resistant.

Preparation 506, *dandelion blossoms (Taraxacum officinale):* In the fall, moistened dandelion flowers that have been gathered in the spring and dried, are folded into the mesentery (the membrane that holds the intestines fast) of a cow. This is buried into the soil until the spring. It helps to regulate the silica processes in relation to the potassium processes.

Preparation 507, *valerian, or garden heliotrope, blossoms (Valeriana officinalis):* This final one of the compost preparations is made from the squeezings of valerian flowers. The juice, diluted in rainwater, when sprayed on the compost, will regulate the phosphorus processes.

The compost preparations, which are admittedly difficult

to make, are used in very minute amounts. A teaspoon-sized amount of each (502 through 506) suffices for a normal garden compost of three cubic yards. Traditionally, the small amounts are placed into holes poked into the compost about a foot or two deep, in the following order, as one looks at the compost from the top. Valerian preparation, made from a drop of valerian stirred rhythmically in a bucket of water for an hour, is sprayed over the entire compost.

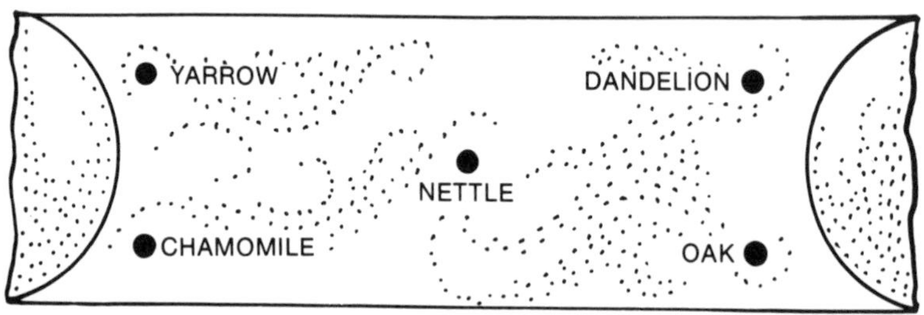

Once the preparations are made, the supply of them will serve to treat many composts, for many seasons. After they have been dug up in the spring, they can be kept in glass jars, packed in a box lined with peat. The valerian preparation is kept in a tinted, corked bottle in the same manner.

Preparation 508, *horsetail (Equisetum arvense):* A tea is made by boiling the horsetail for 20 minutes. This tea can be stored and later diluted with water. It is used as a prophylactic against mildews and other fungal disorders.

There are, of course, other possible preparations. Any *materia medica botanica,* if understood in its relation to the etheric forces, has potential for agricultural-horticultural use. To find other preparations is even a necessity in those parts of the world where climate and ecology do not permit the growing of the standard preparation herbs. What is one to use in place of stinging nettle, yarrow, valerian, etc. in Africa, Australia or South America? Much research needs to be done and the traditional "wortcunning" of our ancestors and of native medicine men, brujos and witchdoctors, needs to be investigated again.

How Can One Explain the Preparations?

For those trained in current scientific agriculture, it is easy to understand why bio-dynamics has been referred to as "muck and magic." The author himself, when first introduced to the preparations, thought that if there was any virtue to them at all, it would be found in the psychological feeling of participation with the garden that one experiences while making and applying them.[2] For are not the feelings and thoughts of the gardener one of the factors that make up the totality of the farm or garden organism? However, to say that psychological projection is all there is to it would be incorrect. This has been shown by experimental evidence.[3] For a comprehension of the preparations (the

---

[2]The author was reminded of the Russian story of a young heir to a run-down, indebted estate. The young man, at a loss about what to do, consults an old wise woman who gives him a bag of magical sand. "If you want your land to prosper," she advises him, "traverse your land each morning and strew a few grains of this magic sand on the fields and into each barn." He takes the advice to heart and, in a few years, the estate is prosperous and healthy again. Why? To the normally lazy peasants, the new master appearing in fields and barn early each day seemed to be a man who meant business. Not wanting to be shamed, they worked hard. In a similar way, from a Freudian perspective, one could interpret much of the spraying, dusting, and burning that goes on in agriculture, not so much in view of its rational effectiveness, as from its psychological effect.

[3]See Koepf, Pettersson, Schaumann, *Bio-Dynamic Agriculture* (1976) and Kolisko, *Agriculture of Tomorrow* (1939).

same holds for a comprehension of Steiner's *Agricultural Course),* one must have a grasp of the whole picture before the parts make sense. One must be an observer of subtle interconnections in Nature and share an understanding of Steiner's conception of the world, his anthroposophy, as is painfully spelled out in a number of his lectures and books, before one can realize that one is not dealing with a number of arbitrary and abstruse practices which one is asked to blindly believe.[4] Instead, one is given something that is rooted in a wide conception as to the nature of the Universe, and one is asked to constantly employ critical intelligence to come to grasp with the bio-dynamic practices.

We will try to look a little closer at the possible rationale of the preparations. Why, in the horn-dung and horn-quartz preparations, are the horns of a cow used? To answer, we must look once again at the nature of the cow, this animal with a four-chambered stomach that processes its food for 18 days, digesting and utilizing cellulose and roughage with the aid of the most varied intestinal flora. The resultant cow dung is a highly astralized substance containing numerous animal secretions in the form of digestive juices. It is as though the cow being, in its chewing of the cud and slow digestive process of taking apart the fodder, is meditating on the energies set free from the herbage, experiencing inwardly the forces that had been bound into the plants. Perhaps that is why the cow is outwardly so dull, much like the proverbial guru in meditation. The horns and hoofs at the cow's extremities keep the forces from raying outward

[4]For a simple introduction, see A. P. Shepherd, *A Scientist of the Invisible* (London: Hodder and Stoughton, 1954).

and dissipating themselves. The horns are thus a device that concentrates and throws back what is pressing into it, like a condenser.[5] At first glance, this seems far-fetched, but when we look at the importance of shapes per se, it is certainly a probability. Spatial relations alone account for the smooth running of an automobile, as in the setting of the valves or the spark gap in the internal combustion engine. The tone quality of instruments, such as violins, trumpets, or drums depends on the shape of the instrument. If the shape is off, the sound vibrations are disharmonious. Recent studies on the shape of pyramids indicate that the pyramidal containers made after the exact geometric relationships of the great Cheops of Giza, can naturally mummify carcasses, keep maggots out and seem to collect alpha waves.[6] Czech engineer Karel Dbral took out a patent for sharpening dull razor blades inside a pyramidal box, and Czech brewers found that the quality of their beer lessened when they switched from the traditional round barrels to more functional rectangular containers.[7] In optics, it is the shape of the lens that focuses light waves. Suggestions have been made that bees could not make honey were it not for spending their larval stage in hexagonal cells, and humans would not be able to think were it not for a spherical cranium. Perhaps, then, it is possible that the architectural form of the cow's horn concentrates the earth's forces as

[5]Kolisko, in *Agriculture of Tomorrow,* sees in this a key to the treatment of the dread hoof-and-mouth disease.

[6]Pat G. Flanagan, *Pyramid Power* (Davores Co., 1973).

[7]Sheila Ostrander and Lynn Schroder, *Psychic Discoveries Behind the Iron Curtain* (New York: Bantam Books, Inc.), chap. 27.

they work on the dung or on the pulverized quartz.

The embryologist and pediatrician, Dr. Karl Koenig, in his discussion of the compost preparations, makes the point that it is not so much the substances of the animal sheaths that surround the vegetable matter, but that it is the tectonics of the sheaths that concentrate and amplify formative forces which are essential. These organs do so in the animal and continue this function in the soil when handled properly.[8]

Most of the preparations are buried into the ground: the horn-dung, dandelion, yarrow, chamomile, and oak bark are buried into the ground over the winter; the stinging nettle stays in the ground both winter and summer, and the horn-quartz preparation is buried during the summer. This is not an arbitrary arrangement, either, for different forces work in the ground in the summer than in the winter. In the winter, the earth becomes, contrary to casual thought, more alive. The plants retreat into the ground in the form of seeds, tubers, roots and rosettes that closely hug the earth; leaves fall off and the external picture of summer vegetation disappears. Animals such as frogs, insects, mammals tend at this time to burrow into the soil to hibernate. During January and February, the crystallization forces are the strongest, even penetrating the ground in the form of frost and ice to a degree. It is this concentrating force that is captured by the horn-dung preparation which will eventually aid root formation.

The horn-quartz, on the other hand, will aid the fruiting and flowering and is related to the forces of light and

---

[8]Karl Koenig, *On the Sheaths of the Preparations* (England: Glencraig Printery, Reprint 1968).

warmth. For this reason, a mountain quartz crystal is preferred, to obtain the silica. When it is put into the ground in the summer in its cow-horn sheath, it makes use of the expanding, centrifugal forces of nature when the vegetation is shooting upward and outwards toward the sun.[9]

The horn preparations are used at the rate of a few pinches per acre, and the compost preparations at the rate of a teaspoon per compost.[10] Regarding these minute quantities, one might find it presumptuous that they should have an effect. Yet, what has been discovered about the effects of trace minerals, micronutrients, catalysts, hormones and enzymes should lend credibility to the possibility of such effects. In homeopathy, for example, dilutions so fine that they are not grasped by conventional physics and chemistry are known to have curative effects. Usually these are substances that are very poisonous in larger doses, while in homeopathic dilution they stimulate the organism. Swiss cheese makers know that just one milking from a cow that has had a penicillin injection will spoil vats of a thousand liters or more, making it no longer usable for their cheese. This is even after the small amount of substance has traveled through the large cow organism. More than an ounce of molybdenum per acre will make the plants so toxic that the animals will not eat them. The phenoxy herbicide

---

[9]For similar reasons, the Preparation 501 is sprayed out in the morning, for then, too, as Wachsmuth noted, the centrifugal forces are at work, shooting sap into stems and leaves, with maximum secretion and assimilation occurring. The cow dung, Preparation 500, is, for the opposite reason, sprayed on the ground in the late afternoon as the earth goes into its daily "in-breathing" phase.

[10]Anyone interested in exact measurements can contact the Bio-Dynamic Association or consult the book *Bio-Dynamic Agriculture* (Koepf, Pettersson and Schaumann).

2,4,5,-T that is sprayed on roadsides and forests contains an impurity created as a by-product of manufacture called dioxin. Scientists currently testing it in dosages of parts per trillion find that even in this infinitesimally small amount it is carcinogenic and mutagenic to animal organisms.[11] Pfeiffer illustrates the concept of minutest quantities in his *Bio-Dynamic Farming and Gardening* by showing that copper sulfate in a solution of 1 part to 1,000,000,000 water will hurt the Spirogyra algae, that 1 part per 700,000,000 hinders wheat from sprouting and so on.[12]

One must not think of the preparations in the same terms as one does about trace minerals or radioactive substances. They are simple, common substances that have been *potentized,* or dynamized, much like homeopathic medicine where forces are released by shaking and stirring.

In three of the preparations, horn-dung, horn-quartz and valerian, homeopathic portions are given into water which is stirred rhythmically as previously indicated. This stirring sensitizes the water and makes it receptive to imprints even if the substance dissolved therein is very minute. That matter can be sensitized is shown in phonograph records, magnetizing metals, etc. Theodor Schwenk shows in his researches the extreme receptivity and impressionability of water that is kept in rhythmic motion.[13] Water in rhythmic motion is also opened up to the workings of the planets.[14]

---

[11]William Boly, "Sweet Dioxin," in *Oregon Times Magazine* (Sept. 1977), p. 39.

[12]E. Pfeiffer, *A Condensation of Bio-dynamic Farming and Gardening.*

[13]T. Schwenk, *Sensitive Chaos, Grundlagen der Potenzforschung.*

[14]T. Schwenk, "Wassernot und Wasserrettung," in *Soziale Hygiene* (Stuttgart: Freies Geistesleben, 1973).

This is one of the reasons for daily stirring one's liquid manures (Russian tea, chicken manure, nettle, seaweed, comfrey, shepherd's purse and cabbage ferments). It is likely that the constant motion of blood through the body, of currents and tides in large bodies of water have a similar effect of opening up the water to cosmic forces and potencies of dissolved substances.

A Closer Look at the Herbs

All of the herbs used in the preparations are of known medicinal value, and in the system of the older science of signatures, they are associated to planets by virtue of their physiognomy of growth, the color of flowers, the geometric arrangement of leaves and petal placement and other criteria. Of course, all of the planets, and indeed the entire cosmos, work in every plant, but in some, one or the other planet's signature predominates.

In the yarrow, Venus predominates; Culpeper assigns it to Venus and in the Middle Ages, it was known as *supercilium veneris*, the eyebrows of Venus. From the fragrance and fine lacy leaves, one can tell that the sulphur process penetrates the yarrow, so that "as a medicine it is drying and binding. A decoction of it . . . is good to stop the running of the reins in men and whites in women."[15] Reins (kidneys) and bladder are of course under the rule of Venus, so it is no wonder that the hart's bladder is to be used. The hart excretes large amounts of potassium, an element found in large amounts in the yarrow. The drying action of yarrow is indicated in its Latin appelation, *Achillea*,

[15]*Culpeper's Complete Herbal*, p. 397.

named after the Greek warrior Achilles because warriors used the herb to dry the bleeding of wounds. An old English divination relates to the venereal aspects of the yarrow in the following way:

Thou pretty herb of Venus tree
Thy true name is Yarrow
Now who my bosom friend may be
Pray tell thou me tomorrow.

The answer would come in a dream. Sexuality has to do with the relating of the astral to the etheric and, in a wider sense, we can expect this function to be fulfilled by the yarrow as a compost preparation.

The chamomile, a tough little herb with flighty, lacelike foliage and a strong smell, is recognized as one of the most potent medical herbs. It grows on compacted, alkaline soils. Culpeper assigns it to the Sun; so did apparently the Germanic tribes, who "dedicated it to their sun god Baldur because to them the chamomile's yellow center and white petals around it seemed to convey sun forces."[16] It helps to relieve pain, stop inflammations, and soothe troubled intestines. Its name *matricaria (L. mater)* refers to its use during childbirth to lessen the labor pains. In the preparations, the herb is given into intestines, where its Mercury processes are called upon to keep the ethereal in flow and harmonize the astral.[17]

The stinging nettle is truly a Mars plant, ready to inflict a jab at anyone who dares touch it, forming a special relation to iron, so that it can be used as medicine for iron deficiency

---

[16]*Rodale Herb Book*, p. 389.

[17]C. B. J. Lievegoed, *The Working of the Planets and the Life Processes in Man and Earth* (Stourbridge, Worcs.: Broome Farm, Clent, 1972).

anemia. It makes a good spring tonic when eaten like cooked spinach, an excellent hair rinse, and brings martian heat to arthritis and rheumatism. Placed into liquid manure pits, it helps the slurry break down fast and smoothly. It contains so much astrality (containing histamines and formic acid in its needles) that it does not need an animal organ as a sheath in the preparations.

The white oak is a Mars or Jupiter tree, but its bark contains so much calcium (78% ash content), that the bark can be assigned to the moon. This moon calcium, given to the compost after having been excreted by the oak, is activated in the skull cavity of a domestic animal, to help the plants be resistant to a number of diseases. In naturopathic medicine, oak bark has been used to counter ulcers of the stomach and other forms of internal bleeding, for it is astringent due to the tannin content. In ancient Europe, each farmstead or village had a sacred oak to protect against sorcery and lightning. Plant fungi and parasites, which appear by the excess of lunar forces, will be stayed by the use of the oak bark preparation.

Dandelion is under the rule of Jupiter as indicated by its yellow head, and its use against jaundice and liver ailments. It is a good spring tonic. Its long tap root deeply penetrating into compacted soil and its crystalline seed-formation after blooming indicate the strength of penetration by Jupiter forces in this preparation.

The valerian, the last of the compost preparations, is assigned to Saturn for its warmth-generating ability.[18] The roots can be made into a sedative tea and *valium* is a syn-

[18]Culpeper assigns it to Mercury, probably because of its many medical uses, it being known in England as "heal-all."

thetic made in imitation of the valerian root. If grown in the garden, it attracts earthworms. Sprayed over the finished compost, this preparation regulates the phosphorus processes, making it possible for the spiritual archetypes to work into the mass of materia.[19]

Having briefly discussed the herbs that go into the compost, we obtain a greater appreciation of what a compost is, and what goes on in it. The compost is a great digester; it breaks down substances completely and builds them up into a different form. It takes organized matter, plant and animal structures, returns them to chaos (unformed matter) and then rebuilds them into complex life carrying molecules. We are dealing with the mysteries of life and death. In the breaking down process and in the building up process, the wider cosmos is involved, the planets accompany each step. This is outlined beautifully in *The Working of the Planets and the Life Processes in Man and Earth,* written by the Dutch physician, C. B. J. Lievegoed. Whenever matter is returned to chaos, it becomes once again impressionable to new influences; this is so even microcosmically when people's lives are in shambles and they become open to numerous suggestions and influences. The bio-dynamic gardener provides anchoring places for the working of the planets with his preparations. These insertions into the compost become focal points through which the planetary forces can enter chaotic matter and work into the etheric, astral, and even spiritual aspects of soil, plant, animal and eventually man. We see that the use of the preparations is much more encompassing than mere compost starters.

---

[19]Lievegoed, p. 31.

We can understand the compost in another light, that of an extremely generalized organism, more generalized than the lower plants or amoeba, whose life activity is diffused throughout its substance. Just as worms and starfish, some roots and leaves can be cut in half and each part regenerates, because nowhere is life focused into specific vital organs, so one can divide the compost, seeing it as the most primitive of such generalized organisms. A continuum could be set up from the compost through the lower plants and animals to the mammals and man, the latter with their highly specialized life organs.[20] Although such highly specialized life organs are not found on the lower end of the scale, the functions of respiration, metabolism, circulation, secretion, etc. are still carried on because predispositions, *Anlagen,* of such organs exist. Cosmic rhythms, tides, temperature cycles, light rhythms and other factors work macrocosmically through these predispositions or anlagen. Such anlagen are to be found in the compost, for the compost, as we have seen, carries on complex life functions. The bio-dynamic preparations amplify these anlagen, so that the compost can become more receptive to the various cosmic impulses that work upon it. Instead of the seven major sets of endocrine glands that send hormones throughout the body regulating body chemistry, growth, calcium usage, reproduction, etc., the preparations create the proclivity for this. The preparations become anlagen for the major organs, the yarrow becomes the kidney and bladder with their Venus function, the oak bark becomes the brain with its moon function, the nettle becomes the red blood

[20]As we recapitulate phylogeny, humans can be split at an early, generalized stage, creating twins.

with its Mars function, and so on. The structuring influences of the planets can flow into our food sources again, into our fields and gardens, something that the use of artificial fertilizer salt prevents. This is why the quality of bio-dynamically raised produce is excellent, because the formative forces can flow into the plant unimpeded. In a deeper sense, then, the bio-dynamic gardener is creating a helpful being, by creating a compost and fitting it out with "organs" and skin, letting it live through its three stages, and then sacrificing it to the earth where it fertilizes and imparts its macrocosmic strength.[21] In the same vein, Koenig proposes that the compost preparations bring about a living process, where the compost heap is a "becoming being" endowed with a physical and etheric body.[22] It means providing a basis on which the archetypal plant can manifest itself.

The preparations are difficult to make, but once they are made, they will last a long time. It is best if each farmer and gardener can make his own in order to develop that personal relationship to his farm-garden organism. Often bio-dynamically interested farmers and gardeners of an area will get together and jointly make the preparations on a weekend, such as at fall equinox, and dig them up together in the spring, perhaps at spring equinox. Each participant then receives a portion. In the opinion of the author, the preparations, as any medicine, should not be bought and

[21]The creation of such a compost reminds one of the homonculus of the alchemists as described by Paracelsus when he describes "the being developed without the aid of the female organism by the art of the experienced spagyricus," which is treated by a mysterious *arcanum sanguinis hominis*, kept in horse manure for forty weeks, and so on (Hartmann, Paracelsus, p. 174).

[22]Karl Koenig, *On the Sheaths of the Preparations*, lecture 4, pp. 4-5.

sold. Most traditional healers, medicine men, and even the great doctor Paracelsus considered medicines to be gifts of the gods for the blessing of creation, not for making a profit. Such blessings should be freely given.

A less complicated way of preparing the herbs used in bio-dynamic preparations has been developed by Miss Maye Bruce of England. She suggests simply cooking the bio-dynamic herbs in honey and then applying them to the compost. Miss Bruce's method of composting is called the "Quick-Return" and the herb extracts are known in England as "Humofix."[23] Simple comparative experiments carried on in the Aigues Vertes garden showed no immediate differences in the quality of the composts thus prepared; however, that does not mean that there is no long-range effect which might be indicated by more involved studies.

Other Herbal Preparations

All medicinal plants have potential for use in the garden. A number of fermentations have already been discussed in the chapter on composting. Ferments can be made from comfrey, shepherd's purse, cabbage, nettle, thistles and many common weeds. The ferments must be stirred daily to open them up to the air and to sensitize, or potentize, the water. Each gardener should carry on his own experiments with these substances. The common bracken fern *(Pteridium aquilinum)* can be made into a tea that will drive off red mites and as a mulch it will provide potassium to the potatoes and other crops.

---

[23]M.E. Bruce, *Common Sense Compost Making* (London: Faber and Faber, 1946).

CHAPTER XIX

BIO-DYNAMIC COOKING, NUTRITION AND FOOD HANDLING

Now that we know a little bit how happy, healthy vegetables are grown, we should know how to turn them into good food without losing food value.

When it comes to eating, human beings have lost the sureness of instinct that marks the animals. This is so because the human being has evolved out of the intimate connection with nature that characterizes beings still closely tied to the macrocosm. Primitive people seem to have much more sense when it comes to eating. This is so because food practices are regulated by complex traditions, taboos and rituals that were evolved at a time when human consciousness was much more closely tied to its spiritual origins, the macrocosm. Modern human beings, if they rely on their "instincts" overeat and become obese, become hyperactive and rot their teeth due to excess sugar intake, damage their nerves and circulatory system by taking too many stimulants, create sluggish stool by eating too many soft, processed foods, and help no one except their doctors. Growing a nice garden is not enough; we must become conscious of what we ought to do with the produce.

What is food? All foods are derived from *living* organisms. Man, with all of his technology and long years of research, has not been able to create one single lettuce leaf. All food, including animal substances, is based upon plant life. "You live because we live!" the plant admonishes us in a quiet way every time we take a bite to eat or draw a breath of air.

What is it that the plant does, in that it becomes food for other living organisms? One can set up the equation of assimilation and photosynthesis in which 12 parts water (H_2O) and 6 parts carbon dioxide (CO_2), in the presence of sunlight, warmth and certain catalytic minerals, yield sugars ($C_6H_{12}O_6$) which can be converted to starches and lipids, and yield oxygen (O_2) and water. A more goetheanistic way of looking at this is to see how the plant organism can combine the "dead" elements, earth (soil), water, air (carbon dioxide) and fire (light and warmth); and, in combining them, *vitalize* (L. vita=life) them. The energies that bring these elements together in an orderly form are cosmic energies, as they come to us primarily from the sun, but also from the moon, the planets and the stars. Thus when we eat a plant (and all food is ultimately plant), we are eating the entire universe, that is, the elements as they are arranged by cosmic impulses. One can say that the plant captures celestial life and fixes it into a physical form using the elements. When we eat, we take that celestial life into ourselves and it becomes our own life.

Actually, eating food is only one form of nutrition available to us. Breathing fresh air nourishes us, as do all the impressions that pass our senses. A garden is a source of health not only because of the nutritious food it provides, but also because of the fresh air, and the sights and sounds that nourish body and soul.

We *transform* the macrocosmic, celestial and terrestrial impulses, by means of the process of digestion, into microcosmic impulses. Our digestion breaks the substances down completely and releases the forces that had been fixed into it. Animals use these forces for running, springing, frolicking

and giving expression to their astrality. The human being does this, too, but takes it a step further, using the energy to think and reflect, to intuit and imagine, to speak and to love. He has the free will to decide what to use these energies for that the plants have given him; to do good or to do works of evil, to give of himself, like the plant, or to self-indulge.

In order to have the cosmic energies available to carry on a healthy culture and sustain the life of our body, soul and spirit on earth, we must see to it that we have the right kind of food . . . Food which comes from plants that have been grown under the best natural conditions and which is eaten with only minimal loss of vitality through cooking and preparing. Inadequately grown food and badly cooked food will not only harm the body, but make it impossible to think, feel and will in a holistic manner.

Pfeiffer, in his foreword to the *Agricultural Course* by Steiner, relates a conversation he had with Dr. Steiner about the shortcomings and faults so typical in all sorts of spiritually oriented movements. Pfeiffer asked: "How can it happen that the spiritual impulse, and especially the inner schooling for which you are constantly providing stimulus and guidance bear so little fruit? Why do the people concerned give so little evidence of spiritual experience, in spite of all their efforts?" Why, he continued his questioning, are people having such trouble carrying out their intentions without being pulled off the right path by personal ambition, illusions and petty jealousies? The thought-provoking and surprising answer that Steiner gave was that: "This is a problem of nutrition. Nutrition as it is today does not supply the strength necessary for manifesting spirit in physical life. A bridge can no longer be built from thinking to will and action. Food plants no longer contain the forces people need for this."[1] Elsewhere, Steiner states that if current developments continue, the time will come when people will starve at a fully-decked table, which seems entirely possible with our denatured, processed food.

With this as a background, we can see how bio-dynamics has vital consequences for the future of humanity. In order to have the right kind of food that fully supports our thinking, feeling and willing functions; we must have foods full of vitality. This starts, for one thing, with healthy, living soil as Are Waerland, J. I. Rodale and Jethro Kloss[2] also have

---

[1]Ehrenfried Pfeiffer, in preface to Steiner's *Agriculture* (London: 1974), p. 7.

[2]Jethro Kloss, *Back to Eden* (Santa Barbara, Ca.: Woodbridge Press, 1975).

realized. But the proper soil and growing techniques are not enough; our cooking must not devitalize the food. Loss of vitality can be incurred during:

a. storage
b. processing
c. cooking
d. eating habits
e. seasoning

Freshness

The fresher the food, the better, the more etheric properties are available. Leaf crops are best harvested in the morning hours as the vitality rises with the sap into the plant in the morning hours in its daily rhythm.[3] Root crops are best harvested in the evening as the vitality draws into the roots in the "in-breathing" phase of the daily cycle. Plants, as living organisms, are constantly changing and growing. Never are they exactly the same. Alan Chadwick states that a fruit is ripe only for one moment; before that the fruit is still green and ripening, and after that, it is already starting to decompose. Thus vegetables, especially fruits, must be picked at the right moments. Plants that have been picked a long time previously usually wilt and eventually rot, and even if artificially preserved, will not be able to transmit vitality well.

Processing

The Swiss nutritionist, W. Kollath, emphasizes *wholeness*

[3]Wachsmuth, *Erde und Mensch,* Chapter 6.

and *freshness* as criteria for good food.[4] By that criteria, a fresh carrot is better than carrot juice; whole wheat is better than white, processed flour.

	Fresh	**Whole**	**Vitalized (Alive)**
Ripe Apple	+	+	
Fresh Carrot	+	+	
Carrot Juice	+	–	
Preserves	–	–	
Refined Sugar	–	–	Mineralized (Dead)

The further away one gets from freshness and wholeness, the closer one gets toward *mineralization,* the state at which substances fall out of the cycle of living matter. We have seen this falling out of the living cycle in our study of composts and manures, which are normally full of etheric and astral life, and mineral fertilizers which are quite lifeless in comparison and which are salts, dead end-processes fallen out of the living cycle. Studies with rats show that whole wheat grain keeps the animals healthy; ground wheat is not quite as good, and modern processed flour will eventually lead to the animals' demise. Modern milling techniques remove bran and germ, leaving the flour so denatured that synthetic nutrients have to be added to create fortified flour. In earlier times, it was possible to keep prisoners healthy on bread and water, but today, because of the mismanagement of the soil and the processing of the flour, the poor prisoners would starve. Like flour, sugar is devitalized by excessive processing, causing tooth decay and a host of other

[4]Werner E. Loeckle, *Bewusste Ernahrung und Gesunde Lebensfuhrung* (Freiburg, i. Br.: Verl. Die Kommenden, 1970), p. 105.

problems. Good sweeteners are honey, malt, molasses, date sugar, or fruits.

Loss of wholeness results from unnecessary peeling, skinning and grinding of the vegetables. Often most of the vitamins are in the rinds and skins.

Canning has become a popular way of preserving foods for the winter months. It goes along with the pioneer mystique that many modern "folksy" people are trying to recapture and it takes a lot of work and ruins many of the nutrients. Rather than canning, winter gardening and storage of whole foods, roots and tubers in the root cellar is perhaps a better way to go. In the Rogue Valley region of southern Oregon, for example, it is possible to have a full diet of garden vegetables all winter long, and not have to eat the same vegetable for two weeks. (See Appendix, WINTER GARDENING IN OREGON.) Variety on the winter plate includes cabbages, brussel sprouts, kale, collard greens, mustard greens, turnips and turnip greens, rutabagas, Swiss chard, beets and beet greens, leeks, parsnips, hamburg parsley, carrots, osyter plant, Jerusalem artichokes, celeriac, florence fennel and others. Most of these plants can be kept in the ground over the winter with minimal protection of mulch or plastic tents. Potatoes should be dug up and stored separately from other vegetables because their respiration causes others, especially apples, to rot more quickly.

In the winter months, tasty salads need not be lacking. *Sugarhat*, a tender salad vegetable developed in Switzerland, is frost hardy. This salad, which grows into a football-sized head of tightly packed blanched leaves, can be garnished with the frost hardy corn salad (maches). As a cooking vegetable or as a fine salad, *witlof* can be used. Witlof, a chicory, is grown all summer long and in the fall the leaves are cut and fed to animals or composted, while the roots are placed in cool storage. The former hot bed that has been emptied of its by-now well-rotted manure, can be used for such a storage. After winter solstice, at periodic intervals, the roots of the witlof can be planted by fitting them tightly next to each other in a container which is put into a warmer room, such as a basement or a heated garage. A mixture of sand and peat or sawdust is placed over these planted roots to a depth of about one foot. The witlof responds to the warmth and watering by growing a thick, white terminal bud. When the bud starts to peek out above the sand-peat mixture, it is time to harvest this delicious vegetable.

These winter salads can be augmented by greens and herbs growing in the fallowed beds. (Also complemented with boiled eggs, as they are not as sweet as summer salads.) Added as spices and flavoring, the herbs include: ground ivy *(Glechoma hederacea);* chickweed *(Stellaria media);* plantain *(Plantago major, P. lanceolata);* wild mustards *(Brassica arvensis, B. albus, B. nigra);* winter cress

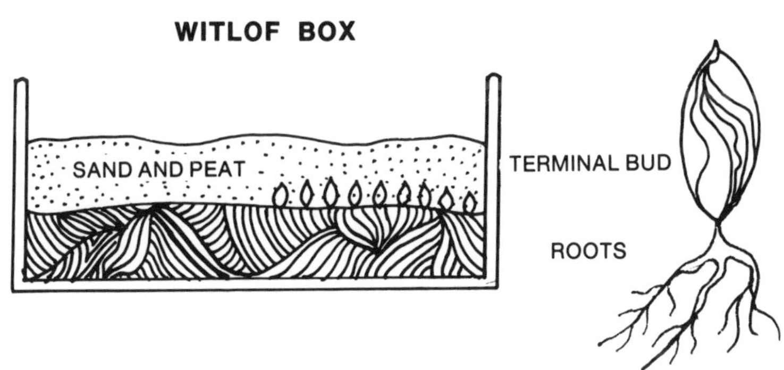

(Barbarea vulgaris); sheep sorrel *(Rumex acetosella);* dandelion *(Taraxacum officinale)* and others. The number of greens increases toward the spring.

Of course, pumpkins, squashes, onions and a number of fruits can be stored for the winter, also.

Given all of these plants, one can achieve a good, wholesome variety in one's winter diet without relying on processed, canned, or imported foods. Perhaps the only canning that needs to be done is to save some of the good summer fruits such as strawberries, raspberries, and blackberries, which make a delicious winter treat. Eating the fruits and vegetables in their season keeps us aware of the rhythms of the macrocosm, supplying us with the etheric energies we need at specific times of the year. The experience of a stronger connectedness with the forces that pervade our garden will be ours if we follow the plant cycle in our diet into the root, bud and seed in the winter months, enjoy the tonic of greens in the spring, and round out the summer and autumn with ripe fruit and seed crops. Although as human beings we have greatly emancipated ourselves from the dictates of the cosmos in the course of evolution, we still respond to the seasonal cycles, such that we become more inward, reflective and indoor oriented in the winter and we become more open to the outer world when the days lengthen. The recognition of our soul's response to the changing rhythms of the earth is expressed in the meditations given in Rudolf Steiner's *Calendar of the Soul.*

Cooking

It goes without saying that cooking is one of the most important parts of food preparation. It is proverbial that food should be cooked with love in order to become us well. The Chinese, with family farms of a few acres, not only grow their food intensively, but know not to ruin the food through excessive cooking. They steam and quick-fry with very little flavor or nutrient loss.

Steaming is one of the best ways to prepare vegetables. The water collected in the steaming pan should always be saved, for it contains most of the water-soluble vitamins. This water can be served as a soup, flavored with minced herbs, butter, egg, soy sauce, nutritional yeast, or whatever is preferred.

Different processes of food preparation unlock different nutrients. In Aigues Vertes this was taken into account by steaming or cooking two-thirds of the vegetables and quick-frying the other third in vegetable oil. (It is important to add water occasionally during the frying process to keep the oil from heating too much.) The cooked and quick-fried vegetables were always served around a *staple* such as rice, millet, barley and other grains or potatoes. Some salads made of lettuces and of raw vegetables provided the fresh greens with the meal, or were served as hors d'oeuvres along with sprouts (wheat, lentil, bean or alfalfa) in the winter. A diet of this nature, along with an assortment of herb teas, kept the people of the village extraordinarily healthy.

Important is the idea of a staple. A staple (AS. stapol = post or pillar) is a total food containing all the nutrition needed by human beings; it is the "daily bread," the "staff of life," the food wherein all the elements are balanced according to macrobiotics. All cultures have had their staples, and for most societies it has been a grain, though for some people in the southern hemisphere the staple has been a

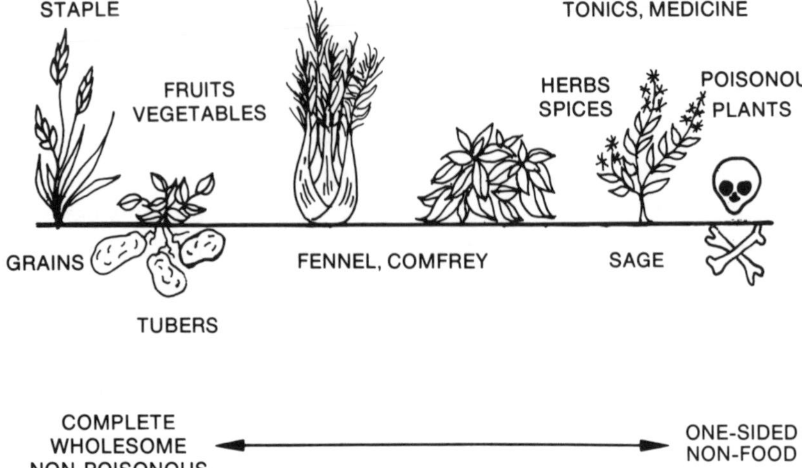

tuber (yam, taro, manioc, potato). The great civilizations of the East depended on rice, the American Indian on maize, Africa largely on millet, West Asia and the Mediterranean basin mainly on wheat, while the colder countries depended on barley, rye and oats. The grain plant, rooting firmly in the earth, stretching its ears toward the sun and sacrificing abundant leaf and flower development, is truly the nutritional foundation of human civilization. Modern people, especially 20th century Americans, tend to forget this and prefer the trimmings (meat, vegetable, fruit) to the staple. (Compare American pizza to Italian pizza.) This can have an unstabilizing effect on human health.

One can indicate the distance of a food from the staple by a continuum in the following manner:

Any grain, such as wheat berries, barley, rye, etc. can be soaked overnight for softening (lunar process) and then slowly cooked, simmered to simulate a continuing ripening process (solar process). Other foods are served in combination with this.

Some of the cooks in Aigues Vertes made sure that the "whole plant," meaning some root, some leaf and some fruit or seed was eaten every day, in order to provide wholeness for the human organism. The rule of thumb is that roots stimulate the head and nervous system, leaves the respiration and blood circulatory system and the flowers and fruits affect mainly the metabolic and limb system, whereas the staple has an overall balancing effect.[5]

Foods should not be overcooked, which leads to loss of vitamins and decreased salivating due to lack of chewing, which in turn creates weak digestion, constipation and eventually loose teeth. Loss of flavor results also from overcooking, creating a need for strong spices, pepper and salt, with the possible effect of constipation and kidney damage.

Good Food Habits

A meal must look, smell and taste good for it to be becoming and worthy of the long process of growing. We do not just eat with our taste buds but our eyes have a part in the feast. Our other organs "taste" the food also, it is just that this "tasting" does not reach the threshold of consciousness. If the other organs do not like the food, they make themselves noticed in the form of heartburn, indigestion, fatigue and even sickness. An aesthetic atmosphere

---

[5]One cook used a method of "planetary cooking:" On Sunday, there should be something white on the plate for the light of the sun; on Monday something purple, Tuesday something red for Mars; Wednesday something multicolored for Mercury; Thursday a yellow food for Jupiter; Friday green fruits or vegetables for Venus; and Saturday something dark or bluish. The grain was always there as the "Sun" and other foods as planets that periodically went into conjunction with it. Quaint as it may seem, this provided interest and nutritional variety.

with flowers, a tablecloth and pretty serving dishes aid in this sensible taking in of the meal. Traditionally, a prayer before and after the meal has created a sacred temporal space at mealtimes. A brief meditation of following with one's mind's eye the path of the food from where it came to how it got on the plate and what all was involved, connects the meal with the greater parts of the universe. Course choices and variety (e.g. raw food appetizer, soup, main meal and dessert) are provided by the many cultural traditions of food preparation.

Seasoning

Locally grown *herbs* can substitute for harsh spices. They create a delicate palate of flavors that go excellently with bio-dynamically grown vegetables. Harsh spices (which numb the taste buds to more delicate flavors after prolonged use), the overseasoning with salt, pepper, sugar, ketchup, or soy sauce, is usually due to the lack of flavor in chemically grown foods, as it is to processing, overcooking and long storage. For organically grown foods one needs merely to accentuate the innate flavors.

Herbs used as seasoning aid digestion, causing better saliva, pepsin, gall and pancreas secretion. They also help to balance certain one-sidedness in foods. Heavy cabbage is made more digestible with caraway seed; dill balances cucumbers; the watery nature of sauerkraut is aided by the fragrant, fiery nature of juniper berries; chervil and caraway are good with moony cheeses; beans are accentuated by savory and tomatoes are complemented by basil and parsley. What good is the Christmas goose without the mugwort in the dressing? Most spices bring cosmic forces into the terrestrial-lunar nature of some vegetables. Spices of the umbelliferae family show especially the effect of light and warmth ether in their delicate, lace-like leaves and aromatic seeds. The labiatae, or mint family members, retain much of the aromatic flowering processes within the realm of the leaves, leaving them aromatic, full of essential oils. All of these herbs which can be grown in the home garden are mentioned in the Rodale Herb Book (1974).

UMBELLIFERAE	LABIATAE	OTHERS
Anise	Basil	Borage
Chervil	Oregano	Chives
Fennel	Mints	Horseradish
Dill	Sage	Tarragon
Caraway	Marjoram	
Celery	Thyme	
Coriander	Rosemary	
Parsley	Savory	
Lovage		

All of the preceding list of herbs can be grown locally.

Storage

The problem of storage involves finding the best way to keep the ether body of the plant connected with its physical substance. One ought to use only the best vegetables for storage. They should not have received any substantial nitrogen fertilization late in the season. They should be harvested in dry weather and in the waning moon. Specific factors involved in storage are optimal *temperature, ventilation* and *humidity*.

Temperature: Sweet potatoes, pumpkins, squashes are warm storers (around 50°F). Cool storers (around 35°F) are potatoes, cabbages, carrots, beets, turnips, celery, oyster plant, parsnips, kohlrabi, leeks, and endives. Some of the latter can be left *in situ* in the garden in regions where it does not freeze too much.

Humidity: Onions, sweet potatoes, pumpkins, squashes, and fennel bulbs should be stored in dry places. Onions can be braided and hung in cool, dry rooms such as an unheated attic. Fennel must be stored in a dry, cool place to prevent rotting. Other vegetables prefer to be stored in a somewhat moist environment (75 to 90% humidity) as is provided by a root cellar.

Types of Storage Places

One can leave root crops (parsnips, salsify, hamburg parsley, carrots, beets) directly in the ground where they grew and cover them with a thick *mulch* of straw or leaves. Mustard, spinach, cabbages, endives, maches, leeks, kale, brussel sprouts and sugar hat can be left in the ground also, and a plastic tent can be built over the beds to protect from heavy freezes. Root crops, potatoes and cabbages can be placed into *mound storage*. The crops are placed on a wire mesh, bedded into straw, and a layer of sand and earth is put over them. They are dug out as needed. One has to be careful not to make a compost out of this. Cabbages can be uprooted and stored upside down in *trenches* which are covered with leaves or straw.

Whatever kind of storage place one may choose, simple comparative tests will show that organically grown vegetables keep a much longer time than those grown with chemical fertilizers. The latter are usually not stored in a live form, but must be frozen or canned in order to last.

Empty hotbeds make good underground storage. They

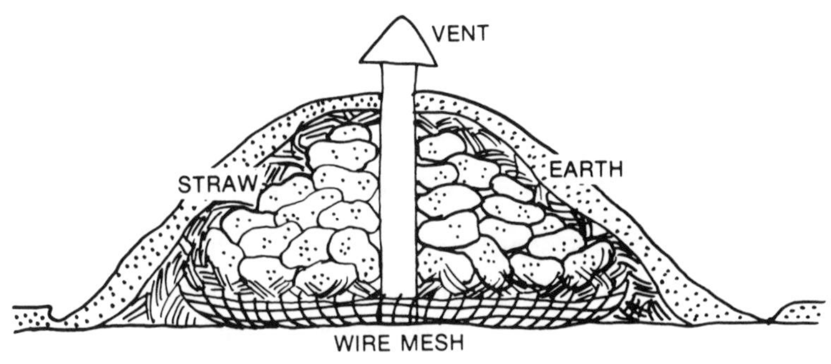

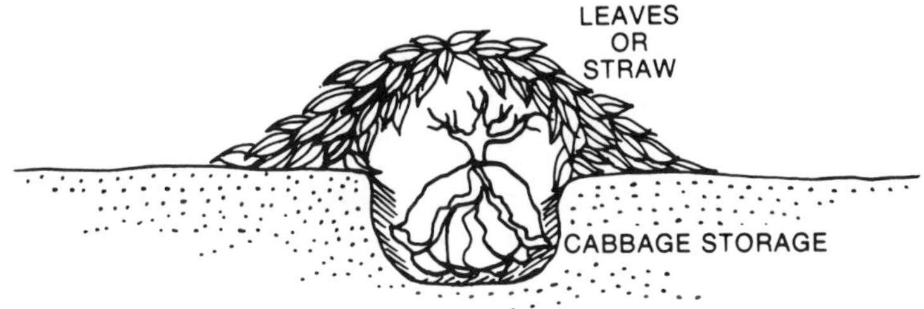

can be covered by boards and mats and are easily accessible.

Other forms of storing fruit are *drying* (fruits, beans, tomatoes), *pickling* (beans, cucumbers, pumpkins), *souring* (cabbage, beets, radish) and last and least *canning*. A number of good publications are available on all of these techniques.

CHAPTER XX

SOCIAL IMPLICATIONS

Growing food is not just a matter of biology, or even economics, but of the interrelationships among people, the use of their time, energy and resources. It is a social concern. Any use of land, any method of growing food, of assigning work and distributing products includes the human element. It requires a social arrangement.

These social arrangements, until recently in history, had been safeguarded by religious institutions, rituals, and traditions which were felt to be embedded in the very nature of the universe. From anthropological studies of simple, precolonial horticultural societies, we know how carefully these social arrangements were handled.

In most of these societies, the work of planting, hoeing, and harvesting was done by women belonging to the same blood-kin group, lineage or clan. The land was the property of the clan, not of the individual, and the highest level of social organization was the autonomous village unit. War, hunt, and the heavier work of clearing land were the domain of the men within a ritually prescribed sexual division of labor. These simple societies did not hover on the edge of starvation, but ethnologists point out that even with the simplest hand tools they were able to create a comfortable standard of living. The surpluses regularly produced were consumed in redistributive rituals and special festivals. Sometimes animals were kept by these gardening tribes, such as pigs and chickens in Melanesia and Southeast Asia.

Rites and traditions, still tied into blood lines and kin

groups (extended families at this point), continued to be the structuring principle of agricultural societies. As opposed to horticultural societies, agricultural societies utilize more animal power, grow grain, use irrigation, and the plow replaces the dibble stick and hoe. In these emergent peasant societies women still gardened, in what would become the kitchen vegetable gardens, while the men farmed in a village and community context, not yet as individuals competing in a market enterprise system. Surpluses, redistributed through barter, secured the services of specialists such as potters, tanners, weavers, cartwrights and the like.

This pattern of agriculture proved very successful and became standard as a basis of the great civilizations of the West, India, and the Far East. The land was not only a place of production, but was a place for the majority of people to live. These people were tied personally and spiritually to the land which nourished them and took their dead into its bosom. This profound tie to the land assured more or less that the life-sustaining ecology was kept intact, that love and care was lavished on it and not just profit extracted.

For the city dweller, the land became a place of refuge in war, social chaos and pestilence. This was partially true even in the United States where during economic depressions the family farm, or close relative's farm, was a place to weather the difficulties.

With the coming of an international market economy, these traditions and sympathies connected with the land no longer hold. As our anthropological studies indicate, they are becoming everywhere decadent and fading rapidly. The Industrial Revolution with its end of the commons, its turning of peasant communities (Gemeinschaft) into proletarian societies (Gesellschaft), its widening gap of the rich and poor, its creation of colonialism and the plantation system (whether growing potatoes in Ireland, sugar cane in the West Indies, cotton in Egypt or the ante-bellum South, makes little difference), the decline of functional village life and crafts with the coming of imported, cheaply manufactured goods, the consequent alienation from land and meaningful work, all of this indicates the changing relationship of man and his world. All of this has been lamented, studied and documented, and numerous attempts at solutions have been proposed. Attempts to return to an idealized past have revealed themselves as effete romanticism.

Great thinkers have tried to deal with these fundamental problems all along. Jefferson, eager to throw off vestiges of feudalism with its special privileges and stifling rigidness, envisioned the new United States as the place where the dignity of each individual was to be guaranteed by the establishment of an independent, self-reliant people based firmly on yeoman agriculture and tied into a network of functional town communities. Private ownership would guarantee the dignity of labor and that responsibility and personal interest pervaded the management of the land. Freedom to experiment and universal education would ensure continual progress and betterment of the people. Stifling centralized control and exploitative hierarchy were to be avoided, being replaced by grass-roots democracy where voting guaranteed that the voice of each household was made known.

Jefferson could not have foreseen the impact of industrialization and its implicit centralization of power and control. He could not have foreseen that the principle of private initiative was to be misused by monopolies working against the interest of society as a whole, merely for self-aggrandizement and profit, while passing the costs (pollution, resource depletion, urban sprawl and other pathologies) on to the public as a whole.

A century later, Marx, realizing the scope of the Industrial Revolution, analyzed the phenomenon of alienation, the condition of a humanity cut off from its roots, its meaning, where the worker has neither a relation to his tools nor his products and experiences himself as a commodity and the owner is alienated from the actual process of labor and involved in abstract notions of capital and ownership. Marx foretold that a rectifying revolution would of historical necessity come about, in which people would regain the dignity of their work and become socially responsible again. He did not foresee the effect of unions, automation, the mechanisms of co-option and the adaptability of the corporations. In overestimating industrial production, he did not understand the sanctity of the soil and he was limited by the materialistic Zeitgeist of the nineteenth century.

The mechanisms of the world market and the Industrial Revolution rambled on, creating masses of dispossessed peasants and reducing others to cheap labor sources for commodities, while the mounting pressures of an international economy with global networks of markets, resources, and power stiffened the competition and increased the monopolistic hold of the corporations or centralized state structures.

The Soviet "corporation" controlled production on 97 percent of the land of the Russian empire in both horizontal and vertical monopoly. Its trading partners and competitors in the western world have grown increasingly powerful also.

Currently, corporations are opting for control of food production and, as Dow Chemical, ITT, Coca-Cola, Gulf & Western, Kaiser Aluminum, Aetna Life Insurance, Goodyear, Tenneco, Ralston-Purina, and Monsanto increase their acreage of land,[1] family farmers, people who have a personal stake and a lifestyle invested in the soil, are being forced out of farming at a rate of 100,000 farms per year.[2]

Corporations envision a worldwide network of supply and demand, as already seen in huge shipments of wheat, fertilizer, raw fiber, coffee, tropical fruit, latex, and other commodities. Mechanized production of genetically engineered tomatoes and other vegetables in northern Mexico for the tables of North America, leaves substantial portions of poor campesinos deprived of land and hungry. The same is shown in the selling of the rich Peruvian catches of anchovies to U.S. chicken batteries and cattle feedlots for fodder, while the Peruvian Indio suffers protein deficiency and the guano fertilizer industry is laid still because the seagulls that feed on the anchovies and produce the guano are starving.[3] Purex and United brands own about a third of the U.S. green leaf vegetable production. Green Giant owns about 25% of the canned pea and corn production.[4] Year after year, five crops of heavily chemicalized, mechanically grown iceberg lettuces are

---

[1]Michael Perelman, "Efficiency in Agriculture: The Economics of Energy," in *Radical Agriculture* (New York: Harper and Row, 1976), p. 71.

[2]Sheldon L. Greene, "Corporate Accountability and the Family Farm," in *Radical Agriculture,* p. 53.

[3]E. N. Anderson, Jr., "The Life and Culture of Ecotopia," in *Reinventing Anthropology,* ed. Dell Hymes (New York: Vintage Books, 1974), p. 268.

[4]Perelman, "Efficiency in Agriculture," in *Radical Agriculture,* p. 71.

produced in Salinas Valley, California, amounting to about a quarter of the iceberg lettuce sold in supermarkets across the country. More awesome figures could be cited of the trends and developments and a number of books and articles exist to this effect.[5]

It has been shown that large-scale corporate farming is not as efficient as small-scale family farming or gardening; it does not achieve better, cheaper and more production per acre.[6] The same can be said of the former Soviet state-owned "factory in the fields," the *sovkhoz,* and the collective farm, the *kolkhoz.* On small, private plots, where personal judgment and responsibility can be exercised, the Russian peasant significantly out-produced the government supported kolkhoz and sovkhoz.[7] Small farms are more tuned to the specific needs of the land, providing better stewardship of the land ecologically, upon which all increased production must be ultimately based.

It is the tax write-offs, government favoritism, exploitation

---

[5] Michael Allaby and Floyd Allen, *Robots Behind the Plow (*Emmaus, Pa.: Rodale Press, 1974).
Jim Hightower, *Hard Tomatoes, Hard Times* (Cambridge, Mass.: Schenkman).
Perelman, *Radical Agriculture,* ed. Richard Merrill (New York: Harper & Row, 1976).

[6] Perelman, *Radical Agriculture,* pp. 62, 82.

[7] "Household plots, ranging in size from six-tenths of an acre up to one and one quarter acres, continued to be a major source of food for the nation. In 1959 this private sector produced over 80 percent of the eggs, 46 percent of the vegetables and 60 percent of the potatoes consumed in the Soviet Union. In 1963, 45.6 percent of meat and milk products came from private husbandry, which occupied a scant 3.1 percent of the total land under cultivation. . . The Party wanted to abolish private plots, but as no formula had been found to produce adequate food supplies through the kolkhoz and sovkhoz farms alone, such drastic action could not be taken," from Ian Gray and Editors of Horizon, *History of Russia* (New York: American Heritage, 1970), p. 392.

of migrant workers, and monopolistic practices that put the corporate farmers at an advantage, not more efficiency. If one were to calculate the ecological damage to the soil, the destruction of natural habitats of beneficial animals, the genetic impoverishment of crop varieties, the unbridled squandering of fossil fuel energy in the making of and using labor-saving machinery, insecticides, fertilizer, herbicides, the processing, packing, transporting and storing, not to mention the social costs and health costs throughout the world of people deprived of meaningful employment, the creation of slums and urban sprawl as a result of rural depopulation, the continuing nutritional decline and increase in cancer and degenerative disease, then one can see that this kind of farming is not progressive at all, but the tool of unsocial, special interests.

The rapid depletion of fossil fuel brings humanity to the point of making a decision, whether to continue the trend of corporate, large-scale, industrial farming, or whether to evolve into a different direction. To continue the trend implies the development of nuclear energy, which, in turn, necessitates increased centralized control (to handle financing, distribution, guard against sabotage, "safeguard" plutonium wastes, etc.). Organic and bio-dynamic farming and gardening can be seen in this regard as a means of showing a different direction, a vote for human dignity and independence, a highly powerful social and political statement in the decision about where human evolution is going next.

At this point in history, only in China does there seem to be the semblance of adjustment. Mao Tse Tung, with a pragmatic mixture of Chinese tradition and reinterpreted Marxist theory, has been effective in inspiring people to help themselves in creating livable conditions. In his stress of community self-reliance and decentralization, he broke with the Soviet model in 1958. No stifling obligatory production quotas were imposed, since the peasants on the grass-roots level should make the decisions about production. The peasants organized themselves into teams consisting of several households or a hamlet which, having combined their land holdings, work it in common. So-called brigades consisting of a village or of several hamlets work together in projects that require a larger organizational unit, e.g. irrigation or reforestation. The commune itself consists of several brigades, including a town where light manufacture of such items as tools or clothes can occur. It is only in the sector of national defense and heavy industries that the state is involved. As a result of this revolution, the Chinese have freed themselves from the burdens of landlord, moneylender, and the abject poverty and starvation that characterized the country before.[8] The revolution consisted primarily of social reorganization, not of a new technology, akin to the "Green Revolution."[9]

The Chinese experience is admirable, but is not necessarily applicable in the highly urbanized, industrialized West. For Americans, it is probably much closer to their folk-spirit and history to reconsider the ideas of Jeffersonian

---

[8]Herbert Franz Schurmann, *People's China: (The China Reader)* (New York: Vintage Books, 1974), Part I, "Communes."

[9]Michael Perelman, "The Green Revolution: American Agriculture in the Third World," in *Radical Agriculture*, p. 123: In China agricultural production has more than doubled since 1949 without any appreciable change in the level of technology. It has been achieved largely by the intensification and improvement of traditional techniques within the new institutional framework.

democracy. A number of thinkers, such as Wendell Berry,[10] Robert Rodale,[11] and Charles Walters, Jr.[12] are urging a reconsideration of this approach. E. F. Schuhmacher's ideas on intermediate technology go in the same direction.[13]

Wendell Berry gives convincing evidence that our social problems, urban riots, idle, drifting youth, unemployment, and lack of meaning in our lives are related to the loss of our Jeffersonian foundation, our alienation from the land. Agri-business has succeeded in replacing some 40 million people from the land between 1920 and 1970, to be absorbed into the sprawling city and its slums, where jobs, due to automation, are increasingly difficult to get. Why not make it possible for people to get back to the land, if they want to, where meaningful work can be done? Why not revitalize local skills? Why not use local energy, such as animal and human energy, wind, solar, wood, water and methane energy wherever applicable, instead of costly polluting fossil fuel which is finite and creates international tensions, or nuclear fuel which is unbelievably expensive and so toxic that life-destroying wastes will have to be guarded for hundreds of thousands of years.

Berry cites the Amish community, which shows no men-

---

[10]Wendell Berry, *The Unsettling of America: Culture and Agriculture* (San Francisco: Sierra Club Books, 1977).

[11]Robert Rodale, as editor and publisher of the *Organic Gardening and Farming Magazine* (Emmaus, Pa.: Rodale Press, Inc.), presents articles and editorials that are in line with grass-roots American tradition.

[12]Charles Walters, Jr. is the publisher of the farming Journal, "Acres, U.S.A.," *The Case for Eco-Agriculture* (Raytown, Missouri: Acres, USA).

[13]E. F. Schuhmacher, *Small Is Beautiful: A Study of Economics as if People Mattered* (London: Blond Briggs, 1973).

tal breakdowns, alcoholism, alienation, sexual problems, crime, or pollution, as an example of local economic independence. The large households of extended families are independent economically in gardening, cooking, simple technology, and energy, while at the same time highly responsible to the community as a whole. There are no neglected poor, sick and old, and the young are given community support to start out on their own. In case of fire or catastrophe, the entire community is there to give assistance.

It is within a social organization that is based on local independence, operating in freedom from stifling centralized regulations, that the farm-garden organism discussed in this book has the best chance of unfolding. Often such a farm-garden organism is more of a far-off ideal striving for realization than it is a present possibility. Though it may seem utopian, it is still a direction that can be taken in any garden, no matter how small.

The Implementation of Bio-Dynamic Gardening

Gardening can be carried out in a number of social contexts. There are, first of all, the small, home gardens that provide relaxation and fresh food to the family unit. Americans are familiar with the "Victory gardens" of the war years, and "inflation gardens" and retirement gardens are becoming popular at this point in history. The worker's gardens or allotment gardens along railroad tracks and on the outskirts of European cities, function in a similar fashion, providing contact with nature, relaxation and fresh fruit and vegetables to the white collar and blue collar urban workers. As outgrowths of the socialist movement of the late 19th century, they could be rented by anyone for a nominal fee. It is in the context of these small plots that the French Intensive Method was developed.[14] Workers saved their garbage, ashes and coffee grounds and dutifully carried them to the allotment garden composts; they planted berries, vegetables, and fruit trees, and whole families spent weekends picnicking in these little oases.

Besides these small privately owned or rented gardens, there are commercial gardens growing vegetables for a competitive market, communal gardens belonging to communes or alternative societies, institutional gardens, and finally, gardens integrated into a larger farm organism. Biodynamics can be practiced in each of these instances; one need not wait for a social revolution in order to garden. Gardening itself is so basic and fundamental that it does not need the energy input and monetization that is required for so many other undertakings. It is simple and inexpensive in spite of the distorting claims of salesmen and writers for industry.

The small garden, if handled right, can satisfy nutritional needs, save on food bills, provide for essential contact with nature and serve aesthetic purposes. One does not need expensive equipment for this at all. With permanent, double-dug beds, one does not even need a rototiller. A shredder is helpful but not necessary, and could be held in common by a neighborhood or a group of allotment gardeners, since there is no need for everyone to use it at the same time. The only tools needed are a spade, a digging fork, a wheel-

[14]Small entrepreneurs around Paris originated the "French Intensive Method" or *culture maraicher*. Small plots of land with double dug beds, fertilized with composted horse manure from the city stables, produced unusually great amounts of superior vegetables for the Paris markets.

barrow, a rake, a trowel, a hoe, a pendulum, or stirrup hoe, barrels, string for marking rows, a good pocket knife, and, in the drier regions, the greatest expense might be the sprinklers or watering system. Another expense might be mulching material, manure, bean poles, and tomato stakes, but more often than not these can be locally procured or bartered for. Watering can be reduced by 70% of what is customary by following the indications given in this book. Fertility can be stretched by composting and the use of liquid ferments, so that independence from commercial fertilizer is achieved. Proper cultivating and planting practices will eliminate the need for expensive and dangerous bug and weed killers. Seeds, which are becoming increasingly costly, can, for the most part, be grown by the gardener himself, or seed exchange with other local gardeners through a garden club can eliminate dependence on commercial seed companies. Local garden clubs can be useful for mutual exchange of information, tools, seeds, and good company. (See Appendix II, SEEDS.) Even a small home garden can supply itself with manure and balance the vegetation with animals such as rabbits, chickens, ducks, and bees. On slightly larger acreage, a goat or milking sheep might be added, and on land exceeding an acre, a pig or cow, or a fish pond might be feasible depending on the overall climate and ecology.

A well-balanced bio-dynamic garden might be more difficult for a commercial gardener to achieve. Organic and bio-dynamic gardens are diversified. Diversification guarantees the maintenance of a sound ecology, good soil structure, increasing fertility, insect resistance and easy weed control. It serves long-range goals, but cuts into short-term profits. Diversified gardens also need more human care; they are labor-intensive. In the marketplace, human care becomes "labor," and labor is expensive. The competition with huge, mechanized outfits makes it impossible to pay for the greater labor force required for working the composts, mulching, companion planting, cover-cropping, stirring preparations, etc. The commercial gardener, in order to compete successfully, is forced into growing only a relatively few crops that have high market value, and growing these in sufficient quantity. This often eliminates proper rotation and companion planting. He is forced to cut corners by spraying herbicide to save time weeding, applying NPK to avoid composting, and mechanizing to eliminate the cost of human labor. At this point, commercial gardening is an alienating form of labor, in which there is not much joy and satisfaction left. To survive as a commercial gardener on the treadmill of a highly monetized, competitive marketplace, and still be organic or bio-dynamic, one must specialize to serve a specific clientele, people who shop at health food stores, or institutions that need specific diets such as hospitals, homes for the aged, or vegetarian restaurants. Some commercial gardeners solve their problems by setting up a delivery route of steady customers who are willing to give financial support to future crops; others take apprentices or draw on a large family to supply the labor needed. The troubles of the organic commercial gardeners lie not so much in the quantity and quality of production, but in trying to stay solvent, keeping up with the cost of capital inputs, taxes, bad marketing, competition from big outfits, and inflation that cut into the ability to make a decent living. In a simpler economy, such as that of a simple market or bartering system, such a garden would do exceedingly well. In some instances such structural difficulties have been dealt with successfully by the formation of cooperatives that establish resource pools and secure marketing outlets for themselves in big cities.[15]

Perhaps the best way to do organic, bio-dynamic gardening (and farming) is to quit the marketplace altogether and produce for a social group that is interested in a guaranteed supply of fresh, wholesome, unprocessed, high-quality fruits and vegetables. This might be done in conjunction with independent food co-ops, schools, hospitals, homes for the handicapped and old folks, or in the context of a small community or commune. In this way, the production can be geared directly to the needs of the institution or community, which, in turn, provides the necessary capital to operate the garden. An example is the numerous Waldorf Schools,[16] where bio-dynamically grown food provides the best nutritional basis for the developing child. Helping to work in the garden teaches the children fundamental facts about where and how food is grown and who produces it. School gardens are much more realistic biology lessons than dissecting formaldehyded frogs under a lens. Hospitals and clinics can eliminate some of the high operational costs and provide the best nutrition possible for those who need it the most. Research indicates how many of our current ills are related to faulty nutrition or poisonous residues in our food. In progressive hospitals, such as the Arlesheim Clinic in Switzerland, crops and medical herbs are grown bio-

15Robin Myers, "The National Sharecroppers Fund and the Farm Co-op Movement in the South," in *Radical Agriculture*, p. 129.

16For information on the Association of Waldorf Schools of North America, one may contact the following address: Education as an Art, Green Meadow School, Hungry Hollow Road, Spring Valley, New York 10977.

dynamically to fulfill the specific needs of the patients. In such hospitals or clinics, ambulatory patients can convalesce by spending an hour or two in the garden, doing light, stimulating work, or sitting in the sun amidst the relaxing atmosphere of flowers, butterflies, birds, and greenery. A similar garden could be incorporated into a community college, where it can serve as apprenticeship training, provide food for the cafeteria, and biology lessons for ecological and biological sciences. The therapeutic value of gardening in the context of mental hospitals and juvenile homes, when carried out in a conscientious and loving way, has been proven in a number of instances.

A final form of gardening occurs within the structure of an entire community. A number of such communities have been set up, some more and others less successfully, as models for post-industrial society as refuges from competitive, industrial society. Structural difficulties are quick to show up. One difficulty occurs when the community is based on the individuality of one charismatic leader. Especially after such a person is gone, squabbles and rivalries destroy the community. Another difficulty in many social experiments of this nature is the danger that personal individuality and the initiative of the members is stifled. A final source of trouble occurs in the area of assigning roles and sharing responsibilities. Communal gardens, for example, are often the place where people "do their own thing," so that overall planning is lacking, responsible care is sporadic and less pleasant chores such as watering and hoeing are often neglected. If a community can structure itself to avoid these pitfalls, then such a group will stand a better chance of weathering social chaos, inflation and other disintegrative forces, than, say, the family of the "individualist" who hordes food and guns and goes it alone. In the context of such communities, firmly based on bio-dynamic, organic farming and gardening, there can be a revival of culture, of arts, crafts, medicine, good child rearing, and of the aesthetics that give charm and warmth to life.

Camphill Communities

One successful model for a modern community based on bio-dynamic agriculture can be seen in the villages of the Camphill Movement.[17] Dr. Karl Koenig (1902-1966) of Vienna, founded these villages as places where human beings at a disadvantage in competitive society, such as the mentally handicapped, could flourish and develop their own potential beings, their *imago dei.* The first community was set up in Camphill, Aberdeen, Scotland, and in the mean time there are a number of such villages in Europe, North America and South Africa which have been developed.[18] Koenig utilized Rudolf Steiner's conception of the Threefold Social Order (1919),[19] combining this with the structural features of such well-worked out small community systems as the Hutterite Bruderhof, a functional communal system that has survived for nearly four hundred years. Included also was the utopian model of Robert Owen's "Villages of Cooperation" (e.g. New Harmony,

---

[17]Although a number of other successful communities could be examined in this context, the Camphill Village is chosen because of the author's familiarity with the subject based on participant-observation research (1971-73).

[18]Information about such communities in the United States can be obtained from: Camphill Village, U.S.A., Copake, NY 12516.

[19]Rudolf Steiner, *The Threefold Social Order* (New York: Anthroposophic Press, 1972); *The Social Future* (New York: Anthroposophic Press, 1972).

1825), which rejected the ideology that one man's loss is another man's gain.

Steiner wrote *The Threefold Social Order* as a proposal for social reorganization after the collapse of the central and eastern European social systems at the end of the First World War. He proposed abandoning the nation state idea in favor of a threefold division of the social body into an *economic* realm, a *rights-judicial* realm, and a *spiritual-cultural* realm. In essence, the economic realm is to function with associations of producers and consumers as its constituent units. The basic needs of all people ought to be satisfied regardless of whether they are able-bodied or sick, young or old, male or female, weak or strong. This is a basic human right. There should be complete freedom in the flow of the goods and services as the market, determined by human needs, demands it. The key word in the economic realm is "brotherliness." Land, tools, and other means of production should not abstractly be owned as private property, but ownership should be coupled with stewardship and responsibility. It is the people who work the land who "own" it; if they cannot care for it, the "ownership" should be transferred to someone who can manage responsibly.

The rights, or judicial, realm is to function as the legal institution that guarantees the equitable relationship of each person relative to every other person. The key word is "equality." The wealthy should not have more rights than the poor, the men more rights than the women, producers more rights than the consumers, or the entrepreneur more than the worker. Though each person's role and social function might be different, and the responsibilities lighter or heavier, openness and mutual trust based on social parity are needed. The work relationships are part of the rights realm, not part of the economic sphere, because they are the relations of human beings and not of goods. Labor cannot be treated as a commodity or as capital without violating human rights. It happens that workers and managers are producers in some instances, and consumers in other instances.

For Steiner, the spiritual-cultural sphere is not just "superstructure" that has evolved as a mere epiphenomenon out of an economic basis. It is a realm of its own importance, involving all the endowments and talents of the individual person, and each human being's individual connectedness with the Spirit of the universe. In this sphere people are *not* equal, but everyone is unique and irreplaceable. Some people are more gifted intellectually, some more artistically, some excel in crafts and some contribute by promoting good humor. This creative, spiritual life cannot be dictated by the state and should not be dominated by economic interests, but should be left free to develop. Each person must be able to unfold his individual capacities as his unique contribution to humanity and the world, without fear or economic pressure. The arts, sciences, religion, and education belong to this realm. The key word here is "freedom."

Brotherhood, Equality, and Freedom, as the slogan to characterize a just social order, is a deliberate reinterpretation of the ideals of the Enlightenment and the impulse of the French Revolution. This is something that Jefferson could have lived with.

Just as the body consists of three major systems, the

metabolic system, the rhythmic system of blood circulation and breathing, and the nervous system, which are dependent on each other, but function relatively independently, so in the social organism, the economics sphere, the rights sphere and the spiritual-cultural sphere should be independent but function together. Where is the nexus for these three spheres of social life? It is in each individual person that makes up the society, as he daily participates in each of the three realms.

Just as in the biological organism, when the nervous system interferes with the metabolic system or rhythmic system (or vice-versa) illness results, so there is social pathology in the social body if the separate realms interfere with each other. In the western world, the economic realm (capitalism, market mechanisms) dominates all other areas, and in the Communist world, the state controls and stifles the economic system and the development of creative spirit.

The dialectic of individual needs and the needs of the society as a whole is expressed in the motto regarding the social ethic: "The healthy social life is found, when in the mirror of each human soul the whole community finds its reflection, and when in the community the virtue of each one is living."[20] In other contexts Steiner comes to the conclusion that revitalization of civilization must come from the land.

The Threefold Social Order in Practice

Karl Koenig adopted these ideas and reformulated them

---

[20]Inscribed by Steiner in a copy of *The Threefold Social Order*, Nov. 1920 for Edith Maryon.

to be applicable to the scale of a small village, such as the Camphill Village. How does this work in practice?

The economic sphere is based on bio-dynamic farming and gardening that provides for the material needs of the members of the community and produces goods to be sold outside of the community. The entire community works in various workshops, on the land or in the households. The goods produced, such as bread, vegetables, cheese, candles, cloth or carpentry output are made freely available wherever they are needed in the village. Wages are not paid, because the work is not done for money, but for the satisfaction of real needs. However, everyone can satisfy extra needs, vacation money, money for eating out or going to a concert, for example, by tapping the resources of a common fund. The community is small enough that the conscience of the individual is a reliable guide.

The means of production, land, tools, and workshops are owned by the community as a whole; they do not become the source of status differences. However, they are assigned to individuals of ability, so that a qualified farmer farms, the gardener gardens, the beekeeper keeps bees, and the learned carpenter does carpentry. If the farmer quits farming or the gardener gardening, he cannot sell the land or the tools, but the responsibility is turned over to someone else.

The rights sphere guarantees equal rights to all the people. A village council composed of all co-workers meets every week to discuss problems, make announcements, set up study committees for special problems, and make decisions. Everyone has an equal right to speak his mind. Decisions that are made, are made on the basis of unanimous consent, after each item has been thoroughly discussed and weighed. If there is any dissent, this must be taken into consideration and analyzed for its reasonableness. If the dissenting person has a valid point of contention, then the majority can be swayed; if he does not have a reasonable point, then this is made clear. In this manner, derisive factionalism and the party mentality is avoided. The village council is flexible and can repeal the decisions any time it is necessary, so that the "laws," as they are made by the people, serve the people, and not the people the laws. Because there are no special interests to protect and there are no individual insecurities generated in the economic sphere, which would make the equitable function of such a council impossible, the decisions can be made on a basis of reasonability. Since the common good becomes also the personal good, the individual works for the common good.

It is in the spiritual-cultural realm that the sense of self and individual achievement are satisfied. Each person takes pride in personal skills that are necessary for the well-being of the whole community. He need not depend upon a sense of self based on the accumulation of material goods or property, on special privileges or on domination. Positive social sanction for the performance of vital work roles, and freedom to express initiative, talent and creativity is enough to ensure a sense of individual being. This applies to the handicapped villager who takes pride in the amount of firewood he can saw, the mechanic who can fix any broken device, or the gardener upon whom the entire village depends for vegetables. By virtue of personal endowment, each person works in the area where he feels best qualified and most responsible. This is a nonalienating means of role assignment.

To this sphere belongs the right of the individual to arrange his personal living space and lifestyle, each household's right to cook its food and arrange its after-work hours to its own preference, and the parents' and teachers' rights to determine what the schools should teach their children. It includes the formation of art, craft, and study groups, where thought and creativity are free to find expression, and it includes each person's personal relationship to his innermost source of meaning.

All of this provides for a model of small scale society, which works successfully in practice.

Regarding specifically the agricultural sector, some of this has been discussed in the introduction. The farm and garden work together, with the farm providing necessary manures for the compost and the garden taking care of making the preparations used on the farm. The various workers can simply agree to exchange roles in such a community setting, so that if the farmer wants to take a vacation, the gardener or an apprentice can keep the farm running during that time. If there is a lot of weeding, berry picking, or harvesting to be done, workers can be pulled from the workshops, whereas if the workshops have a major sale coming up, the farmers and gardeners can lend a helping hand. In this situation, there is no worry about the high cost of labor, for the community provides a flexible, skilled, non-capitalized labor pool. The weavers, carpenters, gardeners and other workers always enjoy the change in routine and benefit from a variety of experience.

Many of the inputs that would have to be purchased on a commercial farm or garden are locally produced and need not be shipped far or paid for. Examples are making fence posts, constructing tool sheds, digging ponds, or raising seed. In this setting, appropriate and intermediate technology can usefully be employed. Another major advantage for the farmer and gardener is that the market for the produce is guaranteed. Each day the households order fresh vegetables, milk, bread, meat or potatoes directly from the garden, farm or bakery. The households are benefited by the freshness, known quality, and also the personal relation to the producer and his land. The producer is benefited by an assured outlet for his produce and by the knowledge of exactly what and how much needs to be produced each season. Surpluses are usually sold outside of the community and make the financing of projects (greenhouse, root cellar, fruit driers, or irrigation pipes) possible.

The garden and farm serve also the social function of training handicapped persons to do useful and important work, and the handicapee gains a sense of self-respect, knowing that he is fulfilling a vital function within the total community. In the same manner, other apprentices (juvenile delinquents, drug rehabilitees, prisoners, and other socially handicapped persons) can be trained successfully under these circumstances without recidivism.

One of the problems with modern farmers and commercial gardeners within the competitive social system of today is the lack of time and of meaningful social life. The traditional peasantry was replete with customs, processions, folk dances, and other sundry forms of social interaction, but this is no more. In a community such as Camphill, a sense of social meaningfulness is restored in a modern way, without a mere nostalgic rehashing of outmoded traditions. Festivals that are community affairs are celebrated in these villages in a traditional manner, but with a revitalized meaning and rekindled spirit. The problems of the Russian model of the kolkhoz is that of creating a rural proletariat that has no personal interest in its work except that of pay and a few material incentives. Lagging farm production in the Soviet Union on the state-owned and centrally administered collective farms, when compared with the little bit of private land that the peasant is allowed to retain, is a strong argument for the need for personal involvement, responsibility, and a sense of meaning. This is satisfied in the functioning of a community as here described.

---♋---

It is in a healthy, socio-cultural system that the needs of the ecology, the proper stewardship of our soils, plant and animal companions, can be done justice. Where unbridled greed, unconcern and decadence characterize a society, there one will surely find ecological catastrophe, pollution, endangered wildlife, agricultural crisis, and people alienated from the land.

Our conclusion must be that culture and horticulture, or culture and agriculture, are not merely linked by verbal coincidence, but that one implies the other: A healthy culture that fills people with a sense for the good, the beautiful and the true, will be characterized by a healthy land, whereas, a culture torn by exploitation, colonialism, speculation, social contradiction, and other pathologies will surely be characterized by a crisis in agriculture. Gardening organically and bio-dynamically is just one small way to start on the road to health, for both nature and man.

APPENDIX I

WINTER GARDENING IN OREGON

With occasional exceptions, Oregon has the relatively mild winters that make winter vegetable gardening possible.

Our gardening practices developed in northwestern Europe were carried to the East Coast and eventually to the Midwest of this continent. Each of these geographical regions has in common a climate of distinct spring, summer, fall and winter. In the winter the earth is frozen solid and covered by feet of snow in these regions and only a fool would think of gardening at that time. With the coming of spring and summer, it is time to "put in a garden" and after it has grown during the summer, by Michaelmas (Fall Equinox) it is time to harvest, to dry fruits and vegetables, can them and put them up for winter use. The garden gets a dressing of manure and lies fallow until it is time, once again, to put a garden in. Thus, we have a different gardening tradition which makes sense in the regions where it developed, but here in Oregon, we can do things differently.

The famous nutritionist, Bircher-Benner concludes that food is always most nutritious when it is *whole* and *fresh*. If we can eat vegetables that are whole and fresh from the garden in the winter, then we are able to spend much less time canning and preserving, except for some of our special favorites such as berries or peas.

There are so many fresh vegetables that can be enjoyed in the winter that one need not worry about having the same dish day after day. Here is a list of vegetables that like cooler weather and should be in Oregon winter gardens:

I. The following should be planted in *coldframes* during the waxing moon of July, or August at the latest. This will permit them to grow strong before the days get cooler and darker when their growth will slow down. The coldframes should be specially prepared with the following mixture:

2 parts good garden loam
1 part mixed peat and sand
1 part very ripe (humified) compost

The seeds should be kept moist and a lattice (burlap, cheesecloth) should shade the young seedlings. They are transplanted when they are about 6 inches tall.

1. *Cabbages:* just about all cabbages like cooler weather. *Kale* and *brussel sprouts* even taste better when nipped by frost. *Boc choi* can be grown also.

2. *Swiss Chard.*

3. *Leeks:* can take very cold weather.

4. *Endives.*

5. *Sugarhat:* forms tightly packed head the size of a football of tender, slightly bitter leaves that can be eaten all winter as a winter salad. It can take severe frost; with the outside leaves frozen it will still be good inside (available from Burpee's).

II. The following should be sown into their own beds directly, as they do not transplant easily. Germination being a problem in July and August, they should be kept moist. This holds true especially for the umbelliferae (parsnips, carrots, hamburg parsley). The umbelliferae should be companion planted in alternating rows with members of the lily family (leeks, onions) for symbiotic effects.

6. *Parsnips.*

7. *Hamburg parsley:* This is grown mainly for its

carrot-like root. The greens can be used like regular parsley. *Skirret,* closely related, is also a root crop.

8. *Turnips:* the tops are good winter greens.

9. *Rutabagas.*

10. *Beets:* the tops are good winter greens.

11. *Carrots:* companion plant with leeks.

12. *Oyster plant* (salsify): smells like oysters when cooked.

13. *Mustard greens.*

14. *Corn salad* (maches — in Nichol's catalog, lamb's lettuce, fetticus, *(Valerianella locusta var. olitoria):* This delicious, tender salad plant can be eaten by itself or in combination with witlof or sugarhat, or with hard-boiled eggs as the Swiss eat it. It should be sown out in August or September. It is sensitive to heat and grows all winter long.

15. *Rockett:* sown in September.

16. *Spinach.*

17. *Florence fennel:* Fennel sown late in July or early August, kept moist and cultivated, will have large, bulbous edible leaf bases the size of a hand when harvested by the first frost. When harvested, the foliage is cut off, the leaf bases are stored in a dry, airy environment where they will keep until the New Year.

III. The following are ready for eating during the winter months, but have been planted already the previous spring.

18. *Celeriac,* or root celery: These are started in the coldframe in spring, then transplanted. They like wood ashes for their potassium needs and much water, and need the entire growing season to make their football-sized roots. Leeks are good companions and can also be planted in the spring where they can make the best use of the growing season.

19. *Witlof:* a chicory that is sown in the spring and harvested for its roots in the fall. The roots are put into dormancy in a cool, somewhat dry storage. When needed, they are placed into soil in boxes in a warmed cellar or garage. A foot of sand/peat or sand/sawdust is added on top. When they are watered, they will send the terminal bud growing through this light mixture. When this blanched terminal bud becomes visible, the witlof, a superior salad and cooking vegetable, is ready for the table. The root itself is then discarded (composted, fed to livestock or chopped, dried, ground, and roasted as a coffee additive).

20. *Jerusalem Artichokes:* an alternative to the potato, delicious raw in salads.

The list could possibly go on to include some of the herbs, such as *horseradish, comfrey, mint* and other plants that continue for some time if it does not freeze too harshly, such as *Chinese Cabbage* (michihili) and *New Zealand Spinach*.

On colder, freezing days, the plants in the winter garden should be protected by covering them loosely with straw, or by putting plastic tents over them. The plastic tunnels can fit the beds easily and are cheaply constructed with PVC pipe as supports. Doubling the plastic creates dead air spaces that help insulate.

Beginning in February, a new impulse for growth exists in Nature. By this time it is advantageous to have put many of the root crops into a root cellar to prevent them from becoming woody (leeks, parsnips, hamburg parsley, turnips, beets, carrots, celeriac, oyster plant, and rutabagas). By this time, free beds are needed for early peas, snow peas, fava, or broad beans, onion sets, spinach, etc.

Oregon has garden weather the year round and can provide fresh vegetables in their respective seasons.

APPENDIX II

SEEDS

In many instances it is worth one's while to raise one's own seeds. At the cost of seed in inflationary times, it saves money, but also it brings one closer to an appreciation of the mystery of life as the plant moves out of and into manifestation in continuous rhythms. It is still a miracle how the tiny seed, this little, round microcosm can become the focal point of the forces that build up the stately plant. Some seeds are easy to save, while others are tricky, requiring much skill and patience. Like keeping bees, it is something for which one must almost have a special predilection.

Seed Selection

Pick the very best of plants, such as the lettuce plant that bolts last, the spinach that has the lushest leaves, the corn that has the first and largest ears, or the cabbage that forms the tightest head. These plants should have been grown on organic, bio-dynamic soil, so that the greatest vitality can assist them and the least amount of seed degeneration results.

Let the seeds ripen on the plants as much as possible. As they are about to mature, paper bags can be tied over the heads to prevent them from being eaten by birds or falling to the ground. The entire stalk is then cut, the seeds shaken off and thrashed in the bag and then winnowed. Some, like peas, beans and corn can be left to dry in the shells or husks. Let fleshy fruits, such as tomatoes, squash, cucumbers, or eggplant overripen on the vine, then scrape the seeds out of the fruit, soak for a couple of days in water until they ferment slightly, free the seed from the pulp by washing and rubbing, and then dry on paper blotters or on screens.

Storage

It is useless to save seeds if one does not label, date and store them correctly. The seeds should be thoroughly dried and then placed in cool, dry storage, so that they will not become moldy or mildewed. Glass containers (e.g. small jars) or snuff boxes (e.g. Copenhagen lids) which are sealed airtight with wax and contain traces of tobacco which discourages seed-eating bugs, are the best for storing.

Germination Test

If one would like to be sure that the seeds are viable, especially after long storage, one can make a germination test to determine the *germination ratio.* Ten to 20 seeds are counted and sprouted on blotter paper or cotton which has been moistened and covered. The number of seeds that germinate versus the number that are dead gives the percentage of the germination ratio. For example, if one out of twenty does not germinate, the ratio is 95%; if only ten out of twenty germinate, then the ratio is 50%. From this percentage, one can determine if it is worth sowing the seed out, or how thickly one must sow for an even stand.

Some seeds are *quick sprouters,* such as cress, beans, sunflowers, mustards, lettuce, and most members of the brassica family. *Slow sprouters* include most of the umbelliferae (carrots, parsnips, parsley, celery), New Zealand spinach and most herbs. These can take from three weeks to over a month to germinate.

Most vegetable seeds sprout soon after they have been dried; some, however, have to be cured for some time before they germinate. The umbellifers need at least a month before they are ready to grow, and the germination ratio of beets and Swiss chard is increased if the seeds are stored for a couple of years.

Some seeds, such as many weed species, might not even grow when moisture, temperature and soil conditions are right. This is known as seed dormancy. Dormancy might be caused by chemical inhibitors which have to wear off the coat (they prevent tomatoes and squash from sprouting while within the fruit). It might be related to lunar and planetary positions as suggested by Maria Thun for many weeds, it might need the corrosive effect of a fungus on the seed coat, or the seed needs to go through a cold period before it germinates. Some weed seeds last for several decades in this way while buried in the soil.

Seed Viability

Is it necessary to grow seeds or to buy them in a store each year? Some seeds have very long viability. For example, one can keep cucumber and endive seeds for over ten years; celery and celeriac seed lasts seven to eight years; beets, eggplant, melons and squash last six years before the germination ratio starts to drop off; most cabbages (incl. cauliflower, kohlrabi, broccoli, kale), lettuce, pumpkin, spinach and turnips are viable up to five years; asparagus, carrot, mustard, pepper and tomato last for four years; beans, leeks, parsley, and peas can be stored for three years; and it is best to replenish corn, onions, oyster plants and parsnips every other year.

Hybrids

For raising one's own seeds, unless one is really fanatic about it, it is best to use *standard varieties* which will breed true. Hybrids contain latent and recessive genes which become manifest in the next generation, so that at least three-fourths of the next crop will deviate considerably from what one expects.

Pollination

Pollination comes about when the haploid pollen combines with the haploid gametes of the female flower to form a new diploid seed. Some plants are pollinated by wind and insects, while others are self-pollinating. Self-pollinated vegetables include tomatoes, beans, peas, and corn, which makes it extremely easy to save seed from them, because they tend to come out true and they are not easily *cross-pollinated.* Lettuce tends to self-pollinate, but can be crossed with a nearby wild-growing, tough, spiny compass plant or wild lettuce *(Lactuca scariola).* Oyster plant, chicory, and dandelion can be self-fertilized although bees and other insects do cross them with others of their own species. Their seeds should be shaken into bags every few days, to keep the finches from eating the ripe seed. Most other plants are fertilized mainly by insects.

Peppers must be watched because the sweet peppers can cross with the hot peppers. Cucumbers, melons and cantaloupes will not cross, but different species of squash and pumpkins, both of the genus *Cucurbita,* can cross into strange combinations, such as crook-necked, zucchini pumpkins. Beets, Swiss chard, sugar beets and mangels cross-pollinate each other by means of wind. The cabbages, which all belong to the species *brassica oleracea* (cabbage, cauliflower, collard, kohlrabi, kale, brussel sprouts) are cross-pollinated by bees and butterflies creating throwbacks that are of little use to the gardener. Carrots cross easily with their wild relative, the Queen Anne's Lace; leeks cross with onions; celery with celeriac. For any vegetables that are threatened with the loss of desired characteristics because of cross-pollination, extreme caution must be taken. Either the plants grown for seed are placed in plots very far removed from their cousins (a quarter of a mile), or the flowers have to be hand-pollinated by using a soft-haired brush to transfer the flower dust from the stamen to the pistils of the female flowers. All the while a paper bag is tied over the flowers to prevent unwanted pollen from fertilizing the pistils. The bags can be removed when the fruit is starting to set.

Annuals and Biennials

Annuals produce seed within a season's span and include the beans, peas, corn, fava, or broad bean, tomatoes, peppers, eggplant, cucumbers, melons, squash, lettuce, spinach, rocket, radish, Chinese cabbage, broccoli, orache, cress, and New Zealand spinach.

Biennials, on the other hand, take two seasons to produce seed. The first year's growth is vegetative and a winter rest-period intervenes before the seed formation occurs in the second year. In the mild climate of the Northwest coastal region, chosen plants can be left in the ground over the winter and let to go to seed the next summer. In climates with cold, icy winters, these plants must be carefully removed from the field and put into cold storage by being packed into peat moss and put into a root cellar.

Fennel and oyster plant often make seed in the first year. It is best, however, to obtain seeds for the next crop from those plants that have gone through the biennial cycle.

Other Means of Propagation

Not all plants in the garden are propagated by means of seeds. With potatoes and Jerusalem artichokes, tubers are cut and the eyes planted to produce the next season's crops. With strawberries and many herbs such as nettle, mints or tansy, runners are cut and replanted; while for others, such as comfrey, horseradish, valerian or rhubarb, cuttings of the roots multiply the number of plants.

Sources

The Encyclopedia of Organic Gardening, Rodale Press, 1975.

Farmer's Almanac, 1978; Yankee, Inc., Dublin, N.H., 1977, p. 64.

Seeds, The Yearbook of Agriculture, 1961; USDA, Washington, D.C.

APPENDIX III

TOOLS

While the technology of intensive gardening is simple, the techniques are sophisticated. The opposite can be said of an agriculture which is dependent upon complicated and expensive machinery and chemicals, but simplifies the technique to the point of creating boring, alienating work routines and at the same time harmfully simplifies the ecology (monocultures, destruction of a wide range of fauna and flora).

The tools for gardening are ancient, not having changed substantially since the early neolithic when the first crops were deliberately planted and sowed. Even then the digging stick, used as an all-purpose tool for furrowing the ground for seeding, poking the ground for planting, weeding and eventually harvesting tubers, had a precursor in the ancient dibble stick with a fire-hardened tip used by mesolithic hunters and gatherers as an extension of their fingers. From this ancient, simple tool, the digging fork, spade, trowel, and eventually, the plow, are derived. The hoe, too, is an ancient tool found in nearly all horticultural societies, used for weeding, cultivating, aerating and dry mulching the soil. Shells, bones, flat stones and deer scapulae preceded the use of metal in the making of hoes. Rakes for smoothing the beds (and later, harrows derived from the same principle) and blades (sickle, scythe and knife) for harvesting and pruning are nearly as ancient and universal for gardeners and still make up the core technology of intensive horticulture.

The tools one needs for successful gardening:

1. The *digging fork* for double digging, harvesting potatoes, carrots, salsify, etc., and for turning in compost.

2. The *space* for double digging, trenching, chopping compost material, etc.

3. The *hoe* for weeding, clearing, cultivating. The triangular hoe makes it possible to work close to the individual plants, and the stirrup, or pendulum, hoe which can be dragged backwards and forwards between rows reduces some of the toil. The ordinary hoe is also used for furrowing and for mounding up potatoes, peas, beans, leeks, fennel, corn and tomatoes.

4. The *rake* for smoothing the newly-prepared beds and for sowing (making furrows, covering the seeds with earth and pressing the soil firmly onto the seeds).

5. *Pegs, line and measuring tape (or yardstick)* are used for marking the beds, rows and paths. A nylon line will not rot.

6. A *trowel* for transplanting seedlings. Make sure the seedlings have been watered before transplanting, and that a deep enough hole is made by the trowel, so that the roots of the transplants are not bent.

7. A *pitchfork* is handy for pitching compost material, manure and mulch.

8. A *wheelbarrow* is needed for transporting earth, compost, mulch, lime or tools.

9. A *sickle or scythe* for collecting mulching and composting material. Working rhythmically with a well-sharpened scythe, one can smoothly and quickly mow large areas. It is definitely more relaxing than a fume-spewing, noisy lawn mower.

10. *Barrels* for collecting and brewing Russian tea, nettles, comfrey and other liquid fertilizers and preparations. Wood or crockery barrels are preferred to plastic or metal containers. Metal tends to chemically interact with the brews while the plastic does not last long.

11. *Watering equipment* includes a *watering can* for the seed beds, *hoses, drip irrigation* or *soaker hoses* for those plants that do not like water on their foliage (tomatoes, beans and some other warm-weather lovers) and *overhead sprinklers.* This equipment might well be the most expensive paraphernalia needed.

12. *Hand, or knapsack, sprayer* for foliar feeding and application of preparations.

13. *Plastic tents* and their frames (easily made from willow or pine saplings, or PVC pipe) for covering early or late beds. Old plastic can be used to cover composts to prevent them from leaching and to trap the sun's heat for the compost.

14. A *hatchet* and *mallet* might come in handy for cutting, sharpening and driving bean poles, tomato stakes and fence posts for pea and cucumber fences.

15. A *pocket knife* should be carried by every gardener for sharpening pegs, pruning and harvesting.

16. *A thinking cap.* Ever wonder why the garden gnomes and dwarfs always wear pointed caps? Proper concepts are as important as tools made of wood and steel.

As we see, garden technology is simple, quiet and ancient. It does not lend itself readily to capital intensity, being invented before money was ever thought of. Usually it is only the gimmicks that cost a lot and they are not really needed. *Advanced technology* such as rototillers, mini-tractors, electric compost tumblers and compost shredders can be useful but are not absolutely necessary. This is true especially in smaller gardens where costs outweigh the benefits. Stalks, twigs and haulms that are usually shredded can be chopped up with a spade and composted for a longer time, or they can be placed into the bottom of a newly double-dug bed where they will have ample time to decompose. Double digging and raised beds generally preclude rototillers.

The work with ordinary garden tools is quiet and rhythmical, an activity conducive to an open, receptive frame of mind. One can hear oneself think, so to speak, and one can meditatively apprehend the aliveness of the soil, the plants and the many creatures with whom we share a garden. This frame of mind is necessary to be in empathy with the biological and ecological needs of the garden. In contrast, loud machinery and commotion close the gardener's chakras off from this important contact.

Gardens where people with simple tools but sophisticated techniques predominate instead of expensive machinery, re-create a human environment for young and old. In African hoe-agricultural societies, the fields are filled with song, rather than motor din and fumes, as many people in social activity work the soil.

Tool Care

Gardening tools are inexpensive. However, it is advisable not to buy the very cheapest of these, for often bargain basement tools break very quickly whereas better-wrought tools might last a lifetime. Though we live in a throwaway culture, replacing tools is going to cost more as our resources become more expensive. Like our forebears we ought, once again, to learn to respect and care for what we have to make it last. Garden tools, for example, should not be left laying in the field overnight. Exposure to rain or dew inevitably weakens the handles as microorganisms digest wood fiber and the unprotected, moist metal rusts. Tools should be put into a tool shed clean and dry. The handles should be treated with boiled linseed oil to give them durance. Garden hoses and plastic tents should be put out of the sun and the elements when they are not in seasonal use, as should be stakes, posts and poles. Garden hoses should not be dragged around so that kinks develop, which over a period of time create weakened spots and eventually cracks.

After a while, it is possible even to develop a fondness for one's long-worn tools with their sweat-stained handles, much as one has a liking for a favorite coffee cup or cooking pot. Here, too, it is possible to establish a personal, soul-filled relationship with one's world.

BIBLIOGRAPHY

Adams, George. *Physical and Etheric Spaces.* Rudolf Steiner Press: London, 1965.

Adams, George. *The Plant Between the Sun and the Earth.* Stourbridge, 1952.

Agrippa of Nettesheim. *De Occulta Philosophia – Magische Werke.* Druck A. Hain: Meisenheim Glan, 1530.

Airola, Paavo O. *Health Secrets from Europe.* ARC: New York, 1970.

Albrecht, William A. "The Albrecht Papers." Acres, USA: Raytown, Mo., 1975.

Allaby, Michael, and Floyd Allen. *Robots Behind the Plow.* Rodale Press: Emmaus, Pa., 1974.

Anderson, Edgar. *Plants, Man and Life.* Little, Brown & Co.: Boston, 1952.

Anderson, Jr., E. N. "The Life and Culture of Ecotopia" in *Reinventing Anthropology.* Dell Hymes, ed. Vintage Books: N.Y., 1974.

Attracting Birds to Your Garden. Editors of Sunset Magazine. Lane Books: Menlo Park, Ca., 1974.

Baer's Agriculture Almanac. Grosset & Dunlap Publishers: N.Y.

Balfour, Lady Eve. *The Living Soil.* Devin-Adair: New York, 1950.

Baranger, Pierre. "Science et Vie" Nr. 499, April, 1959.

Barrett, T. J. *Harnessing the Earthworm.* Boston: Bookworm: Ontario, Ca., 1976.

Barthelemy de Glanville. "Le Proprietaire des Choses." 1487.

Basic Book of Organic Gardening. R. Rodale, ed. Ballantine Books: N.Y., 1974.

Bernus, Alexander V. *Alchemie und Heilkunst.* Verlag Hans Karl: Nuremberg, 1969.

Berry, Wendell. *The Unsettling of America: Culture and Agriculture.* Sierra Club Books: San Francisco, 1977.

Boly, William. "Sweet Dioxin." *Oregon Times Magazine:* Sept. 1977.

Borror, Donald J., and Dwight M. De Long. *An Introduction to the Study of Insects.* Holt, Rinehart & Winston: N.Y., 1974.

Brown, Frank A. "Hypothesis of Environmental Timing of the Clock" in *The Biological Clock.* Academic Press: N.Y., 1970.

Bruce, M. E. *Common Sense Compost Making.* Faber & Faber, Ltd.: London, 1946.

Callahan, Philip. *Insects and How They Function.* Holiday House: N.Y., 1971.

Carroll, J. B., and Benjamin Lee Whorf. *Language, Thought, Reality.* MIT Press: Cambridge, Mass., 1956.

Chardin, Teilhard de. *Man's Place in Nature.* Harper & Row, N.Y., 1956.

Christian, James. *Philosophy.* Rinehart Press: San Francisco, 1977.

Clark, Wilson. "U.S. Agriculture is Growing Trouble as Well as Crops." *Smithsonian:* January, 1975.

Cloudsley-Thompson, J. L. *Insects and History.* St. Martin's Press: N.Y., 1976.

Cocannouer, Joseph A. *Weeds, Guardians of the Soil.* Devin-Adair Co.: N.Y., 1971.

Comfrey, Was ist das? Abtei Fulda: 1972.

Cook, Gordon J. *On Living Soil.* The Dial Press, N.Y., 1960.

Culpeper, Nicholas. *Culpeper's Complete Herbal.* Foulsham: London, 1960.

Darwin, Charles. *The Formation of Vegetable Moulds Through the Action of Worms.* 1882.

Daubenmire, Rexford. *Plant Communities.* Harper & Row: N.Y., 1968.

Dethier, V. G. *Man's Plague: Insects and Agriculture.* Darwin Press: Princeton, New Jersey, 1976.

Dobzhansky, Theodosius. "On Genetics and Politics" in *Heredity and Society*. A. S. Baer, ed. MacMillan Co.: N.Y., 1973.

Eliade, Mircea. *Patterns of Comparative Religion*. Meridian Books: N.Y., 1963.

Encyclopedia of Organic Gardening. Jerome Olds, ed. Rodale Books: Emmaus, Pa., 1975.

Farmer's Almanac 1978. Yankee: Dublin, N.H., 1977.

Findhorn Garden, The. The Findhorn Community. Harper & Row: N.Y., 1975.

Flanagan, Pat G. *Pyramid Power*. Davores Co.: 1973.

Fletcher, John. *Russia: Past, Present and Future*. New Knowledge Books: London, 1968.

Frazer, Sir James. *The Golden Bough*. MacMillan Co.: N.Y., 1951.

Fyfe, Agnes. *The Signature of the Moon in Plants (Die Signatur des Mondes im Pflanzenreich)*. Verl. Freies. Geistesleben: Stuttgart, 1967.

Geertz, Clifford. "Two Types of Ecosystems" in *Environment and Cultural Behavior*. A. P. Vayda, ed. Natural History Press: Garden City, N.Y., 1969.

Gilstrap, Marguerite. *Seeds*. Yearbook of Agriculture, USDA: Washington, D.C., 1961.

Glob, P. V. *The Bog People*. Ballantine Books: N.Y., 1975.

Golueke, Clarence G. *Biological Reclamation of Solid Wastes*. Rodale Press: Emmaus, Pa., 1977.

Gray, Ian, and eds. of Horizon. *History of Russia*. American Heritage: N.Y., 1974.

Greene, Sheldon L. "Corporate Accountability and the Family Farm" in *Radical Agriculture*. Harper & Row: N.Y., 1976.

Grohmann, Gerbert. *Die Pflanze als Lichtsinnesorgan der Erde*. Verl. Freies Geistesleben: Stuttgart, 1962.

Grohmann, Gerbert. *The Plant*. R. Steiner Press: London, 1974.

Hale, Nathan Cabot. *Abstraction in Art and Nature*. Watson-Guptill Publ.: N.Y., 1972.

Harris, Marvin. *Cows, Pigs, Wars and Witches*. Vintage Books: N.Y., 1975.

Hartmann, Franz. *Paracelsus: Life and Prophecies*. Rudolf Steiner Publications: Blauvelt, N.Y., 1973.

Hauschka, Rudolf. *Heilmittellehre*. Vittorio Klostermann: Frankfurt/Main, 1965.

Hauschka, Rudolf. *The Nature of Substance*. Vincent Stuart, Ltd.: London, 1966.

Hauser, Albert. *Bauernregeln*. Artemis Verl.: Zurich, 1973.

Hawken, Paul. *The Magic of Findhorn*. Harper & Row: N.Y., 1975.

Hightower, Jim. *Hard Tomatoes, Hard Times*. Schenkman: Cambridge, Mass., 1972.

Holmyard, E. J. *Alchemy*. Penguin Books: Middlesex, England, 1968.

Hottes, Alfred C. *Garden Facts and Fancies*. Dodd, Mead: N.Y., 1949.

Howard, Sir Albert. *An Agricultural Testament*. Oxford University Press: New York and London, 1949. (Special Rodale Press Edition, 1972.)

Howard, Sir Albert. *The Soil and Health*. Schocken Books: New York, 1972.

Huntington, Ellsworth. *Mainsprings of Civilization*. Mentor Books: N.Y., 1962.

Hyton, William H. "The Companionable Herbs" in *Rodale Herb Book*. Rodale Press: Emmaus, Pa., 1974.

Insects. Life Nature Library, Time-Life Books: N.Y., 1968.

Janick, Jules. *Horticultural Science*. W. H. Freeman & Co.: San Francisco, 1973.

Jeavons, John. *How to Grow More Vegetables*. Ecology Action of the Midpeninsula: Palo Alto, Ca., 1974.

Jensen, William A., and Frank B. Salisbury. *Botany: An Ecological Approach*. Wadsworth: Belmont, Ca., 1972.

Johnson, Jerry Mack. *Country Wisdom.* Anchor Press/Doubleday: Garden City, N.Y., 1974.

Kammerer, P. *Das Gesetz der Serie.* Deutsche Verlags Anstalt: Stuttgart, 1919.

Kervran, Louis C. *Biological Transmutations.* Swan House: Binghampton, N.Y., 1973.

King, F. H. *Farmers of Forty Centuries.* Jonathan Cape: London, 1933.

Klett, Manfred. "Untersuchungen von Licht und Schatten Qualitat" Bio-dyn. Land und Gartenbau II. Darmstadt, 1973.

Kloss, Jethro. *Back to Eden.* Woodbridge Press: Santa Barbara, Ca., 1975.

Koenig, Karl. *On the Sheaths of the Preparations.* Glencraig Printery: England, Reprint, 1968.

Koepf, Herbert, Bo Pettersson, and Wolfgang Schaumann. *Bio-Dynamic Agriculture.* Anthroposophic Press: Spring Valley, N.Y., 1976.

Koestler, Arthur. *The Case of the Midwife Toad.* Vintage Books, N.Y., 1973.

Koestler, Arthur. *The Ghost in the Machine.* MacMillan Co.: N.Y., 1967.

Kolisko, L. *Agriculture of Tomorrow.* Kolisko Archives: London, 1939. *(Landwirtschaft der Zukunft.)* Schaffhausen, Switzerland, 1953.

Könemann, Ewald. *Düngerstatten, Kompost und Düngersilos.* Siebeneicher Verl.: Berlin, 1941.

Koxloff, Eugene N. *Plants and Animals of the Pacific Northwest.* U. of Wash. Press: Seattle, 1976.

Kranich, Ernst Michael. *Die Formensprache der Pflanze.* Verl. Freies Geistesleben: Stuttgart, 1976.

Landmann, Michael. *Philosophical Anthropology.* Westminster Press: Philadelphia, Pa., 1974.

Liebig, Justus v. *Chemie und ihre Anwendung auf Landwirtschaft und Physiologie.* 1840.

Liebig, Justus v. *Chemische Briefe*. 1859.

Lievegoed, C. B. J. *The Working of the Planets and the Life Processes in Man and Earth*. Broome Farm, Clent, Stourbridge: Worcs., 1972.

Linder, Maria. "Compost" in Acres, USA, April, 1975, Vol. 4, No. 5.

Lindholm, Dan. *Wie die Sterne Enstanden*. Verl. Freies Geistesleben: Stuttgart, 1973.

Loekle, Werner E. *Bewusste Ernährung und Gesunde Lebensführung*. Verl. Die Kommenden: Freiburg, 1970.

Messegue, Maurice. *Of Men and Plants*. MacMillan Co.: N.Y., 1973.

Muenscher, Walter Conrad. *Poisonous Plants of the United States*. MacMillan Co.: N.Y., 1958.

Myers, Robin. "The National Sharecroppers Fund and the Farm Co-op Movement" in *Radical Agriculture*. Harper and Row: N.Y., 1976.

Neel, James V., and Arthur D. Bloom. "The Detection of Environmental Mutagens" in *Heredity and Society*. A. Baer, ed. MacMillan Co.: N.Y., 1973.

Organic Plant Protection. Yepsen, Roger, B., Jr., ed. Rodale: Emmaus, Pa., 1976.

Ostrander, Sheila and Lynn Schroeder. *Psychic Discoveries Behind the Iron Curtain*. Bantam Books: N.Y., 1973.

Pank, C. J. *Dirt Farmer's Dialogue*. B-D Press: Sprakers, N.Y., 1976.

Pelikan, Wilhelm. *The Secrets of Metals*. Anthroposophic Press: Spring Valley, N.Y., 1973.

Perelman, Michael. "Efficiency in Agriculture: Economics of Energy" in *Radical Agriculture*. Harper & Row: N.Y., 1976.

Perelman, Michael. "The Green Revolution: American Agriculture in the Third World" in *Radical Agriculture*. Harper & Row Publ.: N.Y., 1976.

Pfeiffer, Ehrenfried. *A Condensation of Bio-Dynamic Farming and Gardening.* Conservation Gardening and Farming – Series A: abstracts. B. Rateaver, ed., Pauma Valley, Ca., 1973.

Pfeiffer, Ehrenfried. Preface in *Agriculture* by Rudolf Steiner. London, 1974.

Pfeiffer, Ehrenfried. *Weeds and What They Tell.* Bio-dynamic Gardening & Farming Assn., Inc.: Stroudsburg, Pa., 1960.

Philbrick, H. and R. Gregg. *Companion Plants.* Devin-Adair Co.: N.Y., 1966.

Philbrick, John and Helen. *The Bug Book.* Garden Way: Charlotte, Vermont, 1974.

Piccardi, G. *The Chemical Basis of Medical Climatology.* Thomas: Springfield, Ill., 1962.

Poppelbaum, Hermann. *New Light on Heredity and Evolution.* St. George: Spring Valley, N.Y., 1977.

Rappaport, Roy A. "The Flow of Energy in an Agricultural Society." *Scientific American,* 225, Sept. 1971.

Rasmussen, Elstrup. "Lebendige Erde." 5/1962: Darmstadt.

Rateaver, Bargyla and Gylver. *The Organic Method Primer.* Pauma Valley, Calif., 1973.

Remer, Nicolaus. *Lebensgesetze im Landbau.* Phil-Anthr. Verl. Goetheanum: Dornach, Switz., 1968.

Riotte, Louise. *Companion Planting for Successful Gardening.* Garden Way: Charlotte, Vermont, 1975.

Rodale Herb Book. W. H. Hylton, ed. Rodale Press Book Division: Emmaus, Pa., 1976.

Rodale, J. I., ed. *Encyclopedia of Organic Gardening.* Rodale Books: Emmaus, Pa., 1973.

Rodale, J. I., ed. *The Complete Book of Composting.* Rodale Books: Emmaus, Pa., 1975.

Rodale, Robert. "Making Enemies into Friends." *Organic Gardening and Farming Magazine.* Feb. 1977.

Roszak, Theodore. *Unfinished Animal.* Harper & Row: N.Y., 1975.

Roszak, Theodore. *Where the Wasteland Ends.* Vintage Books: N.Y., 1969.

Salisbury, Frank B., and Cleon Ross. *Plant Physiology.* Wadsworth: Belmont, Ca., 1969.

Sauer, Carl O. *Agricultural Origins and Dispersals.* American Geographical Society: N.Y., 1957.

Scheler, Max. *Man's Place in Nature.* Noonday Press: N.Y., 1962.

Schiller, P. E. "Untersuchungen an der freien schallempfindlichen Flamme" Akustische Zeitschrift, 1938.

Schmidt, F. C. L. *Landwirtschaftlicher Impuls und Seine Entfaltung.* W. Müller Verl.: Birenbach.

Schuhmacher, E. F. *Small is Beautiful: A Study of Economics as if People Mattered.* Blond Briggs: London, 1973.

Schulz, Joachim. "Blattstellungen im Pflanzenreich als Ausdruck kosmischer Gesetzmassigkeiten" in *Lebendige Erde,* Bd. II. Darmstadt, 1973.

Schurmann, Herbert F. *People's China* (The China Reader). Vintage Books: N.Y., 1974.

Schwenk, Theodor. *Grundlagen der Potenzforschung.* Verl. Freies Geistesleben: Stuttgart, 1972.

Schwenk, Theodor. *Sensitive Chaos.* Schocken Books: N.Y., 1976.

Schwenk, Theodor. "Wassernot und Wasserrettung" *Soziale Hygiene.* Freies Geistesleben Verl.: Stuttgart, 1973.

Shepherd, A. P. *A Scientist of the Invisible.* Hodder & Stoughton: London, 1954.

Sloane, Eric. *The Seasons of America Past.* Funk & Wagnalls: N.Y., 1958.

Soper, John. *Studying the Agricultural Course.* Bio-Dynamic Agricultural Association: London, 1976.

Spencer, Edwin Rollin. *All About Weeds.* Dover Publ. Inc.: N.Y., 1974.

Spindler, H. Bull. Lab. Maritime de Dinard XXVIII and Bull. Lab. Maritime de Dinard XXXI, 1948.

Steele, Dorman J. *A Fourteen Weeks Course in Chemistry*. A. S. Barnes: N.Y., 1868.

Steiner, Rudolf. *Agriculture*. Bio-Dynamic Agricultural Association: London, 1974.

Steiner, Rudolf. *An Outline of Occult Science*. Anthrop. Press: Spring Valley, N.Y.

Steiner, Rudolf. *Goethes Naturwissenschaftliche Schriften* Verl. Freies Geistesleben: Stuttgart, 1972.

Steiner, Rudolf. *Macrocosm and Microcosm*. Rudolf Steiner Press: London, 1968.

Steiner, Rudolf. *Man as a Symphony of the Creative Word*. Rudolf Steiner Press: London, 1970.

Steiner, Rudolf. *The Social Future*. Anthroposophic Press: N.Y., 1972.

Steiner, Rudolf. *The Threefold Social Order*. Anthroposophic Press: N.Y., 1972.

Sternkalender 1971-2. Goetheanum, Dornach, Switzerland.

Stone Soup, Ltd. *The Green World, A Guide and Catalogue*. A Berkeley Windhover Book: N.Y., 1975.

Storl, W. D. *Shamanism Among Americans of European Origin*. Unpublished Dissertation. University of Bern, Switz., 1974.

Stout, Ruth. *The Ruth Stout No-Work Garden Book*. Rodale Press: Emmaus, Pa., 1971.

Thaer, A. D. *Grundsatze der Rationalen Landwirtschaft*. 1809.

Thun, Maria. "Kosmische Wirkung im Boden und Pflanze im siderischen Mondrhythmus" in *Sternkalender 1974*. Dornach, Switz., 1973.

Thun, Maria. *Work on the Land and the Constellations*. Lanthorn Press: Peredur, G.B., 1977.

Todd, John. "A Modest Proposal: Science for the People" in *Radical Agriculture*. Richard Merrill, ed. Harper & Row: N.Y., 1976.

Tomkins, P. and C. Bird. *The Secret Life of Plants*. Penguin Books: Harmondsworth, Middlesex, England, 1974.

Wachsmuth, Gunther. *Erde und Mensch*. Philos. Anthrop. Verl.: Dornach, Switz., 1945.

Walters, Charles, Jr. "The Case for Eco-Agriculture." *Acres, USA*: Rayton, Missouri, 1975.

Ward, Ritchie R. *The Living Clocks*. Alfred A. Knopf: N.Y., 1971.

Watson, Lyall. *Supernature*. Bantam Books: N.Y., 1974.

Weather. Life Science Library, Time, Inc.: N.Y., 1965.

Wescott, Cynthia. *The Gardener's Bug Book*. Doubleday: Garden City, N.Y., 1964.

Whicher, Olive. *Projective Geometry*. Rudolf Steiner Press: London, 1961.

Wigginton, Eliot. *The Foxfire Book*. Anchor Books: Garden City, N.Y., 1972.

Wortman, Sterline. *Agriculture in China. Scientific American*. June, 1975.

Yates, Frances. *Giordano Bruno and the Hermetic Tradition*. Vintage Books: New York, 1964.

INDEX

D

Darwin, 105, 132, 173

E